Law for Civil Engineers

An Introduction

Keith Manson

Longman
London

Longman Scientific & Technical
Longman Group UK Limited
Longman House, Burnt Mill, Harlow,
Essex CM20 2JE, England
and Associated Companies throughout the world.

British Library Cataloguing in Publication Data
A catalogue record for this book is available from the British Library

ISBN 0582 06131 8

Set by 5 in 10 on 11pt Baskerville
Printed in Malaysia by PA

Contents

Preface

In recent years the volume of law has increased at a rapid rate, affecting many who in the past have felt no need to make a study of law. Members of all the professions are now aware of the risk of a claim being made against them for professional negligence, and new safety provisions may also impose liabilities on them. In addition there are the numerous legal provisions which a professional person must be aware of in order to meet particular work requirements.

To meet the needs of professional civil engineers in this area, universities and other higher educational establishments are now including in their undergraduate syllabuses courses in relevant aspects of the law. Those civil engineers whose courses of study did not include such legal studies are increasingly availing themselves of short courses and other opportunities to acquire that legal knowledge their professional duties have shown to be necessary.

I have sought in this book to address the needs of the student and young professional engineer in these respects. To achieve this I have tried to explain the law in simple terms, and described cases in some detail in order to assist in the understanding of legal principles. The subjects considered in the book are those the civil engineer is most likely to encounter in the course of his professional work.

In an introductory book of this nature it is not possible to cover particular topics in the way some might believe to be necessary. I hope, however, that I have provided an introduction which will meet the requirements of most readers, and establish a foundation for further detailed study from the standard textbooks, should that be necessary.

Keith Manson
November 1992

Acknowledgements

We are grateful to Thomas Telford Publications Ltd for permission to reproduce copyright material in extracts from the ICE Conditions of Contract, 6th edition (1991), copyright of the Institution of Civil Engineers, the Association of Consulting Engineers and the Federation of Civil Engineering Contractors.

Table of statutes

Table of cases

1

General law

Nature of law

Every society requires a system of laws. The more developed the society the more complex the laws will be, and the greater that body of law will have to be. Rules that govern the conduct of society, when given the appropriate authority, take the status of laws which have to be obeyed. The failure to obey laws carries with it the possibility of a sanction being imposed, such as a fine or a period of imprisonment.

Laws are not static: they are amended frequently and at times fundamentally. As social attitudes and conditions change so the law accommodates these changes. Laws which are no longer relevant can be repealed; new situations are dealt with by new laws. The law-making process is criticized at times as being too slow to meet changes in society: this may be justified by the need to change the law only when it is certain alterations are really needed.

English law comprises public law and private law. Public law seeks to protect and benefit society generally. Examples are statutes such as the Highways Act 1980 and the Town and Country Planning Act 1990, where the rights of private individuals have to give way to the greater need of public benefit. Private landowners may wish to resist the acquisition of their land for highway construction but if, after the proper procedure, the public benefit is held to be the greater need the rights of the private landowners are overriden. Private law concerns disputes between private individuals, where the state is not involved. The state provides the means for resolving those disputes but the individuals concerned decide whether to use those means; a contractual dispute between two individuals is a private matter for them alone.

English law has a history going back before the Norman Conquest but the records for the earlier time are scanty. England, unlike a number of other countries, has not had its law separated from earlier law because of a revolution or a declaration of independence.

English law means the law that applies in England and Wales only. Scotland has a different legal system, but it does share the House of Lords as its final court of appeal and the British

Parliament legislates for Scotland; it also now legislates for Northern Ireland.

Sources of law

English law has developed over the centuries and consequently has a number of sources. We need to examine only those which are relevant to construction law.

Common law

In the mid-eleventh century the legal system consisted of local courts, where disputes were settled by the application of local laws. After the Norman Conquest, a central system gradually developed: judges appointed by the King journeyed from London to the provinces to administer justice in the King's own courts.

These judges made decisions on disputes arising from general custom law (which law applied throughout the country) and local custom law (which varied from one area to another). A body of common law evolved; this was law applied to all as uniform law throughout the country. Through the centuries the common law changed to accommodate a developing society. This was not always possible: parliament then amended the law by passing a statute, for example the Occupiers' Liability Act 1957 rectified the inadequacy of the common law in dealing with the duty that occupiers owe to those who come on their land.

Common law is sometimes referred to as unwritten law; the written law is contained in statutes passed by Parliament. Although common law has diminished in importance, giving way to other sources, it is still important in certain respects. The crime of murder is a common law offence; civil wrongs such as trespass to land and nuisance are common law matters.

Equity

In the middle centuries the common law proved to be inadequate to deal with the difficulties created by an increasingly complex social and commercial life. The population of the country had increased; people travelled more and traded more. The common law had developed in a rigid way, so that new forms of claims were difficult if not impossible to fit into the existing framework; common law could not provide a remedy even though the justice of the claim demanded a remedy.

The practice arose of seeking royal justice by presenting a petition for a remedy to be granted. These petitions were dealt with by the Lord Chancellor, who was and still is the senior law officer. In time these petitions were dealt with by a court of chancery.

The Lords Chancellors and their courts built up a body of equitable principles which allowed justice to be done and remedies to be granted which were not available to the common law. These principles are known as the maxims of equity and seek to provide a decision which is fair, reasonable and just. Unlike the common law, the conduct of the person bringing the action is a relevant fact that the court must take into account. Even if individuals prove their case, but the court forms the opinion that their conduct in the matter was not what it ought to have been, the court will refuse a remedy. At common law people who prove their case must be granted the common law remedy of damages: it is their right. With equity the remedies are at the court's discretion. There are a number of equitable remedies, for example the injunction, which may be granted by the court to restrain a trespass to land. Before granting an injunction the court must be satisfied that the common law award of damages is not appropriate.

With the development of equity courts there were two separate courts administering two branches of law; a person might start an action in a common law court only to find that it ought to have been brought before an equity court; that person would have to discontinue the action and start afresh in an equity court.

The Judicature Acts 1873–75, which set up a single court system, removed this anomaly. Any court thereafter could apply either equity or common law; the laws themselves were unaffected. Parliament was aware of the difficulty a court may face when a dispute could be resolved by applying either common law or equity, and decided that in the event of a conflict the rules of equity were to prevail. That is still the law, by the provisions in Section 49 of the Supreme Court Act 1981.

Statute

The most important source of English law is statute law, in the form of Acts of Parliament. Parliament's power here is unlimited: it may make laws on any matter or to affect any person as it wishes. No English court, unlike some other countries, has power to declare an Act of Parliament to be unconstitutional or illegal.

Parliament makes statute law in the form of public Acts, which change the general law of the country, and private Acts, which are restrictive as they affect only an individual or group of individuals or apply to only one area. These Acts often give local authorities powers in their own areas which exceed the general law; in the past some highway authorities obtained legal powers to deal with highway matters which were greater than the general highway law provided.

The most important changes to statute law are when the government introduces into the House of Commons the proposed Act, which is known as a Bill. This is examined and discussed in principle, then in detail and voted upon. The House of Lords then consider the Bill using a shorter and simpler procedure. The Bill finally receives the Royal Assent, thereby becoming an Act of Parliament but not necessarily immediate law.

Statute law is prepared by lawyers known as parliamentary draughtsmen. Acts of Parliament are laid out in the same way. They have a short title, for example the Highways Act 1980, and a long title which explains the purpose of the Act. An Act is divided into parts, dealing with related matters; parts are reduced into sections, dealing with a particular legal topic. A section may be divided into sub-sections, paragraphs and sub-paragraphs.

Two sections in an Act of Parliament are of particular importance. First, the interpretations section defines words and clauses where the parliamentary draughtsman had either extended or restricted the usual meaning of words or clauses used in the Act. Second, the last section states when the Act or parts of it will come into force. Where the legal change is straightforward it will probably come into force one month after the Royal Assent; Acts of more complexity are brought into force in stages by a minister or secretary of state using power given to them under the Act.

Statute law may become outdated or not deal adequately with a situation. The Law Commission, which has a membership of a High Court judge and academic and practising lawyers, considers problems that appear to warrant examination. Its recommendations may then be adopted by Parliament and result in new statute law.

Delegated legislation

Parliament recognizes the need for detailed law on specialized matters and has given others power to make such law, by expressly providing in an Act that individuals shall have delegated to them that power.

An example of delegated legislation is in section 1 of the Building Act 1984: the Secretary of State for the Environment was given power to make building regulations, which have been amended from time to time.

Where Parliament considers a matter it has delegated to be of some importance, it may require the delegated legislation to be subject to Parliament's approval; it may also reserve the power to disapprove the delegated legislation.

Judicial precedent

Judicial precedent is also known as case law (and inaccurately as judge-made law); the giving of a decision in a case by a court creates a precedent. The interpretation of a statute, common law or equity, if given by a court of proper judicial standing, creates a precedent. Although the system is not intended to allow judges to make laws as they would wish them to be this has happened in the past, hence the expression 'judge-made law'. It is claimed that this makes the law certain and, with the number of judicial precedents, allows lawyers to advise clients how courts are likely to deal with their cases.

Judicial precedent is governed by two doctrines: binding precedent and persuasive precedent. Binding precedent requires inferior courts to apply decisions of superior courts; they have no choice. If, however, an inferior court finds it is dealing with some difference on an important point it may decline to apply the precedent: this is known as 'distinguishing'.

The House of Lords is the most superior court in the English court system; its decisions therefore bind all other courts. In order to create the necessary certainty the law requires, decisions of the House of Lords are not intended to be changed by them except in exceptional circumstances. Until 1966 the House of Lords was bound by previous decisions, but this no longer applies, for example in *Murphy v Brentwood District Council 1990* (see p. 176), the House overruled a decision made thirteen years earlier.

Persuasive precedent allows a decision of one court to be quoted to a court of the same standing as a guide as to how that court should reach a decision, but does not bind that court. Judges can adopt the precedent if they agree with it; they can also refuse to adopt it and decide the case in a totally different way. When there are two conflicting decisions on the same point of law, one of the cases is taken to appeal for a decision by a superior court.

Another form of persuasive precedent is decisions of courts of other countries which have similar common law systems; this means that decisions of former colonies and dominions can be quoted to English courts as a course of reasoning they should adopt.

Law reports

Judicial precedent can operate properly only if there is an adequate system of recording decisions made by the senior courts. It is not the usual practice to report decisions of the lower courts.

The modern system of law reporting started in the mid-nineteenth century. Before this private individuals prepared law reports which they sold to lawyers, which was an unreliable system.

A law report is prepared by a barrister who has been in court to hear the case; the draft is sent to the judge to read through and sign. It is published in the form of a weekly booklet and later put into a bound volume. There are usually three volumes of law reports for each year.

In addition to the official law reports, others are produced as commercial ventures. An example of specialized law reports is the Building Law Reports, which deal solely with construction law disputes. These specialized reports are often the only means of reference to a decision in a particular case.

Judicial decisions are also reported in journals and newspapers, which may be quoted to courts provided they were prepared by barristers who were present when the cases were heard.

Law reports are usually referred to in a shortened form. For example the case of *Murphy v Brentwood District Council*, which was decided by the House of Lords in 1990, is reported in the All England Law Reports. It is quoted as *Murphy v Brentwood District Council 1990* 2 All E.R. 908, which means that Murphy brought an action against Brentwood District Council and the case was in the second volume of the 1990 All England Law Reports starting on page 908.

In reading a law report two particular features need to be noted: the *ratio decidendi* and *obiter dicta*. The *ratio decidendi* is the reason for the decision or the principle of law which governs the decision; *obiter dicta* (sayings by the way) are words spoken by the judge which are not part of the *ratio decidendi* but are of importance in indicating the judge's opinion on matters which did not need a decision.

European law

Parliament passed the European Communities Act in 1972 which made Britain a member of the European Economic Community and so subject to Community laws. These laws override national laws where Community matters are concerned.

The European Commission and the Council of Ministers are allowed to make laws in the form of regulations, directives and decisions. Regulations are binding on all member states. Directives are orders or requirements which individual states have to apply in accordance with their own legal system. In Britain this is done by delegated legislation, for example the Control of Substances Hazardous to Health 1988 was made under powers in the Health and Safety at Work etc Act 1974 in order to implement Council Directive No 80/1107/EEC. Decisions bind the person or body who is the subject of the decision.

As Community law overrides the national laws of member states, the central court which decides cases on Community law is the European Court of Justice situated in Luxembourg; it is not to be confused with the European Court of Human Rights in Strasburg which deals with infringements of human rights and is not part of the Community. Decisions of the European Court of Justice are binding on the courts of member states. For example, in the case of *Allen and Hanburys Ltd v Generics (UK) Ltd 1988*, the House of Lords acting under the European Economic Community Treaty referred a case for a ruling on the law regarding a patent in a drug. The court's ruling bound the House of Lords.

Structure of the courts

The structure of the courts in the English legal system is the result of development over many years. The structure has changed substantially at certain times and contains some anomalies; for example, some criminal courts have civil jurisdiction. A diagram of the court structure is set out in Figure 1.

The structure is in the form of a pyramid with the House of Lords at the apex with courts of lesser importance below. The base consists of the Magistrates Courts dealing with, mainly, criminal cases and the County Courts dealing with civil cases.

The courts are intended, in principle, to deal with either criminal or civil matters.

Criminal courts

Magistrates Courts

Magistrates deal with the vast majority of criminal offences: most are of a minor nature and need to be dealt with as summary offences. An

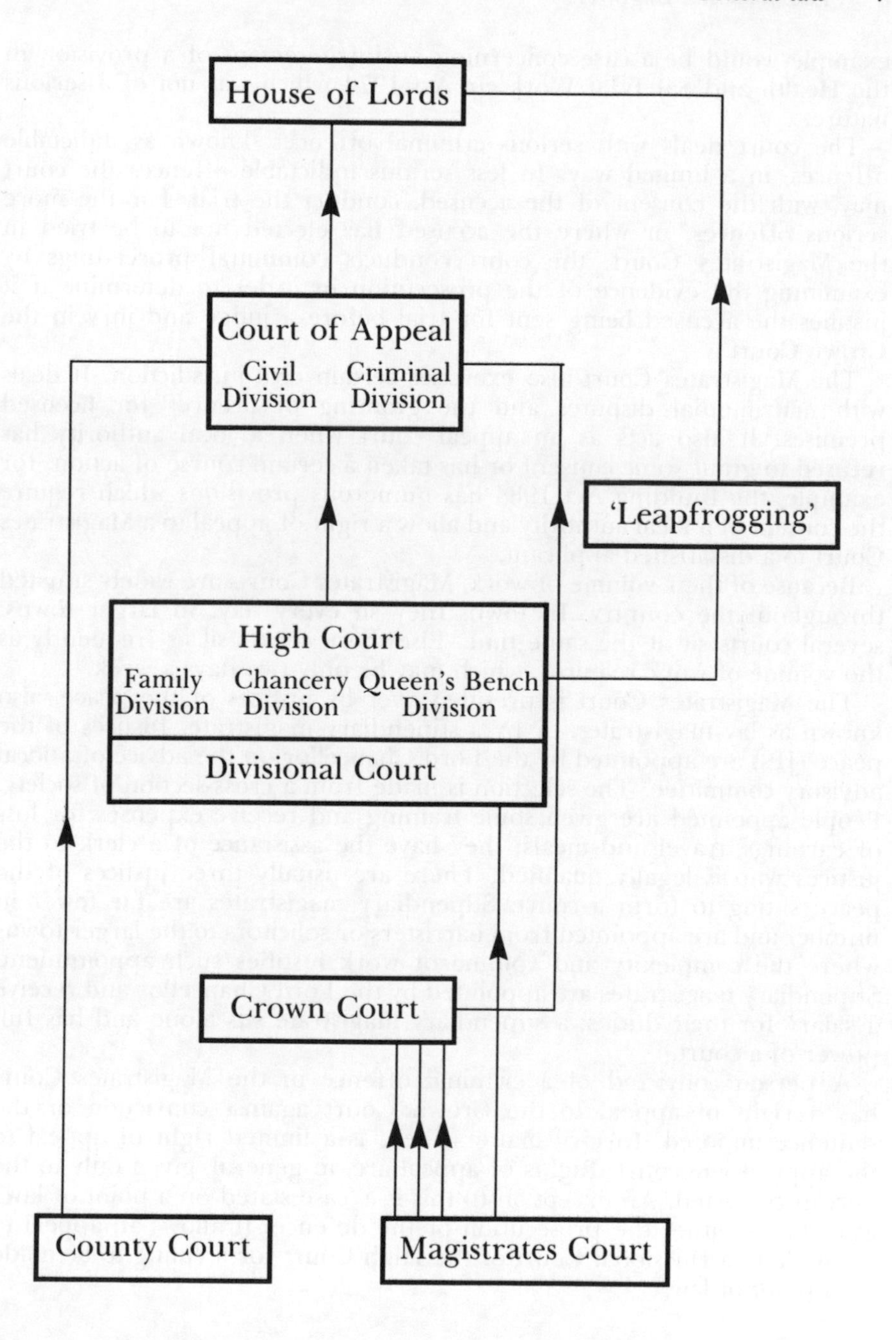

Figure 1 Structure of the courts in the English legal system

example would be a case concerning an infringement of a provision in the Health and Safety at Work etc Act 1974 which was not of a serious nature.

The court deals with serious criminal offences, known as indictable offences, in a limited way. In less serious indictable offences the court may, with the consent of the accused, conduct the trial. For the more serious offences, or where the accused has elected not to be tried in the Magistrates Court, the court conducts committal proceedings by examining the evidence of the prosecution in order to determine if it justifies the accused being sent for trial before a judge and jury in the Crown Court.

The Magistrates Court also exercises certain civil jurisdiction. It deals with matrimonial disputes and the granting of licences for licensed premises. It also acts as an appeal court when a local authority has refused to grant some consent or has taken a certain course of action; for example, the Building Act 1984 has numerous provisions which require the consent of a local authority and allow a right of appeal to a Magistrates Court to a dissatisfied applicant.

Because of their volume of work, Magistrates Courts are widely situated throughout the country. In towns they sit every day; in larger towns, several courts sit at the same time. Elsewhere courts sit as frequently as the volume of work requires, which may be only two days a week.

The Magistrates Court is presided over by justices of the peace, also known as lay magistrates, or by a stipendiary magistrate. Justices of the peace (JPs) are appointed by the Lord Chancellor on the advice of a local advisory committee. The selection is made from a cross-section of society. People appointed are given some training and receive expenses for loss of earnings, travel and meals; they have the assistance of a clerk to the justices who is legally qualified. There are usually three justices of the peace sitting to form a court. Stipendiary magistrates are far fewer in number and are appointed from barristers or solicitors to the larger towns where the complexity and volume of work justifies such appointment. Stipendiary magistrates are appointed by the Lord Chancellor and receive a salary for their duties; a stipendiary magistrate sits alone and has full power of a court.

A person convicted of a criminal offence in the Magistrates Court has a right of appeal to the Crown Court against conviction or the sentence imposed. In civil matters there is a limited right of appeal to the appropriate court. Rights of appeal are, in general, given only to the person convicted. An exception to this is a 'case stated on a point of law', available to either the prosecution or the defence. It allows an appeal to be made to a Divisional Court of the High Court for a ruling to be made on a point of law.

Crown Court

The Courts Act 1971 replaced the old courts of Assize and Quarter Sessions, which had been shown to be inefficient and unsuitable for the present time, with Crown Courts, which sit on a continuous basis (apart from holidays) and so are able to deal with cases more quickly.

The Crown Court is a criminal court dealing with the serious, indictable crimes the Magistrates Court cannot deal with. It also acts as an appeal court, with regard to conviction or sentence, from a decision of a Magistrates Court. Crown Courts impose sentences on those convicted in a Magistrates Court of certain indictable offences where the magistrates consider their powers of punishment to be insufficient.

Crown Courts have certain limited civil jurisdiction. For example, in Section 56 of the Highways Act 1980 the court is empowered to decided whether a way or a bridge is a highway maintainable at public expense, and if it is, and it is out of repair, to order its repair.

When a Crown Court is acting as a court of first instance, that is conducting a trial of a person sent to the court by the Magistrates Court, there is a judge and jury. The judge will, depending on the case, be a High Court judge, a Circuit judge or a recorder. A recorder is a barrister or solicitor who is appointed by the Queen on the recommendation of the Lord Chancellor to act as a part-time judge. When the court is dealing with an appeal from a Magistrates Court the judge will be assisted by two, three or four justices of the peace.

A High Court judge is appointed by the Queen on the recommendation of the Lord Chancellor from those who have had a right of audience before the High Court in relation to all proceedings for ten years or who have been Circuit Judges for at least two years. In order to preserve the independence of High Court judges, the power to remove them from office is extremely limited.

A Circuit judge is appointed by the Queen on the recommendation of the Lord Chancellor from barristers of at least ten years' standing or solicitors who have acted as recorders for at least three years.

Crown Courts are arranged in three tiers: each tier has certain classes of criminal offences allocated to it, the top tier being the court responsible for dealing with murder trials. The courts are situated throughout the country with the lower tier courts in small towns and the top tier in large towns or cities.

An appeal from the decision of a Crown Court may be made to the Court of Appeal, Criminal Division, by defendants against their conviction or sentence. Both the prosecution and the defence may ask the court to state a case on a point of law. This special type of appeal goes to a Divisional Court of the Queen's Bench; the effect of this court's ruling is either to confirm the correctness of the decision in the Crown Court or to disapprove it with the result that the conviction is quashed.

Divisional Court, Queen's Bench High Court

This court is specially created to deal with appeals by either the prosecution or defence on cases stated on a point of law. The court is made up of at least two High Court judges, who give an authoritative ruling on a legal point which the person bringing the appeal believes was misapplied by the Magistrates Court or Crown Court. A right of appeal against this ruling may be made to the House of Lords, with the permission of the Divisional Court or the House of Lords.

Court of Appeal, Criminal Division
This court hears appeals on criminal matters by defendants against their conviction or sentence by a Crown Court. There is also now a limited form of appeal by the Attorney General when a sentence is considered to be out of line with normal sentencing for that type of offence. The court comprises three members but the number may be greater if the case is of particular importance. The members are the Lord Chief Justice and Lords Justices of Appeal, who are appointed by the Queen from those who have had a right of audience before the High Court in relation to all proceedings for ten years or those who are High Court judges. When the court is particularly busy, High Court judges are brought in to assist.

An appeal from a decision of the Court of Appeal, Criminal Division, may be made to the House of Lords, for which the court must grant permission by certifying that a point of public importance is involved. If the court refuses permission it is possible to present a petition to the House of Lords and ask to be allowed to make an appeal to them.

House of Lords
This refers not to the whole House but to a group of members who are appointed by the Queen on the Prime Minister's advice. Appointments are made from barristers of fifteen years' standing or, more usually, from those who have been High Court judges for at least two years especially from the Lord Justices of Appeal. They are known as the Lords of Appeal in Ordinary or as the Law Lords. The Lord Chancellor may also sit, and others who are members of the House of Lords in their own right and have held high judicial office. The number making up the court is usually five, but appeals of particular importance may be heard by a greater number (which is an uneven number).

Civil Courts

The Civil Courts deal with less important cases in a simpler, shorter and less expensive way than the important cases. Because of increased work in the High Court and the lengthy delay in getting a case heard various measures have been adopted to reduce this delay.

County Court
County Courts were established in the mid-nineteenth century to provide an inexpensive means of dealing with simple civil disputes. The success of this can be seen from the many extra duties given to the court.

A County Court is presided over by a Circuit judge, whose use in the County Court as well as the Crown Court indicates the efficient use of judicial time. The judge almost always sits without a jury but in certain circumstances a jury of eight members may be used. Every County Court has a District judge and may have an assistant district judge and deputy district judge. District judges have similar powers to a Circuit judge but their jurisdiction is limited to claims up to £5000. They also have certain administrative duties. A District judge, assistant or deputy is appointed by the Lord Chancellor.

The jurisdiction of the County Court is based on the claim being brought in the area where defendants live or carry on their business or where the cause of action arose, subject to a claim for money which may be made in any County Court. The jurisdiction of County Courts is set out in the County Courts Act 1984 and rules made under that act.

County Courts have been given jurisdiction over a wide range of judicial matters. Claims may be made for breach of contract or tort where the amount claimed is less than £25 000; this, however, is a presumption only. Claims for damages for death or personal injury must be dealt with in the County Court if the claim is for less than £50 000. Other claims are dealt with by the County Court if the claim is for less than £25 000, unless the criteria in Section I of the Courts and Legal Services Act 1990 leads the County Court to transfer the case to the High Court (and the High Court agrees to the transfer). Any claim for £50 000 or above is dealt with by the High Court unless, with regard to the criteria in Section I, the High Court thinks that the case ought to be transferred to the County Court. If, however, a claim for £50 000 or above is started in the County Court it may be dealt with by that court provided, and considering the Section I criteria, it does not think that it should be transferred to the High Court.

A more recent development is that where a claim is made for a sum not exceeding £1000 it is automatically referred to arbitration within the court system, not under the Arbitration Acts. The arbitration may be conducted by a Circuit judge, the District judge, assistant or deputy or some other official. This system, usually referred to as the Small Claims Court, has the advantage of being conducted privately with, in general, no liability for the loser to pay the other side's legal costs.

High Court

This court has three divisions: Queen's Bench, Chancery and Family. Under Section 4 of the Supreme Court Act 1981 there is a maximum of eighty High Court judges but this number may be changed from time to time. High Court judges are appointed by the Queen on the advice of the Lord Chancellor.

The Queen's Bench Division is the largest, with some fifty judges. The court deals with those common law matters the County Court is unable to deal with. So claims in contract and tort for amounts greater than £25 000 may be dealt with here. Usually a single judge deals with a case; juries are now seldom used. Within this division the Commercial Court handles disputes of a commercial nature, for example those concerning insurance.

The Official Referee's Court also comes within the Queen's Bench Division; it deals with civil matters which come to it direct or which are transferred to it from the Queen's Bench or the Chancery Division. The business of the court involves a prolonged examination of documents or accounts or of a technical scientific nature where it is more convenient to have an Official Referee deal with the case. The vast majority of cases dealt with by the Official Referee's Court concern the construction industry. The small number of Official Referees, who are Circuit judges even though the court is part of the High Court, is supplemented by other Circuit judges, deputy circuit judges and recorders.

The Chancery Division deals with mortgages, trusts, revenue matters and the estates of deceased persons; it includes the Companies Court and the Patents Court. Judges appointed to this division are selected from barristers practising in these specialized branches of law.

The Family Division deals with matters concerning marriage, children, adoption and wardship.

Each division of the High Court has divisional courts, which comprise not fewer than two judges and hear appeals from lower courts. The divisional court of the Queen's Bench hears the appeals of cases stated on a point of law from Crown Courts and Magistrates Courts; it also has the power to control and correct mistakes made by lower courts and local authorities.

Court of Appeal, Civil Division

This court deals solely with appeals from the High Court and the County Courts. The court has a senior judge, the Master of the Rolls, and the Lords Justices of Appeal: the usual number is three but a greater uneven number may be used with appeals of particular importance. High Court judges are also used to assist the court; sometimes the delay in dealing with cases is reduced by having two judges form a court. An appeal may be made from a decision of this court to the House of Lords, subject to permission being granted by either the Court of Appeal or the House of Lords.

Some cases that come before the High Court are of such importance that a decision of the House of Lords will be necessary whichever way the High Court decides the case; an arrangement known as 'leapfrogging' allows an appeal to be made direct to the House of Lords. The omission of the appeal to the Court of Appeal, Civil Division, saves both time and expense. Both parties to the action must give their agreement in writing and the High Court judge must certify that this is an appropriate action.

House of Lords

An appeal from the Court of Appeal, Civil Division, is heard by Law Lords; usually five Law Lords hear an appeal but a greater uneven number may be used. When the House of Lords in the case of *Murphy v Brentwood District Council 1990* overruled a previous decision the number of Law Lords was seven, which gave the decision even greater authority.

Legal profession

The legal profession in England and Wales is divided into solicitors and barristers, each with their own training system, examinations and professional authority. The justification is that each profession performs different functions which leads to greater expertise.

A person who wishes to become a solicitor usually has a law degree but this is not essential; the examinations of the Law Society must be passed and the required period of training undertaken. After this the person is admitted as a solicitor by the Law Society and is then subject to its rules.

Professional negligence insurance and contribution to the compensation fund are required for practising solicitors.

The work of solicitors includes conveyancing, preparing wills, acting as executor and trustee, giving general advice and preparing cases for trials. Solicitors now have greater rights to act as an advocate in the courts than previously. Many solicitors are employed by public bodies, companies and other bodies, providing legal advice and undertaking legal work for their employer. All large construction companies employ their own legal staff.

Barristers are lawyers who have been called to the bar by the Inn of Court to which they belong; the four Inns of Court – Gray's Inn, Lincoln's Inn, the Middle Temple and the Inner Temple – are societies of great antiquity governed by Masters of the Bench. The examinations of the Council of Legal Education must be passed and students must also dine in the hall of their Inn the required number of times. Before newly called barristers can practise they must first undertake twelve months' pupillage with a senior barrister in chambers, and then become members of a set of chambers if they wish to practise. Barristers cannot form companies or partnerships; they group together as individual lawyers in a set of chambers.

A barrister who over a period of years has shown great ability may apply to the Lord Chancellor to be appointed a Queen's Counsel. If satisfied as to that person's suitability the Lord Chancellor recommends the Queen to make the appointment. Queen's Counsels deal only with the most important cases and then as advocates; they will usually be assisted by an ordinary barrister who is referred to as their junior.

The work of the barrister is mainly to act as an advocate in any court in the country. Additionally barristers may become specialists in a branch of law and their opinions will be sought based on their special knowledge. In large cases the barrister works closely with the solicitor in the preparation of the preliminary work.

Barristers originally could take work only by being briefed by solicitors; now they may be briefed by members of certain professions. Barristers, as a result of the decisions of the House of Lords in the cases of *Rondel v Worsley 1967* and *Saif Ali v Sydney Mitchell and Co 1978*, cannot be sued for professional negligence in the conduct and management of court cases.

Court procedures

There are different procedures for the Criminal and Civil Courts; however, both seek to reduce the matter in issue to its bare facts. Defendants have to know in clear and sufficient detail what is alleged against them. The procedures, particularly with civil cases, allow the court to deal with the matter as smoothly and speedily as possible.

Criminal procedure

This procedure requires the production of the individual charged with an offence before the Magistrates Court. A person may be arrested either with or without the use of a warrant. Most prosecutions however result from the service of a summons, which is issued by a justice of the peace after a person has laid information that a criminal offence has been committed. The person named in the summons, which may be a company, is required to attend at a named Magistrates Court on a stated day at a stated time. The summons must state what criminal offences are alleged against the person. If a person fails to answer a summons a warrant may be issued for the person to be arrested.

If a person is charged with a criminal offence which only a Magistrates Court may deal with, a summary offence, or if it is a serious criminal offence, an indictable offence, which by agreement can be tried in the Magistrates Court, then the person is required to plead guilty or not guilty in the Magistrates Court.

Where the plea is guilty, the prosecuting lawyer gives brief details of the case and the court is told of the defendant's previous criminal record, if any. The defendant's lawyer addresses the court in mitigation, explaining as favourably as possible how the defendant was involved in the crime, the defendant's personal circumstances and the likely outcome of a conviction. Character witnesses may give evidence in this respect. The court may postpone sentence until social reports have been obtained. If the offence was an indictable offence the defendant will have agreed to the matter being dealt with in the Magistrates Court and warned that if the magistrates, having heard of any previous convictions, decide that their powers of punishment are inadequate that the defendant would be sent to the Crown Court for sentence.

Where the plea is not guilty, the prosecution lawyer, who may be either a barrister or a solicitor, outlines the case to the magistrates and then calls the witnesses. Each witness swears an oath or makes an act of affirmation before giving evidence. This is known as evidence in chief, after which the witness may be cross-examined by the defendant's lawyer, who may seek to prove that the witness was mistaken in some important respect or ought not to be believed. The prosecuting lawyer may then re-examine the witness, to restore the credibility of the witness if it has been damaged by the cross-examination. After all the prosecution witnesses have been heard the defendant's lawyer may submit that there is no case to answer, that the prosecution evidence is insufficient to support the case against the defendant. If the magistrates agree the charge is dismissed; if not the case proceeds.

The defendant's lawyer then calls the witnesses for the defence who, after swearing an oath or making an act of affirmation, give evidence in the same way as the prosecution witnesses. At the end of the defence case the defendant's lawyer may address the court. The prosecuting lawyer occasionally has a right to address the court. The magistrates then retire to consider their verdict. If the decision is not guilty the defendant is discharged and usually receives legal costs. If the defendant is found guilty, the court is told of any previous convictions, hears the defendant's lawyer in mitigation and then imposes sentence.

Committal proceedings are conducted where the Magistrates Court is asked to determine whether the prosecution case constitutes a prima facie case against the defendant, that is whether the prosecution evidence is sufficient to justify the accused being sent for trial before a judge and jury at the Crown Court. The Magistrates Court does not decide the guilt or innocence of the accused. The proceedings may be in one of two forms. The first, now seldom used, is where all the evidence is given by the witnesses, at the end of which the court makes the decision. The second form consists of the evidence being in documentary form only. Defendants have to agree to this and must be legally represented; if they are committed for trial they may, if the offence so justifies, be committed for trial in custody. Otherwise they are granted bail.

Crown Court

Crown Courts are presided over by a High Court judge, a Circuit judge or a part-time recorder, depending on the seriousness of the matter. Where an appeal is made from the Magistrates Court by the defendant against conviction or sentence any of these judges may hear the appeal. In addition there is a bench of two, three or four magistrates; there is no jury. In the case of an appeal against conviction there is a complete rehearing of the case. With an appeal against sentence the court is told of any previous convictions, to be made aware of any reports regarding the defendant and to hear the defendant or the defence lawyer speak in mitigation. In an appeal against conviction or sentence the court has power to increase the sentence.

When the court is called on to sentence a person there is no jury but a court similarly comprised. The court is told briefly of the facts of the case, of the defendant's record, hears the defendant or the defence lawyer in mitigation, considers any reports and then imposes sentence.

In a trial before the Crown Court a jury is used. Jurors are selected randomly from those over eighteen years of age and not more than sixty-five; people who have been sentenced to imprisonment are disqualified.

The trial starts by the indictment, a formal document in the name of the Queen charging the accused with the offence, being read to the accused, who is then asked to plead guilty or not guilty to the indictment. If pleading guilty the court is told of the accused's record, hears the barrister's speech in mitigation, considers any reports about the accused and his or her social position and then imposes sentence.

If, however, the accused pleads not guilty the jury is sworn in; twelve members are randomly selected from a larger number. Both the prosecution and defence can object to a person serving on a jury. The defence is limited to objecting to not more than three without giving any reason, and to an unlimited number if good cause can be shown.

The trial starts by the prosecuting barrister outlining the case to the court and then calling the prosecution witnesses. Each swears an oath or affirms and gives evidence in chief, may be cross-examined and re-examined. At the end of the prosecution's case the defence barrister may submit that the accused has no case to answer, that is the prosecution evidence does not satisfy some essential feature of the offence or the prosecution case is so weak or discredited that no reasonable jury would convict the accused. If the judge agrees, he or she will direct the jury to return a verdict of not guilty.

If the judge rejects the submission, the defence takes over the case. Defence barristers calling the defendant and other witnesses may make an opening speech, otherwise they are not entitled to make one. The defence witnesses, after swearing oaths or affirming, give their evidence in chief and may be cross-examined and re-examined. The defendant may give evidence or may decide not to do so; this is not to be commented on by the prosecution.

When the defence has called all its witnesses the closing speeches are made. The prosecution barrister speaks first to the jury followed by the defence barrister; the strength of each side's case is pointed out to the jury. After this the judge sums up to the jury, indicating that it is the prosecution's duty to prove the case against the defendant beyond reasonable doubt; the judge explains the law relevant in the case so that they understand it clearly, examines the evidence and concludes by indicating to the jury that they must make their decision on the facts of the case and they should endeavour to reach a unanimous verdict.

The jury then retire to consider their verdict. They may take as long as they wish, but they may be discharged if the judge believes that they have spent an adequate time without being able to reach a verdict. Provided the jury have been out for not less than two hours and ten minutes (or a longer time if the judge thinks it reasonable) the judge may accept a majority verdict; at least ten of the jury have to agree on the verdict, although if the jury has been reduced to ten then nine have to agree.

If the verdict is not guilty the defendant is immediately freed. Where the verdict is guilty the judge is told of any previous criminal convictions, and then hears the defence barrister's mitigation speech. Witnesses as to character may also speak. The judge, with the assistance of any special reports, then imposes the sentence appropriate for the offence.

Civil procedure

The procedure to be described relates to court actions. The procedure used in arbitrations is similar and is considered in Chapter 5. The procedure before a trial is not some minor part of a claim leading to a court judgment. It forms the substantial preparation of the later battle in the court room, clarifying the facts of the dispute between the parties. During the preparatory work it may become apparent that it is in the interests of one party to settle the action on the best terms. It is also possible for a decision to be reached without a court hearing.

This procedure has to be conducted in an orderly way and is regulated by County Court Rules for County Court actions, and the Rules of the Supreme Court for High Court actions; the latter are arranged into Orders, divided into rules and sub-rules.

An action in the High Court starts by the plaintiff (the person bringing the action) issuing and serving a writ, which names the defendant, who is called on to acknowledge service of the writ. An exchange of documents, known as pleadings, then sets out the dispute between the parties. Documents in the possession of the parties are declared, known as discovery, and inspected. Other necessary evidence is obtained. After all these measures, which will take months or even longer, the dispute goes before the High Court for trial.

An action before the High Court would normally begin only after the parties had, through their solicitors, negotiated with a view to a settlement of the dispute. Where this has been unsuccessful the plaintiff's solicitor would issue a writ, which is a formal document issued under the authority of the Lord Chancellor and prepared by the plaintiff's solicitor; it states the names of the plaintiff and the defendant and sets out a statement of the case against the defendant. This is usually a brief statement, known as a general indorsement, of the nature of the claim and the remedy or relief sought. If the writ contains the statement of claim in detail it is known as a specially indorsed writ. The writ is then placed on record by being taken to the Central Office of the Law Courts in London or outside London the District Registry. Here the writ is given a number and sealed.

The writ may now be served on the defendant either by post or personal service. The writ is required to be served within four months of its issue, unless the court grants an extension of time; it must be accompanied by an acknowledgement of service form. The defendant must complete this and return it to the issuing office, thus indicating an intention to defend the action. Failure to do this means that the plaintiff could obtain judgment without further action. Under the Companies Act 1985 a writ is required to be served by sending the writ to the registered office of the company, but in practice the defendant's solicitors indicate that they will accept it.

Following the service of the writ the process known as the pleadings takes place; this sets out the points of dispute between the parties. By this process the dispute is reduced to its true facts and the supporting evidence is known to both parties before the court hearing. Although changes may be permitted at a late stage, in general the parties are required to prepare their pleadings on the basis that that is the issue the court will be required to decide.

Pleadings

The pleadings consist of a statement of claim made by the plaintiff with a defence from the defendant. The plaintiff may answer points in the defence by a reply. A defendant may then make a counter-claim against the plaintiff. In a contract dispute a defendant who is being sued for the contract sum may counter-claim for defective work under the contract which the defendant has had to have remedied.

A statement of claim must set out the full nature of the claim and the remedy sought from the court. A simple example of a statement of claim is shown on page 18. This shows that the defendant has admitted that a written contract was made on 2 November 1990, with an express term as to a fall to the car park. The defendant denies that the car park was constructed without a fall and if there is not a fall as specified that has been caused by a failure to specify adequate foundation and/or it has been caused by using the car park for the parking of heavy commercial vehicles. The loss or expense alleged by the plaintiff is expressly denied and the defence concludes by denying all the allegations. The rules (to p. 19)

In the High Court of Justice 1992 No 5 1911
Queen's Bench Division
(Writ issued 2 February 1992)
Between
Blanktown District Council Plaintiff
and
Alpha Construction PLC Defendant
Statement of Claim

1. By a contract in writing dated 2 November 1990 the Defendant agreed to construct a car park for the Plaintiffs for the sum of £50 000.
2. It was an express term of the said agreement that the surface of the car park should be laid to a fall.
3. In breach of the aforesaid term the Defendant constructed the surface without the specified fall.
4. By reason of the matters aforesaid the Plaintiff has incurred loss and expense and suffered damage.

Particulars of Loss and Expense

Cost of remedial work	£5000
Loss of revenue from car parking fees	£500

5. The plaintiff claims interest upon such damages as may be awarded pursuant to Section 35A of the Supreme Court Act 1981.

And the Plaintiff claims damages and interest.

Served this last day of November 1992
by Alpha and Beta of 5 Plumtree Walk, Blanktown.
Solicitors for the Plaintiff.

To this the defendant is required to make a defence. Failure to do so would allow the plaintiff to obtain judgment in default. The defence may take the following form:

Defence

1. Paragraphs 1 and 2 of the Statement of Claim is admitted.
2. Paragraph 3 is denied. If the surface of the car park does not have the specified fall, which is denied, this has been caused by the plaintiff failing to specify adequate foundation to the car park and/or to the plaintiff permitting the use of the car park by heavy commercial vehicles.
3. The defendant does not admit that the plaintiff incurred all or any of the loss and expense set out in paragraph 4.
4. Save as here before expressly admitted, the defendant denies each and every allegation contained in the Statement of Claim as if the same were here set out and specifically traversed.

Served this twentieth day of December 1992
by Gamma and Co of 10 Apple Drive, Blanktown.
Solicitors for the Defendants.

---

stipulate that if an allegation in a statement of claim is not expressly denied, known as a traverse, it is deemed to have been admitted.

Order 14 Judgment

The defendant's failure to enter a defence to a statement of claim allows the plaintiff to apply for judgment in default. The plaintiff wins the case without having to prove the claim by a court trial. In addition to this, the provisions in Order 14 allow the plaintiff to make an application on the ground that the defendant has no triable defence to the statement of claim. Evidence, of course, has to be produced which is sufficient to justify the application. Defendants need do no more than prove that they have a triable defence in order to have the plaintiff's application dismissed.

Order 14 procedure is widely used in construction disputes, for example a main contractor may refuse to pay a sub-contractor on some ground, such as delay, with the result the sub-contractor has to issue a writ. By the use of Order 14 procedure the sub-contractor may be able to obtain judgment without having to wait for a court hearing.

The use of Order 14 procedure is to be seen in the case of *Ellis Mechanical Services Limited v Wates Construction Limited 1976*. Ellis Mechanical Services were sub-contractors for heating, pipes and mechanical services for Wates, the main contractors for a large development. The main contract was determined which automatically determined the sub-contract. The sub-contractors believed that they were entitled to some £187 000; they thought that they had an undisputed claim to £52 437, while the balance of the £187 000 they recognized as open to agreement.

The sub-contractors obtained an Order 14 judgment for the £52 437, with the balance to be dealt with by arbitration. The main contractors appealed against the Order 14 judgment. The Court of Appeal was, however, satisfied that the judgment was correct, because certificates for payment for this sum had been issued by the engineers and surveyors of the Greater London Council for whom the work was being done. The Court of Appeal indicated that if a person was able to produce satisfactory evidence that a certain sum can be shown to be due then Order 14 judgment is appropriate.

Other provisions

If neither summary judgment in default nor Order 14 judgment is appropriate the pleadings continue. If a defendant served with a statement of claim or a plaintiff served with a defence believes that document does not provide them with the necessary information to deal with the matter they may make a request for further and better particulars. This sets out in detail the points of uncertainty and requires answers to be made to those questions.

A further procedural measure is that of discovery of documents: each side is entitled to know the documents in the possession of the other party which will be used in the case. An exception to this requirement is the class of privileged documents, which have passed between one of the parties and their legal adviser. Privileged documents are disclosed as being in existence but their contents are not inspected by the other party.

In the course of the pleadings it may become apparent to defendants that the claim concerns some matter which is not entirely their responsibility: defendants may involve the other person whom they believe has some liability by serving a third party notice, which makes that person a party to the action; the person's liability is considered as part of the court hearing.

The final action before the trial is a summons for directions. This is heard by a Master of the Supreme Court, a senior legally qualified official who considers the papers in the case and issues any directions necessary to allow the case to come to trial. The case is then placed in the court list for hearing.

The majority of matters where pleadings are exchanged do not in fact go before a court for trial. Both before and after a writ is served it is usual for negotiations to be going on with a view to a settlement. Defendants, or more likely their insurers, could be offering a sum of money as settlement without however admitting liability. A defendant may also seek to obtain a settlement by making a payment into court. If it is refused and in the subsequent trial the court awards a smaller sum, the defendant is responsible not only for the defence costs but also for the plaintiff's costs from the date of payment into court. From the pleadings it may become apparent to one of the parties that their case is weak and unlikely to succeed; they may then decide to discontinue the action.

Trial

The practice in civil trials, with one or two exceptions, is for the judge to hear the case without a jury. The judge decides whether or not the plaintiff has proved the case, which means that the trial is conducted at a faster pace, the decision is more likely to be correct and the sum awarded by the judge will be within the accepted range and so less likely to be the subject of an appeal.

The trial starts with the plaintiff's barrister making an opening speech, setting out the events which led to the case being brought, taking the judge through the pleadings and making reference to the documentary evidence.

The plaintiff's witnesses are called to give evidence. They swear an oath or affirm and give their evidence in chief, then they are cross-examined by the defendant's barrister. If in the course of cross-examination the evidence of the witness has been discredited the plaintiff's barrister may re-examine the witness. If a witness produces a document or a plan this becomes an exhibit in the case. When the plaintiff's case has been concluded the defendant's barrister may submit that the defendant has no case to answer.

The defence barrister may make an opening speech provided defence witnesses are to be called. After their evidence the defence barrister addresses the court, followed by the plaintiff's barrister. The judge may give a reserved judgment (that is the judge takes time to consider his or her decision, which is given later) or gives judgment immediately.

Costs are at the judge's discretion but generally the successful party are awarded their costs, which are subject to taxation by a court official.

The items in the bill of costs are examined in order to see that they are neither unreasonably incurred nor unreasonable in amount: this frequently means that the successful party will not receive a sum sufficient to meet the amount they owe to their solicitors.

County Court
The procedure just considered is followed in a case brought before the County Court. Because of the nature of the cases brought before the court and the practice of parties acting without the assistance of lawyers, the procedure is much simpler.

Court remedies

Damages

Damages, which are the common law remedy available to the civil courts, consist of an award of money to compensate the plaintiff. The award is made both for claims for breach of contract and for actions in tort.

In breach of contract, the principle is that the plaintiff is to be compensated only. In the case of *British Westinghouse v Underground Electric Railways 1912* the House of Lords stated that as far as money could do so the plaintiff is to be put in the situation he or she would have been in as if the contract had been performed. There is, therefore, no element of the plaintiff being put in a better position than would have been the case if the contract had been properly performed. At one time the fact that a plaintiff had suffered inconvenience or injured feelings was something the court could not take into account in making an award of damages. The decision of the Court of Appeal in the case of *Jarvis v Swan Tours Ltd 1973*, however, allowed an element of damages where there was inconvenience and injured feelings from a holiday which turned out to be unsatisfactory.

In an award of damages for tort, say negligence, the court is required to make an award that puts plaintiffs in the position they would have been in if the wrong had not taken place. This means that a number of factors must be considered by the court. If, for example, a plaintiff suffered personal injury in an industrial accident as a result of her employer's negligence, in assessing the damages the court would have regard to her pain and suffering, loss of enjoyment of life and loss of earnings.

This calculation of damages requires the court to fix sums which the court believe to be appropriate; a claim of this nature is a claim for general damages. Where some of the claim can be calculated precisely, for example a claim for loss of earnings for three months, that claim is for special damages.

When a court makes an award of damages it is invariably some considerable time after the event which gave rise to the action. The plaintiff should therefore be able to have an amount added to that award for the delayed payment, and a claim for interest may be added to the damages awarded by the court. If the action is with regard to a delayed payment under a contract and the contract expressly provides for interest to be paid, the court will add interest to the debt. In general, however, the award of interest is governed by the provisions in Section 35A of the Supreme Court Act 1981, which gives the High Court a discretion to include simple interest at a rate the court thinks fit or as rules of the court may provide.

In making a claim, whether in contract or tort, plaintiffs must show that they mitigated the loss, that is they took reasonable steps to keep the loss to a minimum. For example an employee who has been dismissed and claims that his dismissal was wrongful and in breach of his contract of employment would have to show that he made reasonable efforts to obtain similar employment. If he can prove this he has minimized his loss and may claim for the time he suffered loss of earnings from the wrongful dismissal.

Injunctions

In addition to damages, the court may also, at the court's discretion, grant an injunction. An injunction is an equitable remedy granted at the court's discretion, unlike the common law remedy of damages which is the plaintiff's right if the case is proved.

The High Court's approach to the granting of an injunction is governed by the case of *American Cyanamid Co v Ethicon Ltd 1975*, where the Law Lords altered the traditional approach that an injunction would be granted if the plaintiff proved that a prima facie case exists and that if an injunction was refused the plaintiff would suffer damage greater than the inconvenience and nuisance suffered by the defendants in having their activities restricted. The Law Lords said that the approach should be whether the plaintiff could show that there was a serious issue to be tried. Once a court is satisfied on this point it has to decide whether on the facts of the case an injunction ought to be granted. There is no requirement on the court to consider the likely outcome of the claim: the court is required only to be satisfied that the injunction being sought is based on a serious issue.

Injunctions may be granted by the court as either perpetual or interlocutory. Perpetual injunctions are granted after a full hearing of the claim and where plaintiffs have proved their case to the satisfaction of the court. Interlocutory injunctions are granted after proceedings have started and before the court conducts a trial of the dispute, with the intention of restraining the defendant from continuing a course of action which the plaintiff claims is unlawful. Recent examples have been injunctions to control the trespass of jibs of contractors' cranes swinging over adjoining property. In practice, the granting of an interlocutory injunction may lead to the parties settling the action without recourse to a trial.

The granting of an interlocutory injunction can have a serious effect on the defendant: it may limit or close a business operation. There is, therefore, a need to provide some protection for the defendant. The court requires plaintiffs to give an undertaking that if their claim ultimately fails they will compensate the defendant for any financial loss the defendant has incurred because of the interlocutory injunction having been granted.

Injunctions, whether interlocutory or perpetual, may be in the form of prohibitory or mandatory injunctions. Mandatory injunctions are less usual since they require the defendant to take some action which is likely to require the expenditure of money.

Other equitable remedies

Other forms of equitable remedies the court may grant are specific performance, rescission and rectification. The decree of specific performance is an order of the court that the parties to a contract shall perform the contract. The court is aware of the difficulty in some circumstances of enforcing an order for specific performance and so will not make an order of specific performance if the contract is one of personal service. Thus a contract of employment will not be made the subject of such an order. Because specific performance is granted only when the award of damages would be inadequate, the order is in practice confined to contracts for the sale of land or for articles of rare value.

The decree of rescission is an order that a contract be set aside and the parties to the contract to be put back into the position they were in before the contract was made. The court will not make this order if a third party to the contract would be affected by an order. The court would then have to make an award of damages, the common law remedy.

The decree of rectification is granted by the court where a written contract has a term which does not comply with the earlier oral contract. When a court is satisfied that this is so, the court may make an order putting right the written contract so that it conforms to the terms of the original oral contract.

Failure to observe one of these equitable remedies constitutes contempt of court, when the court may impose appropriate punishment, including imprisonment.

Legal status

English law recognizes that there are different capacities which persons may occupy when involved in legal matters. English law deals with the situation where a group of people join together to form an independent body in order to conduct a business, by accepting that there can be artificial persons as well as natural persons.

English law draws distinctions in both criminal and civil law according to age. A child under ten years of age is held to be incapable of committing any crime; a child between ten and fourteen years can be held to be capable of committing a crime only if it can be shown that the child was capable of forming a criminal intent. So far as civil law is concerned minors under the age of eighteen may make a valid contract only for those goods and services necessary for their existence. Subject to these exceptions, ordinary persons have that legal status to be responsible for their actions.

A civil engineer who set up in business as a consultant is liable personally for all the liabilities of that business, and also liable for any civil wrong committed by any person employed in that business. Because of this personal liability, business people who get into financial difficulties could be made bankrupt and their personal assets, such as their house, be taken by the trustees in bankruptcy in order to meet their business debts. This is the risk a sole trader or professional person runs.

Another way of conducting a business is to form a partnership, which is defined in Section 2 of the Partnership Act 1890 as 'the relation which subsists between persons carrying on a business with a view to profit'. There has to be agreement between two or more persons as to the carrying on of a business with a view to making a profit. The Companies Act 1985 fixes an upper limit of twenty members to a partnership. A number of professions, including consulting engineers, are by concession allowed to exceed the maximum of twenty.

In law a partnership is an unincorporated association which does not have a legal existence separate to those who make up the partnership: the partners are each personally liable for the conduct of the partnership. Great care should be exercised in accepting a person as a partner; the failure of one partner to act properly can bring down the whole partnership, with the consequence that the personal assets of all the partners can be called upon to meet a claim. Actions may be brought against a partnership, by suing the partnership in the firm's name or suing the names of all the partners.

The risk found with unlimited liability can be reduced by using the provisions in the Limited Partnership Act 1907. A limited partnership consists of one or more general partners who are liable for all the debts and obligations of the firm, and one or more limited partners who when they enter the partnership contribute money or property to a stated value and whose liability for debts or obligations of the firm shall not exceed that value. The Limited Partnership Act requires registration to be made and other administrative requirements to be observed. Limited partnership allows individuals to put money into a partnership and to limit their liability to that amount, but it has no great advantage over an ordinary partnership and is not greatly used.

A company is different from individuals in business on their own and from a partnership in that it has a separate legal existence to the members making up the company. A company may be referred to as an artificial person, and can be sued and sue in its own name; it has full legal responsibility for its actions, including criminal offences. Companies are frequently prosecuted for breaches of safety laws. In order to prevent a company being prosecuted as the sole offender when senior officers of a company have some responsibility, Section 37 of the Health and Safety at Work etc Act 1974 allows a director and other specified officers to be prosecuted in addition to the company. Similar provisions are found in certain other Acts of Parliament.

A company has perpetual succession: its life continues until the existence of the company is brought to an end by action under the Companies Act 1985. A company also has a common seal: the company indicates its agreement to important contracts and other documents. The Companies

Act 1989 now allows a company to operate without a common seal if the company so decides.

Probably the most important advantage is that it may operate as a limited liability company. The members of the company (the shareholders) have their liability for the company's debts and obligations limited to the unpaid part of the shares they hold. As most shares are now issued as fully paid up, members are at no greater risk than the loss of the value of their shares, unlike sole traders and partnerships where the personal assets of those concerned are at risk.

Evidence

The law of evidence is a set of rules dealing with the way in which facts may be proved in courts. These rules are found in common law and in Acts of Parliament. The responsibility for the production of relevant evidence falls on the parties to the dispute since it is their duty either to prove or to disprove the issue in dispute. The court's function is to reach a decision based on the evidence of the parties.

The obligation that the law places on a person bringing an action is known as the burden of proof. It is the duty of the prosecution in a criminal case to prove the guilt of the accused; accused persons are not required to prove their innocence. Failure of the prosecution to prove guilt means that the accused must be acquitted. In a civil case the rule is 'he who alleges must prove'. Failure to satisfy this requirement means the claim made must fail.

The standard of proof required to discharge the burden of proof depends on whether it is a criminal case or a civil case. In a criminal case the prosecution must prove the case against the accused beyond reasonable doubt. Juries are told that if they have a reasonable doubt, it must be exercised in favour of the accused, who must be found not guilty. In a civil case the required standard is not so stringent; even though the evidence may not be wholly convincing, if the balance of probabilities falls in favour of the persons bringing the claim then they have succeeded in their claim. If the balance of probabilities falls on the other side the plaintiff has failed to discharge the burden of proof and the claim must fail.

In the preparation of the pleadings in a civil case the object is to clarify the issue for the court hearing; the parties may make certain admissions or agree evidence in order to avoid argument on points which do not justify that course of action.

Evidence given to a court in order to prove or disprove the facts in issue may take a number of forms. These are: testimony, hearsay, documentary, real and circumstantial.

Testimony

Testimony is evidence given on oath or by affirmation by a witness who may be an ordinary witness or an expert witness. Ordinary witnesses tell the court what they saw, so the court is given a sworn testimony of an event by a person who saw what happened. Ordinary witnesses are not allowed to give their opinion. It is the court's duty to form an opinion on the evidence put before the court.

Ordinary witnesses tell the court what they saw or experienced; the side calling them is not, in general, allowed to 'lead' them to say certain things by putting to them leading questions, which are those which suggest answers. The other side in the cross-examination may ask leading questions in order to discredit the witness. Ordinary witnesses may be required to give evidence on an event that occurred some time earlier; they may 'refresh their memory' by consulting notes or a report they prepared regarding the event, subject to the notes or report being prepared at the time of the event or shortly afterwards.

In circumstances such as death, illness or absence abroad, the evidence of a witness may be read to the court provided it has been obtained by means of a deposition; this does not give it any special significance. It is for the court or jury to assess it in the same way as any other evidence.

Expert witnesses are by reason of their training, qualification or experience experts in a particular matter. Unlike ordinary witnesses, expert witnesses can give their opinion, which is evidence that the court may accept or reject. In civil cases expert witnesses are used by both parties to the dispute, for which they receive fees for preparation of their reports and attendance at court. In giving evidence expert witnesses may consult textbooks, reports and other sources in order to enable them to give their opinion.

Witnesses may be compelled to attend civil trials by the court issuing an order. Individuals may also be required to bring to court documents which are relevant to the trial.

Hearsay evidence

Hearsay evidence is when people give evidence on a matter which they have been told about by somebody else but which they themselves did not witness. For example X may be injured in an industrial accident, witnessed by Y. Y is an original witness to the accident since she saw what happened. If Y told Z of the accident, Z would be giving hearsay evidence if he told the court what he was told by Y.

For many years there has been a reluctance to allow hearsay evidence to be given to courts, because it was considered to be unreliable in that people giving evidence did not themselves witness the events, they cannot therefore be properly cross-examined and a story retold is often a story changed. However, without the use of hearsay evidence some cases could not proceed properly, and now exceptions are permitted under common law and in several Acts of Parliament.

Documentary evidence

Documentary evidence consists of the production of documents for the court's inspection. The documents are evidence of their existence and of their contents. For example the production of the employer's accident report book in a claim for damages for an industrial accident would be documentary evidence of the existence of the accident report book and of the entries in it. Courts expect to have the original document produced but are allowed to accept secondary evidence both of the document's existence and its contents.

Real evidence

Real evidence often consists of the production of some material object for the court's inspection. It can also be the physical appearance of persons, the demeanour of witnesses or views. If a physical object is too large to be taken into the court it is permissible for the court to go to view it, for example a large machine which had caused an industrial accident could be visited at its place of work in order to assist the court to understand its working.

Circumstantial evidence

Circumstantial evidence consists of relevant facts from which the existence or non-existence of a fact in issue may be inferred; the proof of the facts the court is to decide may be proved or disproved by other evidence which is relevant. For example, skid marks would be circumstantial evidence in a case concerning a road accident. The evidence from the skid marks would assist the court as to the position of the vehicle, its direction and its possible speed. Circumstantial evidence can be a good source of evidence and need not be inferior to direct evidence. The more circumstantial evidence there is, the less likely a court will come to the wrong decision.

Without prejudice

'Without prejudice' negotiation is a rule of evidence that negotiations made with a view to a settlement of a civil action cannot be referred to in any subsequent court action provided those negotiations had been conducted under the privilege of 'without prejudice'. The rule is based on public policy, with the intention that the parties to a dispute are to be encouraged to settle their dispute without going to litigation. The statements made in the course of seeking a settlement are privileged and cannot be used against a person in later litigation: without this privilege few settlements would be achieved.

The privilege given by the rule applies not only to written documents, such as the exchange of letters, but also to discussions provided the circumstances are ones where possible litigation is the subject of those discussions. For example in *Rabin v Mendoza and Co 1954*, Rabin sued for negligence in the survey of a property. Before the action had started the solicitors of Rabin and a partner of the surveyors' firm had a meeting to see if it was possible to settle the matter without litigation. The partner agreed to make inquiries to see if there was the possibility of obtaining insurance cover for possible damage to the house which would avoid the need for litigation. The surveyors obtained a report from another surveyor with a view to obtaining the insurance cover. No settlement was reached and legal action followed. The surveyors claimed privilege for this report on the ground that it was the result of a discussion which came within the rule. The Court of Appeal agreed that the rule applied in these circumstances.

There must, of course, be a dispute with possible litigation if the rule is to apply. The marking of documents with the words 'without prejudice' when no dispute exists does not bring the rule into operation. The rule does not apply to a document or statement made in the course of without prejudice negotiations if it has no reference to the dispute.

The privilege given by the rule may be removed only if both parties agree to its removal. A party can, however, protect their position to a certain extent by marking an offer 'without prejudice save as to costs'. Under the rules of the Supreme Court that letter of offer may be referred to by the court when it considers the award of cost after the court hearing.

2

General contract law

Nature of a contract

In English law a contract is an agreement made between two or more parties which is intended to have legal obligations. Every contract is an agreement but not all agreements are contracts. A contract is an agreement which gives rise to obligations which will be recognized by law and enforced in the courts. A party to an agreement cannot have the assistance of the courts in the event of a dispute arising, as the essential features of legal obligation and enforcement are missing.

The law accepts that agreements are made without any intention that they should have legal consequences; social or domestic arrangements are agreements only. Parties may wish to make agreements which would usually be contracts but they have chosen to avoid forming a contract. In the case of *Rose and Frank Co v J R Crompton and Bros Ltd 1925*, two commercial companies made an agreement which expressly said that it was not entered into as a formal or legal agreement, was not to be subject to legal jurisdiction in the law courts and was to be held to be an expression and record of the intention of the parties to honourably pledge themselves. The House of Lords decided that the agreement was not a legally binding agreement: there was no intention that it was to have the effect of a contract.

An agreement which usually contains express provision that it is not to have legal consequences is the normal letter of intent. A contract will come into existence only when the parties have proceeded in a manner which the law accepts converts the letter of intent into a contract.

A contract in English law is in the nature of a bargain: each party is expected to derive some advantage. The advantages for each party do not have to balance each other, but in general the courts will not enforce a contract against a party who would receive no benefit from the contract.

There are two types of contract: a simple contract and a contract by deed. A simple contract may be formed by word of mouth, in writing or by conduct; it is how all common transactions are conducted. A contract by deed, usually known as a contract under seal, is a more formal contract made in a prescribed manner. It is used for contracts of a substantial nature, for example a construction contract.

Since a contract is an agreement made between individuals they can include what terms they wish. They may make a contract with short simple terms or one with complex terms. They may, and frequently do, make use of contracts prepared by some professional or trade organization which contains terms appropriate to the contract obligations; a range of standard forms of contract prepared specially for use in construction work is extensively used.

At one time the parties to a contract could make it without restraint to its terms. Parliament has increasingly passed statutes which restrain the terms used in certain contracts: if terms conflict with certain statutes they are ineffective. Contracts of employment were originally made with the terms agreed with the employers and employees. Now, as a result of the extensive provisions in the Employment Protection (Consolidation) Act 1978, contracts of employment are made up mainly of statutory terms. The freedom of the parties to contract as they wish has been substantially reduced.

Contract law is comprised of case law and statutes. A number of cases were decided in the nineteenth century when important principles were being established by the courts. Parliament has strengthened contract law by passing statutes to deal with deficiencies which have been revealed by judicial decisions. The Unfair Contract Terms Act 1977 was passed to strengthen the law controlling, among other things, contract terms which are unreasonable against one of the parties to the contract.

Essential elements

The essential element of a contract is that the agreement must have been made with the intention that it would have legal obligations. In addition the following elements must be present:

1. *Offer and acceptance.* A contract is formed by one person making an offer to another person who then accepts the offer. An offer may be made in writing or by word of mouth and may be made to unknown persons. Acceptance may be made in writing or by word of mouth. Offer and acceptance may also be held to have occurred from the conduct of the parties. Negotiation may take place to obtain an agreement which is acceptable to both parties. There is then an offer on the agreed basis and an acceptance of that particular offer.
2. *Form or consideration.* English law requires that a contract not made in a particular form must have consideration if it is to be a contract. A contract by deed or under seal has a special status since, historically, it was made by a man of honour affixing his personal seal into molten wax on the contract document. Over the years persons without their own personal seals were able to make this form of contract by affixing to the contract document a red adhesive wafer. Under the Law of Property (Miscellaneous Provisions) Act 1989 the procedure is much simpler: an expression that the contract is made as a deed, supported by the signature of the contracting party and which is witnessed, is sufficient.

Consideration is the reward that persons receive in return for the performance of their part of the contract; it is usually money but it does not have to be. Nor does it have to be a fair reward of the contract performance. Consideration is essential to a simple contract (and without it no contract exists) but not to a contract by deed.

3. *Legality.* A contract will not be one the courts will recognize and enforce if the substance of the contract is illegal. The construction industry has in the past been subject to government licensing: if parties entered into a construction contract for unlicensed work, that was an illegal contract.

4. *Capacity.* In order to enter into a contract the parties must have the necessary capacity. Persons under the age of eighteen cannot, in general, enter into a binding contract. Difficulties have arisen in the past with companies entering into contracts which the objects clause of the company's Memorandum of Association did not allow.

5. *Genuine consent.* A contract is a freely negotiated agreement between the parties with agreed terms. The consent of each party is to be freely given. A party's consent to a contract would not be genuine if they had entered into the contract as a direct result of some misinformation given to them by the other party which was fundamental to the contract. Where there has been a genuine mistake about the substance of the contract, the court will take the view that the consent of the parties was not genuine. Another example would be where a party entered into a contract solely because of threats made to them.

Written contracts

Most contracts can be made orally, but few parties would wish to contract on important topics simply by an exchange of spoken words. Common sense would suggest that the contract be put in writing: reference can then be made to the written terms to resolve any difficulty which might arise. Without any intention to deceive, parties to an oral contract can, especially over a period of time, have different understandings as to the contract.

In two circumstances statute law requires that contracts must be in writing, otherwise they are unenforceable. First, the Statute of Frauds 1677 requires that a contract of guarantee shall be evidenced in writing. A contract of guarantee arises where one person promises to answer for the debt, default or miscarriage of another person. Where A intends to contract with B but, because of some doubt as to B's ability to pay for goods, seeks a guarantor to accept liability in the event of B's failure to pay. A third person C is brought in to act as the guarantor. C will be called upon to honour this promise only if B fails to pay. B is said to be primarily liable and C to be secondarily liable.

A contract of guarantee is different from a contract of indemnity, where a person (C in the above example) promises to be liable unconditionally. So A can turn to B or C for payment as A chooses. There is no obligation, as in a guarantee, for B to default before C can become liable. Contracts of indemnity do not come within the provisions of the Statute of Frauds and so do not have to be in writing to be enforceable.

Second, contracts for the sale of land were originally governed by the Statute of Frauds. Now, section 2 of the Law of Property (Miscellaneous Provisions) Act 1989 requires that a contract for the sale or other disposition of an interest in land must be in writing. All the terms agreed by the parties must be in that document or be incorporated by reference to some other document. The contract must be signed by or on behalf of each party to the contract. If contracts are exchanged, each document must be signed by or on behalf of the party exchanging the document; each party then has a contract document with the other party's signature on it. A contract which does not satisfy the requirement of the Law of Property (Miscellaneous Provisions) Act 1989 is unenforceable.

Two exceptions to this requirement are where the contract is made by auction, and what are termed 'short leases' under section 54 of the Law of Property Act 1925.

Offer and acceptance

An offer is an expression of willingness to contract made with the intention that it shall become binding on the person making it as soon as it is accepted by the person to whom it is addressed. The important feature of this definition is the expression of willingness to contract, which may be stated in a number of ways, such as 'tender', 'price', 'contract sum', 'estimate' or 'quotation'. Whatever word is used the expression of willingness to contract constitutes an offer.

There is the practice of using the word 'estimate' to mean that the person is not making a firm offer on that stated figure. The word 'quotation' is used to indicate that a firm offer is being made. The court will look to see whether there was an expression of willingness to contract whatever word was used.

In the case of *Crowshaw v Pritchard and Renwick 1899*, Crowshaw sent a drawing and specification to Pritchard and Renwick and asked for a tender for alteration work. The reply was marked ESTIMATE and stated that their estimate was for carrying out the alteration work in accordance with the drawing and specification amounting to £1230. Crowshaw wrote next day accepting the 'offer to execute' the works. Pritchard and Renwick, however, refused to carry out the work. The claim was made not only that by using the word 'estimate' there was no offer to do the work, but also that there was a trade custom that such a letter was not to be treated as an offer. The High Court, however, decided that the word 'estimate' was an offer which had been accepted by Crowshaw, so making Pritchard and Renwick liable on the contract. The court also indicated that if there was some custom or well-known understanding that a letter in that form was not to be treated as an offer then it was contrary to law.

Despite this decision it is unlikely that a court would ignore an established contract practice between two parties. If, for example, a sub-contractor regularly responded to a request from a main contractor to supply, quickly, an estimate as a rough figure followed later by a quotation at a firm price the courts would accept that this was the way in which the parties conducted their business. A court would be reluctant to impose a different understanding from the parties' established contract practice. If there was no established practice, the court would look to the intention of the parties based on legal principles.

A number of cases show that this problem has arisen in the haste to start a construction project: it would have been avoided if the offer had been supplemented by an indication that it was not a firm price because of a stated reason.

Invitation to treat

English law recognizes when a person seeks an offer: this is known as an invitation to treat. In the case of the *Pharmaceutical Society of Great Britain v Boots Cash Chemists (Southern) Ltd 1953*, Boots had a self-service store where a qualified pharmacist was situated at the cashier's position. The duty of the pharmacist was to permit or deny the purchase of medicines, some of which could be obtained only on a doctor's prescription. An inspector of the Society visited the store to check that the law with regard to the sale of drugs and medicine was being observed. The inspector selected various items from the open shelves and then sought to pay for them at the cash point. The inspector was told that the payment for certain goods could not be accepted. The Society brought an action on the basis that a contract of sale of the goods had been made when the inspector took the goods from the open shelves: the display of the goods was an offer by Boots which was accepted by the inspector taking them to the cash point with the intention of paying for them.

The court took the view that the display of goods did not constitute an offer, but was an invitation to treat only. Boots were prepared to consider offers being made for the goods. The offer was made by the inspector; the pharmacist's refusal to allow the goods to be paid for constituted a rejection of the offer.

An invitation to treat in construction work may be seen in the practice of public bodies inviting contractors to submit tenders for work. The contractor tenders and offers to execute the work which the public body can accept or reject. Public bodies frequently indicate that they do not bind themselves to accept either the lowest or any tender; this is not necessary since all the public body has done is to indicate an interest in receiving offers to execute work at a stated price. The public body may accept any offer or reject them all, which they could do if the lowest offer was more than they wished to pay for the work.

There may, however, be a duty on the person who invited contractors' tenders. In the case of *Blackpool and Fylde Aero Club Ltd v Blackpool Borough Council 1990*, Blackpool Council owned Blackpool Airport and leased the concession for the operation of pleasure flights. In 1975, 1978 and 1980 the Aero Club tendered for and were successful in obtaining the concession. In 1983 the concession again became available and the Aero Club and six other parties were invited to submit tenders on a form of tender provided by the Council. The form stated that the Council did not bind themselves to accept all or any part of any tender and that 'No Tender which is received after the last date and time specified shall be admitted for consideration'. The Aero Club posted their tender by hand in the town hall before the deadline expired at noon. The letter box was normally cleared at noon, but on that day it was not cleared until later. It was held to be a late submission and although it was the highest tender, the tender of another air operator was accepted.

The Aero Club brought an action claiming damages for breach of contract. The Court of Appeal upheld the decision in favour of the Aero Club: the invitation to selected persons to submit tenders for the concession contractually bound the Council to open and consider all the tenders received in accordance with the tendering procedure. This has not been done and so the Aero Club were entitled to damages for breach of contract. The court noted that a person invited to submit a tender was put to considerable expense in its preparation and there was no recompense if the tender was unsuccessful. The person who had invited the tenders need not accept the lowest or any tender and did not have to give any reason for the decision.

The cost of preparing tenders is a commercial risk. It is recovered by the successful contractor in the contract price. For the unsuccessful tenders the expense is usually irrecoverable; in certain circumstances, however, costs associated with preparatory work may be recovered.

In the case of *William Lacey (Hounslow) Ltd v Davis 1957*, Davis owned certain properties which had been damaged by bombing in the Second World War. In order to obtain damage compensation for rebuilding Davis asked Lacey to submit a tender. In the belief that this tender would be accepted Lacey prepared further estimates and schedules. All these were made use of by Davis in his claim for war damage compensation. Davis then gave the work to another contractor. Lacey made a claim for a reasonable sum in payment for the work they had done, which the court accepted. The judge took the view that both parties had intended that payment for the work would be part of the total contract price when the contract was made. There was no understanding that the work was to be done without payment. There was therefore an obligation at law to pay a reasonable sum for the services obtained.

In the case of *Marston Construction Co Ltd v Kigass Ltd 1989*, Marston, building and civil engineering contractors, were invited to submit a tender for the rebuilding of a fire-damaged factory. This tender offered the best value for money but more detail was needed. Kigass made it clear (at a meeting to discuss the tender) that the factory would not be rebuilt unless and until the insurance money had been paid. No indication, however, was given to the contractors that if the insurance money was not paid all their preparatory work would be at their risk. The contractors proceeded with substantial preparatory work which went over and above the expense of the preparation of the tender. If the contract was awarded to them this cost would be included in the contract price.

A dispute arose as to whether the contractors were entitled to payment for this preparatory work. Kigass contended that the work had been done without charge in an attempt to secure the contract and improve the contractors' ability to complete on time, which meant that there was no obligation to pay. The court decided that the contractors were entitled to a reasonable payment for their preparatory work, because Kigass had implicity requested the preparatory work.

These two cases show that where contractors carry out work such as design, calculations, planning or survey work which goes beyond what is needed for the preparation of the tender, they may be entitled to payment of a reasonable sum for this work. Contractors will be entitled to payment if they have done the preparatory work either at the express or implied request of the person seeking the tender. The contractors' claim for payment will be strengthened if it can be shown (as in Lacey's case) that the other party made use of the preparatory work and thereby obtained a benefit.

Letters of intent

Letters of intent are frequently used with civil engineering work, less so for building work. There is no standard wording used in letters of intent: each must be examined as to its own form, which determines the liability, if any, of the sender of the letter.

Judge Fay, in the case of *Turriff Construction Ltd v Regalia Knitting Mills Ltd 1971*, said 'A Letter of Intent would ordinarily have two characteristics, one, that it will express an intention to enter into a contract in future and, two, it will itself create no liability in regard to that future contract'. Thus an ordinary letter of intent will be a written indication of the intention to enter into a contract at some time in the future, qualified by a further statement that the letter is not in itself to create a contractual relationship.

Using letters of intent gives a contractor or sub-contractor an early indication that a contract is likely and the recipient may therefore wish to order materials, start to make equipment or organize staff, but at the risk of the recipient of the letter of intent. A contract usually follows which puts the parties into a contractual relationship with regard to what has been done. If a contract is not made the issue of whether a contract actually exists has then to be determined.

If a dispute arises, the court looks not only to the terms of the letter of intent but also to the conduct of the parties and may on the basis of the letter or the conduct of the parties hold that a contract exists. For example a stated intention to nominate a party as a sub-contractor, which does not occur, would probably entitle the sub-contractor to payment for the work they have done. If the parties give possession of the site or make an advanced payment this would probably be held to be conduct sufficient to constitute a contract.

In the case of *British Steel Corporation v Cleveland Bridge and Engineering Co Ltd 1982*, Cleveland were successful in their tender for the fabrication of steel work in the construction of a building. The design was for steel beams to be jointed to the steel frame of the building by means of cast-steel nodes. British Steel were approached with a view to manufacturing these cast-steel nodes. Discussions on their manufacture and price took place. Cleveland sent a letter of intent asking British Steel to start work and stating that the contract would be on Cleveland's own standard form, which provided for unlimited liability to Cleveland for consequential loss due to late delivery. British Steel would not have contracted in this way. Cleveland indicated that the nodes were to be delivered in a particular sequence.

British Steel then sent a quotation on their standard form quoting a higher price. This was not accepted by Cleveland. At no time was a formal contract agreed. Work proceeded, however, and all but one node were delivered. Cleveland failed to make any interim or final payments. A dispute arose and Cleveland claimed a large sum for late delivery or delivery out of sequence. British Steel claimed payment of a reasonable sum, *quantum meruit*, for the value of the nodes.

The court decided that no contract existed between the parties. The letter of intent had indicated Cleveland's intention to use their own form of contract, with its terms regarding consequential loss. British Steel had refused to accept this and were unwilling to contract except on their own form of contract. Other evidence showed a failure to agree on details such as price and delivery dates. The parties had been unable to agree a contract, therefore British Steel were entitled to payment of a reasonable sum for the supply of the nodes. Cleveland's claim for consequential loss was dismissed as this was based on a term in a contract which did not exist.

In the case of *Turriff Construction Ltd v Regalia Knitting Mills Ltd 1971*, Regalia asked Turriff to submit a tender for the design and construction of a factory. In December 1968 the tender was submitted. Discussion took place and it became final in May 1969. In June 1969 Regalia told Turriff that they were to be given a contract to cover a programme ending in 1972. This required intensive and extensive preparatory work by Turriff, who therefore asked for a letter of intent to cover them for the work that they would be undertaking. It was not possible to conclude a contract as a number of matters were not then settled. Later that month Regalia sent the letter of intent, which stated the intention to award the contract to Turriff, phased over a period of time, and that it was subject to obtaining all necessary consents and subject to agreement on an acceptable contract.

The building work did not start because of a delay in obtaining planning permission. Turriff were negotiating with Regalia's architect about the form of contract and were preparing their detailed design. By December work had still not started and Turriff asked for payment of £3500 for their design costs. Regalia were then taken over and the project was cancelled. The new company denied any obligation to pay Turriff for their work.

The court decided that Turriff were entitled to payment for the work done. The letter of intent did not create a contract as it was dependent on the obtaining of consents and an acceptable contract being made. Turriff, however, had responded to a request to carry out work urgently required by Regalia. The sending of the letter of intent acted as an acceptance of Turriff's offer to undertake this work. This created an 'ancillary' contract which was separate to the intended project contract.

Making an offer

An offer is an expression of a willingness to contract; it must therefore be definite in its terms. If it is not definite it is probably not possible to make a proper acceptance and so no concluded contract exists.

In the case of *Peter Lind and Co Ltd v Mersey Docks and Harbour Board 1972*, Peter Lind submitted alternative tenders for the construction of a freight terminal. One of the tenders was a fixed-price tender and the other was a 'cost-plus' tender. Mersey Docks and Harbour Board said that they accepted 'your tender' but failed to indicate which of the two tenders they were accepting. Peter Lind carried out the work and then claimed payment not on the basis of either tender but on a *quantum meruit*. The court agreed that there was no concluded contract since the acceptance failed to state which tender was being accepted. The claim for payment on a *quantum meruit* succeeded.

An offer is usually sufficiently definite to avoid any difficulty arising; offers may be made by word of mouth or in writing. Sometimes offers must be submitted in a prescribed way and failure to do so would make the offer invalid. Public bodies for administrative reasons usually require that an offer shall be submitted on a form supplied and in a stated manner.

Termination of an offer

Offerors may withdraw their offer at any time before it is accepted, even if the offeror has stated that the offer is open for acceptance, say for thirty days. This is subject to no payment being made to keep the offer open for a period of time. In the purchase of land it is not uncommon to pay a sum of money in order to keep the offer open in order to obtain, for example, planning permission for development. This is known as purchasing an option.

If contractors withdraw an offer before it is accepted, they do not have to give any reason. It may, of course, be an embarrassment to the offeree to have the offer withdrawn but there is no legal impropriety in the withdrawal.

The rule that an offer can be revoked before acceptance is subject to revocation having to be communicated for it to be effective. In the case of *Byrne and Co v Van Tienhoven and Co 1880*, Van Tienhoven in Cardiff posted a letter on 1 October, offering to sell 1000 boxes of tinplate, to Byrne and Co in New York. The letter was received in New York on the 11th and accepted by telegraphy with a letter of confirmation sent on the 15th. Van Tienhoven, however, decided on 8 October to withdraw the offer and sent a letter to this effect to New York, where it arrived on the 20th. The court decided that Van Tienhoven's letter of revocation could not effectively withdraw the offer since it had been accepted by telegraph on the 11th and by letter on the 15th. Both these events occurred before the letter of revocation was received.

An offer may be open for acceptance for a limited time, for example within seven days, after which time the offer cannot be accepted. Where an offer does not have any time limit, the rule is that the offer lapses after a reasonable period of time, which varies with the nature of the offer. An offer to sell perishable food must, of necessity, lapse in a short time; with an offer to undertake a civil engineering project, a period of weeks would be a reasonable time.

In the case of *Ramsgate Victoria Hotel Co v Montefiore 1886*, Montefiore made an application in June to Ramsgate Victoria Hotel to buy shares.

He heard nothing about his application until November, when he was informed that he had been allocated a number of shares in the company. When he was asked to pay for the shares he refused to do so. The court agreed that he was entitled to refuse the shares, as his offer had not been accepted within a reasonable time.

An offer also comes to an end when it is rejected and in its place a counter-offer is made. This situation (dealt with in more detail on p. 39) arises when an offer, say, to perform work for £1000 is rejected and in its place a counter-offer of £900 is made. The making of the counter-offer extinguishes the original offer.

In the case of an offer which if accepted would give rise to a personal contract, such as a contract of employment, the death of either the offeror or the offeree terminates the offer.

Acceptance

A valid acceptance of an offer is a final and unqualified acceptance to the terms of the offer. No contract therefore comes into existence until the offer is accepted. Difficulties arise when there are negotiations over a period of time. The original offer may be rejected and a counter-offer made, which in turn may be rejected.

An acceptance may be made subject to a condition, such as the completion of a formal document: the acceptance is conditional on the performance of the completion of the document.

The general rule is that acceptance means communicated acceptance. In *Felthouse v Bindley 1862*, Felthouse sent a letter to a nephew offering to buy a horse from him for £30, telling the nephew that if he did not hear from him he would treat the horse as his. The nephew did not reply but withdrew the horse from an auction sale. By error the auctioneer, Bindley, sold the horse. Felthouse sued on the basis that he had bought the horse. The court decided that his offer to buy the horse had not been accepted. Acceptance had not been communicated.

An exception to this rule is the postal rule: where acceptance is expected to be by post, acceptance occurs when the letter is actually posted. This is so even if the letter is delayed or never arrives. In the case of *Household Fire and Carriage Accident Insurance Co Ltd v Grant 1879*, Grant offered to buy some shares from the company. The company secretary made out a letter of allotment for the shares and it was posted to Grant, who never received the letter. Not long afterwards the company became insolvent and Grant was required to pay the amount of the shares allotted to him. Grant disputed that he had bought the shares. The court decided that the contract was made when the letter of allotment was posted.

Some people who make offers stipulate that for a letter of acceptance to be valid it must be received by the offeror at a stated place, day and time. In this way the danger of a delayed letter of acceptance is avoided.

The question of acceptance by telex was considered in the case of *Brinkibon Ltd v Stahag Stahl und Stahlwarenhandels GmbH 1982*, where a contract was made between the two parties, one in business in Austria and the other in England. Wherever the contract was made determined which country's courts had jurisdiction to deal with a contract dispute. Brinkibon in England received an offer to which they telexed acceptance to Austria. The House of Lords held that the postal rule did not apply: the transaction was almost instantaneous thus, in accordance with the general rule that acceptance means communicated acceptance, acceptance was in Austria where it was received. So the Austrian courts had the jurisdiction to deal with the contract dispute.

Battle of the forms

The practice in the civil engineering industry is for suppliers of goods, sub-contractors and main contractors to use their own forms of contract or to alter the terms of the widely used standard forms of contract, to make the contract on the most favourable terms to the party whose form of contract is used. This was seen in the case of *British Steel Corporation v Cleveland Bridge and Engineering Co Ltd 1982* (see p. 35).

The description 'battle of the forms' was used by Lord Denning, the Master of the Rolls, in the case of *Butler Machine Tool Co Ltd v Ex-Cell-O Corporation (England) Ltd 1979*. Ex-Cell-O were interested in purchasing a machine tool and asked Butler if they could supply this machine tool. Butler replied quoting a price of £75 535 and a delivery date of ten months. The quotation was stated to be on the terms and conditions on the back of the document, including a price variation clause which required payment of a higher price if the cost of the machine tool had been increased on the date of delivery. Another clause stated that all orders were accepted only on Butler's terms and conditions, which were to prevail over the terms and conditions in the buyer's order.

Ex-Cell-O placed the order for the machine tool using their own order form which did not contain a price variation clause. At the bottom of their form was a tear-off acknowledgement of the order for signing and returning to Ex-Cell-O; it carried the words 'We accept your order on the Terms and Conditions stated thereon . . .'. Butler completed this acknowledgement and returned it to Ex-Cell-O, together with a letter which said 'This is being entered in accordance with our revised quotation of 23rd May for delivery in 10/11 months'.

When the machine tool was delivered the price had increased by £2892 and this was claimed by Butler. Ex-Cell-O refused to pay and a dispute then arose as to whose terms and conditions applied. Did Butler's with the price variation clause apply or did Ex-Cell-O's without such a clause apply?

The Court of Appeal decided that Ex-Cell-O's terms and conditions applied and so they were not liable to pay the extra £2892. The court's decision was based on an analysis of the actions of both parties. Ex-Cell-O's request was nothing more than an invitation to treat. Butler's response by their quotation was an offer to contract subject to their terms and conditions. Ex-Cell-O's order was a rejection of Butler's offer and a substitution of an offer on Ex-Cell-O's terms and conditions. Ex-Cell-O's order was accepted, and the contract formed, on the completion and return of the acknowledgement slip, even though Butler sent with it a letter which said the order was entered in accordance with the quotation of 23 May. The court took the view that the letter referred only to the price and delivery date and did not bring in the terms and conditions of the quotation.

Acceptance by conduct

An offer may be accepted by the conduct of the person to whom the offer was made: the conduct is treated as equivalent to a communicated acceptance. In the case of *Carlill v Carbolic Smoke Ball Co 1893*, the Carbolic Smoke Ball Co made an offer to pay £100 to anybody who contracted any one of an extensive range of illnesses after using the Smoke Ball in the recommended manner. As an indication of the company's sincerity it was stated that the sum of £1000, to meet any demand, had been deposited at a named branch of a bank. Mrs Carlill purchased a Smoke Ball and used it in the recommended manner. When she contracted an illness she claimed £100. This was refused and she then sued.

In answer to her claim the company said what was said was just mere sales talk, that it was not possible to make an offer to unknown persons and in any case Mrs Carlill had not communicated her acceptance to the company. The court decided that it was not just sales talk and that it was possible in law to make an offer to unknown persons. The matter of acceptance was covered by Mrs Carlill's purchase and use of the device in the recommended way. This constituted acceptance by conduct. There was no obligation on Mrs Carlill to send a written acceptance.

In the case of *A Davies and Co (Shopfitters) Ltd v William Old Ltd 1969*, Davies were invited by a building owner's architect to submit a tender as nominated sub-contractors. Davies were told that they would receive payment through the main contractors on the issue of architect's certificates. The tender was accepted and the main contractors, Old, placed an order with them. This order, however, introduced a new term, that the sub-contractors would be paid only when the main contractors had been paid. Davies started work without making any protest at the introduction of the new term. The building owner became insolvent, which meant that the main contractors had not received moneys to pay the sub-contractors for their work. Davies sued Old.

The court decided that a contract existed between them which included the term that the main contractors would pay the sub-contractors when they had been paid. The contract had been formed by Old's order which was a counter-offer and this had been accepted by Davies's conduct in starting the work. The court also rejected the claim that the term, which was on the back of the order form, did not apply because the main contractors had not done sufficient to draw the sub-contractors' attention to it.

Form or consideration

In English law a contract must be made in a particular form or it must have consideration. This divides contracts into two classes: contracts by deed or contracts under seal, and simple contracts. Contracts of a substantial nature are made as deeds and other contracts are made as simple contracts.

Until the introduction of the Law of Property (Miscellaneous Provisions) Act 1989 the requirement was that a contract made as a deed had to be signed, sealed and delivered: one party signed and put their seal on the document and then delivered the contract to the other party for the same things to be done. Originally the sealing was by pressing the personal seal into hot wax that had been melted on to the document. In more recent times the sealing has been done by sticking on the document a red adhesive wafer.

Now if an individual wishes to make a contract by deed the individual may do so by the document stating it is to be a deed, and the individual signing with that signature witnessed and attested. The Companies Act 1985 allows a company to make the contract by sealing it if the company has a common seal. The company may also make the contract by deed by the signatures of two directors or a director and the secretary.

Construction contracts are usually made as contracts by deed, which is advantageous to the employer since under the Limitation Act 1980 an action may be brought up to twelve years after the breach of contract. With a simple contract the period of time under the Act is six years only.

Consideration is a requirement of a simple contract: individuals who make a promise to another are not bound in a contract unless there is to be something they receive in return for that promise. If X promises to dig Y's garden for £5, X is bound in contract. If X promises to dig the garden without receiving any reward, there is no contract since there is no consideration.

Consideration covers a range of things which in some way are of value as recognized by law. In a construction contract the employer promises to pay the contract price in return for the work being done by the contractors. In return the contractors are promising that in return for the contract price they will perform the contract work. Each provides consideration in return for the promise made.

Consideration need not be a payment of money but can consist of the performance of some service or the loss of some benefit. The range of benefits and detriments recognized by law is such that there is much complexity of the matter. For example, a wayward teenage son who promised his father to change his conduct in return for a sum of money when he became twenty-one has not given consideration recognized by law.

Consideration can be executed or executory. Executed consideration arises, for example, when a seller of goods hands the goods over without payment being made at that time: the seller has performed her obligation under the contract. The buyer's consideration is executory since he has yet to undertake his part of the contract.

Consideration need not be adequate. So if a contractor undertakes a contract for a low price, the contractor, in general, cannot obtain the assistance of the courts to make the reward greater; conversely the employer cannot get the courts to order a contractor to accept a lower price than the contract price if the employer finds that the contractor is going to be 'over-rewarded'.

In *Williams v Roffey Bros and Nicholls (Contractors) Ltd 1990*, Roffey and Nicholls were building contractors who had contracted to refurbish a block of twenty-seven flats. The carpentry work was sub-contracted to Williams for a price of £20 000. Williams was a carpenter in a small way of business; he was to receive interim payments as the work proceeded. After completing the carpentry work to the roof and some of the flats, and receiving interim payments of £16 200, Williams found himself to be in financial difficulties, mainly because his price was too low. Some 80 per cent of the contract price had been paid but much more than 20 per cent of the work remained to be completed. Roffey and Nicholls were subject to a liquidated damages provision in the main contract if completion was delayed. They were aware that the sub-contract had been underpriced and that Williams was in financial difficulties; they agreed with Williams that they would pay him an extra £10 300 at the rate of £575 per flat, to ensure that Williams continued with the work and the need to appoint another sub-contractor would be avoided. It would also secure the completion of the work on time and so avoid any payment of liquidated damages.

On this basis Williams carried on with the work and completed eight more flats; for this he received a further payment of £1500. Williams stopped work on the remaining flats and brought an action claiming £10 847. Roffey and Nicholls denied liability and in particular denied that any part of the £10 300 could be claimed, on the ground that the agreement to pay that was unenforceable since there was no consideration in return for the promise.

The Court of Appeal upheld Williams's claim that he was entitled to eight payments of £575, plus a reasonable proportion of the amount outstanding on the original contract, which came to £1500. The court took the view that if a party to a contract agreed, in the absence of fraud or economic duress, to pay a sum over and above the original contract price that would be binding if in return some benefit was obtained. In return for the promise to pay the additional £10 300, Roffey and Nicholls had obtained the benefit of the avoidance of paying liquidated damages or having to obtain a replacement sub-contractor. This was so even though Williams was not required to carry out any further work than that he had contracted to do under the contract.

This decision ought not to be treated as a general principle that if contractors underprice their tender they can later expect the employer to pay an additional sum. Each case must be considered on its own particular facts. Contractors who had underpriced their tender and having started the contract threatened to leave the work unless the employer agreed to pay an additional sum would very likely be held to have used economic duress, which would disentitle them to that additional sum. In Williams's case evidence was given by a surveyor that the proper price for the original contract ought to have been £23 738 rather than £20 000. There was also evidence that Williams had failed to supervise his workers properly. In total the court was satisfied that Williams's financial difficulties were genuine, that there was a real possibility that Williams would not be able to continue with the work, and this would require the appointment of a replacement sub-contractor with the probability of liquidated damages having to be paid. The additional payment to Williams sought to, and in the main achieved, the avoidance of these events coming about.

A rule with regard to consideration is that it must not be past, that is a promise made after an act. For example, if a person, having been rescued from drowning, promises the rescuer a reward, this does not constitute consideration since the promised reward was after the rescuer had performed the rescue.

A development with regard to consideration is that of estoppel: a person in certain circumstances cannot deny a statement he or she has made. In the case of *Central London Property Trust Ltd v High Trees House Ltd 1947*, Central London leased a block of flats in 1937 for 99 years to High Trees at an annual rent of £2500. In 1940 because of the wartime conditions High Trees were having great difficulty in letting the flats. Central London therefore agreed to reduce the rent to £1250 per annum for the duration of the war. When the war ended Central London demanded the full rent. The Court of Appeal granted this claim but added that if the claim had been for the full rent during the period covered by the agreement this would have been refused: if a person makes a binding promise which another person acts on then the person making the promise is estopped, that is not allowed to go back on that promise.

This principle of estoppel could be used only as a defence and could not form a cause of action on its own. It does now appear that the courts are moving towards a recognition that a promise made in circumstances where another person acts on it to his or her detriment might constitute a cause of action even though it does not come within the present accepted concept of consideration.

Legality

The courts may refuse to give full effect to any contract if it is an illegal contract. Simple examples are contracts to commit a crime, contracts to commit a civil wrong and contracts amounting to a legal wrong. There are two matters of importance: first, where a contract is illegal in itself, and second, where some illegality arises in the performance of the contract.

Since the end of the Second World War there has been a system of licensing of construction work. Construction work above a certain value required a licence issued by a government department. A contract to carry out work at a value which required a licence would be illegal without a licence. A contract to construct a building forbidden by law, such as a brothel, would also be illegal.

In the case of *Bostel Brothers Ltd v Hurlock 1949*, Hurlock obtained a licence for certain works to his house, and appointed Bostel Brothers to carry out this work. By an innocent oversight the builders exceeded the amount of the licence and did not apply for a supplementary licence. The builders made a claim for the value of the work which exceeded the amount stated in the licence. This claim was refused by the Court of Appeal on the ground that there was a prohibition on doing the unlicensed work, which made that work illegal.

In the case of *Townsends (Builders) Ltd v Cinema News and Property Management Ltd 1959*, Cinema News had some alteration work done by Townsend on a plan and specification prepared by a firm of architects. By error the work resulted in a breach of the building byelaws. Cinema News refused to pay, claiming that the work was illegal. The Court of Appeal refused to accept this made the contract illegal. Townsends were required to remedy the work which contravened the building byelaws at their own expense, but they were then entitled to claim this from the architects. The court took the view that it was the architects' responsibility to see that the plans conformed with the building byelaws.

This principle applies in respect of other breaches of law in the performance of the contract. So the prosecution of a contractor for breaches of the Health and Safety at Work etc Act 1974 does not make the construction contract illegal. If, however, both parties entered into a construction contract fully aware that the contract work could be carried out only by breaches of safety law that would be an illegal contract.

Capacity of the parties

English law recognizes that certain parties are restricted in their capacity to enter into a contract. For individuals under the age of eighteen, common law makes minors not bound by their contracts unless they are for necessaries, that is food, clothing, accommodation and essential services.

At one time companies, as corporate bodies, were subject strictly to the *ultra vires* rule: any contract made by a company which went beyond its capacity to make that kind of contract was beyond its powers and so null and void. All registered companies have in their memorandums of association objects clauses, which set out the purposes of the company. Any act by the company, other than one which is incidental to its objects, which goes beyond the objects is subject to the *ultra vires* rule. An early example is the case of *Ashbury Railway Carriage and Iron Co v Riche 1875*, where the company's objects clause was for the construction and sale of railway stock and the business of mechanical engineers. The company entered into an arrangement for the development of a railway line in Belgium. Riche was appointed as its contractor. The company discovered its true legal position and repudiated the contract it had with Riche. Riche sued but his claim was unsuccessful on the ground that the contract was *ultra vires* the objects clause of the company.

Modern practice has been for the objects clause of a new company to be drafted in the widest way so as not to restrict the business activities of the company; there is also power under the Companies Act 1985 for a company to change its objects clause if it so wishes.

The Companies Act 1985, as amended by the Companies Act 1989, was made in order to comply with a European Community Directive and to improve the position of those who contract with companies. Section 35 states that the validity of an act done by a company shall not be called into question on the ground of lack of capacity by reason of anything in the company's memorandum. A contract made by the company itself, by its seal, is not *ultra vires* because the contract is not within the objects clause of the company. Under Section 35A a person dealing in good faith with a company by means of the board of directors is entitled to be treated on the basis that the directors are acting free of any limitation of the objects clause. Under Section 35B a party to a transaction with a company is not bound to inquire whether that transaction is permitted by the objects clause.

To summarize this, a person dealing with a company does not have to inquire whether what is proposed is within the objects clause, in dealing with the directors of a company; provided the person acts in good faith, the person is entitled to act on the basis that they are not limited by the objects clause; when a contract is made with the company itself the contract is not invalidated because of the company's failure to act within the objects clause.

In the case of statutory companies (those created by an Act of Parliament) the powers of the company are set out in detail in the Act. As such Acts are drafted in the widest ways little difficulty arises in practice.

Genuine consent

The consent of the parties to a contract must be genuine consent. Consent which is not genuine may entitle the party whose consent has been improperly obtained to relief from the contract. One means whereby consent may be obtained improperly is by misrepresentation.

Misrepresentation

Misrepresentation arises where a party has been induced to enter into a contract as a result of a misleading statement made to the party. The law recognizes that certain statements are made which are mere sales talk and are not considered to be statements which can form a representation. A person who enters into a contract as a result of sales talk and is dissatisfied with the contract has no redress in law for being misled by that sales talk. A statement to be a representation must be a statement of fact and not of law. The maker of the statement of fact is the person who has that knowledge, whereas a statement of law is a matter of open knowledge since that statement can be checked by reference to appropriate sources.

There is also a distinction to be drawn between a representation and an opinion or belief. Individuals who express an opinion or belief are not making a representation unless they have some special knowledge or skill. In *Esso Petroleum Co Ltd v Mardon 1976*, a commercial manager of the petrol company expressed an opinion to a prospective tenant of a petrol station under construction what he thought would be the potential throughput. The Court of Appeal decided that, having regard to the experience of the commercial manager, he was making a statement of fact. This was held to be a misrepresentation.

It is not uncommon in contract negotiations for one party to be aware of some material fact which is not known to the other party. The general rule here is that there is no duty to make disclosures. However, a person seeking insurance cover is under a duty to disclose all material facts to the insurer (see p. 320). If a party makes a statement which is a material fact to a contract and, before the contract is made, discovers that statement to be incorrect, there is a duty to inform the other party of the change.

A statement made becomes a misrepresentation for which a court may grant remedies when the following are satisfied:

1. a statement of fact was made
2. with the intention to induce a contract
3. the person to whom the representation was made acts on it
4. as a result of his or her action the person to whom the representation was made suffers loss.

Not only must the statement be one of fact, but also it must have been made with the intention of inducing a contract, and it must have been acted on. If a statement was made which did not induce the contract, that statement cannot later be used in order to bring an action. Here the contract was made without any reliance being put on the statement.

In the case of *J E B Fasteners Ltd v Marks Bloom and Co 1983*, J E B Fasteners took over a company after seeing its accounts. The accounts were inaccurate having been negligently prepared by Marks Bloom, a firm of accountants. When J E B Fasteners sued claiming damages for misrepresentation, the claim was dismissed, even though the accounts of the company were material, since J E B Fasteners had not relied on the accounts. They had taken over the company in order to obtain the services of some of its directors and it was apparent that even if the true financial state of the company had been known to J E B Fasteners they would still have proceeded with the takeover.

Misrepresentation may exist in one of three ways:

1. fraudulent misrepresentation
2. negligent misrepresentation
3. innocent misrepresentation.

Fraudulent misrepresentation

Fraudulent misrepresentation does not often arise since it is a claim of a serious nature and is often associated with criminal conduct. The House of Lords in the case of *Derry v Peek 1889* defined fraudulent misrepresentation as a statement made with knowledge of its falsity, or without belief in its truth, recklessly, not caring whether it is true or false. It is where a lie is deliberately told, or something is said which is not a lie but which is not believed to be true, or made recklessly, careless of whether what is said is true or not.

Negligent misrepresentation

Negligent misrepresentation is a form of misrepresentation covering a negligent act or omission and it is less serious than fraudulent misrepresentation, where there is an element of deceit. In the case of

Hussey v Eels 1990, Mr and Mrs Hussey were purchasing the bungalow owned by Mr and Mrs Eels. In the usual inquiries before the contract was made a question was asked for confirmation that the property had not been affected by subsidence. The answer was confirmation that there had been no subsidence; this was not correct as there had been subsidence. On the basis of this confirmation the Husseys bought the bungalow. Not long after moving in they discovered that the foundations needed stabilizing. The Court of Appeal decided that this was negligent misrepresentation for which damages were awarded.

The House of Lords in *Hedley Byrne and Co Ltd v Heller and Partners Ltd 1964* decided that the tort of negligence extended to negligent misstatements. Even though a contractual relationship does not exist there can sometimes be a duty of care not to make a negligent misstatement. A person to whom that duty of care is owed, who suffers loss as a result of that negligent misstatement, may sue for damages even though no contractual relationship exists or was considered.

A case which dealt with negligent misrepresentation in a civil engineering contract is *Howard Marine and Dredging Co Ltd v A Ogden and Sons (Excavations) Ltd 1978*. Ogden were invited to submit a tender for a large sewage works. The excavation works were extensive: material was to be dug out, taken by conveyors to a riverside and dumped into sea-going barges, which were to dump the material a few miles out at sea. Ogden were unfamiliar with this practice and got in touch with a number of firms who had barges to hire. Howard had two German-built sea-going barges which they had recently used for transporting dredged silt from a harbour. Howard had the file of German shipping documents for the barges at their London office. Howard were interested in having their barges hired and sent their manager to inspect the proposed works. He then offered in a letter the hire of the two barges at £1800 a week 'subject to availability and charterparty'. In the letter the carrying capacity was put at some 850 cubic metres; there was, however, no mention of the weight each barge could carry. In two telephone conversations between Ogden and Howard's manager, Ogden sought confirmation that each barge could carry 850 cubic metres of material. This was confirmed but a caution was made that the barges were not to be filled above their load lines. With their limited experience, the importance of this point was not appreciated by Ogden. Ogden were considering the material to be removed, which was heavy clay, and Howard the silt carried by the barges in the last contract.

Ogden, believing that each barge could be used to carry 850 cubic metres of heavy clay, used Howard's quotation to make up their own tender, which was successful. Ogden and Howard had a further meeting and an exchange of letters and telex; the carrying capacity was again confirmed at 850 cubic metres. The order was then placed for the hire of the barges. After six months' hire it became apparent that the barges were not capable of carrying 850 cubic metres of heavy clay as this weight overloaded the barges. Ogden therefore obtained the services of other barges from another hirer. Howard sued for breach of contract. Ogden's defence was that there had been misrepresentation.

In the High Court Howard's manager said that the 850 cubic metre carrying capacity he had given was from Lloyd's Shipping Register, which was actually incorrect. The true figure, which was less, was in German in the barges' documents. This had been seen by Howard's manager but the discrepancy had not been the subject of further clarification.

The Court of Appeal, by a majority, decided that there had been misrepresentation because of the negligence of Howard's representative in not stating the correct weight capacity. The court also considered a clause in Howard's contract of hire that the handing over of the barges was to be conclusive that they were in all respects fit for the intended and contemplated use by Ogden. The court decided that the clause was not fair and reasonable as required by Section 3 of the Misrepresentation Act 1967. Howard's claim for damages for breach of contract was therefore dismissed.

Innocent misrepresentation
Innocent misrepresentation arises when a misrepresentation is made neither fraudulently nor negligently. In the case of *Leaf v International Galleries 1950*, Leaf bought a painting which the Galleries said had been painted by John Constable. Some five years later Leaf discovered that the painting was by another artist not of the standing of John Constable. Leaf brought an action for his purchase money to be returned to him. The court, however, rejected this on the ground that the claim, five years after the contract was made, was too late. The remedy being sought was the equitable one of rescission: the equitable rule that 'delay defeats equity' meant that the court, in its discretion, refused to grant rescission.

The misrepresentation may sometimes become a term of the contract, when a claim may be made for damages for breach of contract. In the case of *Dick Bentley Productions Ltd v Harold Smith (Motors) Ltd 1965* a dealer sold a Bentley car, representing that the car had done only 20 000 miles since a replacement engine had been fitted. This was untrue because the car had done some 100 000 miles. The Court of Appeal decided that the dealers were in a better position than the buyer to know the history of the car and thus the statement was a term of the contract. Damages were therefore awarded against the dealer.

Remedies for misrepresentation
The remedies for misrepresentation are found in the common law, equity and the provisions in the Misrepresentation Act 1967. This Act, now amended by the Unfair Contract Terms Act 1977, was passed with the intention of improving the position of a victim of a misrepresentation; it has produced a set of complex rules which have been the subject of some judicial criticisms.

In the case of fraudulent or negligent misrepresentation the court will award damages against the representor. If a person can show that she entered into a contract after a misrepresentation and has thereby suffered loss, then the representor will be liable provided he would have been liable for damages had the misrepresentation been made fraudulently. The purpose of this provision, contained in Section 2 of the Misrepresentation Act 1967, is to allow a person to claim damages for negligent misrepresentation. Section 2 makes representors liable unless they can prove that they had reasonable ground to believe and did believe up to the time the contract was made that the facts represented were true. It is also possible for the representee to repudiate the contract but this must be done without delay.

In the case of a claim based on a negligent misstatement under the principle of *Hedley Byrne and Co Ltd v Heller and Partners Ltd 1964* (see p. 177) the court will award damages.

Innocent misrepresentation before the Act was passed was subject to the limited right of rescission; this award of the court was not always appropriate. The court may now order a contract to be rescinded where the misrepresentation has become a term of the contract or where the contract has been performed. If the court believes that to rescind the contract would not be appropriate the court also has discretionary power to refuse rescission of the contract and to award damages instead.

Section 3 of the Act deals with the use in a contract of a term which seeks to exclude or restrict liability for misrepresentation or any remedy available to a party by reason of such misrepresentation. This term is to be of no effect unless, in any proceedings, the court or arbitrator accepts that the term is fair and reasonable so far as it satisfies the test of reasonableness set out in Section 11 of the Unfair Contract Terms Act 1977.

In the case of *Walker v Boyle 1982*, Mr Walker, the prospective purchaser of a large house, sent to the vendor the usual preliminary inquiries seeking information regarding the property, including whether there was any dispute concerning the boundaries of the property. The vendor replied that there were none and Mr Walker therefore proceeded with the matter and exchanged contracts paying a deposit of £10 500. The standard form of contract had a provision that 'no error, misstatement or omission in any preliminary answer concerning the property . . . shall annul the sale'.

When Mr Walker learnt of the boundary dispute he disclaimed the contract and brought an action claiming rescission and the return of the deposit of £10 500. The ground for his claim was that there had been misrepresentation in the reply to the preliminary inquiries. The court decided that the failure to disclose the boundary dispute constituted innocent misrepresentation which entitled the purchaser to rescission since if the dispute had been made known to him he could reasonably have refused to exchange contracts. Furthermore the provision which sought to exclude the vendor's liability for misrepresentation could be effective only if it satisfied the requirements as to reasonableness set out in Section 11 of the Unfair Contract Terms Act 1977. As it did not do so, Mr Walker was entitled to rescission of the contract and the return of the deposit.

In addition to the provisions in Section 3 of the 1967 Act which restrict the exclusion of liability for misrepresentation, there is an obligation at common law which disallows a provision excluding or limiting liability if a fraudulent statement is made, in the House of Lords' decision in *S Pearson and Son Ltd v Dublin Corporation 1907*. The contract between the parties contained a term which required the contractors to satisfy themselves as to all things which may have a connection with the works of the contract, and to obtain their own information on all matters which could in any way influence their tender. The corporation's engineers had prepared plans which showed a non-existent wall as being in existence. The contractors based their tender on this information; when they discovered that no wall existed they had to revise their plans and so incurred much extra cost. The House of Lords decided that the statement about the wall was fraudulent and that the common law would not allow the maker of a fraudulent statement to escape liability.

Mistake

The word 'mistake' is used in law in a different sense from its everyday meaning. The courts will not assist a person who in a contract has undertaken to do work which, on reflection, she believes she ought to have priced more highly. Nor will they assist a person who believes he has paid more for contract work than he needed to do.

The forms of mistake of particular interest to civil engineers are where one party makes a mistake which the other party may or may not be aware of, and 'common mistake' where both parties misunderstand the contract. When contractors make a mistake in the pricing of a tender, the general rule is that contractors are bound by their mistake unless before acceptance the offeree becomes aware that there is an error and that it is not intentional.

In the case of *W Higgins Ltd v Northampton Corporation 1927*, Higgins submitted a tender for the erection of fifty-eight houses for the corporation. By mistake Higgins made up the Bills of Quantities in such a way that he believed that he was tendering a price of £1670 a pair. In fact his tender was for a price of £1613 a pair. Higgins sought to have the contract set aside or rectified to take account of the mistake. The court refused to assist Higgins, despite having great sympathy for the contractor, because the mistake was Higgins's alone and the corporation were unaware of the mistake.

The outcome was different in the case of *A R Roberts and Co Ltd v Leicestershire County Council 1961*, where the contractor's revised tender specified a period of completion of eighteen months. The county architect decided that the period should be thirty months; the clerk's department accordingly drew up the formal contract document with the same month but the following year as the date for completion. The contractors were informed by letter that their tender had been accepted, but without telling them that the date of completion had been changed. The contractors sealed and returned the contract without noticing the change of the date. There were two further meetings held with the assistant county architect and the contractors, where the contractors made reference to completion of the contract in eighteen months' time and produced a progress schedule on that basis. The council then executed the contract by affixing the council seal.

The court decided that the contractors were entitled to have the contract rectified to a completion date of eighteen months: if they believed that a particular term was included in the contract, and the other party concluded the contract with the omission or variation of that term, the contractors were entitled to have the contract rectified.

Various decisions have established that contractors are bound by underpriced tenders, unless the offeree becomes aware of the mistake before acceptance. There is no obligation in law for a tender to be examined in detail to determine its accuracy but for practical reasons examinations are made; if a mistake in the tender is revealed, the contractor should be given the opportunity to amend the tender or withdraw it. Acceptance of the tender with the mistake without informing the contractor could mean the contract would be rectified by the court later.

Mistake as to the identity of the subject matter

An example of both parties making a mistake is in the case of *Raffles v Wichelhaus 1864*. Raffles sold to Wichelhaus a cargo of cotton to arrive on the ship *Peerless* from Bombay. Wichelhaus believed that the cargo was on another ship of the same name sailing from Bombay in October, whereas Raffles had in mind a cargo on the *Peerless* which sailed from Bombay in December. Clearly the minds of the two parties were not agreed on the subject matter of the contract and so the contract was held to be void.

Mistake as to the existence of the subject matter

In the case of *Couturier v Hastie 1856* a contract was made for the sale of a cargo of corn being shipped on a boat from Turkey. During the voyage the corn became heated and started to deteriorate. The captain therefore took the ship into a port in North Africa and sold the cargo. The House of Lords decided that the contract was void, because at the time the contract was made the subject matter of the contract, the cargo of corn on that ship, did not exist: it had already been sold.

In the case of *Amalgamated Investment and Property Co Ltd v John Walker and Sons Ltd 1976*, Walker owned a commercial property which was described as suitable for occupation or development. Amalgamated Investment in July 1973 agreed to buy the property for £1 710 000 and made pre-contract inquiries of Walker, including whether the property was listed as a building of special architectural or historic interest. On 14 August Walker replied that the building was not listed.

Unknown to both parties, the Department of the Environment was in the process of listing the building under the Town and Country Planning Act 1971. On 25 September the parties signed the contract. The next day, the 26th, the Department of the Environment informed Walker that the property had been listed as a building of special architectural or historic interest. On 27 September the Secretary of State signed the appropriate document.

The effect of the listing was to make the property have no redevelopment potential, and consequently its value fell by £1 500 000. Amalgamated Investment sought either a declaration that the contract was void or voidable or rescission of the contract on the ground of common mistake. The Court of Appeal refused both claims. At the date of the contract the property was not listed; the fact that it was in the process of being listed was unknown to the parties and so could not form common mistake. The listing of the property did not prevent the performance of the contract; there had not been any warranty that planning permission could be obtained for development of the property. There was a risk, known to Amalgamated Investment, that any property may be listed.

Mistake as to the quality of the subject matter
In the case of *Bell v Lever Brothers Ltd 1932*, Bell was appointed by Lever Brothers to serve for five years as chairman of a company controlled by Lever Brothers. Before this five-year period had expired, Lever Brothers no longer required the services of Bell and therefore made a compensation agreement with Bell for a payment of £30 000 for the early termination of the service contract, which had a term in it forbidding Bell from any activity harmful to Lever Brothers' business interests.

After Bell had received the £30 000 Lever Brothers discovered that Bell had taken part in activities which breached this term. They therefore brought an action claiming the return of the sum. The House of Lords accepted that if Lever Brothers had been aware of Bell's activities they would have been entitled to end the service contract without any payment having to be made. The House of Lords also accepted that when Bell entered into the compensation agreement he had not fraudulently concealed his breach of the service contract; in fact he had not had that in his mind nor had he appreciated the effect of the breach when he made the compensation agreement.

The House of Lords decided that there had been a mistake as to the quality of the subject matter for the contract and that as this was, in the Law Lords' opinion, a mistake which was not fundamental it did not make the contract void. Lever Brothers had got what they wanted from the contract, that is release from the service contract. The fact that if Lever Brothers had known of the breach they could have dismissed Bell without compensation was immaterial.

This decision was made by a three to two majority in the House of Lords after both the Court of Appeal and the High Court had found in favour of Lever Brothers. It has been questioned from time to time, but as a decision of the House of Lords it has the authority of binding precedent.

Undue influence and duress

Undue influence is less likely to be found in construction contracts than duress.

Undue influence arises where a contract has been made as a result of some improper pressure put on one of the parties. The person wishing to dispute the contract has to show that undue influence had been exercised. This burden of proof, however, does not have to be proved where a certain relationship exists, when there is a presumption that undue influence exists. This presumption can be rebutted by evidence that there had not been undue influence. These relationships include parent and child, doctor and patient, priest and parishioner, and solicitor and client. The presumption is rebuffed by showing that the person concerned had independent advice. A solicitor who wished to buy a client's house would have to show that the client had independent advice before making the contract of sale to the solicitor. As the remedy for undue influence is rescission of the contract, equity requires that the remedy shall be sought within a reasonable time.

In the case of *Allcard v Skinner 1887*, a woman entered a religious order which required its members to give up their financial assets to the order. A few years later she left the order and not long after this brought an action for the return of her money. The court decided that there had been delay in seeking to show that there had been undue influence and this defeated the claim.

Duress originally arose when a party had been forced into a contract by actual or threatened physical violence. Later this concept was widened to include compulsion or coercion, for example a person who entered into a contract because of an imminent threat to burn his house down.

A more recent development, likely to arise in construction contracts, is that of commercial pressure or economic duress. In the case of *B and S Contracts and Designs Ltd v Victor Green Publications Ltd 1984* a contractor undertook the erection of stands for an important exhibition. Less than a week before the exhibition was due to open the contractor told the client that if more money was not paid the contract would be cancelled. The contractor claimed the money in order to meet claims being made on him by his workforce. The effect on the client of cancellation would be severely damaging. His reputation would be harmed and he would be liable to pay damage to exhibitors to whom he had let stands. The client's claim for return of the additional sum he had paid was upheld by the court as payment had been paid under duress.

The case of *North Ocean Shipping Co Ltd v Hyundai Construction Co Ltd 1978* concerned a shipbuilding contract made in April 1972; the contract price was payable in instalments. After the first instalment was paid the US dollar was devalued by 10 per cent and the builder sought additional payment. In May 1973 the owners made an advantageous agreement with an important client for the ship to be chartered for three years. They suggested that the claim for the additional payment be dealt with by arbitration. The shipbuilders, however, fixed a date, June 1973, for their claim to be accepted failing which they would terminate the contract. The owners agreed to this 'without prejudice to their rights': they wished to maintain a good relationship with the shipbuilders. They accepted delivery of the ship in November 1974 without protest.

In July 1975 the owners claimed the return of the 10 per cent and nominated an arbitrator. They claimed that the agreement for the payment of the additional sum was voidable because it had been an agreement made involuntarily under economic duress. The court accepted that what had happened could constitute economic duress and so make the agreement voidable, but in this case the court would not order the return of the money paid: the owners had affirmed the agreement, because they had failed to take any action by way of protest until the start of the arbitration in July 1975.

This decision shows that if one party claims that a contract came about because of economic duress it is essential for that party to make protest promptly and properly. Failure to do this may mean that an otherwise good claim is lost by inaction.

Express and implied terms of contract

A contract may contain express terms or implied terms or both. Express terms may be in writing or be made by word of mouth. Implied terms are not expressly included by the parties but were intended to be in the contract by the parties, or are implied by the operation of law, or are implied by custom or usage. If the parties use express terms on a matter, that excludes the implication of a term on that matter. Where there is something which has not been dealt with by the parties in express terms, implied terms may be used to complete the contract.

Express terms

Express terms are those the parties have chosen to include in the contract; they govern the contract and will be applied by the courts in the event of a dispute.

In the case of *Lynch v Thorne 1956*, Thorne, a builder, agreed to sell to Lynch a house which was in the early stage of construction. Thorne agreed by the contract to complete the house in accordance with the plan and specification, which showed that the southern wall of the house was to be built in nine-inch solid brick. Soon after Lynch moved into the house, the solid brick wall allowed damp to enter and the room became uninhabitable. Lynch sued claiming that there was an implied term in the contract that the house would be fit for human habitation. The Court of Appeal refused to hold that there was such a term since the house had been built in accordance with the contract terms. The opinion was also expressed that the court could not imply a term which would be inconsistent with an express term of the contract.

When a court deals with a contract where the parties have put their agreement in writing, it applies the rule against the admittance of extrinsic evidence. Thus neither party can rely on any evidence which is external to that in the contract: the parties are deemed to have put in the contract what they wanted to include and have left out what they wanted to leave out. The courts therefore resolve disputes by reference to the terms in the contract. One judge's interpretation is 'that that is within the four corners of the document'.

This rule is subject to a number of exceptions. The courts will allow external evidence to prove the meaning of certain words, such as technical terms, to prove custom, to identify the subject matter of the contract, and where some warranty had been given by word of mouth.

This rule does not apply when the contract makes specific reference to another document; the additional document is then taken to be incorporated in the contract. The importance of this may be seen in the case of *Davis Contractors Ltd v Fareham Urban District Council 1956*, where the contractors made a contract with the council to build seventy-eight houses for £92 425 within eight months. In submitting their tender they had attached a letter stating that the tender was subject to adequate supplies of labour and materials being available, but this was not included in the contract. Unexpectedly and without any fault on the contractors' part there was a serious shortage of labour and materials; the contract was delayed by fourteen months, with extra cost to the contractors of £17 651. The contractors claimed that the letter was incorporated in the contract making the contract subject to a sufficient supply of labour and materials. The House of Lords, however, held that the letter was not incorporated and so its terms were not part of the contract; the contractors' claim failed.

The position where there are more than one version of the document to be incorporated was considered by the House of Lords in *Smith v South Wales Switchgear Ltd 1978*. South Wales Switchgear had for some years carried out annual maintenance work at a factory. The factory asked for the annual overhaul of the factory electrical equipment and for this purpose sent a purchase note. This said that it was subject to 'our General Conditions of Contract 24001 obtainable on request'. There were three versions all numbers 24001. There was an original one, a 1969 revision and the then current 1970 revision. No request was made for a copy but the 1969 version was sent to South Wales Switchgear. Smith, an employee of South Wales Switchgear, had a accident and the question arose as to the application of an indemnity clause in the General Conditions.

The House of Lords held that the reference to 'General Conditions of Contract 24001 obtainable on request' was sufficient to incorporate that document in the contract. Furthermore the document to be deemed to be incorporated was the 1970 version since it was reasonable to expect that if a request had been made for a copy that would have been supplied to them.

In the case of *A Davies and Co (Shopfitters) Ltd v William Old Ltd 1969* (see p. 40) a failure to read the terms and conditions on the back of an order form did not make those terms and conditions inapplicable. There had not been any special obligation on William Old's part to draw Davies's attention to the clause stating that payment would be made to the sub-contractors only when the main contractors were paid.

Where, however, a term in an invoice or order form is particularly onerous or unusual, there is an obligation to draw the other party's attention to it before the contract is made. In the case of *Interfoto Picture Library Ltd v Siletto Visual Programmes Ltd 1988* the Picture Library loaned photographs to advertising agencies and others. Siletto, who had not previously dealt with the Picture Library, asked to be supplied with a range of photographs from which they would make a selection. When the transparencies were delivered there was a failure to read the terms and conditions. One condition stated that if there was delay in returning the transparencies there would be a charge of £5 a day for each transparency. There was a delay and Picture Library submitted an invoice for £3783. The Court of Appeal decided that this particular condition was so onerous and unusual it ought to have been drawn to Siletto's attention; as this had not been done, the condition could not be enforced. Silletto had, however, to pay an amount which was accepted as a reasonable charge for the delayed return of the transparencies.

The terms of a contract must be brought to the attention of the other party before the contract is formed: terms cannot be imposed after the contract has been made. In the case of *Olley v Marlborough Court Ltd 1949*, Ms Olley stayed at an hotel; the contract was made at the reception desk. When she went to her bedroom she saw a notice on the wall which sought to absolve the hotel from liability for theft and other risks. Some of her property was stolen from the bedroom. The court decided the notice was ineffective since it introduced terms after the contract was made.

The practice of starting work without a formal written contract was considered in the case of *Trollope and Colls Ltd v Atomic Power Construction Ltd 1962*. Trollope and Colls were asked by a letter of intent to start work on a project, as a result of a tender they had submitted, on which negotiations were still taking place when work started. Some ten months later the contract was signed with the essential terms being agreed. A dispute then arose as to whether the terms of the contract applied to work, in particular variations, done before the contract was signed.

The court decided that the contract's terms applied to the work done before the contract was signed, even though there was no term in the contract that it was to have retrospective effect. The court accepted that the parties acted on the understanding that, if and when a contract was made, it would apply to and govern that work already being done.

Implied terms

Implied terms fall into three groups: terms implied in fact, terms implied by law, and terms implied by custom or usage.

Terms implied in fact

Terms implied in fact are those needed to give the contract business efficacy, that is something which is obvious and necessary as the parties must have intended. The courts will not make a contract if one does not exist or make a contract a better contract than the parties made for themselves. As in the case of *Lynch v Thorne 1956* (p. 54) the courts will not imply a term which goes against an express term.

The case of *Courtney and Fairbairn Ltd v Tolaini Brothers (Hotels) Ltd 1975* dealt with the omission of an important term from an agreement. Tolaini Brothers wished to carry out a development of an hotel, a motel and a petrol filling station. Courtney and Fairbairn were developers approached by Tolaini to see if they could be put in touch with someone who could provide the finance. Courtney and Fairbairn were in a position to undertake all the construction of the development, and replied that if they introduced someone capable of providing the necessary finance they would expect to be given the construction work. Tolaini's quantity surveyor would negotiate fair and reasonable contract sums for the development which was to be done in three phases. Tolaini agreed to this. A financial provider was found and negotiations started about the contracts. It was not possible to agree on these and so Tolaini gave the work to another contractor. Courtney and Fairbairn sued claiming that they had a contract to carry out the work.

The Court of Appeal decided that there was no contract in existence: no price had been fixed for the construction work, nor had any means been provided for arriving at a contract price in the event of a failure to agree a figure. The parties had made an agreement only: it could not be a contract since an essential term, the price, was missing. The court could not correct this omission since it was unable to imply a term of a fundamental nature.

A good example of an implied term in fact is the case of *Hancock v B W Brazier (Anerley) Ltd 1966*. Hancock bought a house that was in the course of construction when the contract was signed. The contract referred to the completion of the house in a proper and workmanlike manner; there was no reference to the materials to be used. A few years later the ground floor started to crack and break up. Investigation showed that this was due to the use of unsuitable hardcore, containing soluble sodium sulphate, which had expanded when it came into contact with damp, and exerted force which caused the damage. Hancock sued claiming for the damage to his house. The builders' defence was that their obligation was to perform the work in a workmanlike manner; that this did not include any warranty as to suitability of materials; and that as it was an express term it was not open to the court to make an implication on the same matter.

The Court of Appeal, which found no fault with the builders since they had bought the hardcore in good faith which had a defect not detectable on reasonable examination, decided that a term could be implied into the contract, because the clause in the contract dealt only with workmanship and not materials. The quality of the materials used was left to be implied, that is the hardcore must be good and proper hardcore. It was not and so the builders were liable for breach of contract.

Terms implied by law

Terms implied by law in contract come about by either the application of the common law or some provision in statute law. In common law implied terms in contracts with professional people are that they will use reasonable skill and care in their professional work. In contracts of employment there are implied terms that employees will not conduct themselves so as to harm their employer's business interests and that they have reasonable skill to perform their services. Under statute law, in the Sale of Goods Act 1979 for example, there are terms implied into a contract of sale of goods which protect the purchaser.

Terms implied by custom or usage

Terms implied by custom are where it can be shown that the contract was intended to include any custom of a trade or locality. For example a custom may arise in employment contracts in particular industries. A court will, however, need to be satisfied that such a custom is reasonable before it will imply the custom to be a term of a contract.

Terms implied by usage come about from the practice in particular industries. In the case of *British Crane Hire Corporation Ltd v Ipswich Plant Hire Ltd 1975*, both parties were in the business of plant hire. Ipswich had urgent need for a dragline crane and telephoned British Crane, who had one available for hire; its hire was agreed, the charge hire was fixed but nothing else. British Crane sent their normal printed form to Ipswich for signing. Before it was signed the crane sank into soft marshy ground: this was an accident which was not the fault of anyone. Under the conditions on the British Crane form the responsibility for this mishap fell on Ipswich. These conditions were similar to those used throughout the plant-hire industry and, in fact, were like those Ipswich themselves used when they hired out plant. Ipswich disputed that they applied here since the contract had been made by word of mouth and the printed form had not been signed and returned.

The Court of Appeal decided that the terms were to be treated as being included in the contract, because both parties were in the same business, they were of equal bargaining power, each knew that in the plant-hire industry companies always imposed conditions when hiring plant, and those conditions were similar to the ones in this case.

Exemption clauses

In standard forms of contract one party normally inserts a clause which seeks to exempt the party from liability under the contract or to limit liability. Often the user of the contract form is in a monopoly or near monopoly position so that the other party has not got the bargaining power to remove or reduce the effect of such clauses.

Until the Unfair Contract Terms Act 1977 (see p. 59), the resolution of disputes with these clauses had to be by the use of the common law. To a limited extent this is still the case: common law determines whether such a clause is a term in the contract, and whether it covers the loss or damage suffered.

A term in a contract must be brought to the notice of the other party and provided reasonable steps are taken to bring the term to that party's notice the fact that the term is not read or understood does not exclude it from the contract. The notice must, as we saw in the case of *Olley v Marlborough Court Ltd 1949* (see p. 56), be brought to the attention of the other party before the contract is made.

Over the years the courts, mindful of the unequal position of parties in contracts which contain exemption clauses, have sought to assist the weaker party to the contract. A measure used is the *contra proferentum* rule: if there should be any uncertainty or other doubt in an exemption clause, the matter is to be resolved against the party who made use of that clause. An application of this rule may be seen in a case we have considered in another respect. In *Smith v South Wales Switchgear Ltd 1978*, the House of Lords decided that an indemnity clause in a purchase order which sought to exempt liability for, among other things, personal injury was ineffective. As this clause did not make specific reference to negligence nor could its provisions be read sufficiently to include negligence then the rule applied. This meant that the party's own negligence was not exempt by the indemnity clause.

An exemption clause will also be ineffective if there has been misrepresentation: the misrepresentation has removed the protection otherwise provided by the exemption clause. In *Curtis v Chemical Cleaning and Dyeing Co 1951*, Ms Curtis took a wedding dress to a branch of Chemical Cleaning for it to be cleaned. She was asked to sign a paper marked 'Receipt'; when she questioned this she was told that they would not accept liability for certain risks, including risk of damage by or to the beads and sequins with which the dress was trimmed. She signed the receipt, which contained a clause that exempted the company for any damage howsoever arising. The dress was returned with a stain and Ms Curtis sued.

The Court of Appeal held that the assistant's statement that the exemption related to damage by or to the beads and sequins was a misrepresentation. It was done innocently but nevertheless created a false impression. That in turn meant the exemption clause could not be relied on.

Unfair Contract Terms Act 1977

This Act was introduced as a means of redressing the imbalance of bargaining powers of parties to contracts, and to strengthen the power of the courts in dealing with circumstances where exemption clauses have been used and disputes have consequently arisen.

The Act draws a distinction between 'business liability' and 'deals as a consumer' in order to give a consumer greater protection. (A consumer is defined here as a person who makes a purchase as an ordinary individual not for any business purpose.) 'Business liability' is liability arising from things done by a person in the course of a business or from the occupation of business premises. The Act's most important provision is that a person who comes within the definition of business liability cannot exclude or restrict by a contract term or notice liability for death or personal injury resulting from negligence.

For other loss or damage individuals who come within the definition of business liability cannot so exclude or restrict their liability for negligence except in so far as the term or notice satisfies the requirement of reasonableness. In deciding whether the requirement of reasonableness has been satisfied the court has to have regard to guidelines set out in the Act.

Where parties use their own standard form of contract they are not allowed to exclude or restrict their business liability in the event of a breach of contract, or claim to render a contractual performance substantially different from that which was reasonably expected of them or, in fact, to render no performance at all. In all these circumstances the clause is subject to the requirements of reasonableness.

These provisions set out to prevent parties who use their own standard form of contract, with clauses which seek to protect them if they fail to perform their contract, from benefiting in every circumstance. The clauses, however, will apply and protect the party if they satisfy the requirement of reasonableness. It is for the court to decide if they do so.

The Act does not apply to contracts of insurance and contracts relating to the transfer of land.

Privity of contract

There is a general rule in contract law that it is only the parties to a contract who have rights and obligations under the contract. This has been the subject of criticism for some time: there are a number of circumstances, not recognized by the law, where a person who is not a party to a contract ought to be able to bring an action based on that contract.

The case of *Dunlop Pneumatic Tyre Co v Selfridge and Co 1915* was an instance of privity of contract. Dunlop sold tyres to a firm of wholesalers, Dew and Co, with a stipulation in the contract that the tyres were not to be sold below a fixed price. Dew and Co sold some tyres to Selfridge on the same terms as existed in their contract with Dunlop. Selfridge, however, did not observe these terms and instead sold tyres below the price fixed by Dunlop. Dunlop brought an action against Selfridge. The House of Lords decided that Dunlop could not succeed in their action since they were seeking to sue on a contract to which they were not a party.

Two exceptions to the rule which are of importance to the construction industry are, first, where a person knowing of but not a party to a contract (say, of employment) induces a party to that contract to break it. The innocent party to the contract of employment, usually the employer, can sue the third person even though that person is not a party to the contract. The second exception is where a restrictive covenant is made which affects land. Here a later owner of the land which benefits from the restrictive covenant can sue to enforce it even though that person was not a party to the original contract which created the restrictive covenant.

Privity of contract prevents a building owner suing a sub-contractor, because in construction work the building owner or employer usually makes a contract only with the main contractor. The main contractor then makes sub-contracts with the sub-contractors and suppliers. Applying the rule of privity of contract the employer can sue in contract the main contractor, but the employer cannot sue the sub-contractors or suppliers since the employer is not a party to those sub-contracts. Attempts are made to overcome this problem by the use of collateral contracts.

Collateral contracts

A collateral contract arises when a contract is made between two parties and then one of those parties makes a contract with a third party which is dependent on the existence of the first contract. It is collateral to the first contract.

In the case of *Shanklin Pier Ltd v Detel Products Ltd 1951*, the owners of the pier were to have certain work done to it including repainting. Contractors were appointed for this work. The specification stipulated that the pier was to have two coats of bituminous paint, with the right to vary the specification. A director of Detel wished to secure the contract for supplying the paint; he assured the representatives of Shanklin Pier that his company had a paint which was suitable for use in marine conditions and would have a life of seven to ten years. Shanklin Pier accepted this representation and varied the specification instructing the contractors to use the paint produced by Detel.

The paint in a matter of a few months proved to be unsuitable. Shanklin Pier then sued Detel claiming a contract existed between them. The basis of the claim was that in return for the promise of the suitability of the paint Shanklin Pier nominated Detel as suppliers of the paint to be used in the repainting contract. The High Court accepted the submission of Shanklin's claim; the nomination of Detel provided the consideration needed to satisfy the promise of suitability. Shanklin Pier were therefore successful in their claim.

The principle established in Shanklin's case has been applied in later cases, but it depends on the facts of the transaction. It is too uncertain to rely on when an employer wishes to be able to proceed, if necessary, against sub-contractors and suppliers. A more assured position is secured by the use of a document to create the collateral contract. In 1969 a form of warranty was introduced for use with the JCT 1963 edition standard form of contract. Since then more refined forms have been introduced for use with different standard forms of contract used in the construction industry. Some employers have their own forms specially drafted for them.

Assignment

Assignment in contract law is a transaction whereby the party in a contract entitled to the benefit of the contract transfers that benefit to a third party. The third person, the assignee, having acquired the benefit from the assignor, is then entitled to sue the person liable under the contract, the debtor. The debtor is not involved in the transaction and his or her consent is not needed to make the transaction valid. So a contractor who is owed money under a contract can transfer the right to that payment, the benefit, to a third party. The third party can then sue for payment of the money due. It is important to note that it is the benefit of the contract that is assigned and not the burden.

In the case of a construction contract, it makes no difference to employers whether they pay their debt for the work done, the contract price, to the contractor or to, say, the bank which has accepted an assignment of the contractor's right to that payment provided that payment is a valid discharge of the debt. It is, however, very different if contractors sought to transfer the burden of their contract, the performance of the work, to another contractor. Here employers would be faced with the contract being performed by a contractor they had not selected and, possibly, would not have selected for good reasons.

Standard forms of contract used in the construction industry usually contain clauses prohibiting or restricting the assignment or sub-letting of the contract. Contractors are agreeing that their right to assign the benefit of the contract will no longer be available or, more usually, be subject to the written consent of the employer.

In the case of *Helstan Securities Ltd v Hertfordshire County Council 1978*, the county council made a contract with Renhold Road Surfacing Ltd for certain road works to be carried out. The contract form used was the Institution of Civil Engineers' Conditions of Contract 4th Edition. Clause 3 stated: 'The contractor shall not assign the contract or any part thereof or any benefit or any benefit of interest therein or thereunder without the written consent of the employer'. The contractor got into financial difficulties and without obtaining the council's consent assigned to Helstan Securities the amount (£46 437) the contractor claimed was due to them under the contract; when Helstan Securities claimed payment for this sum the council refused to pay on two grounds. First, they had not agreed to the assignment and under the contract their consent in writing was necessary. Second, they claimed that they had been defrauded and consequently were owed more than the £46 437. Their intention was to set-off and counter-claim against this sum.

The High Court decided that the council did not have to pay the £46 437 to Helstan Securities. There had been an agreement between the parties to the contract that the contractor's right of payment could not be validly assigned without the council's consent. The council had not given their consent and so they were entitled to refuse payment.

Method of assignment

The right to sue in court to enforce a contract is known as a 'chose in action', which is different from a 'thing in possession' in that to secure payment of a debt it is necessary to sue an action. A chose in action may be either legal or equitable, for historical reasons. A legal chose in action, for example a contract debt, could be sued for only in the common law courts. An equitable chose in action was a matter which could be dealt with only in the Court of Chancery. Originally an assignment was made at common law but it became necessary for equity to assist so that assignments could be made.

Assignments now are made by the provisions in various statutes. Section 136 of the Law of Property Act 1925 requires that the assignment must be absolute, that is for the whole of the debt and not part of it; that it is not by way of charge only, that is using the debt as security; that it is in writing; and that express notice of the assignment must be given in writing to the debtor.

An assignment which fails to meet the requirements of Section 136 does not necessarily mean that a valid assignment has not taken place. Equity may provide the required authority provided there was a clear intention to make the assignment and it is fair and reasonable to uphold the assignment.

Discharge of contract

A contract is discharged when the parties are released from their obligations under the contract. It can be discharged in one of four ways: performance, agreement, frustration and breach.

Performance

Most contracts are discharged by performance: the contractor performs the service and the employer pays the contract price. Both have done what the contract required and the contract is now at an end. The question of what constitutes performance is one that the courts have often been called upon to answer.

The general rule is that performance means performance in accordance with the terms of the contract. If therefore a person has undertaken to perform an obligation of a contract which requires great accuracy that is what is required and a lesser performance does not satisfy the contract obligation. In this circumstance the person cannot sue successfully for payment since there has been a failure to perform his or her obligation under the contract. An old case demonstrates the harshness of the rule that performance means complete performance. In *Cutter v Powell 1795*, Cutter made a contract to serve as a second mate on a ship sailing from Jamaica to Liverpool. The contract required him to perform his duty from Jamaica to Liverpool in return for payment of 30 guineas. The ship sailed from Jamaica on 2 August and on 20 September Cutter died. The ship arrived in Liverpool on 9 October. His widow's claim for part of the payment was refused. His contract required complete performance. It was an entire contract, that is one which must be fulfilled completely before payment is due.

This general rule is subject to one party to the contract not preventing the other party from performing their work. If contractors were told to stop work because the employer was in financial difficulties, the contractors were entitled to payment for the work done even though there has not been complete performance. The contractor could sue for breach of contract or claim on a *quantum meruit*.

It is possible for a party to accept partial performance and to pay for the work done. A party cannot, however, partially perform their contractual obligation and then, without fault on the part of the other party, claim payment. In the case of *Sumpter v Hedges 1898*, Sumpter contracted to build two houses in Hedges' land for £565. He completed part of the work to the value of £333 and then abandoned the work. Hedges then completed the remaining work. When Sumpter made a claim for a *quantum meruit* for the work he had done it was refused. Hedges had not accepted the abandonment. Nothing could be implied from his going back on to his own land and completing the building work. Hedges, however, had to pay Sumpter for the materials on the site which he had used in completing the building work.

Substantial performance

The general rule that performance means complete performance can give rise to circumstances where payment would be denied but justice demands that some payment should be made. The courts developed the doctrine of substantial performance: if a contract has been substantially performed the court can order payment of the contract price, less the amount needed to complete the contract.

In the case of *Hoenig v Isaacs 1952*, Hoenig was an interior decorator who made a contract with Isaacs to decorate and furnish his flat. The agreed price was £750, with some payment by instalments and the balance on completion. Hoenig was paid £400 but the balance of £350 was refused on the ground that some workmanship was defective. Hoenig sued claiming the balance of £350. The Court of Appeal decided that the contract had been substantially performed. Hoenig was entitled to the balance of £350 less £56 which was the sum needed to remedy the defects.

Substantial performance of the contract is required if contractors are to be successful in their claim. In *Bolton v Mahadeva 1972*, Bolton had contracted for the price of £560 to install central heating in Mahadeva's house. When the work was completed it was found that the promised temperatures were not attained and fumes leaked from the flue into the house. Attempts were made to remedy the defects but without success. Bolton sued Mahadeva for £560. The Court of Appeal decided that there had not been substantial performance: the work done was generally ineffective and could not be put right by some minor work.

The courts have not laid down a percentage figure which can be used as the yardstick of measurement in deciding whether or not there has been substantial performance of a contract. It is left to the court to decide this point on the evidence put before the court. Courts will come to different decisions: in Bolton's case the County Court decided that there had been substantial performance but the Court of Appeal was firmly of the opinion that this was not the case.

Time of performance

If a contract does not contain a date for completion the requirement is that completion shall be within a reasonable period of time, which depends on the nature of the contract. If the contract is not performed within a reasonable period of time there is a breach of contract for which damages may be claimed. In *Charnock v Liverpool Corporation and Another 1968*, Mr Charnock while driving collided with another car which was being driven negligently. He took his car to a garage for the necessary repairs. A reasonable period for these repairs was five weeks: they took eight weeks owing to a shortage of staff, the garage holiday period and the garage's policy of giving priority to repairs carried out under manufacturers' warranty schemes. These factors were not made known to Mr Charnock. Mr Charnock had hired a car for the period when his car was under repair; he sued the garage for the three weeks' extra hire. The Court of Appeal upheld his claim: there was an implied term in the contract that the work would be completed within a reasonable time.

Where the contract contains a date for completion the question arises as to whether 'time is of the essence', which carries a particular meaning in law. Where the term is used a failure to complete by the stated date allows the other party to treat the contract as ended, even if the delayed performance is only a day over the stated date. Where the term is not used the obligation is to complete the performance by the stated date or within a reasonable time thereafter.

Time may also be of the essence even if not stipulated in the contract. This is done when there has been failure to complete the performance within a reasonable time if no date is stated, or if there is a stated date and performance has not been performed by that date. A notice is served on the defaulting party giving a reasonable time for completion.

Time may also be of the essence, even if not stipulated, if the nature of the contract is such that time should be of the essence, for example a contract to deliver goods to a ship sailing on a stated date.

Agreement

If neither party has done anything under a contract then the promise of each given to the other to agree to discharge the contract is sufficient to bring it to an end. A contract may be discharged by agreement according to a term in the contract. In an ordinary contract of employment there will be an agreed term that each party by giving the required period of notice can bring the contract to an end. If one of the parties brings the contract to an end without giving the required period of notice, in circumstances which do not justify that action, then that will be breach of contract.

If a contract was made which had consideration the agreement to discharge it would also have to be accompanied by consideration or be made by deed. This matter of consideration and the discharge of a contract has presented problems to the court over the years. The difficulty is that if contractors have properly performed their work they are entitled to the agreed contract price. If the client will not or cannot pay the law permits the parties to come to an agreement. The parties can agree that the client will give some new consideration in return for the contractors giving up their rights under the contract. This is known as accord and satisfaction: accord is the agreement of the party and satisfaction is the consideration.

The matter of part payment of a debt – and as to whether that constitutes full redress so that the contract is discharged and there is no right to sue for the unpaid balance – has troubled the courts. In *Pinnel's Case 1602* the law was said to be that 'payment of a lesser sum on the day in satisfaction of a greater sum cannot be any satisfaction for the whole'. This rule was approved by the House of Lords in *Foakes v Beer 1884*: the payment of the less sum on the date it is due does not discharge the debt. So if the lesser sum is paid before the date due the rule does not apply and that would be a discharge of the contract.

In the case of *Central London Properties Trust Ltd v High Trees Ltd 1947* (see p. 43), the Court of Appeal upheld an agreement to accept a lesser sum in discharge of a greater sum. To decide otherwise would be inequitable since it would allow a person to go back on a solemn promise. This principle was also applied by the Court of Appeal in the case of *D and C Builders Ltd v Rees 1966*. D and C Builders were a small firm of jobbing builders. In early 1964 they were employed by Mr Rees to do some work to his property. This was completed in July 1964, and the cost of the work came to £482. No complaint was made about the work, but Mr Rees did not pay the bill. In August and October 1964 D and C Builders wrote to Rees asking for payment but received no reply. In November 1964 Mr Rees was ill and his wife phoned the builders, made complaint about the work and offered £300 in settlement. It was, she said, to be in satisfaction. D and C Builders were in desperate financial straits and without the £300 they would become insolvent; they decided to accept the £300 and see what could be done about the rest. Mrs Rees was told that the £300 would be accepted and the balance could be paid in a year's time. Mrs Rees refused this, saying £300 was better than nothing and that they would never be able to pay the balance.

A cheque for £300 was paid next day. At Mrs Rees's insistence on the receipt were the words 'in completion of the account' as well as the words 'Received the sum of £300 from Mr Rees'. D and C Buildings sued for the balance of the account. The basis of the claim was that they were entitled to sue for the balance under the rule in Pinnel's case.

The Court of Appeal decided that, despite the words on the receipt, D and C Builders were entitled to the balance. It would be inequitable not to allow them to claim the balance since there had not been a true accord and satisfaction. There had not been a voluntary acceptance of the lesser sum which made it a true accord. Mrs Rees had held D and C Builders to ransom, knowing that they needed the money to meet their own commitments. Neither common law nor equity could prevent D and C Builders claiming the full amount.

Frustration

The doctrine of frustration was introduced to provide a fair settlement where there has been a failure to perform a contract without fault on the part of either party to the contract. It is a departure from the original rule that if a party in a contract undertook to do a certain thing that party was absolutely bound to it: events having made that performance no longer possible did not prevent the person being in breach of contract.

The first move away from this strict rule was the case of *Taylor v Caldwell 1863*, where Caldwell agreed to let Taylor have the use of a music hall on four fixed dates for the holding of concerts. Before these dates the music hall was destroyed by fire and Taylor sued on the ground that there had been a breach of contract. The court dismissed the claim: the music hall having ceased to exist, without fault on the part of either party to the contract of hire, both parties were excused their obligations under the contract.

If some event occurs during the existence of the contract which is the fault of neither party, with the result that performance of the contract becomes impossible or illegal or makes the performance of the contract substantially different, the contract is frustrated.

Taylor v Caldwell showed that if the subject matter of the contract is destroyed that frustrates the contract. If the destruction is not total, the contract will still be frustrated provided the damage is sufficient to prevent performance of the contract.

The death of one of the parties to a contract will frustrate the contract provided the contract is of a personal nature. The death of one of the parties to a contract of employment will end the contract; it is also possible for a contract of employment to be frustrated by the illness of one of the parties.

Contracts have frequently been frustrated on the ground that their performance would be illegal, even though they were valid and proper at the time they were made. When war breaks out some contracts become illegal because they would constitute 'trading with the enemy'. Others become illegal because their performance is prevented by legislation, and so are frustrated. For example during recent wars legislation was passed prohibiting building work which was not considered essential to the war efforts.

The fact that a contract becomes much more difficult to perform does not frustrate the contract. In the case of *Davis Contractors Ltd v Fareham Urban District Council 1956* (see p. 55), Davis Contractors had made a fixed price contract which was substantially delayed because of a shortage of labour and materials. The contractors claimed that this shortage had frustrated the contract. Davis Contractors then said that they were entitled to be paid on a *quantum meruit* for all the extra cost they had incurred. The House of Lords rejected this claim: to bring the doctrine of frustration into operation there had to be such a change in the significance of the obligation that the thing undertaken would, if performed, be a different thing from that contracted for. The mere fact that a contract becomes more difficult to perform does not frustrate the contract and so allow the contractor to claim payment as if a contract did not exist.

Contracts sometimes contain provisions which seek to deal with the obligations of the parties to a contract should some event happen which would affect the performance of the contract. By making such promises the parties exclude the doctrine of frustration. The important point is whether the provisions are sufficiently comprehensive to cover the event which occurs. In the case of *Metropolitan Water Board v Dick, Kerr and Co 1918*, in July 1914 (before the outbreak of the First World War) a contract was made for the contractors to build a reservoir for Metropolitan Water Board within six years. The contract provided that if there were delays 'however occasioned' the engineer had power to grant extensions of time. In February 1916 the government used its wartime powers and ordered the contractors to stop work on the construction. The question arose as to whether the contract provision included an event, such as the government action, in which case the contract would remain in force with the engineer giving an extension of time, or whether the contract was frustrated, when a new contract would have to be negotiated. The House of Lords decided that the contract was frustrated: the provision in the contract was meant to apply to the usual temporary difficulties which arose in a contract of this nature. It did not cover an interruption of such a character and duration that it vitally and fundamentally changed the conditions of the contract. It could not have been in the contemplation of the parties when the contract was made.

The doctrine of frustration reached the stage when it was necessary for Parliament to intervene. In the case of *Fibrosa Spolka Akcyjna v Fairbairn Lawson Combe Barbour Ltd 1943*, Fairbairn made a contract in July 1939 to make machinery for the Polish company Fibrosa. The contract price was £4800 of which £1600 was to be an advanced payment. As events turned out only £1000 was paid in advance. The contract provided for delivery of the machinery to the port of Gdynia in Poland. The Second World War broke out on 3 September 1939; on 23 September the port of Gdynia was occupied by the Germans, which meant that some machinery already built could not be delivered. The Polish company reclaimed the £1000 advanced payment. The House of Lords upheld this claim. The contract had been frustrated. The £1000 was payment for consideration, the delivery of the machinery to Gdynia, and that consideration had wholly failed.

This decision, which would apply to other commercial contracts so affected, led Parliament to legislate so as to allow fairer and better decisions to be made where similar circumstances could arise.

Law Reform (Frustrated Contracts) Act 1943

Section 1 provides that all sums paid or payable under a contract before the time when the contract became frustrated shall, in the case of money paid, be recoverable from the party paid that sum, and in the case of sums payable, they cease to be so payable. So an advanced payment, such as was made in the Fibrosa case, can be recovered and the obligation to make payments ends.

There is, however, a proviso: if the party to the contract who has received the advanced payment has incurred expenses before the frustration, in or for the performance of the contract, then a court or arbitrator may allow retention in order to cover the expenses. In the case of sums payable, then the party who has incurred the expenses is allowed to recover the amount of the expenses. In both cases the court or arbitrator has to be satisfied that it is just to allow retention or recovery.

Section 1 also provides for a party who before the frustration has done anything which gives a valuable benefit to the other party, to be allowed to recover that sum. The court or arbitrator has to be satisfied that it is just to allow the amount to be recovered and also has to take account of any expenses incurred by the party who has obtained the valuable benefit and any sums paid or payable to the other party under the previous provision.

The difference between this provision and the previous one is that the first covers the situation where there has been an advanced payment or sums are payable; in the second provision the contract did not provide for an advanced payment or sums payable, or if there were, that that amount is taken into consideration. In addition the court or arbitrator is to have regard, when considering the valuable benefit, to the effect of the circumstances giving rise to the frustration of the contract.

In considering the nature of expenses incurred by one party the court or arbitrator may include overhead expenses. Excluded are any sums which because of the frustration become payable under a contract of insurance, unless there was an express term in the contract to insure.

Section 2 of the Act allows the parties to a contract to insert a provision in the contract to provide for circumstances which otherwise would frustrate the contract: they can agree that the Act shall not apply to their contract. The court or arbitrator may also, when dealing with a contract which has a part which is frustrated and a part which is not, treat the contract as severed.

The Act does not apply to a charterparty (which is a shipping contract for the carriage of goods), a contract of insurance, and a contract to which Section 7 of the Sale of Goods Act 1979 applies (a contract for the sale of specific goods).

Breach

A breach of contract occurs where a party fails to perform or shows an intention not to perform one or more of the obligations the contract places on that party. The first form is an actual breach, and the second form an anticipatory breach, where before the contract is due to be performed the party shows an intention not to perform the obligations under the contract.

Actual breach of contract may take three forms. One form is non-performance, where a contractor fails to carry out the contract work. The second form is that of defective performance, where the party undertakes the contract work but fails to perform it as the contract requires, such as not constructing a building in accordance with the specification. The third form is where a party has contracted as to the existence of something, such as suitability, and if that thing is not so suitable it is breach of contract.

Anticipatory breach of contract is where the breach occurs before the date for performance of the contract; it may come about by express repudiation or by implied repudiation. Express repudiation is where a party under a contractual obligation informs the other party that they have no intention of proceeding with the contract. Implied repudiation is where a party does not inform the other party that they do not intend to fulfil the contract but by their actions shows an intention not to fulfil the contract. An example of this would be someone who accepted an offer of employment but, the day before the agreed date to start work, took up employment with another contractor.

A breach of contract entitles the innocent party to sue for damages. Innocent parties may also treat themselves as no longer bound to perform their obligations under the contract in some cases, and they may also sue for damages. This right is limited to a breach of a condition in the contract, where the breach prevents the innocent party obtaining the benefit of the contract. If the breach is a minor matter, the innocent party can sue for damages; if it is a major matter, the innocent party is no longer bound by the contract and can sue for damages. The innocent party can, however, treat the contract as still existing in all respects and sue for damages.

In anticipatory breach innocent parties either may sue for damages immediately, thereby accepting the breach, or may indicate that they do not accept the breach and press the other party for performance of the contract. In the latter case the innocent party may sue for damages after the date for performance of the contract has passed.

Remedies for breach of contract

The remedies for breach of contract are found in common law, which provides the remedy of damages, and in equity, which provides the remedies of rescission, rectification, specific performance and injunction. A court may also allow *quantum meruit.* Of these remedies damages is the one usually sought and awarded by the courts. The distinction between the common law and equity is that at common law the person making the claim for damages once the case has been proved must be awarded damages: the court has no choice, it is a right. However, in the case of a person seeking an equitable remedy the award is at the court's discretion: if that person's conduct is not what it ought to have been then the remedy sought will be refused. The court is guided by the equitable maxim 'he who comes to equity must come with clean hands'.

Damages

Awards of damages are to put innocent parties in the position they would have been in had the contract been performed, in so far as an award of money can do that. There is no intention in the award of punishing the other party to the contract; the award is compensatory in nature. Breaches of contract may lead to substantial loss, minor loss or no loss at all, thus courts award damages under different heads. If a breach of contract resulted in great loss, this is the amount the court would award once it was satisfied that the loss resulted from that breach of contract. An action for a breach of contract may be brought where there has been no loss but in order to show that there has been a breach of contract by one party. Here the court would award nominal damages, a sum not exceeding £5. When a breach of contract has been proved but the court believes that the case ought not to have been brought, it may make an award for contemptuous damages – the smallest coin of the realm.

There is a duty on the innocent party to mitigate the loss, by taking reasonable steps to minimize the loss and not to take any unreasonable steps which would increase the loss. For example an employee who was wrongfully dismissed is required to take reasonable steps to find another comparable job. What the dismissed employee cannot do is to make no attempt to obtain comparable employment so that the amount that might be awarded is thereby increased. The dismissed employee is not required to accept any form of employment, such as a professional person taking a lowly manual job. The steps to be taken are those that are reasonable, and no more, in the relevant circumstances.

Remoteness of damage
In some cases of breach of contract the innocent party may be awarded a sum of money which is less than the loss actually suffered: in the opinion of the court some loss is so remote from the breach of contract it is beyond contemplation of the court when assessing the damage resulting from the breach of contract.

This is based on the decision in the case of *Hadley v Baxendale 1854*, and is known as the rule in Hadley v Baxendale. Hadley owned a mill at Gloucester where a shaft broke and had to be sent to the makers at Greenwich as a pattern for the production of a new shaft. Baxendale (the carriers) agreed to deliver the shaft to Greenwich next day. In breach of contract the delivery was delayed several days, which resulted in a stoppage of work at the mill. Hadley therefore claimed damages of some £300 for loss of profits. The court decided that Hadley was not entitled to this sum since the carrier had not been told that work at the mill would be stopped until the new shaft was obtained.

In the case the rule, with two branches, was laid down: the damages to be awarded should be such as may fairly and reasonably be considered either arising naturally or such as might reasonably be in the contemplation of both the parties at the time the contract was made as the probable result of the breach. The claim in *Hadley v Baxendale* was dismissed because the special circumstances of the stoppage of the mill were not in the contemplation of the parties at the time the contract was made.

The rule was applied in the case of *Victoria Laundry (Windsor) Ltd v Newman Industries Ltd 1949*. Here a large boiler had been bought by Victoria Laundry, who had secured a profitable government contract. Newman Industries delayed five months in delivering the boiler, despite Victoria indicating that the boiler was to be installed and put into immediate use. The Court of Appeal refused the subsequent claim for loss of extra profit on the government contract, since this was unknown to Newman, but allowed the claim for loss of normal profit. The boiler was purchased for immediate use and it was a natural consequence of the breach of contract that a profit-making body would thereby suffer loss of profit.

In the case of *The Heron 11 1969* the House of Lords considered the two previous cases on remoteness of damage. They questioned the particular words used in the Victoria Laundry case, which were 'loss reasonably foreseeable as liable to result' and instead suggested that there had to be a 'serious possibility' or a 'real danger' or 'very substantial' that the loss would occur. This suggests that a somewhat higher degree of probability is required for remoteness of damage in a breach of contract case than the words 'reasonably foreseeable' usually mean.

Liquidated damages
Standard forms of contract used in the construction industry specify a sum of money payable in the event of a breach of contract occurring. So a delay in completion of a construction contract will lead to the employer being entitled to deduct from money due to the contract the agreed liquidated damages or for the employer to sue for that sum. Employers

may be tempted to insert a large sum to force the contractor to complete on time. Any such clause may be challenged on the ground that it is a 'penalty': if the court is satisfied that it is a penalty, even though the clause is described as liquidated damages, it will not enforce it. The court applies the rules laid down by the House of Lords in the case of *Dunlop Pneumatic Tyre Co Ltd v New Garage and Motor Co Ltd 1915*.

1. If the words 'penalty' or 'liquidated damages' are used they are relevant but not conclusive. It is a matter for the court to determine.
2. It will be a penalty if the sum stipulated is extravagant and unconscionable in comparison with the greatest loss that could follow from a breach of contract.
3. It will be a penalty if the breach is failure to pay a sum of money and the sum stipulated to be paid is greater than the sum which ought to have been paid.
4. There is a presumption that it is a penalty if a single lump sum is made payable on the occurrence of one or more events, some of which may occasion serious and other trifling damage.
5. The sum may be a genuine pre-estimate of the damage even though the consequences of the breach make a precise pre-estimation difficult to make.

To summarize, where an employer puts a clause in a contract for the payment of a sum in the event of, say, delay in completion, provided that sum is a genuine pre-estimate of the loss likely to be suffered by that delay, then that is liquidated damages. The fact that it is less or more than what the true loss turns out to be does not invalidate it.

Rescission

The equitable remedy of rescission is an order of the court that the parties to a contract shall be returned to the positions they occupied before the contract was made. This however is subject to an innocent third party having acquired rights with regard to the subject matter of the contract. If it is not possible for the contract to be rescinded, the matter has to be dealt with by the award of damages. The court can order rescission if there has been misrepresentation (see p. 46).

Rectification

A court may order the equitable remedy of rectification where it is satisfied that a written contract does not fully express the true intention of the parties to the contract. In the case of *Craddock Bros v Hunt 1923*, a written contract was made and the conveyance drawn on it. In both documents there was inclusion of a yard which had been exempt from the sale when the agreement had been made by word of mouth. The court ordered rectification of the contract and conveyance as the documents failed to express the true intention of the parties.

Specific performance

This equitable remedy is an order of the court that the contract will be performed. Before the court will grant the remedy it must be satisfied that damages will not be an adequate remedy. The remedy of specific performance is found with contracts for the sale of land and objects of rarity and value. A building plot in a particular locality has features which cannot be replaced by an award of damages: the seller of the land who refused to proceed with the contract of sale would probably be ordered by the court to perform the contract.

The courts have recognized that sometimes it would not be an appropriate remedy because of the difficulty in enforcing it. A contract of personal service, such as employment, is not a contract for which the remedy should be granted. In contracts which require constant supervision or where the contract lacks mutuality, the courts are unwilling to order specific performance against one party when it could not make a similar order against the other. Specific performance cannot be ordered against an infant, and therefore against the other party in a contract with an infant.

Injunction

An injunction is an order of the court that a person shall do or not do something. It can be used to prevent a party breaking a contract; it cannot compel a person to do something which would not be ordered by specific performance. In the case of *Lumley v Wagner 1852*, Wagner made the contract that she would sing at Lumley's theatre two nights a week and not appear at any other theatre during a three-month period without Lumley's written consent. Despite this contract she agreed, for a greater payment, to sing at another theatre. The court granted Lumley an injunction restraining Wagner from singing at the other theatre.

Quantum meruit

Quantum meruit, 'as much as he deserves', is a remedy where an award of damages would not be appropriate or where a contract has made no provision for payment. The case of *British Steel Corporation v Cleveland Bridge and Engineering Co Ltd 1982* was one where *quantum meruit* was appropriate (see p. 35). In the case of *Davis Contractors Ltd v Fareham Urban District Council 1956*, considered with regard to frustration (see p. 55), if the contractors had been successful in their claim that the contract was frustrated, payment would have been made on *quantum meruit*.

Quantum meruit is appropriate where a breach of contract by the other party prevents performance. It may be appropriate where work has been done under a contract and then the parties have agreed to abandon the contract; it is also the same where a contract is void and a party has performed their obligations under the contract.

Limitation Act 1980

A party to a contract who has a right to bring an action for a breach of contract has a limited time (set out in the Act) within which to start the action. In the case of a simple contract, one not made by deed, the period is six years from when the cause of action arose. For a contract made by deed the period of time is twelve years.

The Act recognizes that a party might not become aware of the breach of contract until the period of six years or twelve years has expired. Section 32 allows an action for breach of contract to be brought outside these periods where there has been fraud, concealment or mistake; the time does not start to run until the breach has been discovered or ought with reasonable diligence to have been discovered.

Agency

Agency is a relationship where one person, the principal, authorizes another person, the agent, to act on his or her behalf. This relationship is found in various areas of law but we shall consider the contract law relationship. Some forms of relationship are similar to agency but do not come within the concept of a contractual relationship. Sellers of goods often describe themselves as an 'agent' of some manufacturer's products. While it is correct that the seller has been appointed as the stockists for those products, the sale to a purchaser is a contract for sale between those two parties. Should the products prove to be defective the purchaser's legal remedy is against the retailer. The use of the word 'agent' in a title, such as estate agent, does not indicate a true 'principal and agent' relationship in law. Estate agents seek to find a purchaser for a property but do not have legal power to make a contract between their client and the prospective purchaser.

One difficulty is settling just whose agent a person is. An insurance broker who helps to complete a proposal form is the agent of the proposer and not the insurers, even though if the proposal is accepted the broker will receive payment from the insurer.

Another difficulty with agency is that some terms are used in different senses. For example the terms 'apparent' or 'ostensible' authority are both used to describe the authority of an agent as it appears to others.

Individuals may act as an agent even though their own contractual capacity is limited: the capacity of the principal determines the contract and is subject to the rules considered earlier. So if the capacity of a principal is limited, that limitation is the deciding factor and cannot be removed by the capacity of the agent.

The relationship of principal and agent is usually that the agent performs the duties of agent in return for a salary or other financial arrangements. There is therefore a contract between them which is separate from whatever contracts the agent makes on the behalf of the principal. Once the agent has been the means of creating the contract between the principal and the third party the agent has performed his or her function and has no liabilities in that contract; the position of privity of contract applies to the principal and the third party.

Creation of agency

The relationship of agency may arise either in the form of agreement or without an agreement being made. Agency by agreement covers express authority and implied authority. Agency without agreement covers apparent authority, usual authority, ratification and necessity. So far as the civil engineer is concerned, express authority is probably the most important form of autthority.

Express authority
This form of appointment of an agent may be made in writing or by word of mouth: no particular form is required. However, an agent appointed to make a contract by deed must be appointed by deed. Express authority may be created for a single transaction or for a series of transactions.

When a professional person is appointed as agent by express authority a standard form of agreement prepared for that purpose is used. For the civil engineer the standard conditions of engagement of the Association of Consulting Engineers may be used. This document deals with, among others, the authority of the engineer: what the engineer can do which will bind the client. In practice some matters not expressly mentioned may be dealt with by the implied authority of the engineer.

Implied authority
This form of authority can be implied from particular conduct or from some form of relationship that exists, for example the wife of a man has lawful authority to pledge his credit for household expenses.

The case of *Carlton Contractors Ltd v Bexley Corporation 1962* is based on the provisions in the Corporate Bodies' Contracts Act 1960, which removed the obligation that local authorities could make contracts only by deed. The Act allowed contracts to be made by local authorities and other corporate bodies by persons acting under their authority, express or implied. Officers of local authorities could make contracts by word of mouth which binds the employing authorities.

Bexley Corporation invited contractors to submit tenders for some building work. Carlton Contractors submitted a tender and a priced bill of quantities. The corporation's surveyor when checking the contractors' documents discovered an error, and called in a member of the contractor's staff to discuss it. The contractors agreed that the price would have to be adjusted to take account of the error and confirmed this adjustment by a letter to the corporation. The contractors were awarded the contract but by some mistake within the corporation it was not understood that the tender price had been adjusted. When the contractors sought payment on the adjusted price, the corporation disputed on the ground that they had not agreed to the adjustment. The court, however, applying the provisions in the Corporate Bodies Contracts Act 1960, decided that the surveyor occupied a position whereby he had the implied authority to bind the corporation in the contract.

Apparent authority
This form of authority arises where persons represent to a third party that they have authorized a person to act as agent on their behalf. This representation binds principals so that they cannot later deny that that person is their agent, even if the agent does an act which the principal

did not authorize or wish the agent to do. In the case of *Summers v Solomon 1857*, Solomon owned a jewellery shop which was run for him by a manager, who regularly ordered jewellery from Summers for sale in the shop; this was paid for by Solomon. The manager left his employment and then ordered some jewellery and absconded with it. Solomon was held liable to pay for the jewellery. He had by his previous conduct led Summers to believe that the manager had authority to order jewellery. Solomon had failed to inform Summers that the manager's authority had been withdrawn.

In order to prevent a person who is no longer an agent securing goods on the basis that the agent's authority has not ended, it is the practice for principals to inform those who had previously done business with the principal that the agent's authority is withdrawn. Notices may be inserted in newspapers and journals but the most effective way is immediate notification to those who have conducted business with the agent.

Usual authority

This is used in a wide sense, including on occasions to mean implied or apparent authority. In employment situations a person appointed to a senior position could be said to have the usual authority of a person occupying that position. Usual authority can have a meaning on its own, as is shown in the case of *Watteau v Fenwick 1893*, where the manager of a public house bought some cigars in his own name without the authority of the owner. The supplier had not received any payments previously for cigars from the owner so there was no ground for apparent authority to exist. Nevertheless the owner was held liable. The court accepted that managers of public houses did order cigars for sale in public houses and that this was usual authority making the owner liable.

Ratification

This is an unusual form of agency since the principal acquires rights and liabilities by ratifying the act of his or her agent when the agent has acted without authority. Ratification is effective provided certain conditions are satisfied. These are that the agent must have indicated that he or she was acting for a principal, who must have the capacity to ratify the agent's action, if the agent acts *ultra vires* the principal cannot correct that by ratification; there must have been a principal in existence when the agent acted; and the principal must ratify in a fixed or reasonable time.

Necessity

This form of agency is not likely to be encountered in construction contracts. It applies in limited circumstances, where the law recognizes that a person in some kind of emergency has to take action. Many cases on necessity were decided in the days when it was not possible for agents to get in touch with their principals to obtain their instructions. In the case of *Couturier v Hastie 1856*, the captain of the ship carrying a cargo of corn from Turkey to Britain sold the corn in North Africa because it had become heated and fermented (see p. 51).

Principal and third party

A principal may be disclosed or undisclosed. A disclosed principal is one who has been named by the agent or whose existence has been disclosed by the agent by words such as 'on behalf of my client'. An undisclosed principal is one the third party does not know exists at the time of making the contract.

A disclosed principal can sue the third party since the contract is between named parties or a named and an unnamed but known party. The third party has not discharged their debt to the principal if they pay the money to the agent unless the principal has indicated that the agent is authorized to receive payment.

An undisclosed principal may sue the third party, subject to limitations: the principal will not be allowed to intervene if that would be inconsistent with the terms of the contract or if there were personal considerations between the third party and the agent; the principal has to accept that if he or she sues the third party any defence the third party might have against the agent can be used against the principal.

Agent and third party

Provided the agent has acted properly, the agent has neither rights nor liabilities under the contract made on behalf of the principal, but if all that was required was not done, the agent may be personally liable.

Agents may contract personally with that intention or they may be held to be personally liable because they failed to convey properly to the third party that they were acting as an agent. In the case of *Sika Contracts Ltd v B L Gill and Closeglen Properties Ltd 1978* Sika Contracts were asked by Gill, a chartered civil engineer, to submit a quotation for repairing structural concrete beams at premises owned by Closeglen. Sika sent a written quotation to Gill, who replied by letter accepting the quotation. Gill had not at any time indicated that he was acting for Closeglen or was acting as an agent.

When the work was completed Sika submitted an invoice for £1628 in accordance with the quotation. At this stage Gill disclosed that he was acting as an agent and had been instructed to accept Sika's quotation by the architects acting for Closeglen.

Sika sued both Gill and Closeglen for the £1628. Closeglen went into liquidation so the action proceeded against Gill alone. Gill's defence was that he had described himself as 'chartered civil engineer' and so was not contracting in a personal capacity. This was not accepted by the court. There was no reference to show that Gill was acting as an agent and this made the contract one of personal liability.

An agent may also be liable if there is a trade usage or custom that the agent shall be liable, and also where the agent is in fact the principal, where the principal has not been disclosed and where no principal actually exists.

Implied warranty of authority

Agents may lead a person to believe that they are acting for a principal when they have full knowledge that they do not have any such authority. This includes where the agent believes that the principal would ratify the agent's action: the agent has led the third party to believe that the agent had authority to act, which constitutes an implied warranty of authority. A breach of this gives the third party the right to sue the agent for deceit and to recover damages.

In order to succeed in such a claim the third party must show that they were unaware that the agent had no authority. This covers actual knowledge and where the third party ought to have known that the agent had no authority. There is no liability on the agent if the representation made by the agent was one of law, or if the third party could sue the principal on the basis of apparent or usual authority of the agent.

Principal and agent

The most important matter between the principal and the agent is probably payment for the agent's services. In many cases payment will be by commission, defined in a properly prepared agreement. Where no amount is stipulated the court awards a reasonable sum, subject to the agreement showing that commission was to be paid.

The right to commission is dependent on its being earned: if a transaction takes place after the agent's authority had ended the agent has no right to commission. In order to avoid the injustice of agents using their efforts to secure transactions which come to fruition only after the agency has ended, agreements can provide for agents to receive payment even if these transactions were concluded outside the agency.

Agents should be given an opportunity to earn their commission. If an agency has a fixed period of duration the principal is liable to the agent if there is premature termination, which deprives the agent of the chance to earn commission. If no period of time is fixed, the principal is not under any obligation to maintain the agency in order to allow the agent to earn commission.

A principal is under a duty to indemnify agents for liabilities which arise from agents' discharging their duties under the agency. Agents must be acting within their duties for the right to indemnify to be present. An agency imposes certain duties on the agent which may be expressed in the agreement or be implied by law from the relationship created between the parties.

If an agent is given instruction under the contract made with the principal the agent is obliged to carry out those instructions. If the agent is a professional person there is an obligation to show the care and skill which a member of that profession could reasonably be expected to provide.

An agent is by the position held a person from whom confidence is expected. As part of this duty to act in a fiduciary capacity agents are not permitted to so conduct themselves as to have their own interests in conflict with their principal's interest. If agents have the same business interests as the principal, the conflict of interest can easily arise.

The agent is prohibited from accepting bribes and secret profits, and cannot without the consent of the principal accept a commission from the third party. Where an agent has accepted a bribe or secret profit, whether or not there was a corrupt motive, the agent is liable to certain measures. The principal can dismiss the agent summarily. The bribe must be paid over to the principal, even if the principal has suffered no loss in the matter. If the bribe has not yet been paid to the agent the principal may recover it from the third party.

In the case of *Reading v Attorney General 1951*, Reading, a non-commissioned officer in the army, used his rank to authorize 'black market' goods to be transported through army checkpoints without examination. For this Reading received substantial payment. After he had been dealt with under army discipline the ownership of the bribe money had to be considered. The House of Lords decided that the government was entitled to it since it had been obtained only because of Reading's position in the army.

In the case of *Horcal Ltd v Gatland 1983*, Gatland was appointed in 1972 as the managing director of Horcal Ltd, who were building contractors. In June 1978 a woman asked Gatland to arrange for some work to be done to her house. She was sent an estimate on the company's headed notepaper. Gatland, however, kept the payment for the work, which amounted to £2524 and was made between July and August 1978. On 24 July Gatland and his employers made an agreement for his employment to end. This agreement provided for him to receive £5000 for his past service. Gatland left on 31 October and received the £5000. Shortly afterwards Horcal discovered that Gatland had kept the £2524. They sued, claiming the £2524, and that the agreement was void because of his failure to disclose that he had kep this money, which entitled them to reclaim the £5000. The Court of Appeal decided that Horcal were entitled to the £2524 but not to the £5000. This was refused since by the agreement Horcal had secured what they wanted. The court did, however, order Gatland to pay £435, in addition to the £2524, for breach of his implied obligation that he should well and faithfully serve the company until 31 October.

A final point is that agents must personally perform their duties. Although agents can use the services of their own employees to do those things necessary to perform their duties, agents cannot simply sub-delegate their duties to another.

Termination of agency

A contract of agency is brought to an end in a number of ways which include performance of the obligations of the contract; if the principal and agent agree to end the contract (proper termination); and death or insanity of either the principal or agent (effective termination). The bankruptcy of the principal also ends the contract, as will that of the agent if the bankruptcy means the agent is unfit to perform the duties.

If the contract of agency provides for either party to end it by notice, giving the required notice is effective termination. If the required notice is not given or if there is no provision for notice, failure to perform the obligations constitutes breach of contract. An action can then be brought for damages.

When the contract of agency ends, principals need to protect their position: principals should give notice to all those with whom the agent has dealt that the agent no longer has any authority to act on their behalf.

3

Contracts for the supply of goods and services

Introduction

The law to be considered in this chapter is mainly statute law with the relevant case law, including the provisions in the Sale of Goods Act 1979, the Unfair Contract Terms Act 1977, the Supply of Goods and Services Act 1982 and the Consumer Protection Act 1987.

The Sale of Goods Act 1979 deals only with contracts for the sale of goods. Contracts for the supply of labour and materials are subject to the Supply of Goods and Services Act 1982. At one time sellers of goods imposed conditions of sale which deprived the purchasers of their statutory rights under the Sale of Goods Act 1893 (later repealed by the 1979 Act). The use of such exemption clauses defeated the aims of the Act. Parliament therefore passed the Unfair Contract Terms Act 1977, which allows a court to declare that an exemption clause is unreasonable and so is ineffective.

The Consumer Protection Act 1987 protects persons, who need not be in a contractual relationship, from defective goods. It is necessary to show that a person suffered damage, which may be death or personal injury or loss of or damage to any property. The Act is therefore concerned with the safety of goods produced.

Sale of Goods Act 1979

The Act protects the buyer of goods by implying that certain terms are to apply in contracts for the sale of goods: the terms overrule the common law rule of *caveat emptor* ('buyer beware') in that the buyer's rights are protected. The Act applies only to contracts for the sale of goods, not to gifts, loans and hire-purchase, which are not contracts for the sale of goods.

Section 2 contains a detailed definition of a contract of sale of goods: in simple terms it is where the seller transfers ownership of goods to the buyer for a money consideration. The contract may be subject to conditions and may provide for the sale to take place some time in the future. The term 'goods' is defined in the Act as including personal chattels, growing crops and things attached to or forming part of the land which are to be severed before sale or under the contract of sale.

In the Act the capacity to buy and sell goods is the same as in the general law. The contract may be made by deed, in writing, by word of mouth, or partly in writing and partly by word of mouth, or may be implied by conduct of the parties. Contracts may be made for goods which are not in existance. The price of the goods is that fixed by the parties at the time of the contract or by some other arrangement agreed between them or on the basis of previous dealings between them. Where none of these provisions applies, the price is to be a reasonable price, which will depend on the circumstances of each case.

Section 10 deals with a matter of importance in contracts for the sale of goods – the time for performance. So far as time of payment is concerned time is not of the essence unless the contract states that it shall be. If payment is required on delivery of the goods, for example, this can be made a term in the contract. If the date for delivery of the goods is made of the essence of the contract, failure to deliver by that date allows the buyer to repudiate the contract and make another contract with a different seller. Even if it has not been stipulated, the circumstances may be such that a court will decide that time is of the essence.

A buyer may choose to waive his or her right to repudiate the contract where there has been delay in delivery: in this case the buyer may sue for damages. A buyer may also, if he or she so wishes, extend the date of delivery: this substitutes a new delivery date when the original date has not been met.

Conditions and warranties

The Sale of Goods Act 1979 implies terms into contracts for the sale of goods; these terms are conditions and warranties. A condition is not defined in the Act: it is a term in a contract which imposes an obligation of substance. It goes to the root of the contract. Under Section 11 a breach of a condition gives the buyer the right to repudiate the contract, but the buyer may choose instead to sue for damages.

Whether a term in a contract is a condition is determined by the importance of the matter in the contract. The use of the term 'condition' is insufficient: the court may decide that something is not a condition and instead may treat it as a warranty.

The term 'warranty' is defined in Section 61: a warranty is collateral to the main purpose of the contract of sale, a breach of which gives rise to a claim for damages but not to a right to repudiate the contract. A warranty is thus of less substance than a condition: the buyer does not have the right, when a breach of warranty occurs, to reject the goods, but only to claim for damages.

The Act allows the parties to the contract of sale to agree that these implied terms shall not apply, subject to the restrictions in the Unfair Contract Terms Act 1977. The restrictions depend on whether the sale is a consumer or non-consumer sale.

Title

At common law persons can, in general, pass a good title to the buyer of the goods only provided they themselves have a good title in those goods. The position may exist where a person has some claim, less than ownership, in goods. In both circumstances, buyers ought to have rights if they, unknowingly, buy goods which have an imperfect title or some person has a claim on them.

Section 12 states that in a contract of sale there is an implied condition that the seller has a right to sell the goods. In the case of an agreement to sell the seller has to have such a right at the time when the property in the goods is to pass.

The leading case on the matter of title to goods is that of *Rowland v Divall 1923*. Rowland bought a car for £334 from Divall, and then sold it for £400 to another person. This person used it for four months when it was discovered that it had never belonged to Divall, who had bought it in good faith from a person who did not have a title to it. The original owner reclaimed the car. Rowland repaid the £400 and then brought an action against Divall to recover the £334 he had paid for the car. The Court of Appeal decided that Rowland was entitled to recover this sum. The court refused to order a reduction of the sum to take account of the four months' use of the car, because Rowland had not received any part of what he contracted to receive, ownership of and the right to possess the car. There had therefore been a total failure of consideration.

Section 12 also deals with goods that are in some way encumbered. There is an implied warranty that goods are free from any charge or encumbrance which has not been disclosed or made known to the buyer before the contract is made; this implied warranty extends to giving the buyer quiet possession of the goods except disturbance by a person entitled to a charge or encumbrance disclosed or known to the buyer.

In the case of *Microbeads A C v Vinhurst Road Markings Ltd 1975*, Microbeads sold a road-marking machine to Vinhurst. Because of dissatisfaction with the machine, Vinhurst refused to pay the balance of the purchase price. Unknown to Microbeads and Vinhurst, there was a possible infringement of a patent. The company holding the patent sued Vinhurst for infringement. The Court of Appeal decided that this action was a breach of the implied warranty that Vinhurst was owed by Microbeads, the seller of the road-marking machine.

Sale by description

Section 13 deals with contracts where goods are bought by description, when there is an implied condition that the goods are to correspond with the description. If the goods are sold by sample as well as description, not only must the bulk of the goods correspond with the sample but also they must correspond with the description. It is still a sale by description if the goods are exposed for sale or hire and are selected by the buyer.

In the case of *Varley v Whipp 1900*, Whipp agreed to buy a second-hand reaping machine which had been described to him as being new the previous year and hardly used. This description was totally inaccurate:

the machine was old, rusty and had been left in a field uncovered for many months. When Whipp discovered the true condition of the machine he refused to pay. The decision of the court was that the machine did not correspond with the description. (Although the case was decided on the Sale of Goods Act 1893, this does not affect the principle as the wording in section 13 is similar.)

Merchantable quality and fitness

Under Section 14 there is an implied condition that where a person sells goods in the course of a business the goods shall be of merchantable quality. This obligation on the seller does not apply when the buyer's attention has been drawn to defects in the goods or where the buyer examines the goods before the contract is made.

Section 14 also provides that where a seller sells goods in the course of a business and the buyer makes known to the seller that the goods are being bought for a particular purpose, there is an implied condition that the goods are reasonably fit for that purpose. This obligation does not apply where the buyer does not rely on the seller or where it is unreasonable for the buyer to rely on the skill or judgement of the seller.

The definition of merchantable quality in the section is one which the courts have had difficulty in applying. Goods are of merchantable quality if they are fit for the purpose (or purposes) for which goods of that kind are commonly bought as it is reasonable to expect having regard to any description applied to them, the price if relevant, and all the other circumstances.

In the case of *Henry Kendall and Sons v William Lillico and Sons Ltd 1969*, buyers bought feeding stuffs for their pheasants. The feeding stuffs were found to be contaminated with a substance in one of the ingredients which harmed the pheasants. The claim by the buyers was met by Lillico, the seller of the feeding stuffs. Kendall, the importer of the ground nuts from Brazil which caused the problem, was sued by Lillico. The claim was breach of Section 14. Kendall appealed to the House of Lords against the decision of the Court of Appeal.

The House of Lords decided that the feeding stuffs were contaminated in such a way as to be a breach of the implied condition as to quality or purpose. The fact that the feeding stuffs could have been safely fed to cattle did not affect the decision. The pheasants were susceptible to the contamination and this was the breach.

A case where the buyer relied only partially on the skill and judgement of the seller is *Cammell Laird and Co Ltd v Manganese Bronze and Brass Co Ltd 1934*. Manganese Bronze agreed to manufacture two propellers for Cammell Laird, who were building two ships. Cammell Laird provided certain specifications for the manufacture of the propellers. Some matters, however, were left to Manganese Bronze to determine, including the thickness of the blades of the propellers. One of the propellers was defective because of defects in matters not included in the specification. This was held to be a breach of the implied condition in Section 14. The House of Lords accepted that there was a substantial area which lay outside the specification where the seller's skill and judgement was the deciding factor.

Sale by sample

Contracts for the sale of goods are often made on the basis of an examination of a sample demonstrated by a representative of the manufacturer. The sample may also be accompanied by some description as to the quality of the goods, when the sale is not only by sample but also by description. Where this is the case, Section 13 provisions apply (see p. 83).

Section 15 states that a contract is a sale by sample where there is an express or implied term to that effect in the contract. In a contract for sale by sample there is an implied condition that the bulk of the goods will correspond with the sample in quality; that the buyer will have a reasonable opportunity of comparing the bulk with the sample; and the goods will be free from any defect rendering them unmerchantable, which would be apparent on reasonable examination of the sample.

Performance of the contract

Sections 27 to 37 deal with the performance of a contract for the sale of goods. The seller of the goods is under a duty to deliver the goods and the buyer is under a duty to accept and pay for the goods. Unless the parties agree otherwise, these are immediate duties. The buyer of the goods is not required to accept delivery of the goods by instalments unless that has been agreed. If an agreement has been made, its terms determine matters regarding delivery and payment.

On delivery, the buyer has the right to a reasonable opportunity to examine the goods to ascertain that they conform to the contract; before this, the buyer is not deemed to have accepted the goods. Acceptance of the goods is an important point in the contract: the buyer is then deprived of any right to reject the goods, and is left with the lesser right of suing for damages. Apart from confirmed acceptance, acceptance occurs when the buyer's actions indicate acceptance, by using the goods, for example, or retaining them for a reasonable period of time without rejecting them.

Buyers who have exercised their right to reject the goods are not under any obligation to return them. In the case of *Kolfor Plant v Tilbury Plant 1977*, Kolfor sold a piece of equipment to Tilbury. Tilbury had the right to reject it, which they did. Kolfor did not take back the equipment reasonably promptly; in order to protect the equipment, Tilbury transported it to a place of safety and incurred storage costs until collection by Kolfor. In the High Court Tilbury succeeded in recovering the expense of moving and storing the equipment: this was a foreseeable loss from the breach of contract by Kolfor.

Rights of sellers and buyers

When the seller of goods has not been paid the whole contract price, the seller may retain the goods or make a claim by a right known as a lien.

However, if the seller has passed to the buyer a document of title to the goods and the buyer transfers the document to another person who bought in good faith and for valuable consideration, then this last person has a claim which defeats the seller's lien or retention of the goods.

The Act allows a seller who has passed the property in goods to a buyer to sue the buyer when the buyer has wrongfully neglected or refused to pay. The same right exists if the buyer has not acquired the property in the goods but agreed a date for payment and has wrongfully neglected or refused to pay the contract price when that date has expired.

Where the seller wrongfully neglects or refuses to deliver the goods the buyer is entitled to sue for damages. If the buyer could buy similar goods elsewhere at a higher price then the damages is the difference between that price and the contract price. The court also has power to order that the contract shall be specifically performed.

Transfer of title

At common law there is a rule that no one can give a better title than he himself has. A seller of goods who has a good title to those goods passes it to the buyer on the contract of sale of the goods. If the seller has a defective title, that is what is conveyed to the buyer.

This common law rule is given statutory authority by section 21, which states that if a person who is not the owner of goods sells them without the authority or consent of the owner, the buyer acquires no better title to the goods than the seller of the goods.

Section 23 deals with the situation where the seller has a voidable title to the goods: if the seller has obtained the goods by fraud and, before action is taken against the seller, sells them to a person who buys them in good faith and without notice of the seller's defect of title, that person acquires a good title to those goods.

Retention of title

There is a well-known practice in the construction industry of sellers of goods retaining title to the goods they sell: they give possession of the goods to the buyer but retain ownership until they are paid the full price. Section 19 provides that where there is a contract for the sale of goods the seller may, by the terms in the contract, reserve the right of disposal of the goods until certain conditions are satisfied. Even though there has been delivery of the goods to the buyer, the property in the goods does not pass to the buyer until the conditions imposed by the seller are fulfilled.

These provisions allow the seller to retain ownership until, for example, payment is made in full. The buyer has possession of the goods but no right of ownership until the condition as to payment is fulfilled. This means that the buyer has not got a good title to the goods and that disposal of the goods before the condition is satisfied is disposal without a good title.

The use of the provision in Section 19 was first given prominence in *Aluminium Industrie Vaassen BV v Romalpa Aluminium Ltd 1976*, usually referred to as 'Romalpa'. Aluminium Industrie (AIV), a Dutch company, manufactured aluminium foil; they sold a quantity of foil to Romalpa, an English company carrying on business in England. The contract of sale contained a number of clauses dealing with various matters. Clause 13 began

The ownership of the material to be delivered by A.I.V. will only be transferred to purchaser when he has met all that is owing to A.I.V. no matter on what grounds.

Other clauses provided for the ownership to be preserved if the foil was mixed with other material so as to produce new objects; it was stipulated that the foil was to be stored separately, in such a way as to indicate that it was the property of AIV, and that the money received from the sale of the foil was to be held accountable to AIV.

Romalpa got into financial difficulties and a receiver was appointed. At the time of his appointment AIV were owed over £122 000. The receiver informed AIV that there was unused aluminium foil to the value of £50 235, plus the sum of £35 152 in a separate bank account, which was money received from the sale of the foil by Romalpa.

The Court of Appeal had to decide who owned the unused aluminium foil and whether AIV were entitled to the £35 152 held in the separate bank account. The court had to determine whether the clauses in the contract were effective to allow AIV to control their ownership of the foil in the way they sought and whether the £35 152 was money which could be claimed only by AIV.

The court relied on a case in equity, *Re Hallet's Estate 1880*, which allows a claim to be made when ownership is established and to trace that claim through to the person who holds the object of the claim. The court accepted that the clause retaining title of ownership was valid, which entitled AIV to reclaim the unused foil. Romalpa did not own this material so the receiver could not lay claim to it as part of Romalpa's assets which he could sell for the benefit of the creditors. The court also decided that the money in the separate bank account came from the sale of aluminium foil and from no other source. That money was being held as money accountable to AIV and was therefore to be paid to AIV.

Although this case did not rely directly on the Sale of Goods Act 1979 the same principle applied, that is the retention of title of ownership. Romalpa's sales of the aluminium foil were not for their own account but for AIV's account, unless and until all the money owing to AIV had been paid.

This case was followed by *Borden (UK) Ltd v Scottish Timber Products Ltd 1979*, where Borden supplied resin to Scottish Timber under a contract containing a clause that the property in the goods would pass to the buyers when payment in full was made for those goods and all other goods supplied up to the date of payment. The sellers of the resin knew that it was to be used in the production of chipboard and that the resin was used within two days of being received at the buyer's premises, after which the resin was simply a component in the chipboard.

The buyers became insolvent; at that time the sellers were owed £318 321. They made a claim to be entitled under the retention of title clause to this amount from any chipboard in which their resin had been incorporated. This meant, they claimed, that they were entitled to trace their resin into any chipboard manufactured from it and the proceeds of the sale of any such chipboard.

The Court of Appeal decided that Borden's claim failed: once the resin was incorporated into the chipboard it ceased to exist as resin and could not be traced. The retention of title clause was effective only so long as the resin remained in its original state. The circumstances differ from the Romalpa case in that here the goods were delivered to the buyers for their own use and not for sale to others. There was no fiduciary relationship since the sellers knew that the buyers would use the resin before it was paid for. There was no right to call for its return.

A further decision of the Court of Appeal concerning the use of retention of title clauses was in the case of *Clough Mill Ltd v Martin 1984*. Clough Mill made a contract to supply yarn on credit terms to a company called Heatherdale Fabrics Ltd. The yarn supplied was to be used in the manufacture of fabric. The sellers made four contracts with the buyers between December 1979 and March 1980. All the contracts included a retention of title clause which retained ownership of the yarn until payment had been received in full. If payment was overdue in whole or in part the sellers had the right to recover or resell the material. There was also a provision claiming the right to goods if the yarn had been incorporated in those goods.

Heatherdale Fabrics got into financial difficulties and Martin was appointed as receiver. At the time of his appointment the buyers had possession of 375kg of unused yarn supplied under the contracts and which had not been paid for. Clough Mill told the receiver they wished to repossess this unused yarn and asked that it no longer be used in the manufacturing process. The receiver, however, allowed the buyers to use the yarn and the balance of the price was not paid.

The Court of Appeal decided that Clough Mill had, as they were entitled to do under Section 19, retained title in the yarn after it was delivered to the buyers until they were paid. The yarn remained identifiable, unused and unpaid for. The buyers had no title to the yarn and so could not retain the goods.

The new point raised was that the buyers claimed that the seller's retention of title clause was a charge which to be valid had to be registered under the provisions in Section 95 of the Companies Act 1948. (A similar requirement now exists in Section 395 of the Companies Act 1985.) The court decided that the buyers had not acquired ownership of the yarn, which meant that there was no charge which required registration under Section 95 as a charge could arise only with regard to a company's own property.

There are clauses in the standard forms of contract used in the construction industry which seek to deal with retention of title clauses in suppliers' contracts. A clause usually provides for the employer to claim ownership of materials and goods, whether on or off the site, once the main contractor has been paid for these items. Such a clause may not be effective, however, and employers may find that they do not have title to the goods because of the suppliers' retention of title clause.

In the case of *W Hanson (Harrow) Ltd v Rapid Civil Engineering Ltd and Usborne Developments Ltd 1987*, Hanson were suppliers of timber and timber products. Rapid were building contractors who were engaged by Usborne to construct a number of dwellings on a site in London. Hanson had been suppliers to Rapid for a number of years. Hanson had contracted using a contract clause that the property in the goods supplied should not pass until Hanson had received payment in full. Rapid made use of a purchasing agency which placed orders over the telephone and then confirmed them by a written order with terms and conditions.

The arrangement between Usborne and Rapid was that interim payments would be made on the valuation of Usborne's manager. Such valuations were to include materials on site as well as work done. A valuation was done in August 1984 but no payment was made. On 16 August Hanson delivered timber materials to Rapid for which Rapid made no payment. On the previous day Rapid had gone into receivership, and Hanson claimed payment or the return of the goods. Usborne were informed of the retention of title clause and asked not to use the goods. Usborne, however, used the goods so denying Hanson's claim to title of the goods.

Hanson sued. The High Court decided that the contract of supply of the goods had been on Hanson's standard terms which contained the retention of title clause, which meant that Rapid had no title to the goods. Usborne sought to show that the provisions in Section 25 gave them title to the goods. (Section 25 allows a person who has obtained possession of goods, by buying or agreeing to buy them, to sell them to any person who acts in good faith and without any notice of any right claimed by the original owner, free from that claim.) Usborne's claim was unsuccessful because the court held that the contract between Rapid and Usborne did not pass any property in the goods until Rapid received payment. As Usborne had not made any instalment payment there had been no sale which brought the provisions in Section 25 into operation.

Finally, Usborne sought to rely on a clause in their contract with Rapid, which allowed them to use 'any materials of the contractor' after the termination of Rapid's employment on the appointment of a receiver. The court refused to allow this since the materials were not owned by Rapid; they remained Hanson's materials.

Apart from the use of retention of title clauses in contracts, there are other circumstances where employers have paid for goods but subsequently find that they are not the owner. In the case of *Dawber Williamson Roofing Ltd v Humberside County Council 1979*, the council entered into a contract (JCT 1963 edition) with a main contractor for the erection of a school. The main contractor made a contract for the roofing work with a sub-contractor, whose form stated that the sub-contractor was deemed to have knowledge of all the provisions in the main contract. A clause in the main contract stated that, subject to certain conditions, the value of unfixed goods or materials which had been included in an interim certificate under which the main contractor had received payment meant that those goods or materials were to become the property of the employer.

The sub-contractor, Dawber Williamson, brought several tons of slates on the site. The value of the slates was included in an interim certificate. The main contractor received payment but failed to pay Dawber Williamson. When the main contractor became insolvent the council claimed ownership of the slates and refused to return them to Dawber Williamson, who sued for the return of the slates.

The judge decided the case in favour of Dawber Williamson: the judge was satisfied that the sub-contract was a 'supply and fix' contract and did not involve a 'sale' to the main contractor. The main contractor therefore had no title to the goods which could be passed to the employer. A further reason was that the provision in the main contract dealing with the unfixed goods and materials, for which payment was made to the main contractor, was a contract between the employer and the main contractor only. The sub-contractor was not a party to that contract and so privity of contract precluded a claim against the sub-contractor's slates.

A point which may come to mind is what would be the position if the slates had been fixed to the roof. This would bring into consideration the presumptive legal rule: 'what is affixed to land becomes part of the land'. Even though the sub-contractor would have no right, under the rule, to remove the slates from the roof they might have a claim against the owner of the building that it would be inequitable to deny some payment to them.

Exclusion and limitation clauses

In addition to retention of title clauses in contracts for the sale of goods, suppliers commonly insert clauses which seek to exclude or limit their liability if the goods should prove to be defective. A supplier may, for example, limit liability only to replacing or repairing goods which are defective. Any other loss will be excluded if in fact the clause is effective in that respect.

Exclusion and limitation clauses have been used for many years; ordinary consumers were frequently denied all the protection afforded by the Sale of Goods Act 1893. A form of manufacturer's guarantee was offered instead. Ordinary consumers frequently could not buy goods without forfeiting their legal rights: the Supply of Goods (Implied Terms) Act 1973 prevented ordinary consumers being deprived of their rights under the 1893 Act.

The present position is governed by the provisions in the Sale of Goods Act 1979 and the Unfair Contract Terms Act 1977. The 1979 Act allows the use of exclusion and limitation clauses but their use is controlled by the 1977 Act. A distinction is made between a consumer sale and a person who makes a contract other than as a consumer, because Parliament recognized that the ordinary individual requires much greater protection than the business person who makes a contract as a commercial venture. However, here we are more concerned with the business contract.

The use of exclusion and limitation clauses in contracts for the sale of goods is permitted by Section 55 of the Sale of Goods Act 1979, which states that where a right, duty or liability would arise by implication of law under a contract of sale of goods it may be negatived or varied by express agreement, or by the course of dealing between the parties, or by usage as binds the parties to the contract. All this is subject to the Unfair Contract Terms Act 1977. Section 55 also states that a condition or warranty expressed in the contract by the parties does not negative an implied condition or warranty under the Act unless it is inconsistent with it.

A condition or a warranty expressly put in the contract by the parties as overruling a condition or warranty implied by the Unfair Contract Terms Act 1977 is effective only if the express condition or warranty is clearly inconsistent with that implied. The conditions or warranties implied by the Act remain in force unless they are removed by express terms in the contract.

Unfair Contract Terms Act 1977

Section 12 of the Sale of Goods Act 1979, which deals with title and encumbrances, cannot be excluded or restricted by reference to any contract term. The exclusion or restriction by contract terms of Sections 13, 14 or 15 of the 1979 Act is allowed but only if the contract terms satisfy the requirement of reasonableness.

Section 6 of the Unfair Contract Terms Act 1977 introduces the requirement of reasonableness; Section 11 states that the requirement of reasonableness is that the contract term has to have been a fair and reasonable one to be included having regard to the circumstances which were (or ought reasonably to have been) known to or in the contemplation of the parties at the time the contract was made. In deciding whether a contract term satisfies the requirement of reasonableness under Section 6, the court or arbitrator is to have regard to the matters specified in Schedule 2 to the Act. Section 11 also requires that where a contract term seeks to restrict liability to a specified sum of money, regard is to be had to the resources which could be expected to be available to a person to meet the liability if it should arise; and how far it was open to the person to cover this liability by insurance. This particular provision allows persons to limit their liability to a stated financial sum in circumstances where their resources are not substantial and it is difficult to obtain insurance sufficient to meet possible liability. Section 11 ends by stating that the person claiming the contract term is under an obligation to prove that the term satisfies the requirement of reasonableness; the other party is not under a duty to prove that the term is unreasonable.

Schedule 2 to the Act provides five 'guidelines' for the court or arbitrator to decide if the test of reasonableness has been satisfied:

1. The bargaining strength of the parties with regard to each other, including the alternative means available to meet the customer's requirements.
2. Did the customer receive an inducement to enter into the contract, or was it possible for the customer to have made a similar contract with someone else without having to accept that contract term?

3. Did the customer know or ought reasonably to have known of the existence and extent of the term, regard being had to custom of the trade and previous dealings between the parties?
4. If the term excludes or restricts liability if some condition is not complied with, whether at the time of making the contract it was practicable to expect that condition to be complied with.
5. Whether the goods were specially made, processed or adapted for the customer.

In the case of *George Mitchell (Chesterhall) Ltd v Finney Lock Seeds Ltd 1983*, Finney supplied cabbage seed to Mitchell using their standard terms of business. The seed cost £201. An invoice delivered with the seed contained a clause which claimed to limit liability in the event of the seed proving to be defective to replacement of the seed or refunding its purchase price. Any other loss was to be excluded. Mitchell planted 63 acres of land with the seed which, unknown to Mitchell, was not of the variety required. It had been supplied negligently by a company associated with Finney. The crop was a complete failure and was ploughed in. Mitchell sued claiming £61 513 for breach of contract.

The House of Lords decided that the clause limiting liability was applicable at common law since seed, even of the wrong variety and inferior in quality, had been provided. The clause, however, was subject to Section 55 of the Sale of Goods Act 1979, which meant that it could not be fair or reasonable to allow the clause to stand. The reasons given by the Law Lords were that in the past Finney had in similar circumstances sought to settle the dispute without relying on the exclusion clause; the supply of the seeds was due to the negligence of Finney's associate company; and Finney could have insured against claims of this nature without materially increasing the cost of the seed.

A second case, *Rees Hough Ltd v Redland Reinforced Plastics Ltd 1984*, concerned the usual kind of contract for the sale of goods in the construction industry on the supplier's own terms of business, and so brought into consideration the provisions in the Unfair Contract Terms Act 1977. Rees Hough were tunnelling and pipe-jacking contractors and were invited to tender for sewerage works, which required pipes to be capable of a maximum load around the end profiles of 400 tons, with the joints capable of accepting an angle of deflection of 1.5°. Redland undertook to produce pipes which would satisfy these requirements. A contract was made on Redland's standard terms of business for the supply of the pipes. One clause, dealing with the matter of liability for the goods supplied, stated:

Quality and Description
The Company warrants that the goods shall be of sound workmanship and in the event of a defect in any goods being notified to the Company in writing immediately upon the discovery thereof which is the result of unsound workmanship or materials, the Company will, at its own cost at its option, either repair or replace the same, provided always that the Company shall be liable only in respect of defects notified within three months of delivery of the goods concerned. Save as aforesaid the Company undertakes no liability, contractual or tortious, in respect of loss or damage suffered by the customer as a result

of any defect in the goods (even if attributable to unsound workmanship or materials) or as a result of any warranty, representation conduct or negligence of the Company, its directors, employees or agents, and all terms of any nature, express or implied, statutory or otherwise, as to correspondence with any particular description or sample, fitness for purpose or merchantability are hereby excluded.

This clause sought to limit, in the event of the goods being defective, Redland's liability to repairing or replacing those goods as they chose. There was a requirement for prompt notification in writing with a maximum of three months from delivery. All other liability, under contract, in tort and under statute, such as the Sale of Goods Act 1979, was excluded.

During the course of the work the pipes were found to be cracking and the jacking process had to be discontinued. Remedial works were necessary and other means had to be adopted in order to complete the contract. The question then arose of Redland's liability with the matter and, in particular, the effectiveness of the above clause which Redland relied on in the High Court action. The judge, who was guided in his decision by observations made by the Law Lords in George Mitchell's case, came to the conclusion that the term was not fair and reasonable.

The Law Lords had indicated that deciding what is reasonable is a matter of balancing a whole range of considerations. The judge took the view that the clause was effective at common law. Rees Hough were capable of looking after themselves: they were aware of Redland's terms; the terms were understandable to any intelligent business person; and Rees Hough had not attempted to negotiate alterations to those terms. Against these considerations were that in the past Rees Hough, who were regular customers, had received compensation from Redland when goods had been found to be defective, Redland had not relied on the clause; there was also an element of gain for Redland from the development of a new pipe; the sum paid by Rees Hough was substantial; the terms had not been negotiated with trade and contractors' organizations; and Redland could, as they had done previously but discontinued the practice, have had insurance.

Taking all these factors into account, the judge held that the clause was not fair and reasonable under the Unfair Contract Terms Act 1977 and so could not be relied on by Redland to exclude and limit their liability for the defective goods.

Implied warranty of quality

The Sale of Goods Act 1979, and its predecessor the 1893 Act, apply only to goods, and not if the contract is one for the supply of labour and materials. Until 1982, the only remedy available to a person who claimed breach of contract for work and materials was to sue at common law. The Supply of Goods and Services Act 1982 now provides a statutory remedy, but it is still worth considering the common law approach to contracts for labour and materials.

The most appropriate case to consider is *Young and Marten Ltd v*

McManus Childs Ltd 1968, where McManus Childs decided to build houses on land they owned. Richard Saunders and Co Ltd, a builder, acted as agent for McManus Childs. A director of Saunders specified a roofing tile, 'Somerset 13', as being appropriate for the high-value houses to be built. The roofing work was contracted to Young and Marten, who sub-contracted the supply and fixing of the roof tiles to Acme Roofing Ltd. Acme obtained the roofing tiles from the only company which manufactured them. The houses were built and not long afterwards the tiles began to show signs of being defective. At first only a few tiles seemed defective; it then became apparent that the problem was substantial and several owners had re-tiling carried out. The tiles were defective because of a fault in their manufacture which could not be detected on any reasonable examination. The owners of the houses who had incurred the expense of re-tiling the roofs sued successfully McManus Childs, who then sued Young and Marten for breach of an implied warranty of quality.

The defence of Young and Marten to the claim was that since the type of tile had been selected by Saunders and there was one manufacturer only of the tiles, there was no implied warranty of fitness or quality. The House of Lords observed that usually an employer might sue the contractor who then might sue the supplier under the Sale of Goods Act 1893: the expense finally comes to be borne by the person at fault. The fact that there was only one manufacturer of the tiles did not affect that position. The only reservation to this belief was where the supplier disclaimed liability and that fact was known to the employer and the contractor. That, however, did not apply in these circumstances and so a warranty of quality was implied. The Law Lords also noted that because of the passage of time it was no longer possible to sue the manufacturer. His contract of supply was a simple contract and as it had been made more than six years previously any claim against them would be statute barred under the Limitation Act 1939.

Supply of Goods and Services Act 1982

Parliament sought to remedy statutory deficiencies by passing the Supply of Goods and Services Act 1982, which adopted many of the provisions of the Sale of Goods Act 1979, so that having dealt in some detail with those provisions we can deal briefly with the 1982 Act.

The first part of the 1982 Act deals with the transfer of ownership of goods, other than, among others, contracts for the sale of goods and a hire-purchase agreement. A contract to which this part of the Act applies may or may not be accompanied by services. So a contract for labour and materials comes within the provisions of the first part of the Act. These provisions, following the pattern of the 1979 Act, imply conditions and warranties with regard to title and encumbrances; description; quality of fitness; and contract by sample. There is also a provision, similar to Section 55 of the 1979 Act, which allows exclusion of implied terms (see p. 91).

The second part of the Act deals with contracts for the hire of goods, which may or may not include the provision of services. The provisions deal with contracts for the hire of goods but not for hire-purchase agreements. A contract for the hire of goods is a contract to have possession of goods for a period of time in return for a payment. A hire-purchase agreement, however, is a contract for the hire of goods with a right to purchase the goods, usually at the end of the hire period. So the hirer obtains possession of the goods with a right, if the hirer chooses, also to acquire ownership. A contract for the hire of goods is subject to implied conditions and warranties with regard to the right to transfer possession; to description; quality or fitness; and sample. All these provisions may be excluded in the same way as Section 55 of the 1979 Act allows (see p. 91).

The final part of the 1982 Act deals with contracts for the supply of a service, that is a person agrees to carry out a service. This does not include a contract of service, the usual employment contract, or a contract of apprenticeship. A contract is still a contract for the supply of services even if goods are also to be transferred. In Section 13 there is an implied term that where suppliers are acting in the course of a business they will carry out the service with reasonable skill and care. In Section 14, if the contract performance time is not fixed, there is an implied term that the supplier will carry out the service in a reasonable time. What is a reasonable time is a question of fact. The matter of payment is dealt with by the provisions in Section 15: if the payment is not fixed by the contract, there is an implied term that the party contracting with the supplier will pay a reasonable charge. What is a reasonable charge is a question of fact. The implied term in the section may be excluded by agreement of the parties.

There have been no cases of importance on the 1982 Act; those decided on the 1979 Act should, however, provide some guidance.

Consumer Protection Act 1987

Passed by Parliament in order to put into effect a Directive of the European Economic Community, this is an Act of some length, with the power to make regulations. There have not been any cases of importance regarding the provisions in the Act, some of which are particularly complex; judicial interpretation will be helpful in understanding their full meaning.

The Act sets out to protect the public against dangers from products which have defects in them; the Act provides both criminal liability and liability for damages to those who suffer injury as a result of the defective product. As the Act is of limited application to the construction industry, a brief consideration will be sufficient.

The Act makes a person liable if that person has supplied a product which has a defect in it and that defect wholly or in part caused damage. The person liable is the producer of the product, or the person who put his or her name, trade mark or other distinguishing mark so as to hold themselves out to be the producer, or the importer of the product. The word 'product' means goods or electricity and includes a product which is comprised in another product, whether by virtue of being a component part or raw material or otherwise. The component parts of a building or structure would appear to be covered by this provision. Liability arises, therefore, when there is a product with a defect which causes damage to a person. The word 'damage' means death or personal injury or any loss of or damage to any property. It does not, however, include liability for loss or damage to the product itself. Liability is limited to products intended for private use, occupation or consumption. In order to prevent claims being made for trivial amounts, no damages are to be awarded for loss or damage unless the amount exceeds £275.

There are three points of importance. First, the liability arises under the Act and is not dependent on a contractual relationship existing; a person may, however, make a claim for breach of contract or negligence if that is relevant. Second, it is a matter of strict liability: it is not necessary to prove that the product was made negligently. Third, the Act prohibits any attempt to exclude liability under the Act to a person who suffers loss or damage caused wholly or partly by the defect in the product.

The Act defines the term 'defect': it is basically that the safety of the product is not such as persons are generally entitled to expect. In this respect regard is to be had, among other things, to the purpose for which the product has been marketed and instructions for or warnings as to the doing or not doing of anything with respect to the product.

Where civil proceedings are brought under the Act in respect of a defect in a product, the Act provides a number of defences. The most important is that when the product was supplied, the state of scientific and technical knowledge was such that the producer could not be expected to have discovered the defect if it had existed in the product.

The Act allows actions to be brought within prescribed times, and for this purpose has changed the Limitation Act 1980. An action claiming damages is to be brought within three years. If for some acceptable reason an action was not brought within three years there is an extension of the time to ten years. No claim may, however, be made after ten years have expired from the producer supplying the product.

4

The Institution of Civil Engineers' Conditions of Contract and the Form of Sub-contract

Introduction

There has been a standard form of contract used in the civil engineering industry for a considerable number of years. The present edition, the sixth, was issued in 1991. Like its predecessors, it sets out to serve the needs of civil engineering contractors and employers by providing for the difficulties which may arise with a civil engineering project. As with all forms of standard contracts it seeks to hold a balance between the interests of the parties to the contract, in order to keep disputes to a minimum. Any dispute is to be resolved by arbitration.

The 6th edition is produced by a joint committee of the sponsoring bodies: the Institution of Civil Engineers, the Association of Consulting Engineers and the Federation of Civil Engineering Contractors. Like its predecessors, it will be revised from time to time to take account of changes in civil engineering practice and judicial decisions.

Many civil engineers are involved in contracts where the standard form of contract used is not the 6th edition. The Joint Contracts Tribunal (JCT) has produced a wide range of standard forms which are designed to deal with particular contract requirements, for example the contractor may be responsible for the design as well as the construction of the building. The form of contract in widespread use is the JCT 1980 edition. Another form of contract with which civil engineering contractors are familiar is that published by Her Majesty's Stationery Office, the General Conditions of Government Contracts for Building and Civil Engineering Works, usually referred to as GC/Works.

Some public bodies, such as local authorities, either produce their own forms of contract for civil engineering works or adapt a standard form to their needs.

Experience has shown that the disputes that arise under the Institution of Civil Engineers' Conditions of Contract have been far fewer than with the use of the JCT forms. This may be due not only to the drafting of the documents but also to the practical approach of the contractors. Civil engineering contractors with a reputation for quality work and a wish to remain on employers' selected tenderers' lists may well not seek to pursue every possible contract claim open to them.

The smaller number of judicial decisions with the Institution of Civil Engineers' Form of Contract means that for guidance as to the likely approach of the courts to a similar dispute, reference will be made to a number of judicial decisions concerning the JCT forms. Although the clauses in the two forms of contract differ, the principles of law are unlikely to be dissimilar.

It is not possible here to consider either all the forms of contract used for civil engineering works or the clauses in the 6th edition in detail, but only in general terms with comment and reference to judicial decisions as appropriate.

Parties to the contract

The 6th edition is a good example of the doctrine of privity of contract (see p. 60). The parties to the contract are the employer and the main contractor, who have rights and obligations under the contract. The engineer who is to run the works is not a party; the engineer's powers are those set out as express terms in the contract or those that can be properly implied from the position held.

The engineer is appointed by a contract made with the employer, who would most likely use the Association of Consulting Engineers' Conditions of Engagements. The agreement exists in various forms, each dealing with a particular situation, such as where no architect is appointed and it is the engineer's responsibility to see to all the supervision and administration of the works. Each form sets out the obligations of the engineer and the employer and provides for any dispute to be settled by arbitration.

Most construction works involve the use of sub-contractors, usually nominated. With the 6th edition the standard sub-contract form used is that produced by the Federation of Civil Engineering Contractors; it is approved by the Committee of Associations of Specialist Engineering Contractors and the Federation of Associations of Specialists and Sub-Contractors. Again the doctrine of privity of contract is applicable. Although the employer nominates the sub-contractor, the sub-contract is made between the main contractor and the sub-contractor, who have the rights and obligations under the sub-contract. If the employer wishes to have a contractual relationship with the sub-contractor it is necessary to secure that by a collateral contract or warranty. Without this the employer will have no legal redress against a nominated sub-contractor in the event of some default. The main contractors may be liable to the employer for the default under the main contract, and may then exercise any right they have under the sub-contract to claim against the sub-contractor for breach of the sub-contract.

Formation of the contract

The principles of law considered earlier for the formation of a contract apply to the making of a civil engineering contract. A contractor who is invited to submit a tender, whether open tendering or selected, is making an offer to undertake that work for a stated sum. In the case of *Blackpool and Fylde Aero Club Ltd v Blackpool Borough Council 1990* (see p. 33), the Court of Appeal decided that where a person submitted a tender in accordance with the tender requirements that tender had to be considered in the same way as all the other tenders. Failure to do this constitutes breach of contract.

The tender remains open for acceptance for a reasonable period, which depends on the circumstances. Contractors have the right to withdraw their tender at any time before acceptance, even if it was stated that it remained open for a given period.

Acceptance of the tender is subject to the general rule that acceptance has to be communicated. Under the postal rule, a letter of acceptance makes the contract even if it is delayed or never arrives.

The 6th edition contains a Form of Agreement which names the parties to the contract, names briefly the works to be constructed, and states that the employer has accepted the contractor's tender for the construction and completion of those works. The Form of Agreement lists those documents which are to form part of the Agreement, which makes these contract documents and in the event of a dispute allows a court or arbitrator to consult them. In the case of *Davis Contractors Ltd v Fareham Urban District Council 1956* (see p. 55) the failure to refer to a letter in the appendix of the contract meant that it was not a contract document and so its contents could not be referred to in order to assist the contractors' claim.

The Form of Agreement provides for the payments made by the employer to the contractor to be the consideration for the contractor's undertaking to construct and complete the works in accordance with the provisions of the contract.

The Form of Agreement concludes by the parties executing the contract, either as a simple contract or as a contract by deed. If the contract is to be made by deed the present wording needs to be read having regard to the provisions in the Companies Act 1985, that is the contract may be made as a deed by the signature of two directors or the company secretary and a director without following the formality of fixing a seal to the document. A contract using a seal is still possible.

The 6th edition contains an Appendix. Part 1 contains information, provided by the employer before tenders are invited, which allows the contractor to calculate the tender price. Part 2 is completed by the contractor and specifies certain matters such as the times of sectional completion. There is also a Form of Bond which provides for the contractor to have a surety, usually a bank or an insurance company, who will pay an agreed sum to the employer in the event of the default of the contractor.

Clauses in the 6th edition

Clause 1 contains a number of definitions and interpretations; sometimes reference has also to be made to the Appendix. For example the 'Defects Correction Period' is a period specified in the Appendix.

Engineer and engineer's representative

Clause 2 sets out the powers and duties of the engineer and the engineer's representative. The clause requires the engineer to carry out the duties specified in or necessarily to be implied from the contract, which makes the engineer subject not only to express terms in the contract but also to carry out those duties which have to be implied from the contract. An implied term cannot exclude an express term (see p. 54).

The engineer may be made to obtain the specific approval of the employer before exercising the authority specified in or necessarily to be implied from the contract; that requirement is to be set out in the Appendix. Unless expressly given authority by the contract, the engineer has no authority to amend the terms and conditions of the contract nor to relieve the contractor of any contractual obligations.

Where the engineer is not a single named Chartered Engineer, within seven days of the award of the contract and before the works' commencement date, the name of the Chartered Engineer who is to act is to be notified in writing. Any replacement is to be similarly notified.

The clause allows for the appointment of an engineer's representative, who is to be responsible to the engineer. The duties of the engineer's representative are to watch and supervise the construction and completion of the works. Clause 2(3)(b) states that the engineer's representative shall have no authority

1. to relieve the Contractor of any of his duties or obligations under the Contract

nor except as expressly provided hereunder

2. to order any work involving delay or any extra payment by the Employer or
3. to make any variation of or in the Works.

The engineer's representative's duties and authority are to make inspections, to detect deficiencies and to report to the engineer. Only if expressly authorized is the engineer's representative able to order work involving delay or extra payment by the employer or to make variation of or in the works.

The engineer is allowed from time to time to delegate to the engineer's representative or any other person responsible to the engineer any of the duties and authorities vested in the engineer. Any such delegation may be revoked by the engineer at any time, has to be in writing and does not come into effect until a copy has been delivered to the contractors or their agent. Any such delegation remains in force until revoked in writing and the contractor so notified. The engineer is not allowed to delegate a decision to be taken or certificate to be issued under Clauses 12(6), 44, 46(3), 48, 60(4), 61, 63 or 66, which deal with matters considered to be of such importance that the engineer ought not to be allowed to delegate their responsibilities. The engineer alone is the person responsible for making the decisions.

Clause 2 also permits both the engineer and the engineer's representative to appoint any number of assistants to assist the engineer's representative to carry out duties. The contractor is to be notified of such appointments. The assistants have limited powers: they cannot issue instructions to the contractor other than those necessary to carry out their duties and to secure the acceptance of materials and workmanship as satisfying the contract requirements. Instructions by an assistant are to be in writing where appropriate and are deemed to be given by the engineer's representative. The possibility of a contractor being dissatisfied by an instruction of an assistant is dealt with by allowing the contractor to refer that matter to the engineer's representative, who then has to confirm, reverse or vary that instruction.

If it is necessary for an instruction to be given orally then the contractor has to comply with that instruction, which has to be confirmed in writing as soon as possible. If the contractor confirms in writing an oral instruction then unless it is contradicted in writing forthwith by the engineer or the engineer's representative it is deemed to be an instruction in writing by the engineer.

If a contractor is dissatisfied by any act or instruction of the engineer's representative, sub-clause (7) allows the contractor to refer the matter to the engineer for his or her decision.

Sub-clause (8) requires the engineer, with the exception of matters requiring the specific approval of the employer under the clause, to act impartially within the terms of the contract having regard to all the circumstances.

Assignment and sub-contracting

Clauses 3 and 4 contain the usual provisions found in standard forms of contract restricting the assignment or sub-contracting of the contract. Prior written consent is required, which is not to be unreasonably withheld, if either the employer or the contractor wishes to assign the contract. The importance of this provision was noted in the case of *Helstan Securities Ltd v Hertfordshire County Council 1978* (see p. 62), where a contractor was prevented from assigning the benefit of his contract. The attempted assignment without written consent was held to be invalid.

In the case of sub-contracting the contractor is not to contract the whole of the works without the prior written consent of the employer. Whether it is reasonable or unreasonable to withhold consent is a matter solely for the employer.

Partial sub-contracting is permitted, unless otherwise provided, both for the works and their design. The engineer should be notified in writing before the sub-contractors' entry on the site or in the case of design on appointment. Notification is not required in the case of the use of labour-only sub-contractors.

Sub-clause (4) of Clause 4 states that the contractor remains liable under the contract for all the work sub-contracted and for the acts, defaults or neglects of sub-contractors, their agents, servants or work people.

Clause 4 ends by empowering the engineer, after giving written warning, to require the contractor to remove from the works any sub-contractors who misconduct themselves, are incompetent or negligent or fail to conform to safety requirements. They are not to be employed again on the works unless the engineer consents.

Contract documents

Clause 5 states that documents forming the contract are to be mutually explanatory; if any ambiguity or discrepancy exists the engineer is to explain and adjust the matter, and then issue a written instruction which is to be regarded as an instruction under Clause 13.

Clause 6 provides for the exchange of contract documents between the contractor and the engineer. In making such exchange the copyright which exists is not to pass from either the employer or the engineer to the contractor or from the contractor to the employer or engineer.

Clause 7 requires the engineer to supply the contractor with modified or further drawings, specifications and instructions as the engineer considers necessary. The contractor is then bound by such change. Where any drawing or specification requires variation to the works then it is to be deemed to be a variation order under Clause 51.

Where the contractor has undertaken, in accordance with the contract, the design of part of the permanent works the engineer has power to call for further documents. The contractor has to submit to the engineer specified documents for approval, but this does not relieve the contractor of the contractual responsibilities.

A contractor who requires further drawings or specification is required to give adequate notice in writing. If the engineer does not issue them within a reasonable time and the contractor suffers delay or incurs costs, that has to be taken into account by the engineer. The engineer may grant an extension of time under Clause 44 and allow for the payment of reasonable costs under Clause 52. Any failure by the contractor to submit the required drawings or other documents is to be taken into account by the engineer in considering any claim by the contractor for an extension of time.

Delay in providing drawings and documents often leads to disputes. In the case of *Neodox Ltd v Swinton and Pendlebury Borough Council 1958*, a claim had been made by a contractor on the ground that there had been delay by the engineer in providing further drawings. The judge said that the engineer was under a duty to give periodic details and instructions within a reasonable time in order to give business efficacy to the contract. Failure to do so would make the employer liable for breach of contract. Contractors are not entitled to have such further details and instructions solely as a matter to meet their convenience and financial interests. Engineers are to be given a reasonable period of time within which they and their staff can prepare what is required. It would not be reasonable for a contractor to call for drawings either too far in advance of their true need, having regard to the order of work, or too soon, so leaving the engineer insufficient time to prepare what is required.

The contractor is required by Clause 7 to keep a copy of the drawings and specification on the site available for the engineer, the engineer's representative and those authorized in writing by the engineer.

General obligations

This occupies the main part of the 6th edition, in Clauses 8 to 35.

Clause 8 sets out the contractor's responsibilities. The contractor is required to construct and complete the works and to provide all the labour, materials and other facilities necessary for the construction and completion of the works. The contractor is not to be held liable for the design or specification of the permanent works, unless expressly provided for by the contract, nor for any temporary works which have been designed by the engineer. The contractor is to exercise reasonable skill, care and diligence in designing any part of the permanent works for which the contractor is responsible.

Sub-clause (3) imposes a duty on the contractor to take full responsibility for the adequacy, stability and safety of all site operations and methods of construction. This is an important provision since it puts responsibility for site matters clearly on the contractor. In the case of *Oldschool v Gleeson (Construction) Ltd and Others 1976*, the contractors excavated for a hoist which caused a failure of clay beneath foundations, leading to a collapse of a party wall. The contractors, who had indemnified Oldschool, claimed a contribution from the consulting engineers, based on two grounds. The first was faulty design and the second was lack of supervision by the consulting engineers. The High Court decided that the collapse was not due to a faulty design. The judge also refused to accept that it was the duty of the consulting engineers to supervise the works: even if there was a duty, it did not extend beyond warning the contractors to take any necessary precautions.

A case where the decision was different was that of *Clay v A J Crump and Sons Ltd 1964*; this concerned an architect but in principle it is applicable to a civil engineer. A redevelopment of a garage was being undertaken and a demolition company had been instructed to demolish some buildings. Part way through the demolition work the owner of the garage asked the demolition contractor if a wall of a building could be left standing in order to act as an obstruction to trespassers. The contractor telephoned the architect, who asked the contractor if he thought it was safe to leave the wall standing. The contractor thought so and, acting on this assurance, the architect agreed to the owner's request. When the main contractors moved on the site a hut for the employees was positioned near to the wall. A few days later the wall fell, killing and injuring several occupants who were taking a meal break. Clay, an injured employee of the main contractors, sued his employer, the demolition contractor and the architect.

The Court of Appeal held all to be liable to differing degrees. The architect was held liable since he had involved himself in a site operation and he had relied on the demolition contractor for an assessment of the safety aspect of leaving the wall standing. Furthermore the architect had visited the site after the decision to leave the wall standing. If he had inspected the wall the court was satisfied that he would have appreciated its unsafe condition and had the wall demolished.

In comparison with the decision in Oldschool's case, the architect involved himself in a change in the contract operation, relied on another's opinion and failed to assess the result of the change when he visited the site.

Clause 9 requires the contractor, if so required, to execute a contract agreement.

Clause 10 allows the employer to call on the contractor to provide security for proper performance of the contract to a sum not exceeding 10 per cent of the tender total. If the employer requires this security it is to be provided within twenty-eight days of the award of the contract from a body approved by the employer. The employer is deemed to be a party to an arbitration in the security in order to give effect to its provisions. The discharge of the security is without prejudice to the settlement of any dispute or difference between the employer and the contractor under Clause 66.

Under Clause 11 the employer is deemed to have made available to the contractor (before the submission of the tender) all the information on the nature of the ground which the employer has obtained. The contractor is responsible for the interpretation of this supplied information and for any design which is the contractor's responsibility under the contract.

Contractors are deemed to have inspected and examined the site, its surroundings and information available in connection therewith. Contractors are deemed to have satisfied themselves, so far as is practicable and reasonable, before submitting their tender as to

1. the form and nature thereof including the ground and sub-soil
2. the extent and nature of work and materials necessary for constructing and completing the works and
3. the means of communication with and access to the site and the accommodation they may require

and in general to have obtained for themselves all necessary information as to risks, contingencies and all other circumstances which may influence or affect their tender.

Clause 11 also states that contractors are deemed to have based their tender on the information provided by the employer and their own inspection and examination of the matters just considered, and before submitting their tender to have satisfied themselves of the correctness and sufficiency of the rates and prices in the bill of quantities. These are to cover all the contractor's obligations under the contract.

In contract law a person who makes a representation which the other party acts on may be liable if it was in fact a misrepresentation (see p. 45). The provision of information by an employer to a contractor for the purpose of enabling the contractor to submit a tender may amount to a misrepresentation, depending on the circumstances.

A case (based on the JCT 1963 form) illustrates the legal position when incorrect information was supplied to a contractor. *Bacal Construction (Midland) Ltd v Northampton Development Corporation 1975* arose from a contract for the erection of six blocks of dwellings. The contractors had been informed by the corporation that the site was a mixture of Northamptonshire sand and upper lias clay. The contractors as part of their tender submitted designs for the sub-structure and detailed priced bills of quantities: these were contract documents. As the work proceeded tufa was found in several places, which necessitated redesign of the foundations and additional work. The contractors claimed that there had been a breach of an implied term or warranty that the ground conditions would be those made known to them on which they had been instructed to design the foundations.

The Court of Appeal agreed with the contractors' submission that there was an implied term or warranty and awarded them damages.

The case of *Howard Marine and Dredging Co Ltd v A Ogden and Sons (Excavations) Ltd 1978* (see p. 47) is also relevant to the supply of misleading information about ground conditions.

Clause 12 is most important to the contractor since it provides a means whereby a contractor may claim extra cost and an extension of time when unexpected physical conditions are encountered.

If the contractor encounters physical conditions (excepting weather conditions or conditions due to weather conditions) or artificial obstructions which could not reasonably have been foreseen by an experienced contractor, the contractor is to give written notice to the engineer as early as practicable. If the contractor also intends to make a claim for additional payment or extension of time because of the condition or obstruction, a written claim is to be made as soon as is reasonable to the engineer.

In making either claim the contractor is to give details of any anticipated effects of the condition or obstruction, the measures to be taken, the estimated cost of those measures and the anticipated delay or interference to the execution of the works.

On receiving notification of the condition or obstruction, the engineer may, among other things,

1. require the contractor to investigate and report upon the practicality cost and timing of alternative measures which may be available
2. give written consent to measure notified under sub-clause (3) of Clause 12 with or without modification
3. give written instructions as to how the physical conditions or artificial obstructions are to be dealt with
4. order a suspension under Clause 40 or a variation under Clause 51.

Sub-clause (5) requires the engineer, having decided that the condition or obstruction could, in whole or in part, have been reasonably foreseen by an experienced contractor, to inform the contractor in writing as soon as the engineer has made that decision. If the engineer has ordered any variation, it shall be calculated in accordance with Clause 52 and included in the contract price.

Clause 13 puts an obligation on the contractor, unless it is legally or physically impossible, to construct and complete the works in strict accordance with the contract and to the satisfaction of the engineer. The engineer's instructions are to be adhered to strictly. The contractor is to take instructions only from the engineer or, subject to the limitations in Clause 2, the engineer's representative.

In contract law a contract may be frustrated (see p. 66). If a contract cannot legally or physically be completed it will most likely be frustrated; neither party will be in breach.

An unusual case is that of *Turriff Ltd v Welsh National Water Development*

Authority 1979, where Turriff were main contractors for a drainage scheme. The contract was for the manufacture, laying and jointing of rectangular pre-cast concrete culvert units. The design of the units was unusual both in shape and the use of a flexible rubber ring joint. The units were manufactured by a supplier. Turriff were required to lay the units with a gap of $^{1}/_{16}$ of an inch. As the units were substantial in size and weight Turriff encountered difficulty in meeting the required standard. They were of the opinion that their difficulty was caused by the failure of the supplier to manufacture the units to a tolerance of plus or minus $^{3}/_{32}$ of an inch. A dispute arose with regard to this. The court held that under Clause 13 Turriff were not able to meet their contractual obligations but were not in breach of contract since what they had been called upon to do was absolutely as well as practically impossible.

Clause 13 requires the materials and labour provided by the contractor under the contract and the mode, manner and speed of construction are to be of a kind and conducted in an acceptable manner to the engineer.

Clause 13 also deals with the situation where the engineer has issued instructions which have delayed the contractor or incurred cost beyond what would have been foreseen by an experienced contractor at the time of tender. The engineer is to take such delay into account in determining an extension of time and the extra cost to be paid to the contractor. Any delay and extra cost that are the fault of the contractor are to be excluded. Any instruction by the engineer which requires a variation is deemed to be a variation order under Clause 51.

Clause 14 requires the contractor to submit the programme within twenty-one days after the award of the contract. With this there has to be information in writing as to the arrangements and methods of construction the contractor proposes to adopt. Within twenty-one days the engineer must inform the contractor that the programme is accepted or is rejected. The engineer may also request further information from the contractor in order to clarify or substantiate the programme. An engineer who fails to accept or reject the submitted programme is deemed to have accepted the programme. Where the engineer has requested further information the contractor is to provide it within twenty-one days or such longer period as the engineer allows. On receipt, the engineer has twenty-one days within which to accept or reject the programme.

If it appears to the engineer that the progress of the works does not conform to the programme, the engineer is entitled to require the contractor to produce a revised programme.

Clause 14 also permits the engineer to require the contractor, at times the engineer considers reasonable, to provide information as to the methods of construction, so that the engineer may determine whether those methods will result in proper completion of the contract. The engineer is required to provide relevant design criteria so as to allow the contractor to meet this obligation. The engineer is to give written notification within twenty-one days that he or she has consented to the proposals or to indicate in what respects they fail to meet the requirements or will be detrimental to the permanent works, when the contractor is to take such steps or make changes as to satisfy the engineer and obtain his or her consent.

If the engineer's consent is unreasonably delayed or any requirement could not have been foreseen by an experienced contractor at the time of tender, then the engineer is to take that into account in granting an extension of time or payment of extra cost.

Clause 14 ends by stating that the engineer's acceptance of the contractor's programme does not relieve contractors of their obligations under the contract.

In the case of *Glenlion Construction Ltd v The Guiness Trust 1988*, which was concerned with the JCT 1963 edition but in principle is applicable to the 6th edition, the contract provided for the completion of the works 114 weeks from possession of the site being given. The programme submitted to the architect by the contractor showed an earlier completion date than the contract date. No objection was made to this. A dispute arose with the contract; one of the points the High Court was called on to decide was whether there was an implied term in the contract that if the programme showed an earlier date for completion than the contract date the employers were under a duty to so act, by themselves, their servants and agents as to allow the contractor to complete the contract by the earlier date.

The court decided that the contractor could complete by an earlier date than the contract date, whether there was an earlier date in the programme or not. The court, however, refused to hold that there was an implied term requiring the employers to so perform their part of the contract as to enable the contractor to complete by the earlier date in the programme. This would allow the contractor to impose a different completion date, which would throw out of balance the whole contract.

Clause 15 requires the contractor to have sufficient superintendence constantly on the site during the construction and completion of the works and as long thereafter as the engineer considers necessary. Such persons are to have adequate knowledge of the operations involved in satisfactory and safe construction of the works. The contractor or other authorized person approved in writing by the engineer is to be constantly on the works. Such persons must give their whole time to and be in full charge of the works; they must receive any direction or instruction from the engineer on behalf of the contractor.

Clause 16 imposes an obligation on the contractor to employ skilled and experienced people; the engineer may object to and require the contractor to remove from the works and not re-employ any employees who in the opinion of the engineer misconduct themselves, are incompetent or negligent in the performance of their duties or whose conduct affects safety or health.

Clause 17 makes the contractor responsible for the setting out of the works. If the engineer or the engineer's representative checks the setting out, this does not relieve contractors of their responsibility. Errors in the setting out are to be corrected by contractors at their own cost. If the error arises from incorrect written data from the engineer or the engineer's representative the cost of correction is to be borne by the employer.

Clause 18 allows the engineer to give the contractor a written requirement to make boreholes or other excavation. This is a variation unless it was included as a provisional sum or a prime cost item in the bill of quantities.

Clause 19 places responsibility on the contractor during the progress of the works for safety and security. Where the employer has taken occupation of part of the works the contractor's responsibility for that part ceases. Employers using their own workmen are to have full regard to safety of persons on the site and to keep it in an orderly state. Other contractors employed by the employer are to have the same regard to safety and the avoidance of danger.

A contractor on a site is under various obligations under the Health and Safety at Work Act 1974, which are criminal matters, and under the common law with regard to civil claims made by those injured on the site.

Clause 20 makes the contractor, subject to certain exceptions, fully responsible for the care of the works and materials, plant and equipment incorporated in the works from the works commencement date until the date of issue of a certificate of substantial completion of any section or part of the works, which removes responsibility for that section or plant from the contractor to the employer. The contractor is fully responsible for the care of outstanding work, materials, plant and equipment for incorporation in the works which the contractor has undertaken to finish during the defects correction period, until the outstanding work has been completed.

Risks for which the contractor is not liable include the usual exceptions such as riot or war breaking out. The two most important ones are the use or occupation by the employer (or others on the employer's behalf) of any part of the permanent works, and any design fault, defect, error or omission, other than where the contractor has provided the design.

Contractors who have failed to exercise the required care are at their own cost to rectify any loss or damage that results. If loss or damage arises from an excepted risk the contractor is required to rectify the loss or damage at the expense of the employer. Where the loss or damage is partly an excepted risk and partly the contractor's responsibility the engineer is to make an apportionment.

Clause 21 deals with the insurance of the works, which does not affect either the contractor's or the employer's obligations under Clause 20. Insurance is to be taken out in joint names of the contractor and the employer: both are parties to the contract of insurance with the insurer. If the insurance were to be in the name of the contractor only then the doctrine of privity of contract would exclude the employer from making any claim on the contract of insurance. The amount of the insurance cover is to be the cost of full replacement of the works, materials, plant and equipment for incorporation in the works plus 10 per cent for incidentals such as professional fees.

The insurance cover is to be against all loss or damage other than the excepted risks and run from the works commencement date until the issue of the relevant certificate of substantial completion. The cover is to extend to cover loss or damage during the defects correction period from a cause which occurred before the issue of any certificate of substantial completion. This also applies to loss or damage occasioned by contractors when complying with their obligations under Clauses 49 and 50.

Clause 21 does not make the contractor liable to insure against the necessity for the repair or reconstruction of any work constructed or workmanship which is not in accordance with the contract requirements unless the bill of quantities makes special provision for this.

Under Clause 22, the contractor is (subject to exceptions) to indemnify and keep indemnified the employer against all losses and claims in respect of death or injury to any person or loss or damage to any property other than the works, which may arise out of the execution of the works and remedying any defects in the works, and against all claims, demands, proceedings, damages, costs charges and expenses whatsoever.

The exceptions cover mainly the circumstances where employers are concerned in some respects with the land and in the use of their own employees and contractors, who are not contractors employed by the main contractor.

All these matters which are the employer's responsibility are to be the subject of an indemnity by the employer to the contractor.

Where the responsibility is shared, the individual responsibility is to be reduced to the extent that each contributed to the death, injury, loss or damage.

Clause 23 requires proper insurance to be provided to support the indemnities provided for in Clause 22. Contractors, without in any way limiting their own or the employer's obligations and responsibilities under Clause 22, are to insure, for at least the amount set out in the Appendix in the joint names of the contractor and the employer, against death or injury to any person or loss or damage to any property, other than the works themselves, arising out of the execution of the contract. What is excluded is death to or injury of any employee or sub-contractors of the contractor. This is a matter of direct concern between the contractor and those individuals.

The insurance taken out under Clause 23 is to include a cross-liability clause such that the insurance is to apply to the contractor and employer as separate insured.

Clause 24 states that the employer is not to be liable or in respect of any damages or compensation payable at law with regard to any accident or injury to any operative or other person employed by the contractor, except where that accident or injury resulted from or was contributed to by an act or default of the employer and the employer's agents or servants. The contractor has, subject to the exception, to indemnify and keep indemnified the employer against claims, damages and compensation.

Under Clause 25 the contractor has, before the works commencement date, to produce satisfactory evidence that the required insurances have been obtained. Insurance policies and current receipts for payment are to be produced for inspection. The terms of the insurances are subject to the engineer's approval, which is not to be unreasonably withheld. Any excess in the insurance policies is to be that set out in the appendix to the form of tender.

If the contractor does not produce satisfactory evidence that the required insurances are in force, the employer is to take out those insurances. The premiums may be deducted from money due to the contractor or be recovered as a debt.

The employer and contractor are required to observe the conditions in the insurance policies. Failure to do so is dealt with by making the responsible person indemnify the other against all losses and claims arising from such failure.

Clause 26 imposes on the contractor the responsibility for giving all notices and paying all fees required under statutory obligations so far as they relate to the construction and completion of the works. Such fees, and rates and taxes paid by the contractor in connection with the site and constructions, are to be repaid or allowed by the employer on certification by the engineer.

Clause 26 also puts responsibility on the contractor to comply with all the statutory provisions applicable to the works. The contractor is to indemnify the employer against the penalties and liabilities for any breach, except where the breach is the unavoidable consequence of complying with the contract or instructions of the engineer. The obtaining of any necessary planning permission is also excluded. Where the contract or an instruction of the engineer is found not to be in conformity with the statutory obligations the engineer is to issue an instruction, including a variation order, to secure conformity.

Clause 27 deals with the contract works and the Public Utilities Street Works Act 1950. The Act regulates the breaking open of streets and other lands for the laying of mains and other apparatus, and the carrying out of work which might interfere with such mains and apparatus, which are given special protection in that notices have to be given to the service authorities whose mains and apparatus might be affected by construction operations. Reference must be made to the Act itself for a full understanding of the control over construction operations.

Before the contract work begins the employer has to notify the contractor in writing whether any part of the works will bring the provisions of the Act into operation. If so, the employer is to serve whatever notices are required under the Act. The contractor undertakes to give not less than twenty-one days' notice in writing to the employer indicating when certain specified works are to start. Failure to start within two months of the date of the notice makes it invalid and a fresh notice must be served.

If compliance with the Act results in work being done in land in which services exist or will exist and a variation order is issued, any resulting delay to the contractor or extra cost incurred thereby must be taken into account by the engineer.

Subject to the employer's obligations, the contractor is obliged to comply with all the requirements of the Act and to indemnify the employer against any liability to meet such requirements.

Clause 28 requires the contractor to indemnify the employer against any claim for infringement of patent rights. If, however, the infringement results from compliance with the design or specification, not provided by the contractor, then the employer is to indemnify the contractor against claims for infringement. The contractor is also required to pay royalty charges for getting stone, sand, clay and other materials required for the works.

Clause 29 deals with the liability for disturbances caused by the carrying out of the works, and allocates responsibility between the contractor and employer as parties to the contract. Any action taken by a third party, such as a local authority, would be in accordance with the relevant statutory and common law provisions.

The contractor is not to interfere unnecessarily or improperly with the convenience of the public or access to public or private roads or properties. The contractor is to indemnify the employer against all liability and claims with regard to these matters.

All work is to be carried out without unreasonable noise or disturbance or other pollution. The contractor is under a number of statutory and common law obligations; any infringement could lead to prosecution or a civil claim being made.

Where noise disturbance or other pollution is *not* the unavoidable consequence of constructing and completing the works the contractor is to indemnify the employer against such claims. If, however, noise disturbance or other pollution is the unavoidable consequence, it is the employer who is to indemnify the contractor.

Clause 30 allocates responsibility between the contractor and employer on the matter of damage to highways. A number of provisions in the Highways Act 1980 put obligations on contractors so far as their activities damage or interfere with the use of highways (see p. 263). Clause 30 does not affect these obligations.

The contractor is to use all reasonable means to prevent highways and bridges being subject to extraordinary traffic, including the subcontractors' traffic. Where loads and the use of vehicles will inevitably lead to extraordinary traffic, then routes shall be selected and vehicles used with load distributions to limit, as far as is reasonably practicable, unnecessary damage or injury to highways and bridges.

Unless the contract otherwise provides, the contractor is responsible for the cost of strengthening bridges or altering or improving a highway which communicates with the site to facilitate the movement of contractor's equipment. The contractor is to indemnify the employer against claims for damage to highways and bridges. If damage does occur to any bridge or highway communicating with the site from the transport of materials or manufactured or fabricated articles in the execution of the works, the contractor is to notify the employer.

If some statutory provision makes the haulier of such items liable to indemnify the highway authority against damage then the employer is not liable for any claims in that respect. If this is not the case, the employer is to negotiate the settlement, pay the sums due and indemnify the contractor. Provided that if the engineer is of the opinion that such claim results from the failure of the contractor to use reasonable means to prevent extraordinary traffic, as required by the clause, then the amount is to be paid by the contractor to the employer or be deducted from any sum due to the contractor.

Clause 31 requires the contractor to afford reasonable facilities to the employer's other contractors and workers and properly authorized persons or bodies who may be on the site or near the site engaged in work not in the contract. If this should cause delay or cost beyond that reasonably foreseeable by an experienced contractor at the time of tender then the engineer is to take such matters into account in granting an extension of time or extra payment. Profit is to be added to any additional permanent or temporary work.

Clause 32 determines the position between the employer and contractor when valuables, antiquities and things of geological or archaeological interest are discovered on the site. Any such find belongs to the employer and not the contractor. The contractor is to take reasonable precautions to prevent any person removing or damaging them, to notify the engineer and, at the expense of the employer, to act on the engineer's orders as to the disposal of the finds.

However, a find of treasure trove belongs to the Crown (see p. 231) and here the provisions in this clause are of no effect. The Crown decides how the find of treasure trove shall be dealt with.

Clause 33 requires the contractor on completion of the works to clear the site and leave everything in a clean and workmanlike manner to the satisfaction of the engineer.

Clause 34 is not used in the 6th edition. In earlier editions the clause required contractors to pay fair wages to their workers, later revised to an obligation to pay the wage rates and observe the hours and conditions of employment for operations not less than those agreed under the Working Rule Agreement of the Civil Engineering Construction Conciliation Board for Great Britain. This is no longer considered necessary.

Clause 35 requires the contractor, if the engineer so directs, to deliver to either the engineer or the engineer's representative in a form and at intervals prescribed a return of contractor's labour and equipment engaged on the site. Contractors are to require their sub-contractors to observe these provisions.

Workmanship and materials

Clauses 36 to 40 of the 6th edition set out what is required of the contractor regarding workmanship and materials. Provision is made for work which is not of the proper standard to be remedied. The engineer is also empowered in given circumstances to suspend the work.

Clause 36 requires materials and workmanship to be in accordance with the contract and engineer's instructions. The engineer may direct that tests be carried out both on the site and off it. The contractor is to give the normal assistance in the conduct of tests, including the supply of samples of materials.

The cost of supplying samples and making tests is to be borne by the contractor if the contract provided for this. Where a test ordered by the engineer is not intended or provided for in the contract, or is not sufficiently described in the specification or bill of quantities, then the cost of the test is to be borne by the contractor only if it reveals workmanship or materials not to be in accordance with the contractor or the engineer's instructions.

Clause 37 empowers the engineer and any person authorized by the engineer to have at all times access to the site and other places where work is being prepared or materials, articles and equipment being obtained for the works. The contractor is to give every assistance and facility in obtaining such access.

Without this provision there could be legal problems in gaining access since the contractor has exclusive possession of the site and others, such as manufacturers, have the same with regard to their own premises.

Clause 38 requires the contractor to give the engineer full opportunity to examine and measure any work about to be covered up. The contractor is to notify the engineer when the work is ready for inspection, which should be done without unreasonable delay unless the engineer informs the contractor that it is considered unnecessary.

The clause allows the engineer to require that any part of the works be uncovered and then reinstated and made good. The cost of this is to be borne by the contractor only if the uncovered work is found to be not in accordance with the contract, otherwise the employer has to bear the cost.

Clause 39 empowers engineers to take action when they are of the opinion that materials or work are not in accordance with the contract. During the progress of the work engineers are to instruct in writing the removal of material which in their opinion is not in accordance with the contract and its substitution with materials which accord with the contract. Any work, even if included in an interim payment, is to be removed and properly re-executed if in the opinion of the engineer materials, workmanship or contractor's design are not in accordance with the contract.

Where a contractor fails to carry out an engineer's instruction, the employer is entitled to appoint another person to do that work. The cost of that work is recoverable by the employer from the contractor and may be deducted from monies due to the contractor. The engineer is to notify the contractor and the employer of the right to make deduction.

In order to prevent any failure by the engineer to disapprove work or materials being used as acceptance of their suitability, Clause 39 provides that that failure shall not prejudice the power of the engineer or any person acting under the engineer subsequently to take action under the clause.

Clause 40 gives power to the engineer to give a written order to suspend the progress of the works, for the time and in the manner that the engineer considers necessary. During the suspension the works are to be properly protected and secured. The contractor is (subject to exceptions) to be paid extra cost incurred in giving effect to the engineer's instructions. The contractor has to give notice for the claim in accordance with Clause 52(4). The exceptions to the contractor's right to payment are: suspension was included in the contract; was necessary by reason of weather conditions or default of the contractor; and was necessary for the proper execution or safety of the works or part, provided that does not arise from any act or default of the engineer, the employer or from any excepted risks defined in Clause 20(2).

Profit is to be added in respect of any additional permanent or temporary work.

In determining a claim for an extension of time the engineer is to take into account the period of suspension, including that caused by an act or default of the engineer or employer, unless the suspension was provided for by the contract or was the result of the contractor's default.

Clearly prolonged periods of suspension will create difficulties for contractors: Clause 40 allows contractors to take action to protect their position. If the period of suspension continues for three months then, unless the contract provided for the suspension or it resulted from the contractor's default, the contractor can serve written notice on the engineer requiring permission within twenty-eight days to proceed with the works. If the engineer within the twenty-eight days does not grant that permission, the contractor may serve a written notice electing to treat the suspension as an omission, if part only of the works is affected, and as abandonment by the employer if the whole is affected.

Commencement time and delays

Clause 41 states that the works commencement date shall be: the date specified in the Appendix to the form of tender; if no date is specified, within twenty-eight days of written notification from the engineer of the award of the contract; or such other date as may be agreed between the parties.

The contractor is required to start work as soon as is reasonably practicable after the commencement date, and to proceed with the work with due expedition and without delay in accordance with the contract.

Clause 42 makes a number of provisions with regard to possession of the site and access to it.

The contract may prescribe the extent and order in which parts of the site are to be made available to the contractor; the availability and nature of the access provided by the employer; and the order in which the works are to be constructed.

The employer is to give the contractor on the commencement date possession of the site and access as may be required to allow the contractor to commence and proceed with the works.

Where the contractor suffers delay and/or incurs additional costs because of failure by the employer to give possession of the site the engineer is to determine an extension of time and any additional cost. Profit is to be added for additional permanent or temporary works. The engineer has to notify both the contractor and employer of his or her decision in these matters.

Should contractors require additional access or facilities then that is to be at their cost.

Clause 43 requires the whole of the works and any section required to be completed by a particular time as set out in the Appendix to the form of tender to be substantially completed within the time stated or extended time, as allowed under Clause 44, from the commencement date.

Clause 44 provides for an extension of time for completion of the contract in prescribed circumstances. These are set out in sub-clause (1):

Should the Contractor consider that
(a) any variation ordered under Clause 51(1) or
(b) increased quantities referred to in Clause 51(4) or
(c) any cause of delay referred to in these Conditions or
(d) exceptional adverse weather conditions or
(e) other special circumstances of any kind whatsoever which may occur
be such as to entitle him to an extension of time for the substantial completion of the Works or any Section thereof he shall within 28 days after the cause of any delay has arisen or as soon thereafter as is reasonable deliver to the Engineer full and detailed particulars in justification of the period of extension claimed in order that the claim may be investigated at the time.

On receiving the detailed particulars from the contractor the engineer is to consider all the circumstances and assess the delay, if any, and notify the contractor in writing of his or her decision. Engineers are also authorized to act without a claim from the contractor if they are satisfied that any of the prescribed circumstances has arisen; they then notify the contractor in writing.

Events in the course of the work may create a situation where a delay fairly entitles a contractor to an extension of time for substantial completion of the works or a section. The engineer may therefore grant forthwith an interim extension. The contractor is to be so informed in writing, and also if the engineer refuses the claim for an extension.

The engineer is required, whether or not requested by the contractor, not later than fourteen days after the due date or extended date for completion, to consider all the circumstances known at that time and make an assessment. If the engineer decides that the contractor is not entitled to an extension, both the contractor and employer are to be notified.

The engineer is required to make a final decision on the matter of the contractor's entitlement to an extension of time within fourteen days of the issue of the certificate of substantial completion of the works or any section. This final decision is to be given to both the employer and contractor.

Clause 45 regulates the hours of work. Unless the contract so provides, or the engineer gives permission in writing, none of the work is to be done at night or on Sundays. The clause provides exceptions where the work is unavoidable or absolutely necessary in order to save life or property or for the safety of the works. In any of these circumstances the engineer or the engineer's representative is to be immediately advised. For example where severe weather had created an unsafe situation, work would probably be necessary without stopping until the danger had been removed. A further exception is where the work is customarily done outside normal hours or by shift working.

Under Clause 46, if the progress of the work is too slow and there is no reason for the contractor to be given an extension of time, so that substantial completion by the time or extended time for completion is not possible, the engineer is to notify the contractor in writing of this opinion. The contractor is then to take the necessary steps, without additional payment, with the engineer's consent to expedite the completion of the works. The contractor may seek permission for night or Sunday working, which is not to be unreasonably withheld.

A contractor may agree with the employer, if so requested by either the employer or engineer, to complete the works earlier than the time or extended time for completion. Any special terms and conditions of payment are to be agreed between the contractor and employer before action is taken for earlier completion.

Liquidated damages for delay

Clause 47, which deals with liquidated damages, is generally considered the most important clause in the 6th edition. Liquidated damages clauses in construction contracts have been the subject of judicial interpretation over a period of time. Although many cases have involved the JCT forms of contract, the court's approach would in principle be the same with the 6th edition. Due regard must be given to the precise wording of the particular contract form used.

Liquidated damages must not be a penalty, or otherwise the court will refuse to recognize it, and must be a genuine pre-estimate of the loss likely to be suffered from the breach of contract (see p. 72). The House of Lords' decision in the case of *Dunlop Pneumatic Tyre Co Ltd v New Garage and Motor Co Ltd 1915* laid down the general principles on liquidated damages and penalties (see p. 72).

Sub-clause (1) of Clause 47 states that where the whole of the works is not divided into sections, the Appendix to the form of tender shall include a sum which is the employer's genuine pre-estimate, expressed by per week or per day, of the damages likely to be suffered by the employer if the whole of the works is not completed by the contract completion date as originally fixed or as extended.

Failure of the contractor to complete the whole of the works in the prescribed time requires the contractor to pay the employer the stated sum for every week or day which shall elapse between the date on which the prescribed time expired and the date when the whole of the works is substantially completed.

Where the engineer has certified under Clause 48 that part of the works has been completed before the whole of the works has been completed, the agreed sum of liquidated damages shall be reduced in proportion to the value of the completed part bears to the value of the whole of the works.

For a liquidated damage provision to apply there must be such a clause in the contract and it must be completed properly. Failure to do so may result in the employer losing not only the right to liquidated damages but also the right to claim unliquidated damages. In the case of *Temloc Ltd v Errill Properties Ltd 1987*, the parties to a construction contract (using the

JCT 1980 form) agreed that there would not be a stipulated sum by way of liquidated damages. The standard form used had the usual provision in the Appendix for the figure for the liquidated damages to be inserted. Instead of an amount the word 'NIL' was inserted. The contractor was late in the completion of the contract and the employer sought to make a claim for unliquidated damages. The Court of Appeal however refused to accept that such a right existed: a clause in the contract dealt in a comprehensive manner with the building owner's right to liquidated damages for late completion. As the parties to the contract had expressly agreed that the liquidated damages should be nil that also excluded an option of claiming unliquidated damages.

An employer is faced with the difficulty that if the amount fixed is too high it may be held to be a penalty and if it is too low the amount the employer will receive will not be adequate recompense. The employer cannot look to the court to fix the amount. The approach of the courts, once they are satisfied that an agreed sum is a genuine pre-estimate of the loss likely to be suffered, is to uphold that sum as liquidated damages. This can result in an employer receiving a sum which is either greater or less than the actual loss at that time.

In the case of *Cellulose Acetate Silk Co Ltd v Widnes Foundry (1925) Ltd*, a contract provided for the construction of a chemical plant. A clause in the contract made provision for late completion by stating that the contractors were to pay 'by way of penalty £20 per working week'. The contractors delayed in the completion by some thirty weeks. During this time the owners of the plant suffered an actual loss of £5850. The attempt to recover this amount was unsuccessful. The House of Lords decided that the owners were entitled to £600 only, which was the figure agreed and the extent of the owners' right to claim.

A liquidated damages provision is effective only if the delay is the contractor's fault. Where a delay is the result in whole or in part of the employer he or she cannot claim liquidated damages unless the contract allows the employer to extend the completion date to take account of this delay. The case of *Peak Construction (Liverpool) Ltd v McKinney Foundations Ltd 1970* concerned a delay caused partly by the employer. Peak entered into a contract with Liverpool Corporation for the construction of some multi-storey flats. The contract (Liverpool Corporation's own form) provided for a payment of £1.25 for each uncompleted flat per week or part of a week. The contract contained a provision allowing the architect to grant an extension of time. McKinney were nominated sub-contractors for the piling work. After the piling work was completed there were found to be serious defects in the work. At a site meeting it was agreed that there should be an investigation, with the work stopped in the meantime, by a consulting engineer. There was a delay of several months by the corporation in the appointment of the engineer. A report was submitted which was not agreed to by the corporation for some time. Work could not be recommenced until fifty-eight weeks after the work had to be stopped. The Court of Appeal decided that the corporation had no right to recover liquidated damages against Peak since the delay was partly the fault of the corporation.

Sub-clause (2) deals with work divided into sections. Where completion of the sections is to be to particular times there is to be a sum in respect of each section by way of liquidated damages. Such sum may be expressed to be per week or per day payable for the period which elapses between the prescribed time expiring and the date of substantial completion of that section. Where a part of a section is certified as complete before the whole section is completed then there is to be a reduction in the proportion of the value the completed part bears to the value of that section.

Sub-clause (3) states that any sums payable by the contractor to the employer are to be liquidated damages and not as a penalty. The court reserves to itself the right to decide whether a provision is liquidated damages or a penalty. What the parties to the contract have expressed can be overturned by the court.

Sub-clause (4) provides for a limitation of the total amount payable as liquidated damages; the limitation should be stated in the Appendix to the form of tender. If no limit is stated, the contractor's liability is unlimited. If no sum is inserted as liquidated damages or any sum payable is stated to be 'NIL', damages are not payable.

Sub-clause (5) allows the employer to deduct and retain liquidated damages from sums due or to become due to the contractor, or to require the contractor to pay such amount to the employer forthwith. If the engineer in a subsequent or final review grants an extension or further extension of time then the employer is no longer entitled to liquidated damages for that period. Furthermore if any sum has already been recovered that is to be returned to the contractor.

Sub-clause (6) deals with the situation where liquidated damages have become payable in respect of part of the works and the engineer issues a variation order which results in further delay to that part of the works. The employer's entitlement to liquidated damages in respect of that part of the works is to be suspended. The engineer is to inform both the employer and the contractor in writing of the further delay and also when the further delay ends. Suspension does not invalidate any entitlement to liquidated damages which have already started to run. Any monies deducted or recovered under sub-clause (5) may be retained by the employer without incurring liability for interest under clause 60(7).

Certificate of substantial completion

Clause 48 sets out the procedure to be followed when the works are substantially completed. When the contractor considers the whole of the works (or any section in respect of which there was a separate completion time) has been substantially completed and satisfied any test laid down in the contract, the contractor may notify the engineer or the engineer's representative in writing and including an undertaking to finish any outstanding work in accordance with Clause 49(1).

The engineer within twenty-one days of delivery of the contractor's notice has either to issue to both the contractor and employer a certificate of substantial completion with the date when the works or section in the engineer's opinion were substantially completed in accordance with the contract, or to issue instructions in writing to the contractor of the work to be done before the engineer can issue the certificate. When contractors have fulfilled those instructions they are entitled to the certificate of substantial completion within twenty-one days of the engineer's satisfaction that the specified work has been done.

Where the employer has occupied or used a substantial part of the works, and that was not provided for in the contract, the engineer is to issue a certificate of substantial completion for that part. The certificate takes effect from the date of the contractor's request. Any outstanding work is to be completed during the defects correction period.

A certificate of substantial completion is not to be taken to certify completion of ground or surface reinstatement unless the certificate expressly states that fact.

Outstanding work and defects

Clause 49 supports the contractor's undertaking given in Clause 48 that any outstanding work will be finished. An agreement may be made between the engineer and contractor as to the time within which outstanding work is to be completed, otherwise the work is to be completed as soon as practicable after the defects correction period.

The contractor is to hand over to the employer the works and each section and part in the condition required by the contract and to the satisfaction of the engineer. Any making good as required by the engineer in writing is to be done within the defects correction period or within fourteen days thereafter as a result of the engineer's inspection within the defects correction period. The cost of such work is to be borne by the contractor unless the engineer is of the opinion that the contractor is not at fault with regard to workmanship or materials. In this circumstance the value of the work is paid for as additional work.

Where a contractor fails to do the remedial works the employer may have that work done by others and recover the cost from the contractor provided it is work that should have been done at the contractor's own expense.

Clause 50 allows the engineer to require, in writing, the contractor to make searches, tests or trials to determine the cause of some defect, imperfection or fault. If this reveals that the contractor has not fulfilled the contractual obligation the cost of the work is to be borne by the contractor, including making good faults that have been revealed; otherwise the cost is borne by the employer.

Alterations, additions and omissions

Almost every construction contract is subjected to some change. Conditions may require a change or the client may wish to amend something after the work has started. Clause 51 provides for such variations. Sub-clause (1) states:

The Engineer

(a) shall order any variation to any part of the Works that is in his opinion necessary for the completion of the Works and

(b) may order any variation that for any other reason shall in his opinion be desirable for the completion and/or improved functioning of the Works.

Such variations may include additions omission substitutions alterations changes in quality form character kind position dimension level or line and changes in any specified method or timing of construction required by the Contract and may be ordered during the Defects Correction Period.

Engineers have wide powers to order variations as they consider desirable. Variation may be ordered to overcome some practical problem revealed in the course of the work, and for any other reason. Variations are to be ordered in writing subject to the right to give an oral instruction, as set out in Clause 2.

Sub-clause (3) deals with a matter of importance:

No variation ordered in accordance with sub-clause (1) and (2) of this Clause shall in any way vitiate or invalidate the Contract but the value (if any) of all such variations shall be taken into account in ascertaining the amount of the Contract Price except to the extent that such variation is necessitated by the Contractor's default.

This provision preserves the contract even though the contractor is called upon to do something which was not originally envisaged. Judicial decisions support the view that if a contractor is called upon to do something which varies the work to such an extent as to go outside the original contract, then it forms a fresh contract to which rates in the original contract may not be applicable. The variation may constitute a new contract which the contractor is not required to perform. For example a substantial omission of work may make a contract totally different from the original and put the contractor in the position of being able to refuse to carry out the work. Individual circumstances must determine whether or not a variation has, in effect, taken the work outside the original contract. A variation order is not required for increases or decreases in the quantity of work as set out in the bill of quantities.

The value of variations ordered by the engineer is to be ascertained after consultation with the contractor on the following principles:

1. Work of similar character and executed under similar conditions at the same rates and prices as in the bill of quantities.
2. Work which is not as above or is ordered during the defects correction period, then the rates and prices in the bill of quantities are to be used as a basis of valuation so far as is reasonable, failing which a fair valuation shall be made.
3. Failing agreement between the engineer and contractor as to any rate or price to be used in the valuation the engineer shall determine the rate or price and notify the contractor.
4. If the variation is such that the rate or price is unreasonable or inapplicable then either the engineer or the contractor are to give notice to the other before the varied work commences. The engineer then fixes the rate or price as he or she thinks reasonable and proper.
5. The engineer may order in writing that additional or substituted work is to be executed on a daywork basis.

If a contractor intends to claim a higher rate or price than that notified by the engineer or an additional payment the contractor is to give written notice to the engineer within twenty-eight days after the engineer's notification or the events giving rise to the claim. The contractor is to keep records to support this claim and to make them available to the engineer. After giving notice to the engineer the contractor is to submit a first interim account; thereafter further accounts are to be sent as the engineer requires.

Failure by the contractor to make a claim in the way required does not disentitle the contractor to payment, subject to the engineer's not having been prevented or substantially prejudiced in investigating the claim.

Any amount claimed under the clause is to be included in an interim payment certified by the engineer provided the engineer has been given sufficient particulars.

Property in materials and contractor's equipment

Clauses 53 and 54 contain provisions which give the employer interests in the contractor's equipment and materials to be incorporated in the works: the employer should be able to make use of them in order to complete the works if the contractor defaults.

Clause 53 states that the contractor's equipment, temporary works, materials for the temporary works or materials owned by the contractor while on the site be deemed to be the property of the employer; they are not to be removed without the written consent of the engineer, which is not to be unreasonably withheld, if they are no longer immediately needed for completion of the works.

The materials have to be owned by the contractor for the employer to be able to lay claim to them. In retention of title clauses with contracts for the sale of goods, difficulties can arise on this matter (see p. 86). The case of *W Hanson (Harrow) Ltd v Rapid Civil Engineering Ltd and Usborne Developments Ltd 1987* is an example of this point (see p. 89).

The employer is not to be liable, other than under Clauses 22 and 65, for loss or damage to the contractor's equipment, temporary works, goods or materials.

If under Clause 33 contractors fail to remove their equipment and other items within a reasonable time after completion, the engineer may allow the employer to sell those items, recover any costs or expenses, and then pay the contractor the balance.

Clause 54 provides for the contractor to be paid for goods and materials not on the site; here the contractor must transfer to the employer the property in the materials and goods listed in the Appendix to the form of tender. The goods and materials must be for, and substantially ready for, incorporation into the works and be the property of the contractor.

The contractor must provide documentary evidence that the property vests in the contractor; marking or identification to show that they belong to the employer and are destined for the site; separate storage; provision of a schedule, listing and giving the value of the goods for the engineer, who should be invited to inspect them.

When the engineer has approved in writing the transfer of ownership of goods and materials they vest in and become the absolute property of the employer. This, however, does not deprive the engineer of the right to reject the goods or materials as not in accordance with the contract. They then revest in the contractor. The contractor remains responsible for loss or damage to the goods or materials and for the cost of storage, handling and insurance.

Once the goods or materials have vested in the employer neither the contractor nor a sub-contractor is to have a lien in them.

When the employment of the contractor ceases before completion of the works, under Clause 63 or otherwise, the contractor is to deliver the goods and materials which have become vested in the employer. Failure to do so empowers the employer to enter either the contractor's or a sub-contractor's premises to remove them.

The provisions in Clause 54 are to be included by the contractor in any sub-contract where payment is to be made for goods or materials before they are delivered to the site.

Measurement

Clause 55 provides that the quantities set out in the bill of quantities are estimated quantities only. Any error in description or omission in the bill of quantities does not vitiate the contract nor release the contractor from any obligations. The error or omission is to be corrected by the engineer and the value of that work ascertained in accordance with Clause 52. If, however, the error or omission is the contractor's fault in inserting rates and prices in the bill of quantities then there is to be no rectification.

Clause 56 provides for the engineer to determine by admeasurement the value of the contract work done in accordance with the contract.

Where the actual quantities executed in respect of any item are greater or less than in the bill of quantities and in the opinion of the engineer warrants change to the rates or prices because they are otherwise unreasonable or inapplicable, the engineer is, after consultation with the contractor, to determine an appropriate increase or decrease and notify the contractor of this decision.

When the engineer is required to measure work, reasonable notice must be given to the contractor, who is then to attend or send an agent to assist. Failure to so act means that the engineer's measurement is to be taken to be the correct measurement of the work.

Where work is done on a daywork basis the contractor is to be paid the rates and prices in the contract daywork schedule. If there is no daywork schedule, payment is to be that fixed by the Federation of Civil Engineering Contractors.

The contractor is to keep records of amounts paid and costs incurred for the engineer in a form and at times that the engineer directs. They are to be agreed within a reasonable time.

When ordering materials the contractor shall if the engineer so requires submit a quotation for approval.

Clause 57 requires that, unless otherwise clearly shown, the bill of quantities is deemed to have been prepared and measurements made in accordance with the 'Civil Engineering Standard Method of Measurement Second Edition 1985' or later or amended edition.

Provisional and prime cost sums and nominated sub-contracts

Clause 58 deals with the use of provisional and prime cost sums. With a provisional sum or a prime cost item the engineer may order either the contractors (with their consent) or a nominated sub-contractor or both to execute work or supply goods, materials or services.

Contractors are to be paid on the quotation which they submit to the engineer for acceptance, otherwise the value is determined in accordance with Clause 52 and included in the contract price. The contractor may object, under Clause 59, to the nomination of a particular sub-contractor.

If a provisional sum or prime cost sum provides for design matters or specification of the works or plant or equipment for incorporation, that is to be expressly stated in the contract and in any nominated sub-contract. The contractor's obligation in this respect is to be limited to what is in the contract.

Clause 59 regulates the position of nominated sub-contractors. Sub-clause (1) states:

> The Contractor shall not be under any obligation to enter into a sub-contract with any Nominated Sub-contractor against whom the Contractor may raise reasonable objection or who declines to enter into a sub-contract with the Contractor containing provisions
>
> (a) that in respect of the work goods materials or services the subject of the sub-contract the Nominated Sub-contractor will undertake towards the Contractor such obligations and liabilities as will enable the Contractor to discharge his own obligations and liabilities towards the Employer under the terms of the Contract
>
> (b) that the Nominated Sub-contractor will save harmless and indemnify the contractor against all claims demands and proceedings damages costs charges and expenses whatsoever arising out of or in connection with any failure by the Nominated Sub-contractor to perform such obligations or fulfil such liabilities
>
> (c) that the Nominated Sub-contractor will save harmless and indemnify the Contractor from and against any negligence by the Nominated Sub-contractor his agents workmen and servants and against any misuse by him or them of any Contractor's Equipment or Temporary Works provided by the Contractor for the purposes of the Contract and for all claims as aforesaid
>
> (d) that the Nominated Sub-contractor will provide the Contractor with security for the proper performance of the sub-contract and
>
> (e) equivalent to those contained in Clause 63.

Contractors may refuse to enter into a sub-contract with a nominated sub-contractor against whom they may raise reasonable objection on any ground or where stated provisions are not satisfied. For example on a previous sub-contract with the nominated sub-contractor the contractor may have encountered bad workmanship and an unwillingness to correct it. The specified grounds are basically where the nominated sub-contractor is not willing to be under the same obligations as the contractor is to the employer under the main contract.

The case of *Fairclough Building Ltd v Rhuddlan Borough Council 1985* (based on the use of the JCT 1963 edition) arose when in the course of constructing a leisure complex a nominated sub-contractor withdrew. After a delay a renomination was made by the architect. The new sub-contract did not provide for the making good of the defective work of the first nominated sub-contractor and, moreover, had a completion date which exceeded Fairclough's (the main contractors) contract completion date. Fairclough would, unless they were granted an extension of time, be liable for liquidated damages for delayed completion. They therefore refused to enter into a sub-contract with the new nominated sub-contractor. The Court of Appeal accepted that Fairclough were justified in this action and were making reasonable objection.

If the contractor refuses to enter into a sub-contract or validly terminates the employment of a nominated sub-contractor, the engineer is to nominate an alternative sub-contractor. Sub-clause (2) details the procedures if the engineer does not nominate an alternative, including contractors securing a sub-contractor of their own choice or the undertaking the work themselves.

Contractors are, subject to Clause 58(3), to be responsible for the work, service or supply of a nominated sub-contractor as if they themselves had executed the work or service, or supplied the goods or materials.

When contractors are of the opinion that they are entitled to terminate the sub-contract or treat it as repudiated they are at once to notify the engineer in writing. If the engineer gives consent in writing, the contractor may by notice expel the nominated sub-contractor or rescind the sub-contract. If the engineer does not consent, the contractor can (under Clause 13) ask the engineer for instructions. When a nominated sub-contractor is expelled from the sub-contract works the engineer is to nominate an alternative.

When the contractor, with the engineer's consent, has terminated a nominated sub-contract the contractor is to take all necessary steps to recover the additional expense incurred, including those of the employer, by the termination. Should the contractor fail to recover all reasonable expenses for completing the sub-contract works and all proper additional expenses arising from the termination, the employer will reimburse the contractor for the unrecovered expenses.

Sub-clause (5) provides that for all work executed and goods, materials or services supplied by the nominated sub-contractor, there is to be included in the contract price the price paid by the contractor under the sub-contract, the sum for labours as set out in the bill of quantities, and a percentage for all other charges and profits. The contractor must produce to the engineer all documents connected with expenditure for work of nominated sub-contractors.

Sub-clause (7) requires the engineer before issuing a certificate under Clause 60 for payment to demand from the engineer reasonable proof that all sums included in previous certificates in respect of things done or supplied to the nominated sub-contractor have been paid. Contractors shall give written details to the engineer of any reasonable cause they might have for withholding or refusing to make payment to the nominated sub-contractor and produce reasonable proof for the engineer that they have so informed the nominated sub-contractor.

Where the engineer is not satisfied that the contractor has properly withheld payment from the nominated sub-contractor, the employer is entitled to pay the nominated sub-contractor direct, on the certification of the engineer, all payments that the contractor has not made. The employer is then entitled to deduct by way of set-off the amount paid from sums due to the contractor. The engineer when issuing further certificates for payment to the contractor is to deduct the amount the employer has paid. The engineer is not to withhold or delay the issue of a certificate when due under the contract.

Certificates and payments

Clause 60 sets out at some length the procedure for payments to be made to the contractor. Sub-clause (1), which introduces the procedure, states:

> The Contractor shall submit to the Engineer at monthly intervals a statement (in such form if any as may be prescribed in the Specification) showing
>
> (a) the estimated contract value of the Permanent Works executed up to the end of that month
>
> (b) a list of any goods or materials delivered to the Site for but not yet incorporated in the Permanent Works and their value
>
> (c) a list of any of those goods or materials identified in the Appendix to the Form of Tender which have not yet been delivered to the Site but of which the property has vested in the Employer pursuant to Clause 54 and their value and
>
> (d) the estimated amounts to which the Contractor considers himself entitled in connection with all other matters for which provision is made under the Contract including any Temporary Works or Contractor's Equipment for which separate amounts are included in the Bill of Quantities
>
> unless in the opinion of the Contractor such values and amounts together will not justify the issue of an interim certificate.
>
> Amounts payable in respect of Nominated Sub-contractors are to be listed separately.

This deals in a comprehensive manner with the right of the contractor to be paid interim payments. Without such a provision a contractor has no right to claim payment for work done as the contract proceeds, and would have to wait until the contract was completed.

Within twenty-eight days of the date of delivery to the engineer or the engineer's representative of the contractor's monthly statement the engineer has to certify and the employer pay to the contractor, after deduction for any previous payment, the amount which in the engineer's opinion is due on the monthly statement, less retention. Other amounts, as the engineer considers proper, are to be paid subject to not exceeding the percentage of the value stated in the Appendix to the form of tender. Amounts certified for nominated sub-contractors are to be shown separately.

Not later than three months after the date of the defects correction certificate the contractor is to submit a statement of final account, including documentation detailing the value of work done and the further amounts the contractor claims up to the date of the defects correction certificate.

Within three months after receipt of the final account and the information reasonably necessary for its verification the engineer is to issue a certificate stating the amount due to the contractor from the employer. Credit has to be given for the amounts the employer has previously paid and also for sums the employer is entitled to under the contract. The amount is, subject to liquidated damages under Clause 47, to be paid within twenty-eight days of the date of the certificate.

Sub-clause (5) and (6) permit retention at the rate indicated and up to the limit set out in the Appendix to the form of tender. The retention is to be paid to the contractor on the basis of one half on the issue of the certificate of substantial completion in respect of the whole works or part of the works. On the expiry of the defects correction period the remainder is to be paid. If there is work outstanding, the employer may withhold payment until that work has been completed. In the case of both releases of the retention, payment is to be made within fourteen days.

Where the engineer has failed to certify or the employer to make payment as required by the clause, or the arbitrator makes a finding to that effect, the employer is to pay to the contractor compound interest on any overdue payment or which should have been certified. The interest is 2 per cent above the base lending rate of a bank specified in the appendix to the form of tender. If the arbitration decides that any sum or additional sum should have been certified on a particular date then that is to be treated as a failure to certify on that date. This sum is to be regarded as overdue twenty-eight days after the date decided by the arbitrator.

Sub-clause (8) gives power to the engineer to omit from any certificate the value of work done, goods or materials supplied or services rendered with which the engineer is dissatisfied. For that reason, and any other which seems proper, the engineer may correct or modify any previously certified sum. In any interim certificate the engineer is not to remove or reduce any sum previously certified with regard to work done or goods, materials and services supplied by a nominated sub-contractor if the contractor has already paid or is bound to pay that sum to the nominated sub-contractor. In the final certificate, if the engineer certifies a deletion or reduction of a sum previously certified for payment to a nominated sub-contractor, and already paid by the contractor, the employer is to reimburse the contractor for the amount overpaid and for any which cannot be recovered from the nominated sub-contractor. Interest is to be added to this amount from the date of the final certificate.

Whenever a certificate is issued the engineer is to send it to the employer with a copy to the contractor together with any necessary explanation.

If the employer pays to the contractor an amount different from that certified by the engineer the employer is to give the contractor full details showing how the amount paid has been calculated.

It should be borne in mind that these provisions govern payments between the employer and the contractor. Even though the contractor has received in a payment from the employer an amount for payment by the contractor to a nominated sub-contractor, contractors may have rights in the sub-contractor which will allow them to retain or deduct from that amount.

The case of *Gilbert-Ash (Northern) Ltd v Modern Engineering (Bristol) Ltd 1973* arose from a building contract for Bradford Corporation (using the JCT 1963 edition) and the main contractors (Gilbert-Ash), who used their own form of sub-contract with the nominated sub-contractors (Modern Engineering). A clause in the sub-contract allowed the main contractors in the event of the sub-contractors' failing to comply with any of the conditions of the sub-contract to suspend or withhold payment of any monies due or becoming due to the sub-contractors. The clause also allowed the main contractors to deduct from any payments certified as due to the sub-contractors for any bona fide counter-claim which the main contractors might have against the sub-contractors in connection with this or any other contract. By three interim certificates the amount of £14 532 was certified as due to the sub-contractors, but the main contractors paid them only £10 000. They claimed that they were entitled to £3137 for alleged delay by the sub-contractors and £1862 for alleged defective work by the sub-contractors. The sub-contractors contested the claim.

The House of Lords decided in favour of the main contractors. The clause in the sub-contract clearly allowed the main contractors to make the deductions provided the main contractors' claims were bona fide, even though the employer had paid the main contractor the sums certified in the certificates as due to the nominated sub-contractors. The Law Lords also stated that the common law right of persons to claim a breach of warranty entitled them to reduce or extinguish a sum due by them by way of set-off could be removed only by clear, unequivocal words. Whether that right had been removed depended on the words used in a particular contract.

Clause 61 requires the engineer to issue a defects correction certificate to the employer and contractors, stating the date when the contractors completed their obligations to construct and complete the works to the engineer's satisfaction. The certificate is to be issued when the defects correction period has expired, either for the whole or parts of the works, and all outstanding works have been made good.

The defects correction certificate does not relieve either the contractor or the employer from liability to each other or in any way connected with the performance of their respective obligations under the contract.

Remedies and powers

Clause 62 gives power to the employer to carry out remedial or other work or repair if there has been an accident, failure or other event which needs to be dealt with urgently. This power may be exercised during the execution of the works or the defects correction period. If the engineer is of the opinion that the contractor was liable under the contract to do the work, the cost incurred by the employer is to be borne by the contractor. This power of carrying out repair work is to be undertaken only if the contractor is unwilling or unable to do it. The contractor is to be notified in writing by the engineer as soon as reasonably practicable.

Clause 63 is used when the contractor is deemed to be in default of the contract. It is the employment of the contractor which is determined and not the contract, which remains in existence; the employer is thereby entitled to pursue any course of action under the contract which is appropriate in the circumstances. Sub-clause (1) states:

If
(a) the Contractor shall be in default in that he
(i) becomes bankrupt or has a receiving order or administration order made against him or presents his petition in bankruptcy or makes an arrangement with or assignment in favour of his creditors or agrees to carry out the Contract under a committee of inspection of his creditors or (being a corporation) goes into liquidation (other than a voluntary liquidation for the purposes of amalgamation or reconstruction) or
(ii) assigns the Contract without the consent in writing of the Employer first obtained or
(iii) has an execution levied on his goods which is not stayed or discharged within 28 days
or
(b) the Engineer certifies in writing to the Employer with a copy to the Contractor that in his opinion the Contractor
(i) has abandoned the Contract or
(ii) without reasonable excuse has failed to commence the Works in accordance with Clause 41 or has suspended the progress of the Works for 14 days after receiving from the Engineer written notice to proceed or
(iii) has failed to remove goods or materials from the Site or to pull down and replace work for 14 days after receiving from the Engineer written notice that the said goods materials or work have been condemned and rejected by the Engineer or
(iv) despite previous warnings by the Engineer in writing is failing to proceed with the Works with due diligence or is otherwise persistently or fundamentally in breach of his obligations under Contract
then the Employer may after give 7 days' notice in writing to the Contractor specifying the default enter upon the Site and the Works and expel the Contractor there from without thereby avoiding the Contract or releasing the Contractor from any of his obligations or liabilities under the Contract. Provided that the Employer may extend the period of notice to give the Contractor opportunity to remedy the default. Where a notice of determination is given pursuant to this sub-clause it shall be given as soon as is reasonably possible after receipt of the Engineer's certificate.

Thus contractors are to be in default, with the consequence to be considered, when they get into financial difficulties of a serious nature, or when they assign the contract without the employer's written consent first being obtained and when execution is levied against their goods which is not stayed or discharged within twenty-eight days. Any one of these events automatically puts the contractor in default.

In (b) of sub-clause (1) before a contractor is to be in default the engineer has to certify in writing that one of the stated grounds applies. The employer may extend the period of time so as to allow the contractor to remedy the default.

Under sub-clause (2) the employer who has entered on the site may complete the works personally or use another contractor to do so. The employer may make use of the contractor's equipment and other items which are deemed to be his or her property under Clauses 53 and 54. The employer may also sell the contractor's equipment and other items and use the proceeds to pay money due from the contractor under the contract.

Sub-clause (3) requires the contractor, after notice from the engineer, to assign the benefit of agreement for work, goods or materials the contractor may have entered into for the purposes of the contract.

Sub-clause (4) deals with the payment to a contractor who has been expelled from the site. The contractor is not entitled to be paid any money until the end of the defects correction period and until the costs of completing the contract and other expenses of the employer have been ascertained and certified by the engineer. If the amount due to the contractor is less than the employer's expenses, the excess is a debt due from the contractor to the employer. The contractor, subject to the employer's right to recover, is entitled to the amount certified by the engineer as due to the contractor upon due completion after deducting the employer's expenses.

Sub-clause (5) requires the engineer to fix the amount at the time of entry and expulsion which the contractor has reasonably earned for work done and the value of the contractor's equipment and other items which are deemed to be the employer's property.

Frustration

The case of *Metropolitan Water Board v Dick, Kerr and Co 1918* was an example of a civil engineering contract being frustrated (see p. 67). Frustration arises without fault on the part of either party to the contract (see p. 66). Clause 64 provides for the contractor to be paid in accordance with Clause 65(5), that is payment for work done at the contract rates and prices with additional sums on specified grounds to compensate contractors for commitments they have entered into in connection with the contract and for expenditure into on the basis that the contractors would complete the whole contract.

War clause

If there is an outbreak of war, work is to continue for twenty-eight days, if possible, with the aim of completing the contract. Clause 65 allows the employer to determine the contract and contractors to remove their equipment; payment is to be made to contractors as prescribed for work executed and expenses incurred in the cost of removal.

Settlement of disputes

The 6th edition advocates that disputes are not to be resolved by the courts (in the form of a claim for breach of contract) but are to be settled by the use of arbitration. The 6th edition also allows a conciliator to be appointed if the parties agree with a view to resolving the dispute without using arbitration. The conciliator may only make a recommendation to the parties. A party who is unwilling to accept the conciliator's recommendation may still require the matter to be determined by arbitration.

Clause 66 contains the provisions for the settlement of disputes. Sub-clause (1) states:

> Except as otherwise provided in these Conditions if a dispute of any kind whatsoever arises between the Employer and the Contractor in connection with or arising out of the Contract or the carrying out of the Works including any dispute as to any decision opinion instruction direction certificate or valuation of the Engineer (whether during the progress of the Works or after their completion and whether before or after the determination abandonment or breach of the Contract) it shall be settled in accordance with the following provisions.

The sub-clause covers not only disputes between the employer and the contractor but also disputes with regard to the various matters which are the responsibilities of the engineer.

Sub-clause (2) states that a dispute begins when one party serves on the engineer a notice of dispute in writing, stating the nature of the dispute. The party must first have taken any steps or invoked any procedure elsewhere in the contract in connection with the subject matter of such dispute. The other party or the engineer has to have taken such steps as may be required or being allowed a reasonable time to take that action.

Sub-clause (3) requires engineers to give their decision in writing of any dispute referred to them under sub-clause (2). Notice of the engineer's decision is to be given to both employer and contractor within the time limits in sub-clause (6).

Sub-clause (4) requires the contractor to proceed with the works with all due diligence, unless the contract has been determined or abandoned. Both the contractor and the employer are to give effect forthwith to the engineer's decision, which is final and binding upon the contractor and employer unless both accept the recommendation of a conciliator or the engineer's decision is revised by an arbitrator and an award made and published.

Sub-clause (5) deals with the use of the services of the conciliator. If the engineer has given a decision or the time for giving that decision has expired and neither party has served a notice under sub-clause (6) to refer the dispute to arbitration, either party may serve written notice requiring the dispute to be considered under the Institution of Civil Engineers' Conciliation Procedure 1988. The recommendation of the conciliator is deemed to have been accepted in settlement of the dispute unless written notice to refer the dispute to arbitration is served within one calendar month of receipt of the recommendation.

The Conciliation Procedure 1988 contains a number of rules dealing with the appointment of the conciliator, the way in which he or she is to act and the effect of any recommendations. An important rule is that the conciliator cannot be appointed as arbitrator in any subsequent arbitration between the parties, whether the same dispute or other under the contract, unless the parties agree in writing.

Sub-clause (6) states:

(a) Where a Certificate of Substantial Completion of the whole of the Works has not been issued and either

(i) the Employer or the Contractor is dissatisfied with any decision of the Engineer given under sub-clause (3) of this Clause or

(ii) the Engineer fails to give such decision for a period of one calendar month after the service of the Notice of Dispute or

(iii) the Employer or the Contractor is dissatisfied with any recommendation of a conciliator appointed under sub-clause (5) of this Clause

then either the Employer or the Contractor may within three calendar months after receiving notice of such decision or within three calendar months after the expiry of the said period of one month or within one calendar month of receipt of the conciliator's recommendation (as the case may be) refer the dispute to the arbitration of a person to be agreed upon by the parties by serving on the other party a written Notice to Refer.

(b) Where a Certificate of Substantial Completion of the whole of the Works has been issued the foregoing provisions shall apply save that the said periods of one calendar month referred to in (a) above shall be read as three calendar months.

Depending on whether a certificate of substantial completion for the whole works has been issued, either the contractor or the employer can serve notice within the prescribed time on the other that the dispute go to arbitration. The grounds are: dissatisfaction with the engineer's decision; failure of the engineer to give a decision within one calendar month after service of notice of dispute; and dissatisfaction with any recommendation of a conciliator.

Sub-clause (7) states that if the parties fail to appoint an arbitrator within one calendar month of one party serving notice on the other to concur in an appointment, either party can ask the President of the Institution of Civil Engineers to make an appointment.

Should an arbitrator decline the appointment, be removed by a court, be incapable of acting or die, then the President (or Vice-President) can appoint another arbitrator.

Sub-clause (8) states:

(a) Any reference to arbitration under this Clause shall be deemed to be a submission to arbitration within the meaning of the Arbitration Acts 1950 and 1979 or any statutory re-enactment or amendment thereof for the time being in force. The reference shall be conducted in accordance with the Institution of Civil Engineers Arbitration Procedure (1983) or any amendment or modification thereof being in force at the time of the appointment of the arbitrator. Such arbitrator shall have full power to open up review and revise any decision opinion instruction direction certificate or valuation of the Engineer.

(b) Neither party shall be limited in the proceedings before such arbitrator to the evidence or arguments put before the Engineer for the purpose of obtaining his decision under sub-clause (3) of this Clause.

(c) The award of the arbitrator shall be binding on all parties.
(d) Unless the parties otherwise agree in writing any reference to arbitration may proceed notwithstanding that the Works are not then complete or alleged to be complete.

The case of *Northern Regional Health Authority v Derek Crouch Construction Co Ltd 1984* was a dispute arising from a building contract using the JCT 1963 edition. The contract contained power for the arbitrator to deal with the architect's decisions and certificates in a similar manner to the power in sub-clause (8). A number of disputes arose from the building contract and an action was started in the High Court. The question arose as to whether the disputes should be dealt with by court action or by arbitration. The Court of Appeal observed that the High Court did not have the power that the arbitrator had to open up and review the exercise of the architect's discretion since the court's jurisdiction was limited to determining and enforcing the contractual rights of the parties. The court did not have the power to substitute its own discretion.

Neither party is limited in the arbitration to evidence or arguments put originally to the engineer. The award is binding on all the parties, so there is no right to refuse to accept that decision.

There is the right to have an arbitration before the works are completed or alleged to be completed.

Sub-clause (9) allows an engineer who has given a decision to be called as a witness and to give evidence before the arbitrator.

Application to Scotland

Clause 67 contains provisions which take account of the different legal system in Scotland.

Notices

Clause 68 deals with the service of notices on the contractor and employer. For a company this is the company's registered office.

Tax matters

Under Clause 69 the rates and prices in the bill of quantities are deemed to include all the taxes and other charges payable by the contractors and their sub-contractors. Under Clause 70 the tender and the engineer's certificates do not include value added tax.

Special conditions

Clause 71 allows for the use as the parties wish of special conditions.

Sub-contracts

The form of sub-contract used with the 6th edition is produced by the Federation of Civil Engineering Contractors and is approved by the Committee of Associations of Specialist Engineering Contractors and

Federation of Associations of Specialists and sub-contractors. The present document was revised in 1984.

The form has twenty clauses and five schedules, with notes of guidance to assist in the completion of the schedules. The schedules contain: particulars of the main contract; details of further documents and the sub-contract works; the contract price, details of retention and the period for completion; details of the contractor's facilities; and details of the sub-contractor's and contractor's insurances.

The contract contains the usual form of agreement between the parties. The sub-contractor undertakes to carry out the sub-contract work to the reasonable satisfaction of the contractor and the engineer. The sub-contractor is deemed to have full knowledge of the main contract, and can request a copy of that document. The sub-contractor undertakes, subject to the provisions in the sub-contract, to complete it so that nothing on the sub-contractor's part puts the contractor in breach of the main contract. In the event of the sub-contractor being in breach of the sub-contract so that the contractor becomes liable, the sub-contractor is to indemnify the contractor.

The sub-contract sets out in some detail the sub-contractor's right to use the contractor's facilities and to the working on the site and means of access to it. The sub-contractor is, in stated circumstances, entitled to an extension of time, and is to comply with instructions given by the engineer or the engineer's representative, which are given to the sub-contractor by the contractor. In addition the contractor may give instructions which the sub-contractor is obliged to abide and comply with.

The sub-contractor can be called upon to vary the sub-contract if ordered by the engineer and confirmed by the contractor; or agreed by the employer and contractor and confirmed by the contractor; and also by the contractor. Any such variation is to be valued in a similar manner to the procedure considered with regard to the 6th edition. Where the contractor is required under the main contract to give any return, account or notice to the engineer or employer the sub-contractor is bound to do the same under the sub-contract in sufficient time to allow the contractor to comply with any obligations in these matters.

If the vesting provisions in the main contract apply with regard to the contractor's equipment and other items, then the same obligations apply between the sub-contractor and the contractor so that the sub-contractor's equipment and other items vest in the contractor.

The sub-contractor is required to indemnify the contractor against all liabilities to other persons for bodily injury, damage to property or other loss that may arise out of or in consequence of the carrying out of the sub-contract works.

Completion of the sub-contract works before the main works are completed requires the sub-contractor to maintain the sub-contract works until completion of the main works. After completion of the main works the sub-contractor is to maintain the sub-contract works for the same period as the contractor's maintenance period.

The sub-contractor is required to take out insurances as detailed in the fifth schedule. The contractor has the usual rights to call for sufficient information to be satisfied that the insurance required has been taken out.

In order to obtain payment for work done, materials and goods on the site, and if the main contract so allows, materials and goods off the site, the sub-contractor is to submit to the contractor a written statement of the claim. That has to be included with the contractor's own application under the main contract. The contractor is given power to withhold or defer payments to the sub-contractor, where there is a dispute between the contractor and the sub-contractor or between the contractor and employer involving any question of measurement or quantities.

If the main contract is determined for any reason before the sub-contractor has completed the sub-contract or if the sub-contractor is in default the contractor may determine the sub-contractor's employment. In both cases the contractor may take possession of the sub-contractor's equipment and other items and use them for the completion of the sub-contract works.

The sub-contract requires that any dispute between the contractor and the sub-contractor shall be determined by arbitration, conducted in accordance with the Institution of Civil Engineers' Arbitration Procedure 1988. The contractor may require that any such dispute shall be dealt with jointly with any dispute under the main contract. A similar power exists if the dispute between the contractor and the employer under the main contract is brought before the courts; the sub-contractor is restricted from having the dispute settled by arbitration unless the contractor agrees.

The sub-contract contains the same provisions with regard to value added tax as exists in the 6th edition.

The form of sub-contract does not make any reference to a nominated sub-contractor; it therefore may be used for a nominated sub-contract and one which is not.

5

Arbitration

Introduction

Arbitration has been a recognized means of resolving disputes for centuries. In English law the first statute was the Arbitration Act 1697; there are now two statutes governing arbitrations: the Arbitration Act 1979, which has amended and strengthened the Arbitration Act 1950. There are also a number of judicial decisions relevant to arbitrations.

The system of arbitration is widely used by many industries as the desirable means of resolving disputes; they have refined the system by introducing rules to take account of their particular needs and practices. The Institution of Civil Engineers' Arbitration Procedure (England and Wales) 1983 may be used in the construction industry, sanctioned by the provisions in Clause 66(8) of the 6th edition. This allows the parties to have a written consideration, instead of a full hearing, with consequent saving of time and expense. For disputes with building contracts the Joint Contract Tribunal produced the JCT Arbitration Rules 1988.

Arbitration does not operate outside the legal system. It is possible to use the powers in the 1950 and 1979 Acts to go to the High Court for assistance and, in limited circumstances, to make an appeal.

Reasons for the use of arbitration

There are a number of reasons why parties decide to have a dispute dealt with by arbitration rather than by an action in the courts, including ability to select the arbitrator, economy, speed, flexibility, privacy and finality.

The parties to a civil engineering dispute have the right to select the arbitrator they believe would be most suited to deal with it. Where the parties are unable to agree, the President would be called on to select a person suited to their particular need. The arbitration will therefore be conducted by a civil engineer who has a deep understanding of all the technicalities of the dispute. If such a dispute were to be dealt with by a court, the judge would usually lack such background and much time would be spent in technical explanations. However, a lawyer may be appointed as arbitrator in a construction dispute where the dispute is concerned with more legal than technical matters.

Costs in a High Court action are substantial and increase greatly if the decision goes to appeal; they may well exceed the sum being claimed in the action. However, no charge is made for the use of the court or the services of the judge. Arbitrators charge for their services and expenses are incurred for the hire of rooms for the hearing. In substantial arbitrations lawyers may be used in the preparation and presentation of each side's case in the dispute. Economy is possible with arbitration as compared with litigation if the parties select the form of arbitration most suited to the dispute and the arbitrator is experienced in all the technicalities of the matter.

An arbitration, if conducted properly in the most suitable form, can be carried out and a decision made more quickly than with a court action. Even in the Official Referee's Court, with a judge experienced in construction contract disputes, there is still the delay before the case progresses to an actual hearing. The arbitrator is probably immediately available and progress depends on the parties' speed in preparing the case.

Arbitration provides a degree of flexibility the courts cannot provide. In the case of *Northern Regional Health Authority v Derek Crouch Construction Co Ltd 1984* (see p. 132) the Court of Appeal drew attention to the power of the arbitrator to open up, review and revise opinions, certificates and decisions of engineers and architects in construction contracts. This a court could not do since that particular power is given to the arbitrator by a provision in the contract between the parties. A contract dispute may involve a sum of a few hundred pounds or hundreds of thousands of pounds. The parties have the right to select a form of arbitration which is most appropriate to both the nature of the dispute and the size of the claim.

What many consider to be the best of reasons for the use of arbitration is that arbitration proceedings are conducted in private. Court proceedings are conducted in public; the power of the judge to allow a private hearing is very seldom exercised. A party to a dispute will wish to avoid having made public matters of commercial confidentiality and how the party had acted in a dispute. The publicity of a court action may leave a permanent feeling of ill-will between the parties, which might not have arisen with arbitration.

The parties to an arbitration bind themselves to accept the decision of the arbitrator. To this extent there is finality. Since the 1979 Act, with its much reduced means of appeal against an arbitration award, the decision of the arbitrator has been more difficult to challenge. Both parties may be dissatisfied with the award of the arbitrator but are unable to challenge it. They chose arbitration as the means to settle the dispute, they chose the arbitrator and they have to abide by his or her decision.

Arbitration agreement

Arbitration may be ordered in three circumstances: where an Act of Parliament so requires; when a court orders that there should be arbitration; and where the parties to a dispute so decide. The last of these is the one with which we are concerned.

An arbitration agreement as defined in Section 32 of the 1950 Act: 'means a written agreement to submit present or future differences to arbitration, whether an arbitrator is named thereon or not'.

A decision to use arbitration may be made either when or before the difference arises. Under Clause 66 of the 6th edition a dispute is to be settled by arbitration in accordance with the Institution's Arbitration Procedure 1983. The award of the arbitrator is to be final, with the power to have an interim arbitration before the works are completed. The arbitration clause in a contract may name the arbitrator but it is more usual in construction contracts for the arbitrator to be named when the decision to arbitrate is made.

Arbitration clauses in contracts set out the period within which one of the parties has to serve on the other party a notice to refer the dispute or difference to arbitration. Under Clause 66 of the 6th edition the period is three months. If the certificate of substantial completion of the whole works has not been issued, a notice to refer may be served by either the employer or the contractor within three months of the engineer's decision; in the case of failure of the engineer to give a decision within one calendar month after service of the notice of dispute; within three months of the expiration of that calendar month; and in the case of the use of the conciliation procedure within one month of the conciliator's recommendation. If the certificate of substantial completion of the whole works has been issued, the same provisions apply except that the engineer is given three calendar months instead of one to make a decision, and the period of time, if the conciliation procedure has been used, is to be within three months.

Section 27 of the Arbitration Act 1950 provides that if there has been a failure to serve notice to refer to arbitration, or an arbitrator appointed or some other step taken within a time fixed in the agreement, that fact shall not debar a claim if the High Court is of the opinion that undue hardship would otherwise be caused. The High Court, if the justice of the case so requires, may extend the time for such period as it thinks proper.

In the case of *Emson Contractors Ltd v Protea Estates Ltd 1987*, Emson (under the JCT 1980 edition) were engaged to construct a number of industrial units. The date of the contract was 23 October 1984. Some disputes arose, the main one of which was whether certain foundation work was a variation. The architect refused to certify that this was a variation. Emson took legal advice but no further action. On 23 December 1985 Emson submitted a final account for £492 339. Between then and mid-1986 discussion took place between Emson and the architect and quantity surveyor about the final account. Emson's claim for the variation could not be agreed. On 29 August 1986 Emson wrote threatening to dispute the matter under the contract. Further discussion did not resolve the matter.

On 16 September 1986 the final certificate was issued for £381 691, which Emson received on 17 September. Emson's employee who dealt with the matter was on holiday and the importance of the certificate was not appreciated by others. By 6 January 1987 Emson was aware of the final certificate but even then steps were not taken to start an arbitration until 26 February. Clause 30 of the JCT contract required an arbitration to commence within fourteen days after the final certificate.

Emson applied under Section 27 of the 1950 Act for an extension of time. The High Court refused to grant the application. Commencement, the court decided, was agreement to appoint an arbitrator or to request the other party to concur in the appointment. The court noted that the amount at stake was substantial but there was no undue hardship to Emson because it had failed to commence the arbitration until 26 February 1987, a delay of some twenty weeks. Furthermore no explanation or mitigation had been given for the delay from 6 January, when the importance of the certificate was known, and 26 February, when the arbitration commenced, a delay of fourteen weeks. Taking into account the fourteen-day period in the contract the delay was not trivial but significant. Protea Estates were not at fault and even though they had not suffered any prejudice the delay was such that the application for an extension could not be granted.

Effect of an arbitration agreement

An arbitration agreement indicates that this procedure is to be used as the means in settling disputes; it does not oust the jurisdiction of the courts, based on the provisions in the 1950 and 1979 Acts. The public policy is that disputes ought not to be settled by bodies which are completely outside the control of the courts. In some arbitration agreements, but not with construction contracts, there may be what is known as a *Scott v Avery 1856* clause. This has a form of words which indicates that the arbitration must take place before there can be a court action on the dispute.

One of the parties to the arbitration agreement may decide that their interests would be better served by an action in the court; the other party may then contest the action by making use of the provisions in Section 4 of the 1950 Act, which allow a party, before delivering any pleadings in the action or taking any steps in the proceedings, to apply to the High Court for the court proceedings to be stayed. That person must however be ready and willing to arbitrate. The court or a judge of the court, if satisfied that there is no sufficient reason why the matter should not be referred to arbitration, may stay the proceedings. This power of the court is discretionary. There are certain grounds on which in the past courts have refused to stay the proceedings and allowed the court action to proceed.

1. Where fraud or charges of a personal character are alleged. The court here takes the view that a party against whom charges of this nature are made ought to have the opportunity to have those matters investigated in open court and have them refuted. Under Section 24 of the 1950 Act where an arbitration agreement provides for any future dispute to be referred to arbitration and that dispute raises a question as to fraud of one of the parties, then in order to have the matter determined by the High Court the court has power to order that the arbitration agreement shall cease to have effect. The court may also revoke the appointment of any arbitrator appointed under the agreement.

2. Where there has been an undue delay in making the application for the stay to the proceedings.
3. Where to stay the proceedings would cause hardship to the person bringing the action. In the case of *Fakes v Taylor Woodrow Construction Ltd 1973*, Fakes, a plumber, was a nominated sub-contractor. A dispute arose under the sub-contract and Fakes obtained legal aid to allow him to bring an action in the court. Legal aid is not available to a person involved in an arbitration. Taylor Woodrow made an application to stay the proceedings and to have the dispute referred to arbitration in accordance with the arbitration clause in the sub-contract. The Court of Appeal refused to stay the proceedings; by a majority, they took the view that Fakes, who was in financial difficulties, would not have the means to go to arbitration. If the matter went to arbitration he would lose by default. He had reasonable grounds for suing Taylor Woodrow, supported by the granting of legal aid, and to stay the action would be justice denied.
4. Where questions of law are involved the court may refuse to stay the action, depending on the type of law and whether the law is mixed with technical facts. If the law is something with which the arbitrator is familiar or the technical facts cannot be separated from the law then the court may well decide to leave the dispute to the arbitrator and so stay the proceedings.
5. Where it is convenient to have the dispute settled by the court. In the past it was feared that if there were a court action and an arbitration on the same contract, a conflict could arise. Now by the Court of Appeal decision in *Northern Regional Health Authority v Derek Crouch Construction Co Ltd 1984* the view has changed. The court allowed a court action to continue, refusing the application to stay it, even though there had already been a reference to arbitration. The court considered that the arbitrator was extremely experienced and, in the event of any possible conflict, could go to the court for a ruling on the matter. This decision was made despite the court expressing the opinion that the arbitrator had powers with regard to reviewing and revising certificates, opinions and decisions, which the court did not have.

Appointment of the arbitrator

Although the Arbitration Act 1950 and arbitration agreements provide for the appointment of more than one arbitrator, in arbitrations of construction contract disputes only a single arbitrator is involved.

Clause 66 of the 6th edition gives the parties to the contract the right to appoint the arbitrator. Failure to make an appointment within one calendar month allows either party to apply to the President (or a Vice-President) of the Institution of Civil Engineers to make an appointment. The Arbitration Procedure (England and Wales) (1983) provides for a similar course of action.

If Clause 66 does not apply, the appointment is dealt with by Section 10 of the Arbitration Act 1950, which allows the High Court to appoint an arbitrator when the parties have failed to agree. This power may also be used when an appointed arbitrator refuses to act, or is incapable of acting, or dies. Arbitrators appointed by the High Court have the same powers to act and make an award as if they had been appointed by the parties. Section 10 of the 1950 Act was amended by Section 6 of the 1979 Act, which allows the High Court to make an appointment when a person, who is not a party to the agreement nor an existing arbitrator, who is to make the appointment directly or in default of the parties, refuses to make the appointment or make it within a specified time. The person appointed by the High Court has the same power to act and make an award as if he or she had been appointed under the agreement.

Under Section 25 where the High Court has exercised its powers under the 1950 Act and revoked the authority of an arbitrator, the High Court may on the application of either party appoint a person to act as arbitrator in place of the person removed, with the same powers to act and make an award.

Disqualification of the arbitrator

An arbitrator is under a duty to act fairly between the parties and to leave the parties satisfied that there has been a properly conducted hearing. The arbitrator must not be a friend or related to either of the parties, and clearly must not have a financial interest in the dispute such as being a substantial shareholder in one of the parties. The arbitrator should not have previous knowledge of the matter in dispute, nor have acted in any capacity in the contract. Where any of these circumstances apply the arbitrator should stand down; if the arbitrator is aware of any matter which could affect his or her impartiality, the arbitrator should refuse to accept the appointment.

Removal of the arbitrator

There are three grounds for the removal of an arbitrator: misconduct, interest or bias. Under Section 23 of the 1950 Act misconduct does not solely mean conduct such as being under the influence of drink at the arbitration. The courts have removed arbitrators for refusing to conduct the hearing properly, including refusing an adjournment when it was right and proper to grant one; improperly refusing to hear the evidence that one of the parties wished to tender; deciding a case which clearly was disregarding the law; and making an award with regard to a contract which was recognized as being illegal.

In the case of *Fisher and Another v P G Wellfair Ltd 1981*, an arbitrator conducted an arbitration into a building contract dispute. The claim was for £93 000, the cost of remedying defects in a block of flats. The builder was not represented at the arbitration. Evidence was given by highly regarded experts on behalf of the owners. The arbitrator awarded £13 600, not revealing that he had special knowledge and used this to reject expert evidence. His failure to indicate why he was rejecting the evidence meant that this could not be challenged nor could contrary evidence be produced. The Court of Appeal agreed to an application to remove the arbitrator and to have his award set aside. By his action the arbitrator has misconducted himself. He ought not to have refused to accept the owners' experts' evidence without putting to them his own knowledge and giving them an opportunity to answer, which might have shown that his view was wrong.

A case where the allegation of misconduct was rejected was in *Three Valleys Water Committee v Binnie and Partners 1991*. Binnie and Partners were consulting engineers engaged by Three Valleys for a tunnelling project; their agreement contained an arbitration clause. Technical problems arose and the project was abandoned. The question as to who was responsible led to an arbitrator being appointed. The pleadings started by the service of points of claim and a defence by way of answer. Before the points of reply could be served the arbitrator died and another was appointed. Three Valleys then attempted to serve points of reply out of time. Binnie and Partners refused to accept service. The arbitrator after a hearing refused to allow service out of time. Three Valleys were dissatisfied and asked him to give reasons for his decision. This he refused to do and so application was made to remove him for misconduct. The High Court refused to do this. There was no rule requiring an arbitrator to give reasons when he gave a ruling in a matter which had to be considered before the award was made.

Under Section 24 the High Court may remove an arbitrator when there is evidence of interest or bias which indicates that the arbitrator may not be impartial. Interest may be a relationship or a financial interest, which must be sufficient to justify the arbitrator's removal. Bias is when the arbitrator has shown some disfavour towards one of the parties. Comment as to the nationality of one of the partners and the inability of persons of that nationality to be truthful witnesses caused a court to order the arbitrator's removal on the ground of bias.

Under Section 13 of the 1950 Act, the High Court may order the removal of an arbitrator if the arbitrator fails to use all reasonable despatch in proceeding with the reference and making an award. Any party to the arbitration may make an application. Arbitrators removed in this way are not entitled to receive any remuneration for their services.

Arbitration proceedings

An arbitration is similar to a court action in that there is the preparatory work, which may be detailed, and the arbitration hearing.

Section 1 of the 1950 Act states that unless there is a contrary intention in the arbitration agreement the authority of the arbitrator is irrevocable, except with leave of the High Court or a judge of the court. This prevents one of the parties bringing the arbitration to an end by withdrawing the arbitrator's authority when the arbitration is going against that party. Section 2 states that an arbitration agreement is not to be discharged by the death of any party to the agreement; it then becomes enforceable against the personal representative of the deceased. The authority of the arbitrator is not to be revoked by the death of any party. Section 3 deals with the situation where a person who has become bankrupt is a party to a contract which contains an arbitration clause. If that contract is adopted by the trustee in bankruptcy, the arbitration clause may be enforced by or against the trustee. This provision comes into effect by the trustee in bankruptcy deciding to allow a contract made by the bankrupt to continue. Under Section 315 of the Insolvency Act 1986 a trustee in bankruptcy has the right to disclaim any contract considered to be unprofitable.

Powers of the arbitrator

When their appointment is complete, arbitrators have jurisdiction to deal with the dispute referred to them. They may conduct the arbitration as they consider appropriate, subject to any agreement that has been made as to the procedure to be used. Under Clause 66 the arbitration is to be conducted in accordance with the Institution of Civil Engineers' Arbitration Procedure (England and Wales) (1983), which gives arbitrators wide powers, additional to any other available to them. Arbitrators may give directions for the preservation of documents or other things concerned with the dispute; they may order the deposit of money or other security to secure the amount in dispute, either the whole amount or any part; they may make an order for security of costs in favour of one or more of the parties; and they may order that their own costs be secured.

In order to assist arbitrators to conduct the hearing properly and to arrive at a proper decision the Procedure allows them to appoint legal, technical or other assessors and to seek legal, technical or other advice. The assessors are to attend the hearings of the arbitration as and when the arbitrator directs. Arbitrators may also rely on their own knowledge and expertise to such extent as they think fit.

The Procedure also gives stated powers to arbitrators with regard to the conduct of the hearing. They may start the hearing immediately after their appointment; they may adjourn the hearing as they think fit; and they may direct that any meeting or summons before them is to be treated as part of the hearing.

Preliminary meeting

It is usual (and a specific requirement of the Procedure) for the arbitrator to hold a preliminary meeting, consisting of the arbitrator and the representatives of the parties, to check that the arbitrator has been properly appointed and that the dispute comes within the arbitrator's field of competence. The terms of the arbitrator's appointment, the procedures, the arrangements and the time-table are agreed with the parties. Coupled with this is each party's form of representation, such as a barrister, and whether experts are to be appointed.

Consideration has to be given at the preliminary meeting by the arbitrator and the parties as to whether the Short Procedure or the Special Procedure for Experts should be used, and whether the arbitration shall proceed by documents only. Consideration is also to be given to determining some of the issues in advance of the hearing.

Procedure before the hearing

An arbitration hearing follows the pattern of a civil action in the High Court in that each party is required to prepare their case adequately so that the other party knows what is alleged against them. There is therefore a system of pleadings; the dispute is reduced to its true facts, and sometimes a settlement is made without a hearing being necessary.

The party who has asked for the arbitration and is making the claim is known as the claimant; the other party is the respondent. The claim is stated in a document known as Points of Claim, which is answered by the respondent sending a document known as Points of Defence. Sometimes the respondent makes a Counter-claim against the points of defence. The claimant may reply to the points of defence by a Points of Reply, which may include a defence if a counter-claim has been made; there can also be a Reply to Defence to a counter-claim.

The points of claim set out all the relevant matters: they identify the parties and state the nature and date of the contract, with its rights and obligations; the matters in dispute under the contract are then stated and a claim made for damages. If a claim has a number of items which while under the same contract stand separately to each other, it is usual to have these set out in a particular form, officially an Official Referee's Schedule, but usually known as a Scott Schedule. It itemizes each claim and sets out the defence to each item. It is a convenient way of setting down these matters and allows for easy reference.

In drafting points of defence the rule is that any claim not expressly denied or otherwise challenged is deemed to have been admitted. Where a respondent has insufficient knowledge of a matter to expressly deny it, the answer may be to 'not admit' it, which puts the claimant in the position of having to prove the point of claim.

If the claimant has not expressed all the details in the points of claim in a clear manner, the respondent may seek clarification by serving on the claimant a request for Further and Better Particulars. The questions so raised have to be answered. A similar right exists for the claimant with regard to the defence or any counter-claim.

When this exchange of the documents – the pleadings – has finished, the procedure moves to the discovery of documents. Each party produces a list of the documents in the possession or power of that party which relate to the dispute; a copy of that list is served on the other party. Each party is thus made aware of the documents to be used at the hearing and has the right to inspect and copy the documents listed. An exception is the list of documents for which the party claims privilege. A privileged document could be one in which the party's legal adviser gave advice on the dispute. Discovery of documents prevents any party being surprised at the hearing when any document is put in as evidence. Without discovery there would have to be an adjournment in order to allow the party surprised to study the document.

Under the Arbitration Procedure the arbitrator has power to order these things to be done. There are additional powers, which allow the arbitration to proceed smoothly and properly. For example the arbitrator can order each party to prepare a summary of that party's case and evidence; an order may also be made that, where possible, the parties shall agree facts and figures.

Whether or not arbitrations are conducted under the Arbitration Procedure, an arbitrator may seek the High Court's assistance under the provisions in Section 12 of the 1950 Act. For example the High Court may order the discovery of documents or may issue a *subpoena ad testificandum*, requiring the witness to attend and give evidence, and a *subpoena duces tecum*, requiring a witness to attend and produce documents.

In the preparatory work a point of law may appear which may well be of substantial importance to the arbitration. The arbitrator may either decide this point of law or seek legal advice. There is a further provision, available whether or not the Arbitration Procedure is used, found in Section 2 of the Arbitration Act 1979. This allows an application to be made to the High Court, with the consent of all the parties, or by one of the parties with the consent of the arbitrator. The High Court has jurisdiction to determine any question of law arising in the course of the reference. The High Court is not, however, to give such determination unless it is satisfied that such determination might produce substantial savings in cost to the parties and the question could substantially affect the rights of one or more of the parties.

The hearing

If the parties have agreed to use other means than the traditional hearing, such as the short procedure or the special procedure for experts as set out in the Arbitration Procedure, the arbitration is to be conducted in accordance with the rules laid down for such procedures. So for the short procedure each party submits a file which contains a statement of the orders or awards they seek and a statement of their reasons for being entitled to such orders or awards and copies of documents on which they rely. After visiting the site, the arbitrator may require further documents or information to be submitted. Within one calendar month the arbitrator fixes a day when the parties may make oral submissions and the arbitrator has the opportunity of questioning the parties, and their representatives or witnesses. Within one calendar month of this meeting or such further period reasonably required by the arbitrator, the arbitrator is to make and publish the award.

Under the Arbitration Procedure the arbitrator is given detailed powers for the conduct of the hearing, including the right when a party has failed to appear to proceed with the hearing in their absence. Before doing so, however, the arbitrator has to be satisfied that all reasonable steps have been taken to notify the party of the hearing; the arbitrator is then to take all reasonable steps to ensure that the issue is decided justly and fairly.

The claimant or the claimant's representative opens the hearing by briefly outlining their case, and then calling their witnesses, who are required either to swear an oath or to make an act of affirmation, depending on their religious beliefs, if any. Section 12 of the 1950 Act gives the arbitrator the power to administer oaths or take affirmations in the arbitration.

The evidence of a witness is examination in chief; the witness may then be subject to cross-examination by the other party or their representative.

There may then be re-examination by the party or their representative who called the witness. The arbitrator may ask any witness questions which he or she feels ought to have been asked of that witness.

When the claimant's witnesses have all given evidence the respondent or the respondent's representative then opens their case. This may be by outlining the defence or dispensing with that and calling witnesses. These witnesses give their evidence, are cross-examined and re-examined as the claimant's witnesses were.

At the end of the defence case presentation the respondent (or the representative) makes a closing speech to the arbitrator, seeking to influence the arbitrator by drawing attention to the strong points in their case and the weakness in the claimant's case. The claimant (or the representative) then makes a closing speech with the aim of influencing the arbitrator's decision. The arbitrator then formally brings the arbitration to an end.

Award of the arbitrator

An arbitrator may make either an interim award or a final award. Under Section 14 of the 1950 Act (unless there is a contrary intention in the arbitration agreements) the arbitrator may make an interim award when it is appropriate to hold a position in its then state until the final award. It may also be used to determine whether there is liability on a person; the amount payable as a consequence of that liability may be agreed between the parties.

A final award concludes the matter, subject to the limited right of appeal; this is set out in Section 16 of the 1950 Act. The arbitration agreement (unless it contains a contrary intention) is deemed to contain a provision that the award of the arbitrator is final and binding on the parties and any person claiming under them.

The time for making the award may be fixed by the arbitration agreement, otherwise the provisions in Section 13 apply; these state that the arbitrator shall have power to make the award at any time. If any time is fixed, under the agreement or under the 1950 Act, for making the award the High Court or a judge thereof may extend that time. On the application of any party to the arbitration, the High Court has the power to remove an arbitrator who fails without reasonable despatch to enter into, proceed with the arbitration and make an award; in this case the arbitrator is not entitled to any remuneration.

The award itself should give an adequate background to the dispute, such as the identification of the parties, the contract, the disputes, the appointment of the arbitrator, the steps taken in the proceedings, the date of the hearing and its duration and any other matter that ought to be recorded. There must then be a detailed account of the facts of the dispute and the arbitrator's decision on those facts applying the law as is appropriate. The award ends by the arbitrator directing that certain things shall be done as a result of his or her decision, that is what amounts are to be paid in respect of the claims and to whom. Under Section 19A of the 1950 Act the arbitrator has discretion to award simple interest to the sum awarded and any sum paid before the award, and to give directions as to costs.

Arbitrators may be asked by the parties to give reasons for reaching their decision; arbitrators may also feel that they should give reasons. In the past arbitrators were reluctant to do so as an error could lead to an appeal being made on that ground; the 1979 Act has now removed that type of appeal. Under Section 1 of the 1979 Act if all the parties consent the High Court may order the arbitrator to state the reasons for his or her award in sufficient detail to enable the court, if called upon to deal with an appeal under Section 1, to consider any question of law arising out of the award. The High Court cannot make this order unless before the award was made one of the parties gave notice to the arbitrator that a reasoned award would be required, or there was some special reason for that notice not having been given. If an exclusion agreement has been made under Section 3 of the 1979 Act, the High Court cannot act in the matter. If there is no exclusion clause, the court can give one of the parties leave to apply to the High Court for an order that the arbitrator give reasons for the award.

As the arbitrator (or the typist) may make a mistake in the award, the arbitrator is given the same power as a judge to correct it. Section 17 of the 1950 Act allows (unless there is a contrary intention in the arbitration agreement) the arbitrator to correct in an award any clerical mistake or error arising from an accidental slip or omission.

The award is said to be 'published' when it has been prepared, signed by the arbitrator and his or her signature witnessed. The arbitrator informs the parties that it is available upon payment by either party of the arbitrator's charges. On receiving payment the arbitrator sends the award to that party and a copy to the other party. In practice it is the winning party who pays the charges and then recovers them from the loser.

Costs

The costs in an arbitration may be substantial, so the award of costs is a matter of some importance, governed by the provisions in Section 18 of the 1950 Act. Every arbitration agreement (unless it contains a contrary intention) is deemed to include a provision that the costs of the reference and award shall be at the discretion of the arbitrator, who may direct to and by whom and in what manner the costs or any part are to be paid. The arbitrator may tax or settle the amount of costs so paid or any part thereof.

Under Section 18 (unless the award otherwise directs) the costs shall be taxable in the High Court. Taxation is the system whereby the costs are examined by a court official in order to determine that they are proper costs. Those which are not are either disallowed or are reduced. For example if one party made use of an expert whose services were not necessary, the expert's fees would be disallowed.

Costs in the reference are all those costs the parties have incurred in the arbitration, including the cost of legal representation, experts' charges and witnesses' expenses. Costs in the award are the arbitrator's fees and expenses.

In awarding costs the arbitrator should follow the rule used by judges, that 'costs follow the event' which means that in general successful parties are awarded their costs. Where, however, as may well be the case in an arbitration, a party is successful with some claims but unsuccessful with others the arbitrator is expected to apportion the award of costs. If both the claim and the counter-claim are successful, the arbitrator has to award the costs with this in mind.

If the successful party has unnecessarily incurred costs these will be disallowed. Failure to deal with matters as required so that expense is also unnecessarily incurred will mean that the arbitrator will order that the person at fault shall pay the costs 'in any event'. Even if successful, that party will have to bear the costs on that particular matter.

In arbitration, as with a civil action in the courts, a party may make an offer to settle the matter, in one of two ways. First, there may be an offer, made without the protection of 'without prejudice', to settle the matter on payment of a sum which is not less than the amount which is eventually awarded, together with costs up to the date of the offer. If the other party refuses this offer, they are to be responsible for the payment of all the costs after the date of the offer. The simple principle here is that the matter has continued for longer than it needed to.

Second, a 'sealed offer' is an offer made in writing to the other party to pay a sum of money in settlement. If the offer is not accepted, a copy is put into a sealed envelope and handed to the arbitrator at the end of the hearing. The arbitrator opens it after making the award but before settling the costs. The envelope is marked 'without prejudice save as to costs', thus giving the letter privilege except as to costs, which are decided by the arbitrator having regard to the offer.

In the award of costs, the arbitrator has to indicate which of two scales shall apply. The first scale is 'Standard Basis', which is a reasonable amount in respect of all costs reasonably incurred; the second scale is 'Indemnity Basis', which is all costs except in so far as they are of unreasonable amount or have been unreasonably incurred. The distinction between the two scales is that with indemnity payment is made unless it can be shown that something is unreasonable; with standard, it is limited to a reasonable amount provided those costs have been reasonably incurred. The indemnity basis is more generous, but usually awarded only when the standard scale is not an appropriate award to make.

Enforcement of the award

The successful party might encounter difficulty in obtaining payment by the other party. Section 26 of the 1950 Act allows an award on an arbitration agreement, with leave of the High Court or a judge thereof, to be enforced in the same way as a High Court judgment or order. If the High Court gives leave then judgment may be entered in the terms of the award. So all the means available to enforce a High Court judgment may, with leave of the court, be used to secure payment of the award: the debtor's goods may be seized, the debtor's land may be charged with the payment of the debt, and money may be obtainable from the debtor's bank account by means of garnishee proceedings.

Appeals

The Arbitration Act 1979 repealed the 'case stated' form of appeal under the 1950 Act and restricted access to the courts by way of appeals. The 'case stated' form of appeal had been widely used as a delaying tactic by the unsuccessful party in order to retain for a longer period the money they had been ordered to pay. Also the parties had chosen to have the dispute determined by arbitration and it was therefore reasonable to expect them to accept the arbitrator's decision as final and binding. It was not, however, thought right to leave parties without any right of appeal, but it is a restricted right. Section 3 of the 1979 Act states that the High Court is not to give leave to appeal under Section 1 of the Act if the parties have entered into an agreement in writing. This is referred to as an 'exclusion agreement' and may be applicable to a particular award, to awards under a particular reference or to any other description of awards. Under Section 4 of the 1979 Act an exclusion agreement is to be of no effect unless it was entered into after the commencement of arbitration in which the award is made or in which the question of law arises. The parties are not to sign away their rights of appeal until the arbitration has started; when the nature and extent of the dispute is known to the parties they can then make an effective exclusion agreement.

Section 1 of the 1979 Act allows an appeal to be made to the High Court on any question of law arising out of an award made on an arbitration agreement. The appeal may be brought by any of the parties with the consent of all the parties to the reference or with the leave of the court subject to any exclusion agreement. Leave is not to be given unless the court is satisfied that the determination of the question of law concerned could substantially affect the rights of one or more of the parties. Conditions may be imposed by the court in granting leave. The court when dealing with an appeal may confirm, vary or set aside the award or remit the award to the arbitrator for his or her reconsideration together with the court's opinion on the question of law which was the subject of the appeal. The remitted award to the arbitrator must, unless the court orders otherwise, make his or her award within three months after the date of the order. Under Section 23 of the 1950 Act, when an application is made to set aside an award, the High Court may order that any money made payable by the award shall be brought into court or otherwise secured pending the determination of the application.

6

Torts

Nature of torts

English law recognizes that there are certain civil wrongs known as torts which will allow a person to sue in the civil courts for damages and other remedies. The word 'tort' comes from Norman-French and indicates a wrong.

Most torts are common law matters but Parliament has from time to time clarified and strengthened the common law where experience has revealed some inadequacy. The Occupiers' Liability Act 1957 was passed in order to resolve difficulties in interpreting the common law obligations that occupiers of land owed to those who came on their land. Judicial decisions on the common law had led to the law on certain points becoming almost incomprehensible. The Occupiers' Liability Act 1984 strengthened the law in that those who went on land as trespassers could be owed a duty of care.

Parliament has also provided that activities, which were previously torts only, shall in addition become criminal offences and subject to the control of public bodies. The Control of Pollution Act 1974 made noise nuisances from construction operations subject to the control of local authorities and punishable by fine in the Magistrates Court. The Act does not alter the rights of people affected by the noise nuisance to sue for the tort of private nuisance if they so wish. The majority of those affected, however, will simply wish to have the noise nuisance controlled and the use of these statutory provisions by a local authority will achieve this purpose speedily and without cost to them.

The class of torts is wide: slander and libel are well known, while others such as passing off, that is passing off goods as being those of another manufacturer, are unknown to the general public.

So far as the civil engineer is concerned, knowledge of those torts connected with land and construction operations is essential; it is necessary to define a tort more precisely in order to avoid confusion with other legal wrongs.

With one exception, that of public nuisance, a tort is not in itself a crime. A crime is an offence against society in that some particular conduct is controlled by the criminal law. A person found guilty by a criminal court is punished by the court, in order to protect society generally and to promote good behaviour. With a tort, for example slander, it is a matter solely for the person slandered as to whether or not to sue; the state is in no way concerned. A number of occurrences give rise to both criminal and tort liability. An industrial accident will probably result from a breach of safety law, for which a criminal prosecution will follow; injured workers will then sue in tort for negligence and breach of statutory duty to recover damages for their injuries.

A breach of contract is also a civil wrong since claims are made in the civil courts and it is left to the injured party to take action or not; the state is not involved. The distinction is that a breach of contract arises from a relationship which the parties have made themselves: tort does not depend on that relationship. A motorist does not make a contract with other road users that she will drive her car in a careful proper way. The tort of negligence, however, puts her under a duty of care to other road users and if she injures them as a result of a breach of that duty of care she will be liable to them. A number of professional people have found that they owed a duty under a contract to a client and a duty in tort both to the client and others. If a civil engineer negligently designed a structure for a client and that structure collapsed damaging property owned by others, then he would be in breach of contract to the client and liable in tort to both the client and the owners of the damaged property.

Trusts have a separately developed legal framework of their own. Relationships have to exist if a breach of trust is alleged. There must be a person who has been appointed as a trustee, or is otherwise recognized, who is in control of property for the benefit of a person known as the beneficiary. Should there be a breach of trust the beneficiary has the right to sue the trustee for his failure. The dispute is settled by the application of trust laws; tort does not come into the matter.

Public nuisance

Public nuisance is a common law criminal offence, arising when there has been an interference with the rights of a section of Her Majesty's subjects. Since it is an interference with public rights, an individual cannot (with one exception) bring an action for public nuisance.

An action for a public nuisance is usually brought by the Attorney-General on behalf of the public. An individual or a group of persons may request the Attorney-General to bring what is known as a relator action. Actions may also be brought by local authorities under Section 222 of the Local Government Act 1972, in order to protect the interests of the local inhabitants.

The exception to the rule that individuals are not allowed to bring an action is where individuals can show that they have suffered an injury over and above that suffered by other members of the public. Injury here means all forms of injury and is not confined to personal injury. To succeed in an action that individual must be able to prove that the injury was substantial, direct and particular.

A question the courts have been called upon to answer is how many members of the public have to be affected for a public nuisance to arise. The case of *Attorney-General v P Y A Quarries Ltd 1957* is a good example of the way in which a public nuisance arises. The quarry company conducted their blasting operations in such a manner as to affect a wide area with dust, splinters, noise and vibrations. Inhabitants of the area, which was rural and sparsely populated, complained of the company's activities to the local council, which in turn made complaints to the company but to no effect. The council then asked the Attorney-General to take action. The quarry company's main defence was that so few people had been affected that no public nuisance had arisen; it was private nuisance only. Lord Denning refused to answer the question as to the number of Her Majesty's subjects who had to be affected before a public nuisance arose. He said that a public nuisance is a nuisance which is so widespread in its range or so indiscriminate in its effect that it would not be reasonable to expect one person to take proceedings to put a stop to it, but that it should be taken on the responsibility of the community at large. Public nuisance was proved and an injunction granted to restrain the quarrying operations.

From Lord Denning's judgment a public nuisance can exist even though a small number of persons are affected; it is usually the case that a considerable number of people are affected.

Public nuisance may take several forms: dust, smoke, fumes, smell, noise, vibrations, obstruction to highways and any other activity which can be the cause of a nuisance. In the construction industry public nuisance can arise from construction operations and obstruction of highways.

Individuals can sue for public nuisance if they can show that they have suffered an injury over and above that suffered by others. In the case of *Halsey v Esso Petroleum Co Ltd 1961*, Halsey owned a house in a street in London. In the same street there was an oil depot belonging to Esso. Oil was received at the depot from tankers on the River Thames and stored in tanks for later transport by road. The oil had to be heated in order for it to be pumped into the road tankers. There was a boiler house with two boilers and a chimney. Emissions from the chimney contained acid smuts which fell on Halsey's house, causing damage to laundry hanging out to dry in the garden, and also to the paintwork of Halsey's car. Halsey further complained about the noise of the boilers and from the 10.00 pm to 6.00 am shift when tankers entered and left the depot. Halsey sued claiming damages for the laundry and the car, and sought an injunction to restrain the work activities which gave rise to the smell and noise. He was successful with all his claims. He was awarded £234 and granted an injunction controlling the noise produced by the depot between 10.00 pm and 6.00 am.

Obstruction of public highways can frequently arise in construction operations. The important case on this matter is *Harper v G N Haden and Sons 1933*, where Haden and Sons erected scaffolding on the highway in order to make alterations to some premises in a cul-de-sac. A temporary pavement and handrail were erected for the use of pedestrians. Harper had a shop lower down the cul-de-sac which meant that his customers had to negotiate the scaffolding. Harper claimed that his business suffered because of this obstruction and sought damages. His claim was dismissed by the Court of Appeal, which commented that the law of the use of highways was the law of give and take. Users had to have reasonable regard to the convenience and comfort of others, and must not themselves expect a degree of convenience and comfort obtainable only by disregarding that of other people. They must expect to be obstructed occasionally: it is the price they pay for the privilege of obstructing others.

Persons can therefore obstruct a highway and not be acting unlawfully even if their neighbours are inconvenienced, but the obstruction must not be more extensive or exist for longer than is reasonably necessary. In the case of *Trevett v Lee 1955*, Lee, who lived in a house not connected to a mains water supply, laid a half-inch hosepipe across a highway during a time of drought in order to obtain water from a source on the other side of the road. The road was not greatly used by traffic and Lee tried to keep a lookout for pedestrians in order to warn them of the danger. Trevett tripped over the pipe and suffered injury. Trevett's claim was unsuccessful, the Court of Appeal deciding that what had been done was reasonable use of the highway and did not constitute public nuisance. This case may be contrasted with that of *Almeroth v W E Chivers and Sons Ltd 1948*, where Chivers and Sons had been carrying out roof repairs to a building by the side of a road. Rubble from the repair work was not removed but left in the gutter. Almeroth, a pedlar, was pushing his cart when he was stopped to make a sale. In going on to the pavement to attend to the customer he failed to notice the rubble and tripped over it. He fell and suffered injury. Almeroth's claim for damages was successful. The Court of Appeal took the view that to leave rubble on a highway constituted a public nuisance. The defence that users of highways should look for hazards and guard against them was rejected. The court held that pedestrians on highways were not under a duty to keep their eyes on the ground to see if there was any obstructions there.

The use of vehicles on highways has in appropriate circumstances been held to be public nuisance. In *Dymond v Pearce and Others 1972* a lorry driver for his own convenience left a large lorry parked on a dual carriageway at 6.00 pm one evening in August. He intended to drive the lorry at 4.00 am the following morning. The carriageway on which the lorry was parked was 24 feet in width. As the lorry was 7.5 feet in width, the carriageway was reduced to about 16 feet. When night came the lorry driver put on the lights; the street lighting was good in any case. A motor cyclist with a pillion passenger drove into the lorry. Dymond, the pillion passenger, recovered damages from Pearce, the driver of the motor cycle. Dymond also sought damages from the owner and driver of the lorry. He was unsuccessful since the court accepted evidence that Pearce's driving was the sole cause of the accident. The Court of Appeal did, however, decide that the parking of the lorry on the carriageway for a number of hours did constitute a public nuisance since it deprived the public of the use of a part of the carriageway.

In the case of the *Attorney-General v Gastonia Coaches Ltd 1977*, the Attorney-General sought and was granted an injunction restraining the parking of coaches on a highway. The coaches never obstructed the highway completely and the parking occurred at certain times of the day. When it did, however, it compelled the drivers of other vehicles to drive on to the grass verge in order to pass or to wait until the obstructing vehicles were moved. This was public nuisance: it was not reasonable use of the highway to obstruct it in that manner for that period of time.

Public nuisance also arises when the owner of the premises adjoining a highway allows them to become a danger to users of the highway. In the case of *Tarry v Ashton 1876*, Ashton owned a house which had a gas lamp fixed to it and which overhung the pavement. Ashton employed a competent gas fitter to repair the lamp. He failed to notice that the securing bolts holding the lamp to the wall were rusting and unreliable. Some months later the lamp fell, injuring Tarry. Tarry's claim was successful. The court accepted that the lamp created a nuisance to the highway. Furthermore Ashton could not plead a defence that the liability was that of the gas fitter. Ashton was under a duty which he could not delegate to someone else. The dangerous state of the lamp would have been apparent to Ashton if he had made a proper inspection.

Private nuisance

Unlike public nuisance, private nuisance requires a person who seeks to sue to show some interest in land, usually occupation, or ownership without actual occupation. With public nuisance, users of a highway may sue simply because their rights as members of the public have been subject to interference. That is not the case with private nuisance: a right connected with the use and enjoyment of land must be affected for liability to arise.

The tort of private nuisance has been defined as 'unlawful interference with a person's use or enjoyment of land, or some right over, or in connection with it'. It is under the first part, concerning the use and enjoyment of land, that most actions are brought, since this covers disturbances caused by smoke, fumes, dust, smell, noise, vibration or dampness. The second part of the definition covers interferences with rights over or in connection with land, that is interferences with easements and similar rights, including interferences with a right to light, a right of support and a right of way. These are considered with land law (see p. 235).

Although private nuisance frequently arises from the activities of the occupier of adjoining land this is not an essential element. Contractors who neither own nor occupy the land on which they are doing their work may be held liable for private nuisance (see p. 160).

Reasonableness

There is a general principle in the law of private nuisance that if persons have acted reasonably they are not liable for nuisance; what is a reasonable use of land by a person depends on the individual circumstances. The court will consider what is the effect on the person claiming nuisance from the activities of the other person: has that person's activities resulted in some oppression on the other person? If so, a claim by the defendants in the action that they were conducting their business in the usual way businesses of that nature are conducted will probably not provide a defence.

The law seeks to achieve a balance between the needs of neighbours; there has to be some 'give and take', otherwise life would be impossible. Minor, isolated interferences are expected to be accepted without recourse being made to the courts; actions brought on such matters would be unsuccessful.

Most claims for private nuisance are made because of some activity which has continued for some time. If the incident complained of is of a major nature then that, even though an isolated occurrence, may also constitute private nuisance. In the case of *Midwood and Co Ltd v Manchester Corporation 1905*, an electric cable of the corporation had faulty insulation which volatized the bitumen giving off an inflammable gas. This exploded and set fire to an adjoining house belonging to Midwood. The corporation were held to be liable in private nuisance.

This principle was applied in the case of *British Celanese Ltd v A H Hunt (Capacitators) Ltd 1969*. Hunt stored on their premises loose metal foil in strips which were light enough to be lifted by strong winds: this had happened some three years previously. About 100 yards away from Hunt's factory was an electricity sub-station which had high-voltage bus-bars in the external air. Some of the strips of metal foil laid in the open air were lifted by wind and coming into contact with the bus-bars caused a short circuit, which cut off the lighting and power supplies to British Celanese's factory. This caused material in some machines to solidify, with cleaning being necessary before they could be put back into production. The High Court decided that the claim by British Celanese for private nuisance, which was one of a number of grounds of claim, was correct. Damages were awarded to them.

The courts have often been asked to consider the locality of the premises subject to the nuisance. This is sometimes put in the form that 'the claimant came to the nuisance and so cannot complain'. In the case of *St Helen's Smelting Company v Tipping 1865*, Tipping had bought a large estate in June 1860. About a mile and half away was a large smelting works, which in September 1860 started extensive operations. Emissions from the works caused physical damage to shrubs and trees on the estate. The defence to the claim was that the area was mainly used for manufacturing purposes and that the smelting works was in a fit place. The House of Lords refused to accept that the locality could constitute a defence when damage had been caused to property. However, the courts accept that localities do vary: what is acceptable in one locality is unacceptable and a nuisance in another.

The courts have also considered sensitivity, that is, are the persons who complain of a nuisance personally sensitive in some way or are their goods sensitive in some respects? Is it right to hold a person liable in nuisance because of some person's sensitivity, without which no nuisance may exist?

The answer to the question is to be found in the case of *Robinson v Kilvert 1889*. Kilvert rented the upper floor of a building to Robinson, who wanted to use the space as a paper warehouse. Kilvert used the lower floor for a manufacturing process which required the air to be hot and dry and resulted in the temperature in the room above being raised to 80°F, which caused damage to brown paper Robinson had stored there, thus reducing its value. This temperature, however, was not so high as to cause damage to paper generally or to inconvenience workers on the upper floor. When Kilvert had rented the upper floor to Robinson he was unaware of the fact that Robinson would use the floor for storing any particular kind of paper.

The Court of Appeal dismissed Robinson's claim that he had suffered injury because of a nuisance. The attitude of the court was that people who carry on an exceptionally delicate trade cannot complain if they are injured by their neighbours' activities which would not cause injury other than to an exceptionally delicate trade.

Malice

As the reasonable use of land is the essential element of the tort of private nuisance, the motive of a person in doing some act must be taken into account. The whole concept of reasonableness must take in the motive of a person with regard to his or her conduct. In the case of *Christie v Davey 1893*, Mr and Mrs Christie lived in a semi-detached house, the other half of which was occupied by Davey. The Christies were a musical family and Mrs Christie, a music teacher, gave lessons to pupils who attended the house. Davey objected to the noise of the music. He retaliated by banging metal trays, blowing a whistle, knocking on the party-wall and shrieking. The Christies were successful in obtaining an injunction to restrain Davey in acting in this manner. Davey's actions were deliberate and malicious and done solely to cause annoyance to the Christies.

This decision was applied in the later case of *Hollywood Silver Fox Farm Ltd v Emmett 1936*. Emmett was a developer on his land of a housing estate; the Farm was established next door. Emmett believed that this would affect his development and asked for the company's sign 'Hollywood Silver Fox Farm' to be removed. On this being refused Emmett threatened to shoot along the boundary, which would disturb the foxes during their breeding season. Emmett's son fired his gun on a number of occasions and the foxes suffered harm. The High Court awarded Hollywood Silver Fox Farm damages and an injunction restraining Emmett from discharging guns or creating other loud noises during the breeding season for the foxes.

What undoubtedly is the leading case on this matter of malice is *Bradford Corporation v Pickles 1895*. Pickles owned land in an area where Bradford Corporation were buying land for the water supply system that was being constructed for the city. Pickles was disappointed that his land was not to be bought by the corporation. Water percolated through Pickles's land in undefined channels; this water would eventually discharge into land belonging to the corporation at a lower level. Pickles with an admitted malicious motive dug a shaft on his land, which reduced the flow of the water and caused it to become discoloured. The corporation sued claiming that Pickles's action constituted a nuisance for which they were entitled to damages and an injunction. The corporation's claim was dismissed. The House of Lords held that digging a shaft in your own land is a lawful activity, which was not made into an unlawful activity because of the admitted malice of the landowner. One of the Law Lords doubted that Pickles's motive was malicious. He took the view that what Pickles wanted to do was to sell his land to the corporation at an advantageous price. However, the decision is generally looked on as one where the malicious motive did not make a lawful action into an unlawful action. In *Christie v Davey* the banging of metal trays,. whistling and knocking on the party-wall was an unlawful act even if the motive of Davey had not been malicious.

In Pickles's case, it is important to note that the water was flowing in undefined channels: it was ground water. If the water had been flowing in defined channels, whether man-made or created by natural forces, at common law such water cannot be extracted if the rights of other landowners are affected in an unreasonable way. The same applies with regard to surface water. The decision in Pickles's case has meant that if ground water is extracted in such quantity as to reduce the water level in adjoining land, with a resulting damage to buildings on that land, then there is no liability on the person who made the extraction. The extraction of the ground water is a lawful action and so any resulting damage on adjoining land is a loss to be borne by that landowner (see p. 238).

Nuisance from natural forces

Until recently it was not thought that a person could be liable for nuisance if it arose from the forces of nature on his or her land. Although the position is not firmly decided, the case of *Leakey and Others v National Trust for Places of Historic Interest or Natural Beauty 1980* provides guidance. Even so the decision in the Court of Appeal was a majority decision; an authoritative ruling of the House of Lords is desirable. In Somerset land owned by the National Trust included a conical hill known as Burrow Mump. Geologically it is composed of Keuper marl, which made it particularly liable to cracking and slipping as a result of weathering. At the base of the hill there were two houses owned by Mr and Mrs Leakey and a neighbour. The side of the hill nearest the houses had been cut away some time in the past, leaving that side steep. Over the years there had been falls of soil, rock, tree-roots and other debris from the bank on to the land where the houses stood. This was the result of natural weathering and not caused by any activity of the National Trust. As a consequence of the exceptionally dry summer of 1976, followed by an unusually wet autumn, a large crack opened up in the hill and a major collapse on the houses looked imminent. The National Trust when notified of the danger declined to take any remedial action. This decision was based on the then valid belief that there was no liability for natural movement of the ground. A serious fall occurred and at considerable expense the fallen material was removed and some protective measures provided. The owners of the houses sued the National Trust for nuisance.

The Court of Appeal decided that there was liability on the National Trust, because the National Trust had to do that which was reasonable for them to do. Included in what is reasonable would be the financial cost of the work needed to remove the nuisance and the financial positions of both parties to the dispute. It was suggested that in the case of landowners who had limited financial means to meet the cost of works that to allow their neighbours to come on their land to execute necessary works might be sufficient or for the landowners to offer a fair share of the expense involved.

Nuisance and construction operations

Having considered the main principles of the tort of private nuisance, we now examine the ways in which private nuisance may arise with construction operations. The person bringing the action will often base the claim on other additional grounds.

The Court of Appeal decision in the case of *Andreae v Selfridge and Co Ltd 1937* demonstrates the court's willingness to accept that some temporary inconvenience which does not cause damage will not constitute an actionable nuisance. The case also showed the court's awareness of developments in construction processes which may result in greater speed and efficiency even though they may cause more noise and interference than older methods.

Mrs Andreae had an hotel on an island site in London; the rest of the site had been bought by Selfridges for development as a new store. On the land stood several buildings which would have to be demolished; then there was to be a deep excavation for a steel framed building. The buildings were demolished with the use of pneumatic hammers, resulting in dust and grit being thrown into the air. After a complaint by a businessman in the area the work was limited to certain hours. Several cranes were installed and initially operated day and night. Mrs Andreae complained at the use of the cranes during the night: the contractors then stopped their use between 10.00 pm and 7.00 am. Mrs Andreae sued claiming that her hotel business had suffered loss of business and that when the works had been completed her loss of custom had not been recovered.

The Court of Appeal awarded Mrs Andreae £1000 for the private nuisance she had suffered from the noise and dust. This had gone beyond the level of inconvenience and discomfort which it was reasonable to expect a person to endure while construction works were being carried out. The court was unwilling to award any damages for the custom not building up after the completion of the works: this was not something that could be attributed to the dust and noise being above a reasonable level. A submission on behalf of Mrs Andreae that an excavation some 60 feet deep and the erection of a steel-framed building was abnormal or unusual use of land was rejected. Had this submission been accepted Mrs Andreae's claim would have been substantially strengthened. The court took the view that new construction methods and inventions meant that bigger buildings could be erected without it being unusual or abnormal use of land. A submission that the loss of sleep for a night was of no consequence was answered by the Master of the Rolls, Sir Wilfred Greene, saying: 'I certainly protest against the idea that, if persons, for their own profit and convenience choose to destroy even one night's rest of their neighbours, they are doing something which is excusable'.

The Court of Appeal in the case of *Mantania v National Provincial Bank Ltd and Elevenist Syndicate Ltd 1936* decided that a private nuisance could occur within the same building, even though it is of a temporary nature. Matania was the tenant of an upper floor of a building owned by the bank, with the Elevenist Syndicate being tenants of the floor beneath, where extensive works of alteration created noise and dust, causing nuisance to Mantania, who sued for private nuisance. His claim was successful: although the works were temporary they affected his occupation as a music teacher. There was liability even though the nuisance was created by the building contractor. The court accepted that what was involved was work of a nature where there was a special danger of a nuisance being caused, otherwise direct responsibility would have fallen on the building contractor.

In the case of *Dodd Properties (Kent) and Another v Canterbury City Council and Others 1980*, Dodd Properties owned a building in Canterbury which was leased to Marlowe Garage (Canterbury) Ltd, who were car dealers and sold petrol and car accessories. In 1968 Canterbury City Council decided to erect a multi-storey car park on land they owned next to the garage. Truscon Ltd were appointed main contractors with Frankipile Ltd as their sub-contractors for the foundation work; it was appreciated that there was a risk of damage to the garage. Pile driving started near to the garage and within a short time severe vibrations caused cracking in the walls and concrete floor of the garage. The building, which had a steel girder frame, was distorted, with the result that the flat roof sloped away from the gutter. Dodd Properties and Marlowe Garage claimed damages for negligence and/or nuisance. Liability was denied until a few days before the trial, when it was admitted. Because of the denial of liability and of financial stringency the necessary repair work was not carried out. The Court of Appeal was called upon to decide whether the damages to be awarded should be assessed on the cost of the repairs in 1970, the earliest possible date for carrying out the repairs, or 1978, the date of the trial before the High Court.

The Court of Appeal accepted the fundamental principle that the injured party was to be put in the position they would have been in if the wrong had not been done. Accepting the financial stringency, it made commercial sense to postpone the repairs until the liability had been determined. The damages were to be assessed on the date of the court action and not the earliest date when the repair works could have been carried out. The cost of the repairs in 1970 were about £11 000; at the court hearing the figure had increased to £30 000.

Who can sue and be sued

The tort of nuisance is an interference with the enjoyment of land: the person who brings an action must have a connection with the land in order to have the legal standing to sue. The person in occupation, whether a tenant or the freeholder, may sue. Tenants may bring an action against their landlord.

It is possible for owners who are not in possession of their land to sue: their standing as the freeholder gives them this right. The right is, however, restricted in that the owners have to show that an injury to the property is such as to affect their interest as the landlord, that is something of a permanent nature. This would include interference to a right of support to a building or obstruction of a right of way. By their nature these are matters which are likely to concern the landlord more than the tenant.

The general rule is that it is the occupier of the land from which the nuisance comes who will be the person sued, subject to a number of exceptions. One example is where the landlord has expressly or impliedly authorized the tenant to do the thing which creates the nuisance. In the case of *Harris v James 1876*, a landlord let a field to a tenant for it to be worked as a lime quarry. The tenant's actions in blasting and allowing the release of smoke from the lime kilns gave rise to a nuisance. Both the landlord and the tenant were held to be liable for the nuisance created by the tenant's activities.

Landlords may also be liable for nuisance from the state of the premises if they have covenanted expressly or impliedly to repair the premises.

In the case of *Sedleigh-Denfield v O'Callaghan 1940* the nuisance had been created by a stranger. A trespasser without permission laid a pipe in a ditch with a grating designed to exclude leaves and other debris; this was so badly placed that it caused an obstruction to the ditch in times of heavy rain. Flooding resulted to adjoining land some three years after the pipe was fixed. The House of Lords held that the owner of the ditch was liable for the nuisance, because the owner had an employee whose duties included cleaning the ditch. He ought to have noticed the pipe and realized the risk of flooding it could cause: his failure made his employer liable for the nuisance.

Independent contractors

At common law an independent contractor is a person who is not an employee but is engaged to perform a given task. In the law of tort a person who engages an independent contractor is not liable for his or her torts, subject to a number of exceptions. So far as nuisance is concerned, with its connection with the use of land between neighbours, occupiers of land have often been held to be liable for nuisance caused by their independent contractors.

In the case of *Bower v Peate 1876*, Peate engaged a builder to carry out rebuilding work on his land. The builder undermined the foundations to the support of Bower's adjoining house. Peate was held liable to Bower for the nuisance created by his independent contractor. In another case, *Spicer v Smee 1946*, Smee engaged an electrician as an independent contractor to rewire her bungalow. The electrical wiring caused a fire which spread to Spicer's adjoining bungalow. The High Court held Smee to be liable for the nuisance created by the independent contractor. Both cases are exceptions to the general rule that independent contractors are liable for their own torts.

The question may be asked as to the importance of being able to sue occupiers of land for the torts of their independent contractors: the occupiers are more likely to have the financial means or insurance with which to meet the damages awarded against them. Many cases, which appear to be two neighbours suing each other for some nuisance damage caused to property, are actions being brought in their names by their insurers. An occupier of land called upon to answer for a nuisance created by her independent contractor could, in turn, sue that independent contractor for breach of contract for failure to perform his duties properly. Whether that course of action is worthwhile depends on the financial resources of the independent contractor or if he has insurance cover.

Defences

The two main defences to an action for private nuisance are that the nuisance has continued for a period of time sufficient to give it legal standing, known as prescriptive right, and statutory authority, that is what is being done is authorized by Act of Parliament.

For a nuisance to become lawful it must have existed as a nuisance openly for a period of not less than twenty years. If the activity has not constituted a nuisance for that twenty-year period, it cannot assume a lawful standing. Two cases illustrate that this defence is difficult to prove in practice. In the first case, *Sturges v Bridgman 1879*, Bridgman was a baker and confectioner who had premises which backed on to the garden of Sturges's house. For many years Bridgman had used a pestle and mortar which created noise and vibrations. Sturges, a physician, built a consulting room in his garden. He then found that the room could not be used because of the noise and vibrations. When he sued for nuisance Bridgman pleaded in defence that his activity had continued for more than twenty years and so he had a legal right to continue. The Court of Appeal, however, held that there was no actionable nuisance until Sturges built the consulting room and then found that a nuisance existed from the noise and vibration. Time started to run only from that date. Sturges was granted an injunction.

In the second case, *Liverpool Corporation v H Coghill and Son 1918*, Coghill had for more than twenty years discharged industrial waste into the sewers of Liverpool Corporation. The discharges were made at infrequent intervals and at night, without permission or knowledge of the corporation. It was only when damage occurred to the corporation's sewage farm that they became aware of the discharge. The High Court decided that as the discharge had been made secretly and unknown, and without any grounds for arousing the suspicion of the corporation, it could not establish a prescriptive right.

Parliament may by passing a statute authorize an activity even though it gives rise to a nuisance: the public interests should override private interests. Private individuals may have to suffer for the benefit of the general public. The availability of this defence depends on either the express words in the statute or the necessary implication to be drawn from the statute.

In the case of *Manchester Corporation v Farnworth 1930*, nuisance was caused by noxious fumes emitted from the chimney of the corporation's electricity generating station, which had been erected by the corporation under statutory powers. The defence of the corporation was that the nuisance was an unavoidable consequence of the operation of the station. Greater precautions might have been possible to reduce the nuisance but, because of their expense, the corporation had not taken this action. The House of Lords took the view that it was reasonable for the corporation to have done more to prevent the nuisance. The corporation were therefore held liable.

In the case of *Allen v Gulf Oil Refining Ltd 1981*, the Law Lords were asked to decide whether there was a necessary implication in a private Act of Parliament that an oil refinery was authorization to commit nuisance. People in the area around the refinery complained of noise, vibrations and smell and brought an action for nuisance. The private Act of Parliament authorized the compulsory acquisition of the land needed for the construction of the refinery but had not expressly dealt with its operation. The House of Lords by a majority decided that it must have been Parliament's intention that the refinery should produce oils. This meant (and this was to be decided later by another court) that it had to be determined whether the nuisance was something which would occur in the operation of any oil refinery or whether the refinery on that site could be operated without causing nuisance. If a nuisance was a consequence of the operation of the oil refinery then there was a statutory defence in that it was to be implied from the Act that Parliament had intended the refinery to operate even if it gave rise to a nuisance.

Remedies

The remedies for private nuisance are damages and injunctions. Damages are awarded in order to compensate the person for the injury suffered. If the injury consists of damage to property or personal injury, the amount may be calculated with reasonable accuracy. Where inconvenience has resulted from noise or smell, for example, judges will award a sum they consider appropriate.

Injunctions are equitable remedies granted by the courts in order to restrain the doing of an act which has given rise to the nuisance, or to order a person to do something to remove a nuisance. Failure to comply with an injunction is contempt of court: the courts have wide powers to punish for contempt of court.

With the tort of private nuisance all forms of injunctions may be used (see Chapter 1). An interlocutory injunction may be granted to maintain the status quo until the issue is decided at the court hearing, where a perpetual injunction may be granted to prohibit recurrence of the nuisance and a mandatory injunction granted if the circumstances require it. Where a nuisance has not yet occurred but there is a real apprehension that nuisance will result the court may grant a *quia timet* injunction.

With the tort of nuisance, there may be the remedy of self-help, that is action by a person to abate a nuisance, usually one of a threatening nature. Self-help is not encouraged by the courts: people may well find that in so doing they have themselves committed a tort.

Statutory nuisances

Both public nuisance and private nuisance are common law torts which require expensive and often lengthy court hearings for their settlement. In the nineteenth century it was recognized by Parliament that some forms of nuisance ought to be dealt with by local authorities rather than individuals, and there was a need to have the matter dealt with speedily, inexpensively and without necessarily involving the courts. The statutory nuisances procedure, now contained in the Environmental Protection Act 1990, is the means used to achieve these aims.

Section 79 of the Act sets out a number of matters which are to constitute 'statutory nuisances'. The ones of most importance to the construction industry are set out in sub-Section 1:

(a) any premises in such a state as to be prejudicial to health or a nuisance;
(b) smoke emitted from premises so as to be prejudicial to health or a nuisance; . .
(d) any dust, steam, smell or other effluvia arising on industrial, trade or business premises and being prejudicial to health or a nuisance;
(e) any accumulation or deposit which is prejudicial to health or a nuisance; . . .
(g) noise emitted from premises so as to be prejudicial to health or a nuisance.

Under Section 80 of the Act, on being satisfied of the existence of a statutory nuisance or that it is likely to occur or recur, the local authority have to serve an 'abatement notice', requiring appropriate action to be taken within a specified period of time. This notice has to be served on the person at fault, or in the case of structural work to premises on the owner, and where the person responsible for the nuisance cannot be found or the nuisance has not yet occurred on the owner or occupier of the premises. A person served with such a notice may appeal against it to a Magistrates Court within twenty-one days beginning with the date on which the notice was served. A person served with a notice who without reasonable excuse contravenes or fails to comply with any requirement or prohibition imposed in the notice is guilty of an offence. On conviction that person is liable to a fine which in the case of an offence on industrial, trade or business premises is not to exceed £20 000. With certain forms of statutory nuisances defendants may plead a 'best practicable means' of defence, that is they did what was reasonably practicable having regard to local conditions and circumstances, to the current state of technical knowledge and to the financial implications.

Under Section 81 of the Act, if more than one person is responsible for the creation of a statutory nuisance each can be dealt with under Section 80 even though what one person did might not on its own amount to nuisance. If an abatement notice has not been complied with then, whether or not the local authority prosecute in the Magistrates Court, the local authority may take steps to abate the nuisance. Expenses incurred by the local authority in abating the nuisance may be recovered from the person at fault. Section 81 contains a power which is extremely effective in appropriate circumstances. This is to bring the matter before the High Court instead of the Magistrates Court, where the proceedings would have provided an inadequate remedy.

The final point to note with the statutory nuisances procedure is the power of an individual to make complaint to a Magistrates Court that that person has been aggrieved by the existence of a statutory nuisance. This power, found in Section 82, has been widely used by individuals where the local authority have been unwilling to take action. The main use has been by the tenants of local authority dwellings which were in a state of disrepair and the authority were slow in carrying out the necessary repairs. Before a person can ask the Magistrates Court for an order the person aggrieved must give twenty-one days' notice in writing of the intention to do so to the person at fault. The Magistrates Court, on being satisfied of the existence of a statutory nuisance, may act in the same way as with a complaint made in the usual way and the same powers of enforcement apply.

Control of Pollution Act 1974

The Control of Pollution Act 1974 is important to the construction industry when dealing with noise and vibrations: these sources of annoyance have caused sufferers to sue in the civil courts for damages and injunctions. In recent years noise has been increasingly recognized as an unacceptable form of environmental pollution; it should not be left to individuals to sue in the civil courts. Parliament passed the Act, placing a duty on local authorities, not dissimilar to that in the Environmental Protection Act 1990, to administer the provisions of the Act. Parliament made specific provisions for controlling noise arising from construction operations, which are contained in Sections 60 and 61 of the Act.

Section 60 empowers a local authority when construction works are being or are going to be carried out on any premises to serve a notice imposing requirements as to the way in which works are to be carried out. The local authority may publish notice of those requirements in any appropriate way. The term 'construction works' covers a range of activities including work of engineering construction. The local authority may make specific requirements in the notice, including specifying plant or machinery which may or may not be used, hours of work, and noise levels generally or at specified hours or places. Where a local authority takes action under Section 60, regard has to be had to any relevant code of practice and the need for ensuring that the best practicable means are used to minimize noise. The need to protect any persons in the locality of the premises from the effect of noise must also be observed.

A local authority notice is to be served on the person who appears to be carrying out or going to carry out the works, and on such other persons who appear to be responsible for or to have control over the carrying out of the works. This allows notices to be served both on the employer and contractor or on the main contractor and a sub-contractor. Whether or not this is done is entirely a matter for the local authority.

A notice served by a local authority may specify the time within which it is to be complied with, it may require the execution of works and the taking of other steps as may be necessary or specified in the notice. A person served with a notice may make an appeal to a Magistrates Court within twenty-one days. Contravention of a requirement of a notice without reasonable excuse is an offence punishable by fine.

First impression of the provisions in Section 60 are that the control given to local authorities will prevent a noise nuisance arising from construction operations or to control such operations so that a noise nuisance is abated. Experience, however, has revealed two deficiencies in the provisions, both of which have been exploited by some contractors. The first is the twenty-one day period for making an appeal, and the second the imposition of a fine which may be inadequate in the circumstances. In order to prevent gross abuse of the appeal system (which stays the operation of a notice once an appeal is made), the relevant regulations, the Control of Noise (Appeals) Regulations 1975, allow a local authority to direct that the making of an appeal shall not suspend the notice. The local authority can give this direction where the expenditure incurred in carrying out works to comply with the notice would not be disproportionate to the public benefit to be expected in that period from such compliance.

In order to make the provisions in the Control of Pollution Act 1974 work effectively, and to prevent work continuing when it ought to be stopped or controlled, local authorities have gone to the High Court and asked for an injunction to be granted.

The first case was *London Borough of Hammersmith v Magnum Automated Forecourts Ltd 1978*, where a 'taxi care centre' operated twenty-four hours a day, providing fuel supplies, washing facilities and vending machines. Local residents complained of the noise and the local authority served a notice under Section 58 of the Act, which deals with general noise nuisances, requiring within twenty-eight days cessation of operations between 11.00 pm and 7.00 am. The notice was directed to stay in force in the event of an appeal. Magnum Automated disregarded the notice and operated the centre as before. The local authority applied for an injunction to restrain the use of the centre between 11.00 pm and 7.00 am. The High Court refused the application but on appeal to the Court of Appeal the local authority secured the injunction.

A case where an injunction was granted to control noise from construction operations but which the contractor disregarded was *Camden London Borough Council v Alpenoak Ltd 1985*. Alpenoak were carrying out work on an hotel they owned in London in such a manner that local residents made complaints about the noise and dirt. The work was being done outside normal hours – early mornings, evenings and weekends. The local authority served Alpenoak with a notice under Section 60 which limited all work which was audible outside the site to the hours of 8.00 am to 6.00 pm Monday to Friday and 8.00 am to 1.00 pm on Saturday. Any work which did not produce this level of noise could be done at any time. Alpenoak ignored the notice and continued working in the same manner. Camden Council, knowing of the Court of Appeal decision in *London Borough of Hammersmith v Magnum Automated Forecourts Ltd 1978*, applied to the High Court for an injunction. If this application had not been made the only course of action available to the council would have been to bring a prosecution in the Magistrates Court.

An injunction was granted by the High Court requiring Alpenoak to comply with the notice. Alpenoak agreed, but the building work continued as before. The council noted many infringements of the injunction in the next two months. In the opinion of the council this was contempt of court by Alpenoak and the matter was brought to the attention of the High Court. Alpenoak contested strongly the allegations of the council and a four-day court hearing followed. Alpenoak were found to be in contempt and were fined £50 000. They were also ordered to pay the costs of the court action.

Parliament when considering the Control of Pollution Act 1974 appreciated the desirability of allowing a person before starting construction operations to consult with the local authority and to obtain consent to those operations so that action will not be taken under Section 60. Section 61 allows a person who intends to carry out works to which Section 60 applies to apply to the local authority for consent. The application must be made at the same time or later than the submission of approval under the building regulations. The application has to contain particulars of the work to be done and the proposed steps to minimize noise from the works. If the local authority is satisfied that what is proposed if properly carried out would not lead to the service of a notice under Section 60 the consent of the local authority is to be given. Conditions may be imposed in the consent and its duration limited. Contravention of any condition is an offence under the Act. The local authority is to give the decision within twenty-eight days. There is a right of appeal to a Magistrates Court both against the failure to give a decision within this period and against any condition in the consent.

The benefit of prior consent for the person undertaking the construction work is that under Section 61 it is a defence to prove in any proceedings brought under Section 60 that an alleged noise nuisance amounted to the carrying out of works in accordance with the consent given under Section 61. So if works are carried out in accordance with the consent a successful prosecution of the person carrying out the works is most unlikely. If there has been a failure by the local authority to assess the possible noise problems then that is their responsibility. By that failure they have deprived themselves of the opportunity of controlling a noise nuisance by a successful prosecution.

The rule in *Rylands v Fletcher*

This rule, generally regarded as an extension to the law of private nuisance, relates to property and activities conducted on that property. The rule is a good example of the way in which the common law can develop from a single case. It also shows how the principle or rule can be extended over the years to an extent where the courts believe that it is necessary to contain it from further development.

In the case of *Rylands v Fletcher 1868*, Rylands and a partner owned a mill and wished to construct a reservoir so as to have a water supply to meet the needs of the mill. They obtained the services of a competent engineer to construct the reservoir; during its construction some disused vertical pit shafts were discovered. These were filled with soil; the presence of the shafts was unknown to anyone. The contractor filled the shafts but in an inadequate manner. Water was fed into the reservoir and soon found its way down the shafts along some unknown disused horizontal shafts and into the shafts of Fletcher's mine, which was a working mine; the flooding disrupted the operation of the mine causing financial loss. Fletcher sued Rylands, but was unable to prove negligence on the part of Rylands and partner. Fletcher was, however, successful in the High Court; Rylands appealed against this decision to the House of Lords, who dismissed Rylands' appeal. In doing so the House of Lords approved the judgment of Mr Justice Blackburn given in the High Court. The rule comes from this judgment:

> The person who for his own purposes brings on his lands and collects and keeps there anything likely to do mischief, if it escapes, must keep it in at his peril, and, if he does not do so, is prime facie answerable for all the damage which is the natural consequence of its escape.

There is no mention of reasonableness in this rule: it is therefore (unlike private nuisance where reasonableness came into the tort) a tort of strict liability. The tort is committed because the thing happened; there is no need to prove negligence or fault on the part of the wrongdoer. Rylands' action caused injury to Fletcher's mine and that made Rylands liable. In the House of Lords reference was made to the use of the land being 'non-natural', so anything which is natural use of the land will fall outside the rule.

Examination of Mr Justice Blackburn's rule shows that there are a number of essential elements present:

1. a person has to bring something on his or her lands and keep it there
2. there must be an escape of that thing
3. it must cause injury by its escape
4. it must be 'non-natural' use of the land.

After the House of Lords' decision the rule was applied in a number of circumstances which if they came before the courts today would probably be decided differently. The case which halted the application of the rule to varying circumstances was *Read v J Lyons and Co Ltd 1947*, which arose from Lyons running a munitions factory in the Second World War. High explosive shells were made for the Ministry of Supply. Mrs Read was employed as an inspector in the factory. While she was in her place of work an explosion occurred in the shell-filling shop; one worker was killed and several others, including Mrs Read, were injured. Mrs Read sued. She did not allege negligence, probably because that would be difficult to prove. She claimed that she was lawfully present in the place where the shells were manufactured, which Lyons knew to be dangerous things, and that while there she was injured when one exploded. In the High Court her claim was successful: the judge held that the rule in *Rylands v Fletcher* applied. Lyons appealed successfully to the Court of Appeal; it was against this decision that Mrs Read appealed to the House of Lords. In dismissing her appeal the Law Lords observed that there had been no escape of the thing which caused the injury. What had happened had been contained within the boundaries of the factory. It was also thought that the manufacture of munitions in wartime could be natural use of the land. Of more general importance, and which cast doubt on earlier decisions, was the observation that the rule did not apply to personal injuries.

Cases are still brought on the basis of the rule, more often linked with some other tort such as negligence. A case involving the application of the rule to escapes of fire is that of *Mason v Levy Auto Parts of England Ltd 1967*. Mason owned a house next to Levy's land, which was used for the storage of spare motor parts and engines; these were protected with greased paper, oil and grease. Inflammable materials including petrol and paints were also stored on the land. On 2 July 1964 fire broke out; because of the dry weather the fire spread quickly. The attempts to control the fire failed to prevent it spreading to Mason's garden and causing damage to a high hedge and plants in the garden. The High Court decided that the probable cause of the fire was a discarded cigarette by one of the workers. The storage of the materials was held to be non-natural use of the land. The rule applied and Mason was successful with his claim.

Defences to the rule

There are a number of defences available to a person sued under the rule, based on cases where in the particular circumstances the court had decided that a defence was available.

Statutory authority is a defence where a statute is interpreted as excepting from liability, usually provided reasonable care is taken. In the case of *Smeaton v Ilford Corporation 1954*, sewage in the corporation's public sewers overflowed on to Smeaton's land in times of heavy rain. Because the Public Health Act 1936 entitled owners of properties to connect to public sewers and the corporation could not prevent such connection, even with an overloaded sewer, no liability fell on the corporation.

A defence exists where something is for the common good of both parties to the action. In the case of *Peters v Prince of Wales Theatres (Birmingham) Ltd 1943* a sprinkler system in a building malfunctioned causing damage to Peters's property. The Court of Appeal decided that Peters, having consented to have the benefit of the sprinkler system, could not, in the absence of negligence, avoid the risk.

In the case of *Rickards v Lothian 1913* the House of Lords decided that if the escape was the malicious act of a stranger then this provides a defence.

Lothian's office in a building occupied by Rickards was flooded over a weekend because some malicious stranger had obstructed the outlet of a wash-hand basin and left a water tap running. Rickards's appeal that he ought not to be held liable for the malicious act of a stranger was accepted as a defence to a claim under *Rylands v Fletcher*.

Act of God had also been accepted as a defence. In the case of *Nichols v Marsland 1876*, a weir was constructed across a stream. During an exceptional storm the weir burst and flooded on to adjoining land: this was accepted as being an Act of God.

A defence is also available where the defendant in the action was the person responsible for the escape.

Trespass to land

Trespass to land is one of the three forms of trespass that exist in common law. The other two are trespass to the person, which is a tort that can exist as assault, battery or false imprisonment, and trespass to goods, which is a tort that consists of some unlawful interference with a person's goods, such as wrongfully detaining them. Trespass to the person has no application to the construction industry; trespass to goods has a limited application in that when contractors become insolvent, and there exists a retention of title clause with regard to goods in their possession, the supplier of the goods may sue for their return. This was considered in the case of *Dawber Williamson Roofing Ltd v Humberside County Council 1979* (see p. 89).

Trespass to land is a tort which arises when there has been a direct interference with the possession of land. It is actionable *per se*, that is actionable without having to prove that damage was caused. The tort arises because the occupier's right to possession of his or her land has been infringed, which constitutes the legal wrong. If during the course of the trespass damage was caused, that will be taken into account in the award of damages by the court.

Despite all the signs which say 'Trespassers will be prosecuted', usually trespass to land remains a civil wrong for which the remedy is a claim in the civil courts. In some circumstances, however, trespass to land is a crime for which a prosecution may be brought in the criminal courts. In ordinary criminal law trespass associated with some other activity makes the trespass a crime. Without such associated activity trespass may be a crime if Parliament has so provided by some statutory provision. For example the act of trespassing on British Rail property is, by Act of Parliament, a criminal offence for which a prosecution is brought in the Magistrates Court. Trespassers are thus dealt with speedily and punished in an appropriate way, compared with the time and expense of bringing a civil action for trespass to land.

An action for trespass to land may, in general, be brought only by the person in possession of the land. The legal right is to possession and any infringement is a challenge to his or her legal rights. For this reason it is possible for tenants to sue their landlord. Even where landlords are not in possession of the land, they can sue for trespass provided they can show that the act of trespass could cause permanent injury to their land. It would not be right, for example, to prevent a landlord bringing an action when an adjoining landowner erected a building which intruded on his land. The landlord's tenant, possibly on a short lease, could hardly be expected to bring an expensive legal action the main purpose of which would be to protect the landlord's interests.

Direct interference is an essential feature of the tort of trespass to land. It is for this reason the branches and roots of trees which intrude into adjoining land constitute private nuisance and not trespass to land. This was decided by the House of Lords in the case of *Lemmon v Webb 1895*. Direct action can take various forms, the usual ones being persons entering on to land, placing or throwing objects on land and persons exceeding the permission authorizing their presence on the land.

If a trespass continues it gives rise to a fresh cause of action each day it continues. In the case of *Holmes v Wilson 1839*, a highway authority without Holmes's permission built buttresses on his land in order to provide support to a road. The highway authority paid compensation for the trespass but did not remove the buttresses. Holmes brought a further action for trespass from the presence of the buttresses on his land and was successful.

The law recognizes that in certain circumstances no right of action for trespass arises:

1 Entry by authority of law, for example a police officer using powers under the Police and Criminal Evidence Act 1984.
2 Entry to abate a nuisance, for example a person who enters the land of his or her next door neighbour in order to extinguish a bonfire which threatens his or her property.
3 Entry to retake goods which were placed there by the occupier of that land.
4 Entry on to land adjoining a highway because the highway has become impassable, provided the land is used solely as a means of right of passage. This is an ancient right which has its origin in unmade highways which frequently become impassable because of bad weather, so that adjoining land had to be used to pass that part of the highway.
5 Entry by an involuntary act, for example a person being thrown or taken on land.
6 Entry by means of licence granted by the occupier. A licence grants permission which makes entry on the land lawful subject to the terms of the licence being observed.

At common law the person in possession of the land has the right to resist not only trespass to the surface of the land, the commonest form, but also trespass beneath the surface of the land and trespass to the air space above the land.

Trespass to the surface of the land

Trespass to the surface of the land can easily arise with construction operations. Site staff may walk over adjoining land, which need not be fenced off or carry any indication that entry is forbidden. Materials or spoil may be deposited on the adjoining land; the fact that this occurred innocently is no defence since intention is not an element required for the tort of trespass to arise. This form of trespass often comes about when scaffolds are to be erected on adjoining land. There is a popular but unsustainable belief that a person can go on his neighbour's land in order to carry out maintenance work to his own property. Entry for this purpose, as for any other purpose, is subject to that occupier's permission.

A case which demonstrated trespass to the surface of land was *John Trenberth Ltd v National Westminster Bank Ltd and Another 1980*, which arose from the state of the stone cladding to a branch office of the bank in Cardiff. The bank was aware of possible danger to the users of the highway on which the branch office stood. The necessary remedial work required entry on to Trenberth's land, which adjoined the branch office. The bank therefore wrote to Trenberth and asked for permission, which was refused even though the bank offered Trenberth full indemnities against any accidents. Trenberth's refusal was not an attempt to obtain some payment for the permission. It was a matter of principle since they were unwilling to allow their property to be entered by the bank or the building contractor engaged by the bank in any circumstance. Further letters from the bank failed to secure the permission. The bank were in the position of having a building which had loose stone claddings which constituted a possible danger to users of a highway. The bank therefore took the decision to go on Trenberth's land even though they had not permission to do so and were aware that this was contrary to Trenberth's wishes. The bank's building contractor erected scaffolding and staging on and over Trenberth's land.

As soon as this trespass occurred Trenberth started an action in the High Court. Two injunctions were sought. A prohibitory injunction was sought to restrain the bank from committing any further acts of trespass. A mandatory injunction was also sought ordering the removal of the scaffolding and staging and the debris and rubbish from the land. The bank's answer to these claims was to admit the trespass but to claim that in the circumstances they had no choice. They also contested the granting of the injunctions, claiming that the award of damages would be sufficient in the circumstances. The bank also claimed that the decision in *Woollerton and Wilson Ltd v Richard Costain Ltd 1970* showed that the judge had power to grant an injunction but to suspend it for a period of time, sufficient for the work to be done, and that in these circumstances this was a proper course for the judge to adopt.

The judge was unwilling to accept any of the submissions of the bank: this was a clear case of trespass for which Trenberth were entitled to the injunctions they sought. The award of damages on its own was not appropriate. He was also unwilling to suspend any injunction: he believed that the decision in the earlier case was unreliable.

Trespass beneath the surface of the land

This form of trespass is not often encountered. Although servicing authorities lay pipes, cables, mains and other apparatus underground they have statutory powers to do these things in the event of occupiers not agreeing to the entry on the land and the laying of the services. In all other circumstances the permission of the occupier has to be obtained. The fact that the intrusion will not disturb the surface of the land, and that the occupier may be totally unaware of what has happened, does not prevent that intrusion being a trespass.

In the case of *Willcox v Kettell 1937*, Willcox and Kettell owned adjoining properties. Kettell wished to redevelop his property, which required the demolition of his property and the erection of a steel-framed building. This would require stanchions along the boundary so as to provide the necessary support to the steelwork. The proximity of this work to Willcox's building meant that the building would have to be underpinned. Willcox gave his permission for the underpinning to be carried out; however, the foundations were laid in such a way that there was intrusion for about twenty inches into Willcox's land. This was not part of Willcox's permission and therefore constituted a trespass in Willcox's opinion. Willcox sued claiming an injunction for the removal of the intruding foundation and damages.

The court accepted that there was a trespass to the subsoil. For this trespass damages were awarded but the injunction refused. The judge took the view that to remove the foundations was not reasonable and that the award of damages was the appropriate remedy.

The judge's refusal to grant an injunction has been followed by other judges but some judges take the view that it is not open to a judge to refuse an injunction and award damages only. Their belief is that occupiers cannot be forced to accept payment of damages for present and future acts of trespass. Higher judicial interpretation is desirable on this point of law.

Trespass to air space

This form of trespass is a more recent development; Parliament has legislated in order to prevent certain legal actions being brought. The Civil Aviation Act 1982 prohibits an action being brought for trespass to air space in connection with a civil aircraft flying at a reasonable height. Traffic regulations make it a criminal offence to fly a civil aircraft below a reasonable height.

The occupier of land can claim trespass only if the intrusion takes place within a reasonable height of the ground, but the courts have not fixed an exact figure for what is a reasonable height. In the case of *Lord Bernstein of Leigh v Skyviews and General Ltd 1977*, Lord Bernstein objected strongly to an aircraft of Skyviews flying over his home and taking a photograph of it. The photograph and negative were then offered for sale to him. Skyviews conducted business in this way. Lord Bernstein sued and the court had to decide whether there could be trespass to air space when an aircraft flew at a height of several hundred feet above the ground. There was a submission made on behalf of Lord Bernstein that the right to air space was unrestricted. The court refused to accept that trespass to air space had occurred: the aircraft flying several hundred feet above the ground was above a reasonable height. The judge expressed the opinion that the right of owners to the air space above their land was restricted to such height as is necessary for the ordinary use and enjoyment of their land and the structures on it; above that height they have no greater right in the air space than any other member of the public.

One case which confirmed trespass of air space was *Kelsen v Imperial Tobacco Co Ltd 1957*. An advertising sign erected by the Imperial Tobacco Company projected some eight inches into the air space immediately above Kelsen's shop. Kelsen was annoyed at this intrusion and asked for the sign to be removed. When this was refused Kelsen sued for trespass. His claim rested solely on trespass since he was unable to show any damage to his property had resulted from the erection of the sign or that any nuisance had been caused. The court agreed that the sign constituted trespass to air space and granted a mandatory injunction requiring removal of the sign. The application of this decision to the construction industry may be seen in the erection of a building or structure which intrudes into adjoining airspace or such things as intruding scaffolds or signs.

In the case of *Woollerton and Wilson Ltd v Richard Costain Ltd 1970*, a 300 foot high building was to be erected on a restricted site in the centre of Leicester. Costain considered that the restricted site would preclude the use of a mobile crane and that a tower crane would have to be positioned in one corner of the site. On this basis the work programme was drawn up and work began. Immediately adjoining the site was a factory and warehouse owned by Woollerton and Wilson Ltd. When the crane was in use its jib swung over the factory and warehouse, and when not in use it was left to swing free in the wind. Woollerton and Wilson objected to this claiming that it was trespass to airspace. When the jib passed over the property it was some fifty feet above the roof level. No damage had been caused and there was no nuisance from the use of the crane. Costain gave assurances as to the adequacy of their insurance in the event of any mishap and offered £250 for past and future trespasses. This was not acceptable to Woollerton and Wilson, who thought that a payment of £50 a week was more appropriate. Unable to reach agreement, Woollerton and Wilson started an action in the High Court claiming an injunction restraining any further acts of trespass by the jib.

Evidence was given to the court by a representative of Costain that he had no knowledge of anyone objecting to the jib of a crane swinging over their property or seeking compensation for that action. The provision of insurance cover against damage, for which no claim had ever been made, was sufficient.

The judge observed that Costain found themselves in this position by mere inadvertence and then issued a warning to contractors in the future not to enter into a contract involving the use of a crane which would swing over adjoining property without first obtaining the permission of the adjoining owner. The judge then took a course of action for which he has been criticized and which judges in later cases have declined to follow. He granted the injunction but suspended it until the contract completion date, which was almost a year ahead. He believed that the circumstances justified the use of his discretion in this way.

This decision was considered in the case of *Anchor Brewhouse Developments Ltd and Others v Berkley House (Docklands Developments) Ltd 1987*. Berkley House were owners of a large development site on which several tower cranes were erected. These cranes oversailed the land of Anchor Brewhouse and others when they were in use and when they were left to swing free. Berkley House obtained a licence to oversail the property of only one adjoining landowner. Anchor Brewhouse and the other landowners issued a writ and sought an interlocutory injunction to restrain further intrusions by the jibs of the cranes. The claim was based solely on trespass to airspace since no damage had occurred or was expected.

Berkley House contested the claim on a number of grounds, chief of which was that the oversailing did not constitute trespass. Other grounds were that no damage had been caused; that Anchor Brewhouse had not objected when the cranes were being erected; and that the award of damages was an appropriate and adequate remedy.

The High Court decided to grant the injunctions sought. The decision in *Lord Bernstein of Leigh v Skyviews and General Ltd 1977*, which was quoted by Berkley House, was of no assistance to them since it dealt with flying aircraft and not intrusion by a structure on adjoining land. The judge rejected the submission that he ought to award damages only since such damages would be nominal and not provide the remedy Anchor Brewhouse were entitled to. The judge also refused to adopt the same course as in the case of *Woollerton and Wilson* and grant an injunction but suspend its operation until the date of the contract completion: once trespass had been proved the injunction should be granted and be effective forthwith in order to protect the rights of the landowner. The fact that Berkley had sought and been granted a licence from another landowner indicated that they believed that a trespass was being committed. The judge also recalled the warning given by the judge in *Woollerton and Wilson* that contractors in the future would be warned about entering into contracts involving the use of cranes which would swing over land of an adjoining owner without first obtaining permission.

After granting the injunctions with their immediate effect the judge, who clearly was aware of the financial and other implications of his decision, reflected on the difficulties of landowners who wished to carry out developments which required the use of cranes. He accepted that an adjoining landowner could adopt a 'dog in the manger attitude' and force the developer to pay an excessive sum for the right to oversail the land. He thought that Parliament could allow the courts to fix commercial rates for oversailing rights when the parties could not agree.

A contractor who intends to make use of a crane which might give rise to trespass to airspace should obtain permission from adjoining landowners. An injunction, a breach of which would be contempt of court, would probably affect the work to such a substantial extent as to lead to financial loss.

Negligence

Negligence in the law of torts means a specific tort; it does not refer to the way in which something has been done. In ordinary language a person may be said to have been negligent when he or she was careless. The use of the word 'negligent' here does not mean that the person has committed a specific civil wrong for which he or she may be called to answer in a civil action before a court.

The modern law of negligence has its starting-point in the House of Lords' decision in the case of *Donoghue v Stevenson 1932*. From that time it has developed as a principle of law. Recently there has been a reconsideration by the courts as to the extent of this development. When economic loss is considered some changes have been of a substantial nature (see p. 177). The effect of such change is to mean that judicial decisions made over a period of years were, accepting present judicial opinion, wrongly made. If the same circumstances were to come before the courts now those decisions would be different. The extent of the change with the application of the principle to economic loss has been so substantial it will probably rank as the biggest change in the common law in the twentieth century.

Donoghue v Stevenson 1932

Mrs Donoghue with a friend went into a café in Paisley, Scotland. The friend bought a bottle of ginger-beer. The liquid was in a dark opaque bottle which had a metal cap crimped on. The shopkeeper took off the metal cap and poured some of the liquid into a tumbler. She then drank some of the contents. The friend then refilled her tumbler from the bottle; floating out came the decomposed remains of a snail. Mrs Donoghue suffered shock and severe gastro-enteritis as a result of the sight of the remains of the snail and the impurities she had consumed. She sued Stevenson the manufacturer of the ginger-beer on the ground that he had manufactured the drink for sale to the public; he had bottled it and labelled it with his own name,; and had sealed it with a metal cap. She claimed that it was Stevenson's duty to provide a system of business which would prevent snails entering the ginger-beer bottles and to have an efficient system of inspection after the bottles were filled. Stevenson's failure to satisfy both these duties, Mrs Donoghue claimed, made him liable to her.

An important point to note before the decision is considered further is that if Mrs Donoghue's friend, the purchaser of the ginger-beer, had been the one affected a similar claim would not have been made. In that circumstance there would have been a claim for breach of contract. The buying of the ginger-beer formed a contract between the friend and the shopkeeper. In contracts for the sale of food and drink there is an implied term that they shall be fit for human consumption. Mrs Donoghue was not able to make a claim for breach of contract and so had to make a claim for a breach of a duty of care owed to her.

The House of Lords agreed with the submission by Mrs Donoghue that Stevenson owed her a duty of care which did not depend on any contractual relationship: there existed in the common law some judicial decisions which supported the approach that in certain circumstances there could be a duty of care owed by one person to another.

From this decision it has been accepted that the tort of negligence is made up of three elements:

1 a duty of care
2 breach of that duty of care
3 injury resulting from that duty of care.

All three elements have to be proved if a claim is to be successful.

The question that must be asked is to whom is this duty owed? This was answered by Lord Atkin, one of the Law Lords in the case:

> The rule that you are to love your neighbour becomes, in law, you must not injure your neighbour: and the lawyer's question, who is my neighbour? receives a restricted reply. You must take reasonable care to avoid acts or omissions which you can reasonably foresee would be likely to injure your neighbour. Who, then, in law is my neighbour? The answer seems to be – persons who are so closely and directly affected by my act that I ought reasonably to have them in contemplation as being so affected when I am directing my mind to the acts or omissions which are called in question.

Consideration of Lord Atkin's statement shows that a duty of care will be owed to those the law believes a person ought reasonably to have in mind as being likely to be affected by acts or omissions. Liability may arise from something done, an act, or something not done, an omission. Such acts or omissions require reasonable care in their avoidance and they have to be reasonably foreseeable.

The use of the words 'reasonable' and 'reasonably' indicate that the tort is not one of strict liability. If a person has done that which is reasonable, no liability falls on that person. If a person has guarded against that which is reasonably foreseeable, again there is no liability.

Initially the decision was applied in a restricted manner even though the courts accepted that there was power for them to apply the decision in circumstances which had not previously been before the courts. This was a gradual process, which in the 1970s and 1980s accelerated to the point where the courts feared that the floodgates were open and control by the courts was being lost. The opening of the floodgates and their closing are to be seen in four House of Lords' decisions.

The first case was *Home Office v Dorset Yacht Co Ltd 1970*, where seven borstal trainees, all of whom had criminal records for burglary, theft and dishonesty, were working on an island in Poole harbour. They were under the care and supervision of borstal officers. One night they escaped, boarded a yacht and caused it to collide with another yacht owned by Dorset Yacht. When Dorset Yacht sued a number of grounds were put forward as defences. The principal one was that the Home Office, employer of the borstal officers, did not owe any duty of care to the public to ensure that the trainees did not cause harm, because there was no previous authority for imposing such a duty. Lord Reid, the senior Law Lord, dealt with this by saying:

> Lord Atkin's speech should I think be regarded as a statement of principle. It is

not to be treated as if it were a statutory definition. It will require qualification in new circumstances. But I think that the time has come when we can and should say that it ought to apply unless there is some justification or valid explanation for its exclusion.

So here the Law Lords were saying that the tort of negligence would apply unless there were circumstances which showed that it ought not to apply. This reversed the previous approach that it had to be shown that negligence ought to apply, based usually on some previous decision.

The second was *Anns v London Borough of Merton 1977*, where the House of Lords decided that both the builder and the local authority whose building control officer had negligently approved foundations as satisfying the standard of the building regulations were under a duty of care to an owner of a flat. The owner's flat had cracks in the walls which meant that underpinning would be required. The Law Lords accepted that Anns was entitled to succeed even though there had been no collapse of the building or damage other than cracks in the walls. This loss was economic loss in that it would mean that the value of the flat would be reduced because of the damage.

In the third case, *Junior Books Ltd v Veitchi Ltd 1982*, Junior Books were having a factory built and nominated Veitchi as specialist sub-contractors for the laying of a concrete floor with a special surface. Two years later the floor was found to be defective and its relaying with consequent disruption to business operations would be costly. Junior Books sued Veitchi for breach of duty of care under the tort of negligence. There was no contractual relationship between them. The Law Lords held that there was liability because of the close proximity between Junior Books and Veitchi which fell just short of a contractual relationship. Furthermore this duty of care extended to a duty to avoid faults being present in the work or articles.

These three cases showed a willingness to apply the principle of *Donoghue v Stevenson* in almost every circumstance. Some members of the judiciary, however, viewed this development with alarm: it created an almost uncontrollable situation. There was also a change in the Law Lords, with retirements and new appointments.

The House of Lords case which turned the clock back to the position prior to these cases was *Murphy v Brentwood District Council 1990*. A construction company submitted plans and calculations for a concrete raft foundation for a pair of semi-detached houses. The local authority used a firm of consulting engineers to check these details. Approval was recommended. Eleven years later Murphy, who had bought the house from the builders, noticed serious cracking in the walls, caused by the foundations being defective. Murphy, who was unable to pay the cost of the remedial work, sold the house for some £35 000 less than its market value. He was successful with his claim in the High Court and the Court of Appeal. The House of Lords, however, overruled the decision in the Anns case and held that a local authority in exercising their functions of building control owed no duty of care for the cost of remedial work needed because of the local authority's negligent failure to see that a building was designed or constructed in accordance with the building regulations.

With this decision the Law Lords indicated their disapproval of previous decisions and pointed to the future of a more restricted application of the tort of negligence.

Economic loss

The courts were unwilling to hold that there could be a duty to avoid causing economic loss. With one important exception, the case of *Hedley Byrne and Co Ltd v Heller and Partners Ltd 1964* (see p. 215), the approach of the courts is that economic loss is not recoverable unless it is associated with physical damage to property or personal injury. So a worker injured in an industrial accident for which he is blameless and which causes a loss of wages may sue for that loss of earnings as well as damages for his injuries. With physical damage an example would be the motorist involved in an accident with another car, the driver of which was to blame. The innocent motorist, provided she could show proper need, could hire another car while her own was being repaired. The cost of the hire would be recoverable as economic loss associated with physical damage.

The House of Lords' decision in *Hedley Byrne and Co Ltd v Heller and Partners Ltd 1964* is important to professional people and in that respect is considered in more detail later (p. 215). Hedley Byrne, who were advertising agents, were approached by a company called Easipower Ltd with regard to advertising Easipower's products. Hedley Byrne had to place an order for advertising for which they would be personally liable; the sum involved was some £17 000. Before committing themselves Hedley Byrne decided to check the financial standing of Easipower; they asked their bankers to obtain this information from Heller and Partners. A favourable report was made by a letter which was headed 'For your private use and without responsibility on the part of this bank or its officials'. On the basis of this report Hedley Byrne placed the order, but the information as to the financial standing was incorrect. Easipower went into liquidation and the expenditure of £17 000 could not be recovered. Hedley Byrne sued Heller and Partners claiming that there was a duty of care owed to them not to make a negligent misstatement and that Heller and Partners had breached this duty which had caused injury to Hedley Byrne.

The House of Lords decided that there was a duty of care in the tort of negligence not to make negligent misstatements. In Hedley Byrne's case, however, the giving of the information had been made under the protection of a disclaimer of liability, which gave full protection to Heller and Partners.

An example of the application of the rule that, with the exception just considered, economic loss is irrecoverable is the case of *S C M (UK) Ltd v W J Whittall and Son Ltd 1971*. Whittall, who were building contractors, were excavating in a road in Birmingham, in an area containing many factories. While excavating a trench in the road an employee cut a high voltage cable, interrupting the power supply for more than several hours to a number of the factories. In the factory of S C M (UK) Ltd, which manufactured office machinery, the loss of power caused molten plastic to solidify in extrusion machines. Machines had to be stripped down and the solidified material chipped off, causing damage to certain parts and required their replacement. There was therefore a loss of value of the parts and of profits from failure to produce goods. S C M (UK) Ltd sued claiming negligence. The decision of the Court of Appeal was that damages would be awarded for the physical damage and the economic loss associated with that physical damage. The economic loss was the loss of profit when the damaged machines were out of production. The court refused to award damages for loss of profits from the undamaged machines which could not produce because of the loss of the electric power. This claim was economic loss on its own and to allow it would be contrary to judicial policy.

Liability for construction works

The substantial change in the approach of the courts to the duty of care where economic loss on its own was concerned has been based on cases where defective building work was at issue. These cases have been considered with regard to economic loss but further consideration as to their application to liability for defective construction works is desirable.

In the case of *Dutton v Bognor Regis Urban District Council 1972*, a builder built a house in accordance with plans approved by the local authority with its construction being subject to the usual inspections by the local authority's building control officer. The house was sold to a Mr Clark, who lived in it for just over a year and then because of a change of employment sold it to Mrs Dutton. Because the house was new she did not have a full structural survey but relied on the building society's valuation survey, which was satisfactory; the building society advanced the mortgage loan. A few months later cracks appeared in the wall of the house. A detailed survey then revealed that the foundations were not to building regulations standard: the building control officer had been negligent in approving the foundations. The cost of the remedial work exceeded the value of the house. Mrs Dutton sued the builder and the local authority. The builder, with whom Mrs Dutton had no contractual relationship, disputed any liability. There was a judicial decision which supported this opinion and so Mrs Dutton accepted a sum of money as settlement of any claim she might have against him. She sued the local authority claiming that a duty of care was owed by their building control officer to her.

The Court of Appeal observed that this was the first time a claim had been made against a council for negligence in approving a house. The court examined the principles of law involved and then decided that the council were liable. There was a duty of care under the statutory provisions dealing with council control over building work. There was a sufficient proximity between the building control officer and Mrs Dutton for that duty of care to be owed to her. There had been a breach of that duty of care which had resulted in injury to Mrs Dutton. The court also decided that the builder too should be liable, so overruling the earlier judicial decision. The matter of the loss being economic loss and so irrecoverable was answered by the Master of the Rolls, Lord Denning:

> The damage done here was not solely economic loss. It was physical damage to the house. If counsel's submission were right, it would mean that, if the inspector negligently passes the house as properly built and it collapses and injures a person, the council are liable; but, if the owner discovers the defect in time to repair it – and he does repair it – the council are not liable. That is an impossible distinction. They are liable in either case.

His Lordship was also conscious that this development could be opening the floodgates to innumerable actions. He among all the judges has been apprehensive of this danger. He said: 'Will it lead to a flood of cases which the council will not be able to handle, nor the courts? Such considerations have sometimes in the past led the courts to reject novel claims. But I see no need to reject this claim on this ground'.

This Court of Appeal decision was confirmed by the House of Lords in the case of *Anns v London Borough of Merton 1977* (see p. 176). This case was similar to Mrs Dutton's case in that there was no collapse of a structure or building or personal injury; there were cracks in the walls of a flat which were caused by inadequate foundations. Again the cost of remedial work was substantial. The Law Lords agreed with the Court of Appeal's approach with regard to a duty of care and breach of that duty of care. The senior Law Lord, Lord Wilberforce, then said that the course of action could arise only 'when the state of the building is such that there is present or imminent danger to the health or safety of persons occupying it'.

These words form the test applied when there was a question of liability for negligent building work. Once it could be shown that a local authority's building control officer had been negligent, the local authority's insurers would settle the claim without resort to litigation. While the floodgates were not thrown wide open they were partly open and claims were made on an increasing scale. Claims were even made against local authorities by persons who had actually been responsible for the defective work: it was the local authority's duty to check the building work and if they were negligent in doing this then the builder could claim.

The House of Lords in the case of *Governors of the Peabody Donation Fund v Sir Lindsay Parkinson and Co Ltd and Others 1984* indicated their disapproval of the way in which the Anns case had developed. Peabody were developing land of their own for residential purposes. Plans had been approved, including those for drainage schemes. Unknown to Peabody or their architects the resident architect and the local authority's drainage inspector changed the drainage plans so that rigid pipes and joints were to be used instead of flexible pipes and joints as had been approved. Rigid pipes and joints were unsuitable for the ground conditions so that they fractured and had to be replaced. Peabody sued the main contractors, the local authority and the architects.

The Law Lords decided that in these circumstances there was no duty of care owed by the local authority and consequently no liability for the cost of the remedial works. Parliament could not have intended in the relevant statutory provisions to have required local authorities to protect owners against their own failure to comply with the provisions. Peabody had failed to conform to the approved plans and this prevented them succeeding in their claim against the local authority.

The doubt raised that there might not be a duty of care for economic loss in construction contracts was strengthened by two decisions of the Court of Appeal. In both cases the decision of the House of Lords in *Junior Books Ltd v Veitchi Ltd 1982* (see p. 181) was unsuccessfully quoted to show that liability existed.

The first case was *Simaan General Contracting Co v Pilkington Glass Ltd (No. 2) 1988*. Simaan were main contractors for the construction in Abu Dhabi of a building which used double glazed units of green glass, incorporated in the curtain walling of the building. The supply and erection of the curtain walling was sub-contracted; the specification required the glass to be supplied by Pilkington. When supplied and installed it was found that the glass was not of a uniform colour; until it was replaced payment to the main contractor was withheld. Simaan claimed that Pilkington owed them a duty of care to avoid defects in the units.

The Court of Appeal took the view that, in the absence of a contract between Simaan and Pilkington, a claim could not be brought for economic loss on its own. Pilkington had not in any way voluntarily assumed direct responsibility for the quality of the glass to be supplied. There was no duty of care to ensure that Simaan's contract did not become less profitable. Simaan had a contractual relationship with the sub-contractor which would have allowed Simaan to sue for breach of contract. The sub-contractor could then have sued Pilkington for breach of contract for the supply of the contract, subject to any exemption clauses.

The second case was *Greater Nottingham Co-operative Society Ltd v Cementation Piling and Foundations Ltd and Others 1988*. The Co-operative Society were extending and altering their office premises and Cementation were sub-contractors for the piling work. Cementation also entered into a collateral contract with the Co-operative Society that they would exercise reasonable skill and care in the design of the works and the selection of materials. One of Cementation's employees negligently operated the piling equipment so causing damage to an adjoining building. Work had to stop and a revised piling scheme worked out, which caused delay to the main contractor and additional costs because of the revised piling scheme. These costs had to be paid by the Society to the main contractor. The Society also claimed a large sum for the delayed completion of the building.

The Court of Appeal dismissed the claim by the Society on two grounds. First, the loss being claimed was economic loss and that only in exceptional circumstances would such a claim be allowed. Second, the parties to the dispute had entered into a contract which did not provide for liability for economic loss; it could have done if the parties had so decided, thus there was no liability.

The move against being able to claim for economic loss for defective construction work gathered momentum with the House of Lords' decision in *D and F Estates Ltd and Others v Church Commissioners for England and Others 1988*. A sub-contractor was appointed by the main contractor for the plastering work to a block of flats being built for the Church Commissioners. Because of the sub-contractor's failure to follow the plaster manufacturer's instructions the plaster was not properly keyed to the walls and ceilings of a flat owned by D and F Estates. This was discovered to affect a room when it was being redecorated and the necessary remedial work cost some £10 676. Later the other rooms were found to be similarly affected and the estimated cost of this work, together with loss of rent while the work was being done, was the subject of a claim principally against the main contractor on the ground that a duty of care was owed by them as to the work of their sub-contractor.

The House of Lords refused to find any liability on the part of the main contractors. There was no contractual arrangement between them and as there was no personal injury or physical damage to other property the cost of repairing the plasterwork was economic loss for which the main contractors were not liable. Added to this was the rule in tort that a person who appoints an apparently competent independent contractor was not liable for their negligence in doing their work. As this decision apparently contradicted the decision in the Anns case clarification was needed.

This clarification came in the case of *Murphy v Brentwood District Council 1990* (see p. 176). As the House of Lords was possibly going to overrule a decision they had made less than fifteen years earlier, seven Law Lords dealt with the case instead of the usual five. The claim was for economic loss since Murphy had sold his house with its defective foundations for some £35 000 less than its market value. The Law Lords overruled the Anns case and the earlier Court of Appeal decision in Dutton's case, because they were unable to support the previous opinion that a local authority in carrying out their statutory functions would be liable for the expense of remedial work to a building which had a dangerous defect as a result of negligence in not ensuring that the building met the appropriate standards. This was a departure from established principle which could not be justified. The Law Lords did, however, leave open the question of liability for personal injury and being able to sue for defective equipment in a building such as central heating boilers or electrical installations provided by other contractors. The Law Lords also drew attention to the fact that Parliament had passed the Defective Premises Act 1972, which made builders liable in certain circumstances.

Junior Books Ltd v Veitchi Ltd 1982

As this case was not overruled by the decision in Murphy's case and was considered in a number of cases leading up to that decision it requires separate consideration. The facts of the case were given earlier (p. 176). The distinguishing factor is that Veitchi were specialist sub-contractors approached by Junior Books to ascertain if they could undertake the laying of a concrete floor with a special finish. Junior Books, on being satisfied that Veitchi were competent, nominated them for the work and the main contractor made a contract with Veitchi: there was no contractual relationship between Junior Books and Veitchi. The Law Lords, however, treated their relationship as being proximate to a contractual relationship and held that there was a duty of care owed by Veitchi to Junior Books. Veitchi knew that Junior Books relied on them to lay a proper floor; that the damage was a direct result of their failure to lay a proper floor; and that they ought to have known that this failure would cause economic loss.

This case stands on its own special facts, but if another case with similar facts came before the courts it could be used as a precedent.

Present position of liability for defective construction works

Lord Denning's belief that the decision in Dutton's case would not open the floodgates was misplaced: the courts became sufficiently alarmed to close the floodgates in a number of decisions culminating in Murphy's case. The present position cannot be stated with general certainty since in Murphy's case some matters were left open, but what does seem certain is that claims for economic loss will be unsuccessful. Where there is physical damage, such as a collapse that causes personal injury, a claim may be possible; a collapse causing damage to an adjoining property or damage arising from the provision of ancillary equipment such as boilers or electrical installations could also form the basis of an acceptable claim. What, however, will not be considered as an acceptable claim would be to treat a building as a complex structure made up of individual parts, so that the failure of one unit which causes damage to another unit would not create liability.

The reference in Murphy's case (and in earlier cases) of Parliament having passed the Defective Premises Act 1972 indicated the Law Lords' belief that future claims would be brought under the provisions of the Act. Any claims made will have to be connected with the provision of dwellings, whether by erection, conversion or extension, since the Act deals specifically with dwellings, despite its title, and not with the construction of industrial and commercial buildings.

Rescuer principle

The courts have been asked to decide what duty, if any, is owed by a wrongdoer who by his negligent act puts a person at risk and another person in coming to the rescue is injured or loses her life. In the case of *Haynes v Harwood 1935*, two horses with a van bolted in a crowded street putting those present at peril. A policeman on duty in a police station ran out and in stopping the horses was crushed when one fell on him. The Court of Appeal decided that there was a duty of care owed to the rescuer.

The rescuer principle is based on public policy: persons should be encouraged to involve themselves in rescue attempts and that if in doing so they should themselves be injured or lose their lives then the person whose negligence created the situation will be liable for that loss. The fact that a person is under no legal duty to make the attempt is no defence. The defence of *volenti non fit injuria* is thus not applicable in rescuer cases; the principle does apply, however, only when persons are in imminent danger to their life or person.

In the case of *Baker v Hopkins (T E) and Sons 1959*, Hopkins were carrying out maintenance work to a water well at a farm using three employees, two of whom were working down the well with the third dealing with operations on the surface. A petrol-driven engine was being used down the well without an exhaust for the fumes to the surface of the ground. The two employees in the well became unconscious and the third man raised the alarm. Among those telephoned was the local doctor, who arrived first on the scene. He tied a rope around his waist and went down the well after giving instructions that if he signalled he was to be pulled to the surface immediately. When he signalled, the rope fouled equipment in the well and he could not be pulled clear. He died and his widow sued.

The Court of Appeal decided that the widow's claim must succeed. The defence that the doctor was under no duty to do what he did, that he had volunteered and so was owed no duty was rejected. Hopkins's negligence had created a situation where the doctor had a moral duty to try to rescue the men down the well. In the circumstance he was owed a duty of care.

Standard of care

If a duty of care is owed, the question that arises is what is required with that duty of care. The person under a duty of care is required to act as a reasonable person would in those circumstances. If reasonable care is exercised, then no more is to be expected of that person: the tort of negligence is based on the duty to take reasonable care to avoid acts or omissions which could be reasonably foreseen as likely to injure the person to whom that duty is owed.

In the case of *Bolton v Stone 1951*, Miss Stone was standing on a highway outside her house. A cricket match was being played on a ground on the other side of the highway. A batsman struck the ball so that it cleared a seven foot high fence by the side of the highway and hit Miss Stone, causing her serious injuries. She sued the cricket club. The playing area was ten feet below the level of the highway; in order to reduce the possibility of balls being hit on to the highway the seven foot high fence had been erected. The ground had been used for playing cricket since 1864, which was before the houses adjoining the highway were built. It was believed that a ball had been hit on to the highway on only six occasions in the last thirty years.

The House of Lords decided that Miss Stone's claim could not succeed: what the cricket club had done to guard against the risk of a ball being hit on to the highway was reasonable care. The risk of injury was remote: it would not be reasonable to require the cricket club to stop playing cricket on the ground or to increase the height of the fence.

Clearly the greater the risk of injury, the more a reasonable person would expect precautions to be taken. Where there is a risk of serious injury, substantial expenditure is necessary to guard against that risk. In the case of *Paris v Stepney Borough Council 1951*, Paris was an employee of the council, which knew that Paris had sight in one eye only. The risk of total blindness if the sight of the good eye was affected was obvious. Paris was working beneath a council vehicle carrying out a task for which it was not normal for the council to provide protective goggles. He struck at some metal and a splinter flew off, entered the good eye and made him totally blind. The House of Lords held the council to be liable. The council's defence that he was doing a job for which it was normal practice not to provide goggles was rejected. Paris was a special risk and so more was needed by way of protection.

People who hold themselves out to have a particular skill are expected to have the skill of the average member of their profession. If their performance falls below the standard of that average member of the profession then they are liable for negligence.

The standard of care is based on the reasonable person: that is the standard (see p. 213). English law does not recognize degrees of standard.

Res ipsa Loquitur

People who sue claiming damages for negligence are obliged to satisfy the burden of proof if they are to succeed: they have to show on the balance of probabilities that they have proved their case. It is, however, possible to plead in their case *res ipsa loquitur*, that the 'thing speaks for itself': something is so obvious that in the absence of an adequate answer the claim will succeed. In the case of *Scott v London and St Katherine's Docks Co 1865*, a customs officer was walking past the Docks warehouse when some bags of sugar fell on him, causing injuries. The customs officer was held entitled to succeed since in the circumstances the absence of explanation of the Docks Co meant that the accident had been caused by negligence.

For *res ipsa loquitur* to apply it is necessary to show that three requirements have been satisfied:

1 control
2 accident must be such as could not in the ordinary course of things have happened without negligence
3 absence of explanation.

First, control means that the defendants or someone for whom they have responsibility must be shown to have control of the circumstances which led to the accident.

Second, what has happened must be something which in the circumstances would not normally happen. Examples accepted by the courts have included vehicles driving on the wrong side of the road or striking a pedestrian on the pavement.

Third, absence of an explanation means that there is no evidence of the cause of accident. Where the facts are sufficiently known and can be established, negligence can be proved on those facts. If the facts known are insufficient to establish negligence on their own, *res ipsa loquitur* may apply. Where this has been pleaded but is unsuccessful, negligence may be proved on the known facts. In the case of *Barkway v South Wales Transport Co Ltd 1950*, a passenger in a bus was killed when the bus left the road and went down an embankment. Evidence showed that the cause of the accident was a defect in a tyre, which might have been discovered if the bus company had had a system of drivers' reporting occurrences which could have caused damage to tyres. The House of Lords decided that the evidence produced was sufficient for negligence to be established, so *res ipsa loquitur* did not apply.

Breach of duty of care

If a person fails to meet the reasonable person standard (see p. 213), then there is by that person a breach of the duty of care, depending on the facts of each case. The deciding factor is whether a reasonable person would have acted in that particular way.

Injury resulting from that breach of duty of care

The injury for which damages may be claimed must be something recognized in law. Furthermore the law puts a limit on the extent of the injury, that is a claim made for an injury may be refused because it is considered to be too remote to the negligence which gave rise to the injury. The principle used to determine the remoteness of damage is based on a case from Australia decided by the Judicial Committee of the Privy Council, which is composed of the same Law Lords as sit in the House of Lords and acts (now in a most limited way) as the final court of appeal from British colonies and dominions.

The case is the *Overseas Tankship (UK) Ltd v Morts Dock and Engineering Co Ltd 1961*, which is usually referred to as *The Wagon Mound No 1*. The ship *The Wagon Mound* was taking on oil in Sydney Harbour. By a negligent act of one of the ship's crew a large quantity of oil was allowed to discharge into the harbour. The oil spread to Morts Dock's wharf where a ship, *The Corrimal*, was undergoing repairs that involved welding work. Morts Dock sought advice as to the continuance of the welding operations and the risk of fire. On being assured that it was safe to continue welding this was resumed. About sixty hours later a spark fell and set fire to some cotton waste or rag floating on the oil. A fire quickly developed and caused serious damage to the wharf.

The question to be decided was whether the shipowners were liable for this damage. The decision was that the test to be applied was whether the damage could reasonably be foreseen. It was decided that it could not reasonably be foreseen that the oil would catch fire which had been negligently discharged.

Another case on the same facts was *Overseas Tankship (UK) Ltd v The Miller Steamship Co Pty 1966*, known as *The Wagon Mound No 2*. The owners of the ship which was being repaired at Morts Dock sued. In the light of new evidence, the decision was that it was reasonably foreseeable that a fire would result from the discharge of oil. The owners of the ship were successful with their claim.

Two cases show the extent to which liability extends to that which is reasonably foreseeable. In the case of *Hughes v Lord Advocate 1963*, Hughes, an eight-year-old boy, and another ten-year-old boy were playing on a street in Edinburgh. A nine foot deep manhole containing cables of the Post Office was open for work to be carried out. A shelter tent was erected over it. At the end of the working day the Post Office workers left; the boys started playing around the paraffin warning lamps which had been left around the tent. Hughes was swinging one of the lamps over the hole, when he stumbled and dropped the lamp into the hole. An explosion occurred from the vaporized paraffin. Hughes fell into the hole and was seriously burned.

The House of Lords held the Post Office to be liable. The fact that Hughes would be injured by some accident or occurrence was a reasonably foreseeable event, though the way in which the events developed could not be foreseen.

In the case of *Bradford v Robinson Rentals Ltd 1967*, Bradford was a van driver for Robinson Rentals. In very severe winter weather Bradford was sent on a long journey in unheated vans. He spent twenty-four hours in two days in the vans and suffered frostbite as a result. He was successful in his claim for damages.

If the personal injury or harm is unusual, however, it is probably not reasonably foreseeable and may be too remote for the affected person to succeed in a claim. In the case of *Tremain v Pike 1969*, Tremain was a herdsman who worked for Pike on his farm. Tremain while working for Pike contracted an unusual disease, Weil's disease, from coming into contact with rat urine. The judge recognized that harm from rats was reasonably foreseeable and cited examples such as rat bites or food poisoning following consumption of food or drink which had been contaminated by rats. Weil's disease, however, in the judge's opinion, was something entirely different in kind. It was a rare disease, it was not foreseeable and so Tremain's claim failed.

In the case of *Lamb and Another v London Borough of Camden and Another 1981*, Mrs Lamb owned a house in Camden. In 1972 she let the house and went to America. In 1973 contractors working for the council were laying a sewer when they broke a water main; the flow of water undermined the foundations and the house subsided. The house was vacated in order for repairs to be carried out. In 1974 squatters moved in but were evicted; in 1975 squatters moved in again and extensive damage was caused. Legal action was necessary to evict them. Eventually extensive works were done to restore the foundations and put the house in a proper state. The cost of remedial work to the foundations was £50 000 for which the council accepted liability. A further sum of £30 000 was claimed as the expense of restoring the house after the damage done to it by the squatters. The council denied liability for this sum. In the High Court the judge decided that squatting was a reasonably foreseeable risk, but that the house stood in an area where it was unlikely to occur. This made the damage caused by the squatters too remote to be recovered.

Mrs Lamb's appeal to the Court of Appeal was dismissed. The reasoning of the judges in coming to this decision varied. The Master of the Rolls, Lord Denning, thought that because it was Mrs Lamb's responsibility to keep squatters out and to evict them when they got in, this meant that the council were not liable for the damage. He also thought that as a matter of public policy some loss should be borne by insurance: Mrs Lamb ought to have been insured against damage to the house and theft and if she were not then that was her misfortune. The other judges approached the matter on the basis whether it was reasonably foreseeable that a contractor's worker breaking a water main would cause a house to be extensively damaged by squatters some time later. They decided that it was not reasonably foreseeable: it was too remote.

Novus actus interveniens

There are circumstances where a person suffers injury as the result of something happening further down the chain of events that started with the act of negligence. Is the person who has been negligent liable for this injury or has there been a *novus actus interveniens* (a new intervening act) which has broken the chain of events? If the new intervening act has broken the chain, there is no liability for the later injury. The break in the chain will occur only if whatever happened was not reasonably foreseeable.

Intervening events may occur in a number of ways; the particular circumstances will determine whether or not what has happened was reasonably foreseeable or not. In the case of *Carslogie Steamship Co Ltd v Royal Norwegian Government 1952*, a ship owned by Carslogie was in collision with one owned by the Norwegian Government, which was responsible for the collision. After temporary repairs, which made Carslogie's ship seaworthy, it set out to go to the United States. Had the collision not occurred then this voyage would not have been made. During the voyage the ship suffered heavy storm damage. On arrival in the United States, in addition to the permanent repairs needed for the collision damage, the storm damage had to be repaired, but this cost could not be recovered. In the opinion of the House of Lords it was an intervening event and not reasonably foreseeable.

In the case of *McKew v Holland and Hannen and Cubitts (Scotland) Ltd 1969*, McKew had suffered an injury in an accident for which Holland and Hannen and Cubitts were liable. As a result of the accident, he occasionally lost control of his left leg. A few days after the accident, together with members of his family, he went to inspect a flat. The approach to the flat was by a steep staircase between two walls, which did not have a handrail. Whilst descending the stairs, holding the hand of his small daughter, he lost control of his left leg and in the emergency threw his daughter back to save her, and jumped hoping to land in an upright position and so avoid falling down the stairs. He fractured his ankle. The Law Lords decided that there had been an intervening event which had been brought about by his own conduct: he ought not to have put himself in the position whereby the emergency arose. He could have descended the stairs on his own, taking care, or he could have had the assistance of his wife or others in the party. His conduct was unreasonable in those circumstances. If he had had no reasonable alternative, then his conduct would not have broken the chain of events.

Nervous shock

A topic which causes difficulty to the courts is the right of a person to claim damages for nervous shock. Initially the courts required that the person claiming for nervous shock had to show that it was reasonably foreseeable, which meant that the person affected had to have been present at the accident that caused the nervous shock. The courts now have a more flexible approach and award damages where a person did not actually witness the accident but the circumstances were such (for example a close relationship and death or severe injuries) that being informed as to what had happened could cause nervous shock which the courts would accept as being reasonably foreseeable. The approach of the courts on this matter varies: this was evident with the claims made by relatives of victims of recent disasters at sports grounds.

The leading case on the topic is *Mcloughlin v O'Brian 1982*. Mr Mcloughlin and his three children were in a car which because of O'Brian's negligence was involved in an accident. All four were injured with one child dying almost at once. An hour later Mrs Mcloughlin, who was at her home some two miles away, was told by a friend of the accident. Mrs Mcloughlin was driven to the hospital where she was informed of the death of her child and she saw the injured members of her family. Mrs Mcloughlin was not a woman of a weak disposition but as a result of these events she suffered severe shock, depression and a change of personality.

The House of Lords accepted that Mrs Mcloughlin was entitled to succeed in her claim even though she was two miles from the accident. The other grounds were given varying relevance by the different Law Lords. They all accepted that there would be liability if the nervous shock was reasonably foreseeable: this was to be decided on the relationship between the injured and the claimant; the nearness to the accident, both in time and place; the severity of the injuries; and the means whereby knowledge of the accident was acquired.

The decision in Mcloughlin's case was considered by the Court of Appeal in the case of *Attia v British Gas PLC 1987*, which was heard as a preliminary point of law, that is the court is being asked to give a decision on a point of law without detailed consideration of all the facts of the case. It may follow that the parties to the action will settle the dispute without further recourse to the courts if liability is held to be possible in the circumstances. It may, however, not be dealt within that way and the parties then take the dispute before the courts.

Mrs Attia had engaged British Gas to install central heating in her house; she returned home one afternoon to see smoke coming from the loft of the house. She telephoned for the fire brigade. By the time the fire had been brought under control the house and its contents were severely damaged. So far as this part of Mrs Attia's claims was concerned, liability was admitted and payment made. Mrs Attia also claimed damages for nervous shock and psychological reaction caused by seeing her house on fire. This was disputed since it was claimed, as a matter of law and public policy, damages for nervous shock could be awarded only if the shock was caused by fear of death or injury to a closely related person, and was not recoverable if the shock was caused merely by damage to property.

The Court of Appeal decided as a point of law that a claim for nervous shock or psychiatric damage resulting from witnessing the consequences of a person's negligence was not limited to the effect of witnessing personal injury. There could be liability where a person suffered nervous shock or psychiatric damage as a result of seeing her home and property destroyed by fire. This finding meant that the case was sent for trial in order to determine whether Mrs Attia had suffered nervous shock or psychiatric damage and whether that had been caused by seeing the destruction of her home by the fire from the negligence of British Gas.

Occupiers' Liability Acts 1957 and 1984

Before the passing of the 1957 Act the duty of an occupier of premises to those who came on his or her premises was governed by the rules of the common law, which put visitors into three categories: invitees, licensees and trespassers. The occupier owed a higher duty of care to invitees, since the occupier had invited them to enter, than to licensees, who were present without an invitation but were permitted to be there. To a trespasser no duty of care was owed other than not to create an additional danger when a trespasser was known to be on the land. Substantial difficulties arose with the common law rules regarding invitees and licensees: courts on occasions sought to move a visitor into the category of licensee rather than trespasser, so that a duty was owed and damages could be awarded. Parliament therefore remedied the situation by the Occupiers' Liability Act 1957, in which new rules were created. Some common law rules were not affected and some judicial decisions remain to which reference is necessary. There are circumstances where the common law tort of negligence is relevant. Claims can be made based on both the duty under negligence and that under the Act.

The Occupiers' Liability Act 1984 was passed by Parliament in order to clarify a decision of the House of Lords which had created a new principle of law with regard to trespassers which was somewhat difficult to apply in practice. The case was *British Railways Board v Herrington 1972*.

Premises to which the 1957 Act applies

Under Section 1 of the Act the duties under the Act apply to land, buildings, fixed or moveable structures, including any vessel, vehicle or aircraft. These also govern liability in respect of damage to property as well as injury, including the property of persons not themselves visitors.

On a construction site, the land, buildings and structures are all features to which the provisions of the Act apply; the inclusion of moveable structures in the definition would cover moveable tower scaffolds, cranes and ladders. In the case of *Wheeler v Copas 1981* Wheeler was a self-employed bricklayer. Under a 'labour only' contract with Copas he undertook work, for which Copas was to provide the materials and equipment needed. A ladder was provided which was unsuitable as it was not a builder's ladder but a fruit picker's ladder. The ladder broke when Wheeler was using it. As part of his claim Wheeler said that Copas owed a duty under the Occupiers' Liability Act 1957 with regard to the ladder. The judge rejected this part of the claim since once the ladder was handed over Copas could not be the occupier under the Act. If, however, this had not been the case, the decision would have been that the Act applied.

Occupier

There is no definition in the Act as to the person who is the occupier; this has to be answered by the use of the common law rules. It is not simply a matter of physical occupation; it is more a matter of the degree of control over the premises, which may not belong exclusively to one person, but may be shared. A person can be an occupier even though that person has not taken possession of premises in any way.

The leading case on this matter is *Wheat v E Lacon and Co Ltd 1966*, where Lacon and Co were a brewery company which owned a public house at Great Yarmouth. Mr Richardson was the manager of the premises. The ground floor was the licensed part and the upper floor was occupied by Mr and Mrs Richardson as their private dwelling. Mrs Richardson had permission to take in private guests. Mr and Mrs Wheat were staying as guests. At about 9.00 pm, when it was getting dark, Mr Wheat fell down the back staircase to the private part of the premises and was killed. It was accepted that there were two causes for the accident: the handrail did not extend to the bottom of the stairs and someone had removed the bulb from the light at the top of the stairs.

The question to be decided was who was the occupier under the Act. The Law Lords decided that the brewery company were occupiers of the ground floor, and also of the upper floor occupied by the Richardsons, because the upper floor had not been formally leased to Mr Richardson but he had been licensed to occupy it. Furthermore they had retained the right to do repairs to the upper floor: this was a sufficient degree of control to make them occupiers. Mr and Mrs Richardson also had a sufficient degree of control to make them occupiers under the Act. All three were therefore occupiers under the Act.

The fact that there may be more than one occupier under the Act is a relevant matter in determining liability for mishaps on construction sites. Sub-contractors are allocated areas for their use and so will be occupiers. The main contractor will be the occupier outside that area and may, depending on the circumstances, be an occupier of the sub-contractors' areas.

In the case of *AMF International Ltd v Magnet Bowling and Another 1968*, Magnet were having a bowling alley built by a main contractor, Trenthams Ltd. AMF were specialist floor layers for the bowling alleys. AMF were not sub-contractors of Trenthams but had a direct contract with Magnet, which provided for AMF to be able to proceed without interruption from a fixed date. The contract between Magnet and Trenthams provided for an indemnity to Magnet against liability in respect of damage to property arising out of the execution of the works if it was due to Trenthams' negligence. The bills of quantities required Trenthams to divert storm water, to protect the works and materials from injury by weather and to prevent the accumulation of water on the site.

A heavy storm occurred and flood water entered the building through a doorway which had been inadequately sealed. The water came from unconnected rainwater pipes. The sixteen bowling alleys were damaged with a loss of £21 453, which AMF claimed against both Magnet and Trenthams. The claims were based on negligence and breach of duty of care under the Occupiers' Liability Act 1957. The claim against Magnet also was for breach of contract.

The High Court decided that AMF could succeed against both as both were occupiers under the Act. Magnet were in breach as occupiers since they had not checked to see that the building would be ready for AMF's work and they had failed to give instructions with regard to anti-flooding precautions. Trenthams were also liable as occupiers because they had failed to take reasonable care to provide temporary precautions against flooding.

The House of Lords' decision in *Ferguson v Welsh and Others 1987* needs to be noted for the suggestion made that in particular circumstances an occupier may be liable for an unsafe system of work used by a contractor on a site. A local authority as part of a sheltered housing development required the demolition of a building. Mr Spence was awarded the contract. The invitation to tender required approval before any sub-contractor could be employed on the site and that any such sub-contractor should have public liability insurance. The demolition was to be done in accordance with 'The British Standards Institution – Code of Practice for Demolition' CP94.

Spence arranged with two brothers, named Welsh, to carry out the demolition. Approval for this arrangement was not sought from the local authority and they did not have insurance. The Welsh brothers offered Ferguson a job on the demolition, which was undertaken in an unsafe manner and a collapse occurred. Ferguson broke his back and was left paralysed from the waist.

Ferguson sued the Welsh brothers, Spence and the local authority. As the Welsh brothers and Spence had no insurance the obtaining of a judgment against them was of no value. The claim against the local authority, if successful, would lead to the award of £150 000 which was the agreed damages for Ferguson's injury.

The Law Lords accepted that the local authority were occupiers of the site but held that they were not liable to Ferguson: an occupier is not usually liable to an employee of a contractor working on the occupier's premises who was injured as a result of an unsafe system of work used by the contractor. Ordinarily an occupier is not under a duty to supervise contractors to see that they are using a safe system of work to protect the employees. In special circumstances, however, where the occupier knows or has reason to suspect that the contractor is using an unsafe system of work, it might well be reasonable for the occupier to take steps to see that the system was made safe.

If a member of the local authority's staff had visited the site while the demolition work was being undertaken in the unsafe way, and had failed to warn the contractor of the danger, then the local authority might have been held to be liable.

Lawful visitors

The 1957 Act overcame all the problems that the courts had been faced with previously in deciding whether a person was an invitee or a licensee by creating a single category – the 'lawful visitor'. Trespassers were left in their common law position until the passing of the Occupiers' Liability Act 1984. The 1957 Act also includes as lawful visitors all those who enter premises by a right conferred by law; a police officer entering by authority of a search warrant or a fire officer attending to a fire are to be lawful visitors.

When a person is invited or given permission to be on premises no difficulty arises in deciding that that person is a lawful visitor. More difficulty is encountered when permission to enter has to be implied, such as when a person enters premises for the purpose of selling something or seeking to talk to the occupier. Examples found with construction sites are workers who enter seeking employment and offer their services to an employer and members of the public who enter a housing development to view houses in the course of construction. Where, however, a notice states that entry is forbidden then a person who enters would be a trespasser.

Common duty of care

Section 2 of the 1957 Act replaced the previous common law duties by a statutory definition, that occupiers owe the same duty to all their visitors, except in so far as they are free to and do extend, restrict, modify or exclude their duty to any visitor or visitors by agreement or otherwise. This is the 'common duty of care', defined in Section 2, sub-section 2:

> The common duty of care is a duty to take such care as in all the circumstances is reasonable to see that the visitor will be reasonably safe in using the premises for the purposes for which he is invited or permitted by the occupier to be there.

This definition is based on reasonableness: the occupier is not required to guarantee safety. If the occupier had done all that was reasonable, the visitor has no claim despite the seriousness of the injury suffered. What is reasonable and what is required to make the visitor reasonably safe must be decided on the particular circumstances of each case.

Visitors must be using the premises for the purpose for which they were invited or permitted by the occupier to be there. So a visitor who fools about and is injured has no claim; a worker who was working on a scaffold and chose to do a handstand on it and fell would have no claim.

Sub-section 3 of Section 2 provides guidance as to the common duty of care. It lays down that the relevant circumstances include the degree of care and of want of care that may be looked for in the particular visitor,

so that (for example) in proper cases:
(a) an occupier must be prepared for children to be less careful than adults; and
(b) an occupier may expect that a person, in the exercise of his calling, will appreciate and guard against any special risks ordinarily incidental to it, so far as the occupier leaves him free to do so.

Paragraph (a) shows that occupiers will have to take account of the presence of children on their premises; this is a matter of importance since children are attracted to construction works.

Children

English law has long recognized that children are unappreciative of dangers and will be harmed in circumstances where an adult would not be harmed. The law classifies things which are dangerous and attractive to children as allurements; persons who have an allurement on their land are under a duty to guard against the risks from that allurement. A leading case on allurements is *Glasgow Corporation v Taylor 1922*, where the corporation had planted in a public park a shrub which produced poisonous red berries. Taylor was a young child who was in the park and attracted to the shrub, ate some berries and died as a result. The House of Lords held that the shrub was an allurement and the claim made was successful.

In the case of *Creed v John McGeoch and Sons Ltd 1955*, a contractor was undertaking the construction of roads, laying of sewers and the levelling of land from Birkenhead Corporation on a site. The contractor used a road trailer for transporting materials. When the roadworks were completed the trailer was not removed from the site but left on land by the side of a completed road. Creed, a five-year-old girl, with some friends was walking on the road when they saw the trailer and played with it, using it as a see-saw. Creed's hand was trapped and a claim was made for the injury. The contractor was held liable: a dangerous and attractive object had been left on land where children were known to play.

The fact that a child was attracted to land and suffered injury as a result does not necessarily mean that the occupier will be liable. In the case of *Latham v Johnson and Nephew Ltd 1913*, Johnson and Nephew, who had been carrying out work, left a pile of stones on a piece of land. Latham, a small child, was attracted to the pile of stones. While playing on the top of the pile he fell off and suffered injury. His claim was unsuccessful: the court took the view that putting stones on land was normal use of land and in any case the pile of stones was not an allurement.

Anyone under the age of eighteen is in law a child. To treat all these in the same way would be to ignore the obvious difference in maturity and appreciation of risks between a seven year old and a seventeen year old. In the case of *Phipps v Rochester Corporation 1955*, Phipps, a boy of five, and his sister, aged seven, went across a piece of land owned by the corporation to go blackberrying. The land was being developed by the corporation as a housing estate. Sewer works were being carried out and the corporation had for this purpose dug a 100 yard trench two to three feet wide and nine feet in depth. The girl crossed the trench safely but the boy fell in and broke his leg. He claimed damages for his injury.

The High Court decided that the trench was not an allurement, but it was a danger to a child of 'tender years', who was not old enough to see the need to avoid the danger or to take special care. The judge considered the duty owed to small children: an occupier of land is entitled to assume that the child would be accompanied by a responsible person. There was no evidence to show that little children frequently went unaccompanied on the land so as to put the corporation on warning that the land was being used in this way. He thought that it was not prudent for the parents to have allowed the children out on an October evening and the parents at least ought to have satisfied themselves that where the children went held no dangers for them. Phipps's claim was dismissed.

This decision was applied in the case of *Simkiss v Rhondda Borough Council 1983*, where Simkiss, a seven-year-old girl, lived in a block of flats which stood opposite to a mountain. Simkiss's father took her and a ten-year-old friend to a picnic spot at the foot of the mountain. He then went back to the flats from where he could keep them under observation. The children went to the top of the mountain and slid down on blankets. The side of the mountain went down steeply to a wall abutting a road. Simkiss lost control and was seriously injured. She sued the council claiming that there was liability under the Act.

The Court of Appeal decided that the mountainside was not a defect or trap but a danger which must have been known to the parents: it was familiar and obvious to them. A prudent parent would have satisfied himself that the children were aware of the danger. The council were entitled to assume that the parents would have taken that precaution. The council were under no obligation to adopt a higher standard of care than that of a reasonably prudent parent. Simkiss's claim was therefore dismissed.

Actions may be brought which are based on the common law tort of negligence in circumstances where the Occupiers' Liability Act is also applicable (see p. 190). Actions may also be brought on both grounds. A case concerning a child based on negligence was that of *Pannett v P McGuiness and Co Ltd 1972*. McGuiness were engaged by Manchester Corporation to demolish a derelict warehouse, which was bounded on three sides by streets and on the other side by a public park. The area was being developed with a considerable number of houses; local children went to the public park to use the playground. When work started in early June 1969, hoardings were erected around the warehouse, the interior stripped and the roof removed. At the end of June the walls remained to be demolished and rubbish to be burned. The hoardings were removed and fires lighted inside the warehouse.

The contractors were aware of the danger that the fires would attract children, and to guard against this risk three men were instructed to feed the fires, control them and watch out for children. Any child that appeared was to be warned off. The system of protection broke down for some unknown reason, so that when school ended and children were coming out of school Pannett went into the warehouse undetected. Pannett was only five years old; he apparently fell into the fire and was severely burnt. Pannett sued claiming negligence by the demolition contractors.

Evidence showed that children had had to be chased away and Pannett was one of these. His mother had warned him not to go there. For the contractors this was claimed to discharge any duty of care: the child was a trespasser and so no liability arose. After noting that McGuiness were not only contractors but also occupiers, and so under that duty, the Court of Appeal held them to be liable to Pannett. The duty owed to Pannett was to use common sense. Ultra-hazardous activities require a person to be ultra cautious in carrying them out. The chasing away of the children, including Pannett, was insufficient. This had been done before fires were lighted: the fires created an extra hazard and called for the contractors to take extra steps.

Since this case, the Occupiers' Liability Act 1984 has been passed and its provisions are those which would be applied if similar circumstances arose.

As civil engineering sites are places of attraction to children a summary of what has been considered may be helpful. A contractor who opens a site on which there will be equipment and other works which could form allurements must provide for children being attracted by them. A site in a built-up area, particularly if a school is close by, must be expected to be an attraction to children. Precautions should therefore take into account their likely presence. Ultra-hazardous operations require extra caution. Children of 'tender years' can be expected to be under the control of a responsible person. Older children, depending on their age, maturity and understanding, can be expected to look to their own safety in a manner approaching that of an adult.

Independent contractors

Paragraph (b) of sub-section 3 of Section 2 (see p. 193) allows an occupier to expect a person in the exercise of his or her calling to appreciate and guard against any special risks incident to it, so far as the occupier leaves the person free to do so. So a householder who calls in a specialist to do repair work can expect that person to guard against the usual risks of the job. The householder is, however, under a duty to warn the specialist of any danger in the house that she is aware of, for example a wood floor which is affected with dry rot and possibly unsafe to walk over.

The case of *Roles v Nathan 1963* demonstrates the application of the occupier being entitled to rely on the independent contractor he has engaged to guard against risks common to his work. Roles was a chimney sweep called in to deal with an old coke-burning boiler which smoked badly; the boiler was in the Manchester Assembly Rooms. Roles and another sweep failed to seal outlets to the boiler so as to prevent poisonous fumes being emitted into the boiler room, despite being warned of the danger both by an expert called in to advise about the boiler problem and the occupier of the building. Both men died from the fumes and Roles's widow sued. The Court of Appeal dismissed the claim. The occupier was entitled to expect them to guard against this risk which was a known risk with that work; in addition the occupier had given them a warning of the danger.

Sub-section 4 of Section 2 states that if damage is caused to a visitor by danger due to the faulty execution of works by an independent contractor employed by the occupier, then the occupier is not liable provided the occupier acted reasonably in giving the work to an independent contractor and had taken reasonable steps to check that the contractor was competent and that the work had been properly done.

In the case of *O'Connor v Swan and Edgar 1963*, an occupier of a building engaged an apparently competent contractor to undertake some plastering work. O'Connor was a visitor to the premises when a section of ceiling plaster fell on him, causing injuries. The occupier was able to avoid liability since it could not be proved that there was anything to suggest that the plasterwork was unsafe or that he had appointed an incompetent contractor.

Warnings

Sub-section 4 of Section 2 also states that if damage is caused to a visitor by a danger of which the visitor had been warned by the occupier, that warning will absolve the occupier of liability provided it was enough to enable the visitor to be reasonably safe.

Notices warning of risks or dangers, and often disclaiming liability under the Occupiers' Liablity Act 1957, are found on all kinds of premises. A warning notice to be effective should be in a prominent position, clearly worded, be of a permanent nature and warn of the specific danger. A notice which simply states 'Danger' without indicating what the danger is will probably be insufficient; the notice should be sufficiently in advance of the danger to enable the visitor to take the necessary precautions.

In the case of *Brayshaw v Leeds City Council 1984*, the council had excavated a trench in the grounds of one of their schools. It was known to the council that local residents used the school grounds outside school hours. Brayshaw, a fourteen-year-old boy, was crossing the grounds one evening in daylight when he came to the trench. Instead of walking round the trench, which would have added about fifty yards to his journey, he tried to leap across. He fell and was injured. He sued the council claiming that they were in breach of a duty to him. He claimed that the council ought to have provided a night watchman, boarded over the trench every night and provided a warning fence.

The High Court dismissed the claim. To have had a night watchman was considered unreasonable; to have boarded over the trench was impracticable. The court agreed that the trench should have had some warning sign. This failure, however, was not the cause of the accident:

it was Brayshaw's fault because he chose to leap across the trench. It was that alone that led to the accident.

In the case of *Rae v Mars (UK) Ltd 1990*, Mr Rae, an experienced chartered surveyor, had an accident while conducting a survey of premises owned by Mars. The premises were a disused factory which it was intended to renovate and let off to an engineering company. The premises were unusual in that a store had been constructed in the form of a pit two feet nine inches below the floor level; the floor consisted of ledges about three feet wide which ran around the sunken area. Access to the store was by means of a door opening from a covered way outside the building. Rae was not told of the sunken area but, knowing that the store was in darkness and not knowing where the switch for the lights was, had a torch. He opened the door, took a pace inside before he had used his torch and fell into the sunken area suffering injury.

Mr Rae's claim for damages was successful. He was owed a duty under the Act and the occupier had breached that duty. The judge considered that warning of the danger should have been given to Rae before he went into the store. He thought that it was a situation where a warning should have been given to all visitors. A specific warning was needed at that entry door to warn of the exceptional hazard; a notice or barrier as a reminder was also needed once entry had been made through the door. The judge, however, considered that as an experienced surveyor, surveying a disused factory, extra care was needed. Mr Rae had not been as careful as he should have been. For this reason he had contributed to the accident, therefore the amount awarded to him would be reduced by one-third because of his own contributory negligence.

Voluntary assumption of risk

Sub-section 5 of Section 2 provides a defence where a visitor has entered premises knowing of the risks involved and willingly accepted them. This defence, *volenti non fit injuria*, applies in common law too. It is necessary to show that the visitor was fully aware of the risks involved and the visitor then willingly accepts to run those risks. Where this is so a complete defence will exist for the occupier.

Exclusion of liability

The Occupiers' Liability Act 1957 makes provision for an occupier to give warning of any danger and that often coupled with it is a statement which seeks to exclude or restrict liability (see p. 192). This provision is now subject to the Unfair Contract Terms Act 1977 which, despite its title, applies to negligence and to the Occupiers' Liability Act 1957.

Section 2 of the Unfair Contract Terms Act 1977 states:

1 A person cannot by reference to any contract term or to a notice exclude or restrict his liability for death or personal injury resulting from negligence;
2 in the case of other loss or damage, a person cannot so exclude or restrict his liability for negligence except in so far as the term or notice satisfies the requirement of reasonableness.

The word 'negligence' used in (1) is given a particular meaning, including the common duty of care under the Occupiers' Liability Act 1957. So occupiers to whom the Act applies cannot exclude by means of a notice their liability for death or personal injury resulting from their negligence. In the case of (2), however, the position is different. Here for other loss or damage it is possible to exclude liability provided it satisfies the 'test of reasonableness', which was considered in some detail in respect of contracts for the sale of goods (see p. 191).

An example of the application of these two provisions would be where a factory owner invited a group of people to visit his factory. If by a notice he sought to exclude or limit his liability for death or personal injury resulting from his negligence and for other loss or damage the position would be that any visitor could claim for an injury suffered because of the factory owner's negligence. The attempt to exclude or restrict liability in this respect would be ineffective. If however one of the visitors had her coat stolen from the cloakroom then the exclusion on that matter may be effective provided the test of reasonableness was satisfied.

Section 2 of the Unfair Contract Terms Act 1977 applies only where the duty arises from things done in the course of a business or from occupation of premises used for the business purposes of the occupier. The definition 'business' includes a profession. This prohibition on the exclusion of liability by businesses means that a private individual can put up a notice excluding or restricting liability and that is effective provided the notice is accepted as fulfilling its purpose.

Occupiers' Liability Act 1984

The 1957 Act did not alter the position of a trespasser, whose rights were found in the common law. Occupiers were liable only if they did some wilful or intentional act to the trespasser or acted with total disregard to the trespasser's presence on the land.

The case of *British Railways Board v Herrington 1972*, which concerned a child going on a railway line and being severely injured, changed the common law. The House of Lords' decision laid down that a duty would be owed to trespassers in certain circumstances. Because the terms created some uncertainty in an important field of law Parliament eventually legislated to put the matter on a proper footing and provide a degree of certainty which many believed was missing in the decision in Herrington's case.

Section 1 states that its provisions are to replace the common law rules. The occupier is to be treated as the same person who is an occupier under the 1957 Act. Visitors are those to whom an occupier under the 1957 Act would owe the common duty of care.

Sub-section 3 of Section 1 states that an occupier of premises owes a duty to another, not being his (or her) visitor, in respect of any risk of suffering injury on the premises by reason of any danger due to the state of the premises or to things done or omitted to be done on them.

This duty is owed if

(a) he is aware of the danger or has reasonable grounds to believe that it exists;
(b) he knows or has reasonable grounds to believe that the other is in the vicinity of the danger concerned or that he may come into the vicinity of the danger (in either case, whether the other has lawful authority for being in that vicinity or not); and
(c) the risk is one against which, in all the circumstances of the case, he may reasonably be expected to offer the other some protection.

The duty is to take such care as is reasonable in all the circumstances to see that the trespasser does not suffer injury on the premises by reason of the danger concerned. This duty may be discharged by the occupier taking reasonable steps to give warning of the danger concerned or to discourage persons from incurring the risk. A person who volunteers to run a risk, *volenti non fit injuria*, is not entitled to the duty of care provided the risk is willingly accepted.

Section 1 also states that it does not apply to people using the highway and does not put an obligation on the occupier to any liability for loss of or damage to property.

Although the Act has been in force since the mid-1980s few cases have been reported. The Court of Appeal in the case of *White v St Albans City and District Council 1990* decided that the question as to whether an occupier owes a duty to trespassers was a question of fact in each case. White, wishing to get to his car in a car park, went across a safety tape on a construction site and in the darkness fell into a trench injuring himself. His claim under the Act failed.

Vicarious liability

The doctrine of vicarious liability has been present in English law for many years. Based on the belief that in appropriate circumstances a person will be responsible for the torts of another person, it is to be seen mainly in the relationship of employer and employee, which was formerly (and occasionally still is) referred to as master and servant. The employer is liable for the torts committed by an employee in the course of his or her employment. Where a person engages an independent contractor, the general rule, subject to certain important exceptions, is that that person is not liable for the torts of the independent contractor. The contract between an employer and an employee is referred to in law as a contract *of* service; the contract with an independent contractor is a contract *for* services. The distinction between an employee and an independent contractor is of great importance: it can be the difference between being fully liable or not liable at all.

Who is an employee?

Over the years the courts have had difficulty in laying down a means of determining whether or not a person was an employee. They have chosen to disregard the form of agreement made between the parties and instead look at the substance of the agreement. The absence of a suitable test has meant that the Inland Revenue, which has to make decisions under the 714 Certificate Scheme for the construction industry, has devised guidelines to determine this question for their own purposes.

Initially the 'control test' was used: was a person subject to such a degree of control that he or she must be the servant of the other? The control test was applied in the case of *Mersey Docks and Harbour Board v Coggins and Griffiths (Liverpool) Ltd 1947*, which arose from the practice of the Harbour Board hiring out mobile cranes together with the skilled drivers to stevedore companies for loading and unloading ships. Coggins and Griffiths hired a crane and driver. The contract of hire provided for the crane driver to be treated as the servant of the hirers, which would mean, if it was effective, that any tort he committed in the course of his work would make his hirers liable. The Board, however, retained the right to pay him and to dismiss him. During the hire period the crane driver was under the control of the hirers, who could tell him which cargo to move and to where. The manipulation of the controls was entirely a matter for the driver. The driver moved the crane in a negligent manner and knocked down an employee of the hirers.

The House of Lords decided that the crane driver, despite the contract of hire, remained the servant of the Board, which had retained a sufficient degree of control, by paying wages and having the power to dismiss, to keep the driver as their servant. As one Law Lord observed, to hold otherwise would mean that the driver would change employers every time he was engaged in the discharge of a new ship, which could be daily. This would introduce uncertainty as to who would be responsible for his insurance for health, employment and accident.

The control test could not be the sole test when it came to considering the work of airline pilots, surgeons and other professional people. All are employees but realistically cannot be subject to the control of their employers. The courts started to look at other factors and a composite test came to be applied; this is the test in use at the present time.

The composite test resulted from the case of *Ready Mixed Concrete (South East) Ltd v Minister of Pensions and National Insurance 1968*. Ready Mixed created a scheme whereby their drivers of concrete delivery vehicles could become self-employed. A detailed scheme was set up which allowed those drivers who wished to participate to buy their own vehicles by means of hire purchase. A contract provided that the drivers would make themselves available for Ready Mixed with the vehicles carrying the appropriate markings; the drivers agreed to be self-employed with responsibility for paying their own income tax, national insurance and providing for holidays and sickness. The scheme was challenged on the ground that the drivers were still employees and so Ready Mixed should pay the employer's contribution to the national insurance. The High Court's decision was that the drivers were no longer employees; they had become self-employed.

In the course of giving this decision the judge held that three conditions had to be satisfied if a contract of employment existed:

1 The servant agrees that, in consideration of a wage or other renumeration, he will provide his own work and skill in the performance of some service for his master.
2 He agrees, expressly or impliedly, that in the performance of that service he will be subject to the other's control in a sufficient degree to make the other master.
3 The other provisions of the contract are consistent with its being a contract of service.

A case of interest to the construction industry was that of *Ferguson v John Dawson and Partners (Contractors) Ltd 1976*. Ferguson was a general labourer with many years' experience in the building industry. He applied for work to the site supervisor, using the name of Goff instead of his real name. He was engaged on the basis that he would be working as self-employed; he agreed to pay his own income tax and national insurance and that no employment cards would be held by Dawsons. He was told that he would be instructed what to do. After starting work he was told to go on the flat roof of a building and to throw down some scaffold boards which were required elsewhere on the site. In throwing down the boards he stumbled over some rubble which had been left on the roof. He fell to the ground and suffered serious injury. He sued claiming that he was an employee and entitled to the protection of the Construction (Working Places) Regulations 1966. If he succeeded in proving he was an employee he would be successful.

The Court of Appeal considered all the circumstances of the making of the contract including its terms. The court said that the parties' expressed intention in the contract was not conclusive: the arrangements as a whole and the realities of the matter also had to be considered. By a majority the court decided that Ferguson was an employee and so could succeed in his claim. Ferguson was paid on an hourly basis, he could be moved from one site to another and the site supervisor had said in evidence that he had the power to 'hire and fire' workers and could tell them what to do. This showed a degree of control which was consistent with a contract of service.

The judge who disagreed with the decision did so on the ground that by using a false name, Ferguson opened the way to the evasion of the payment of income tax on his earnings, which made the contract of service possibly illegal. This judge was of the opinion that Ferguson was self-employed.

Courts reserve the right to disregard what the parties to the contract of service agreed and to look at what exists in fact and make the decision on that basis. All the circumstances are to be examined in making this decision. With the increasing number of people choosing to work as self-employed, in all ranges and levels of employment, it does seem likely that the courts will be more willing than has been the case in the past to accept that a contract for services exists rather than a contract of service.

In the course of employment

The liability of employers for their employees' torts is restricted to those done 'within the course of the employment', which depends on the facts of the matter. Employees who act outside the course of their employment will be liable themselves for their torts; vicarious liability does not arise.

An employee who goes outside his duties of employment, so that the employer is not liable, is referred to as being 'on a frolic of his own'. A common example is the lorry driver who deviates from his proper journey for private purposes. An unusual example is in the case *Heassmans (A Firm) v Clarity Cleaning Co Ltd 1987*, where a contract had been made between the parties for the cleaning of Heassmans' office. The dusting and disinfecting of the telephone was in the contract terms. One of Clarity's employees when at the premises carrying out cleaning work wrongly used the telephone. The use was extensive and increased Heassmans' telephone account by £1499. Heassmans sued Clarity to recover this sum on the ground that the employee had used the telephone dishonestly during his employment, which made Clarity liable for the employee's act. The Court of Appeal accepted that Clarity had no reason to suspect that the employee was dishonest and so were not negligent in employing him. The more difficult question was whether Clarity should be held to be liable when the employee's wrongful act was outside the scope of his employment but where the employment created the opportunity to commit the wrongful act. The court decided that this was insufficient to impose liability on the employer. The employment provided the opportunity to commit the act but no more than this. Heassmans' claim against Clarity was dismissed.

The use of motor vehicles with employment has led to a number of cases. If the journey is within the course of the employment, negligent driving by an employee which causes injury to other employees makes the employer liable. The position is clear when employees are driving between their places of work; it is the use of vehicles in other circumstances which give rise to doubt. The case of *Smith v Stages and Darlington Insulation Co Ltd 1989* gives guidance on this point. Stages and Machin were employees of Darlington Insulation, both working as laggers installing insulation at various power stations. While working at a power station in the Midlands they were sent to do an urgent job at a power station in South Wales, which would entail working night and day over a weekend. They were paid eight hours' pay for travelling to South Wales and eight hours for the return. Travelling expenses were paid at the rail fares rate but the form of travel was not stipulated. After travelling to South Wales they worked twenty-four hours non-stop. Instead of having a break for sleep they drove straight back to the Midlands. The driver, Stages, crashed the car into a brick wall after leaving the road. Machin was seriously injured and died later from a cause not connected with his injuries. His widow remarried and continued the action he had started in her new name of Smith.

Mrs Smith's claim against Stages encountered difficulty since he was uninsured. The claim against Darlington Insulation was on the ground that they were vicariously liable for Stages's negligent driving. This issue depended on whether when driving back from South Wales they were in the course of their employment.

The House of Lords decided that Darlington Insulation were vicariously liable for Stages's negligent driving: where an employee was required to work away for a short time at a different place of work, some distance from his usual place of work, and he was paid wages for the time spent travelling, then when he travelled back to his ordinary residence in the employer's time he was acting in the course of his employment. The Law Lords indicated that employees who travelled from their ordinary residence to their regular place of work would not be acting in the course of their employment.

An employer will be vicariously liable even when an employee acts in a way which may be forbidden or which may defy common sense. In the case of *Century Insurance Co v Northern Ireland Road Transport Board 1942*, a driver of the Board was delivering petrol at a garage. After coupling up the supply from his vehicle to the storage tank and turning on the control valve he lit a cigarette and threw the match on to the floor. The match ignited material on the floor and spread. He then, without turning off the control valve, drove the tanker on to the street. The flame followed the train of petrol; when it reached the tanker, the tanker exploded. The decision was that the Board were vicariously liable for the driver's negligence. When the driver was attending to the transfer of the petrol from his tanker to the garage tank he was acting within the course of his employment. His careless act was part of that employment.

The fact that the employer is liable does not absolve the employee of liability. The House of Lords in the case of *Lister v Romford Ice and Cold Storage Co Ltd 1957* allowed an employer's insurance company to sue an employee for negligence in the performance of his employment. There is of course no point in suing an employee who has no financial resources or insurance.

Independent contractors

The general rule is that the person who engages an independent contractor is not liable for the contractor's torts. Important exceptions to this rule include where the employer has not selected a competent contractor for the work required (for example appointing an ordinary engineering contractor to undertake specialist engineering tasks); where some legal provision puts the liability on the employer and it is applied strictly to the employer; the rule in *Rylands v Fletcher 1868* (see p. 166); the creation of a public nuisance on a highway as seen in *Tarry v Ashton 1876* (see p. 153); and in private nuisance where there is interference with rights of support. If an employer appoints an independent contractor to do something which is negligent in itself, then the employer is liable.

Defences and remedies

We have already considered a number of defences which are relevant to particular torts, so a general consideration of defences will conclude this matter. Persons seeking to prove a tort have the burden placed on them and failure to discharge this burden because of some defence means that this claim must fail.

Volenti non fit injuria

English law accepts that where a person volunteers to run a risk, this fact will often defeat any claim the person may bring. Before the defence can be proved it is necessary to show that the person had knowledge of the risk being undertaken and that knowing of that risk the person freely consented to run the risk. A person who takes part in a dangerous sport knowing of the risk has volunteered to run the risk; if that person receives an injury while the rules of the sport are being observed, the willing assumption of the risk deprives the person of a right to damages. If, however, the injury suffered was a result of a breach of the rules, the person's claim will not be defeated by the defence of *volenti non fit injuria*. In the case of *Condon v Basi 1985* the Court of Appeal agreed that an amateur football player who had been injured in a tackle which was made in a reckless and dangerous manner was entitled to damages: there was no malicious intent, but the tackle had been made in an excitable manner.

In cases where a spectator was injured while attending a dangerous sport, the courts have taken the view that there was a risk which the spectator knew of and willingly accepted. In the case of *Hall v Brooklands Auto Racing Club 1933*, Hall was a spectator at a race meeting. He positioned himself at a corner where the cars had to be driven with great skill and mishaps were likely. A car left the track at that corner, burst through the safety barrier and struck Hall, injuring him. His claim for damages was unsuccessful: he had with full knowledge willingly agreed to the risk in his attendance as a spectator.

The courts have been most unwilling to accept the application of *volenti non fit injuria* in the employment situation: the reason is both sound and obvious. If employees failed to obey an order of their employer which put them at risk, they could well lose their employment. If, however, employees obeyed their employer's instruction and put themselves at risk, then their claim might be defeated on the defence of *volenti non fit injuria*. This reluctance can be seen in the case of *Smith v Baker 1891*, where Smith was a quarryman who worked in a cutting over which a crane swung at intervals with heavy stones. He was not warned when this was about to happen. A stone fell from the crane and injured him. The House of Lords rejected the defence of *volenti non fit injuria* put forward by the employers. Smith had knowledge of what was happening but he had not consented to it.

A decision where the defence was accepted, but in most unusual circumstances, was the case of *Imperial Chemical Industries v Shatwell 1965*, where two brothers, both of whom were qualified shot firers, worked in a quarry. They had bored and filled fifty shot holes, then placed detonators and wired up an electric circuit. One of the brothers, contrary to a statutory provision and clear instructions given to him by his employers, then carried out a test in an improper way. An explosion occurred which injured both brothers. One brother sued the employer on the basis of the negligent act of a fellow employee (his brother) which he claimed made them vicariously liable. The House of Lords decided that *volenti non fit injuria* could apply as an employee deliberately contravened a statutory provision; furthermore an express instruction of the employers had been ignored. Shatwell's claim was therefore dismissed.

Public policy

It is contrary to public policy to allow an individual to succeed in a claim where there is some illegality involved, when a person had been taking part in a crime or when the person knew of the wrongdoer's criminal conduct.

In the case of *Ashton v Turner and Another 1980*, Ashton made a claim after being injured in a car accident. Ashton, Turner and McLure had all been drinking heavily one night; a decision was made to break into a shop. McLure took no part in this, but his car was used as the 'get-away' car. Ashton and Turner broke into a shop; in order to evade capture, Turner drove the car negligently at high speed and crashed. Ashton suffered serious injuries, and sued Turner as the driver and McLure as the owner of the car. Ashton's claim was dismissed in the High Court: the law did not recognize a duty of care owed by one participant in a crime to another in relation to the commission of that crime.

In the case of *Pitts v Hunt 1990*, a claim was made by Pitts for injuries received while riding pillion on Hunt's motorcycle. Despite knowing that Hunt was intoxicated, Pitts encouraged Hunt to ride the motorcycle. Pitts also knew that Hunt was uninsured and unlicensed. The motorcycle was in collision with a car; Hunt was killed and Pitts injured. Pitts's claim was dismissed by the Court of Appeal. He was not entitled to succeed: he had encouraged Hunt to use the motorcycle knowing he was drunk, uninsured and unlicensed and had encouraged him to ride in a reckless manner. It was contrary to public policy to allow his claim to succeed.

Contributory negligence

Until Parliament passed the Law Reform (Contributory Negligence) Act 1945, the position at common law was that if it could be shown that the person making a claim was partly at fault in the accident, that meant the claim must fail. The Act provides that such fault shall not defeat the claim, but the damages to be awarded shall be reduced to such extent as the court thinks just and equitable having regard to the claimant's share in the responsibility for the damage.

Contributory negligence applies to loss of life, personal injury and damage to property. Under the Act 'fault' means negligence, breach of statutory duty or other act or omission which gives rise to a liability in tort or would, apart from the Act, gives rise to the defence of contributory negligence. Despite some attempts to make the Act apply, the courts have decided that the Act does not apply to breaches of contract.

A well-known application of contributory negligence is where a driver or passenger in a motor car fails to wear a seat belt; it also applies to motorcyclists' wearing of helmets.

Contributory negligence frequently comes into operation in industrial accidents where the employer claims that the employee was at fault. In the case of *Jones v Livox Quarries Ltd 1952*, Jones was riding on a tow-bar at the back of a vehicle in order to get to the canteen from his place of work. Another vehicle negligently drove into the towing vehicle, throwing Jones off the tow-bar and causing him injury. Riding on the tow-bar exposed him to the risk of being thrown off and the award of damages was reduced accordingly.

The reduction in the award is entirely a matter for the courts; reductions have been made of seventy-five per cent and more. It is doubted that a person can be 100 per cent contributory negligence since this means that the person was entirely responsible for the accident.

Necessity

The law recognizes that sometimes a person has to take a course of action which might result in some harm being caused to another: any claim for compensation may then be met by the defence of necessity. Examples include pulling down a dangerous building liable to collapse on a highway, throwing goods overboard to lighten a ship and giving medical assistance. Whatever the circumstances, what is done must be reasonable.

The leading case on necessity is *Esso Petroleum Co Ltd v Southport Corporation 1956*, where an oil tanker ran aground in the Ribble estuary. The ship was in danger of breaking her back, thereby putting the lives of the crew at risk. The master ordered that part of the cargo of oil should be discharged in order to lighten the ship. The oil discharge eventually washed up on the shore at Southport. Southport Corporation spent a considerable sum of money in clearing the oil from the shore and claimed this sum. The claim was based on trespass, nuisance and negligence. The House of Lords accepted that as lives were at risk the action in discharging the oil was a necessary act and so formed a defence to the claim.

Remedies

The common law remedy for injury resulting from a tort is damages, a sum of money awarded to compensate the claimant for the injury suffered. To this rule there are certain exceptions:

1 *Contemptuous* here the court awards the lowest coin of the realm to indicate its view of the merit of the case. A danger with this award is that the court might decide to refuse to award the costs of the case to the successful party. Costs are at the court's discretion and normally follow the event.
2 *Nominal* where the parties are contesting a legal right, for example trespass to land, that is the important issue and not the sum of damages to be awarded. For this reason the court awards a nominal amount, normally not exceeding £5.
3 *Exemplary* this is an award rarely made since it contains an element of punishment designed to show the court's feelings about the defendant's conduct. Unless an Act of Parliament permits the award of exemplary damages, there are

two circumstances only where such an award will be made. The first is where there has been some oppressive, arbitrary or unconstitutional actions by servants of the Government, for example where the police have exceeded their authority in arresting and detaining a person. The second case is where the defendant's conduct is such that unless exemplary damages are awarded he will benefit from his wrongful action. Awards have been made under this classification where landlords have acted towards their tenants in an aggressive manner with the intention of forcing the tenants out so that the tenancy will be available to the landlords.

Other than these exceptions damages are to be compensatory: they may be special or general. Special damages are those which may be quantified, for example loss of earnings by a worker injured in an industrial accident. General damages cannot be quantified in the same way and are, therefore, damages which are decided by the court after hearing all the evidence, for example the amount the court believes is an appropriate award for the pain and suffering in a personal injury case.

In the case of damage to property the usual rule is that the cost of repairs is recoverable, which allows the cost to be recovered even if the repairs have not been carried out. If a building has been damaged beyond repair, the amount is to be the cost of reinstatement. If the reinstatement cost exceeds the reduction in value to an unreasonable extent, the court may refuse to award that sum. The cost of repair work can increase substantially over a period of time. The old rule that the sum to be awarded was to be the cost of repair on the day the tort was committed, together with interest, was changed in *Dodd Properties (Kent) and Another v Canterbury City Council and Others 1980*, where the Court of Appeal decided that the date for determining the cost of the repairs was to be the date when, in all the circumstances, it was reasonable for the repairs to be undertaken. In considering this matter it is appropriate to take into account the financial position of the injured party.

A person bringing an action claiming damages for a tort must mitigate the loss: the duty is to do what is reasonable in the circumstances to minimize the loss. Nothing exceptional is required of a person and the particular circumstances determine what was reasonable to expect.

Civil Liability (Contribution) Act 1978

A person bringing an action for tort may sue all those who appear to be involved in the tort even if the proportion of blame is most unequal. The reason for this is that if only one person is sued and that person has insufficient financial resources to meet the damages ordered by the court, there is no other person to whom to look to for payment. A case where an architect, demolition contractor and contractor were all sued by a worker injured by the fall of a wall which ought to have been demolished was that of *Clay v A J Crump and Sons Ltd 1964*. All were found to be liable and on the evidence the court apportioned damages as: architect forty-two per cent; demolition contractor thirty-eight per cent; contractor twenty per cent. If any one of these parties had become unable to pay, the remaining parties would have to pay that portion as well as their own. In a case where two parties were sued and found liable, with one later becoming insolvent, the other party has to pay the full amount that the court awarded.

The Civil Liability (Contribution) Act 1978 contains provisions which allow a person held liable to pay damages, whether for tort, contract or otherwise, to recover a contribution from any other person liable in respect of the same damage. The contribution is to be an amount which the court finds to be just and equitable having regard to that person's responsibility in the matter. The Act does not affect an indemnity clause in a contract between two defendants in an action. For example, a scaffolding sub-contractor may give a main contractor a full indemnity with regard to accidents caused by the scaffold. If a worker of the main contractor is injured by a collapse of the scaffold and that collapse is shown to be the result of negligent erection of the scaffold, then the worker would sue both. The main contractor would recover all they had had to pay to the injured employee from the sub-contractor on the full indemnity.

The Act also allows a contribution to be recovered where individuals have settled a claim against them without a court pronouncing judgment. Thus the persons sued may accept that they are liable and settle the matter on the best terms they can. Provided that settlement was bona fide they can claim a contribution from any other person who would also have been liable.

Injunctions

In the tort of trespass to land an important remedy is an injunction granted by the court (see p. 22). Injunctions may also be granted for other torts. An injunction is a court order and failure to observe its terms is contempt of court which the court may deal with by appropriate punishment.

An injunction is an equitable remedy, granted at the court's discretion: it cannot be demanded as of right. It will be granted only where the court is satisfied the award of damages would be an insufficient remedy. The conduct of the person seeking the injunction is relevant. If he has misled a person by letting her believe that he has no objection to what is happening the application for an injunction may be refused.

An injunction may be prohibitory, which restrains a person from committing some wrongful act; or mandatory, which is granted much less frequently, commands a person to do something and usually requires the expenditure of money.

In the case of *Redland Bricks Ltd v Morris 1969*, Redland excavated on their own land extracting clay; this resulted in a landslip to adjoining land owned by Morris. The county court granted a mandatory injunction ordering the execution of works to restore support to Morris's land. The House of Lords found that the injunction was inappropriate because of the heavy expense involved and that it failed to explain with sufficient clarity what works were required.

An injunction may be granted as interlocutory or as perpetual. An interlocutory injunction is granted before the matter in issue has had a court hearing, in order to maintain the status quo. It is possible that the court will decide that no wrong has occurred; the person seeking the injunction must therefore give an undertaking to pay any loss incurred by the defendant because of the granting of the injunction.

A perpetual injunction is one granted at the end of the court hearing: the case has been proved, a tort has been committed and the court is satisfied that a perpetual injunction is an appropriate remedy to grant.

A form of injunction not often sought or granted is a *quia timet*. This is an injunction granted because although something has not yet happened, substantial evidence exists to show that it is likely to do so unless restrained: there has to be a risk of substantial damage.

In the case of *Hooper v Rogers 1974*, both parties were neighbours in a pair of semi-detached houses. A track fairly near to Hooper's house was lowered and deepened by Rogers. He gave no warning to Hooper of what he proposed to do. This action withdrew support to land adjoining Hooper's house and he feared that the stability of his house was threatened. The Court of Appeal were satisfied that in time unless the excavated portion of the track was restored to its original state the stability of the house would be affected. There was justification to award a *quia timet* injunction. The claim that there was no certainty or immediacy of damage being caused to Hooper's house was dismissed. The requirement of imminent danger meant that the court had to be satisfied that the remedy was not being granted prematurely.

Limitation Act 1980

Under the Act a person who wishes to bring an action for tort must bring it within six years, unless it is a claim for personal injury in which case the period is three years. Failure to bring the action, which consists of issuing the writ, within the appropriate time will defeat the claim. Justice requires any claim to be brought within a reasonable period of time. No one should have to face a claim made many years after the event occurred, with the difficulty of gathering evidence in the form of documents and witnesses in order to prepare a defence.

The limitation period runs from the date on which the cause of action accrues. Where, for example, a worker is injured because of the collapse of a scaffold which had been negligently erected, that is the day on which the cause of action started. Damage to buildings from some negligent action is, however, more difficult to fix with a date.

Until the House of Lords' decision in *Pirelli General Cable Works Ltd v Oscar Faber and Partners (A Firm) 1983*, the rule was that the cause of action accrued on the day the damage was discovered or ought with reasonable diligence to have been discovered. Pirelli had decided to have their factory extended, including the construction of a 160 foot high boiler flue chimney by a specialist sub-contractor. Oscar Faber, a firm of consulting engineers, were engaged to advise on the design and construction of the chimney. The chimney was constructed in 1969; in 1977 the top of the chimney was found to have cracks in it. The cost of remedial work was substantial. There was evidence which was accepted by the court that the cracks must have occurred not later than April 1970. In October 1978 Pirelli issued a writ against Oscar Faber claiming damages for negligence. It was not possible to sue for breach of contract since the six-year limitation period had expired. If the rule with regard to discovery applied then Pirelli had discovered the damage in 1977 and issued the writ the following year, well within the six-year limitation period. The Law Lords, however, refused to accept this rule, which had been created by the Court of Appeal in the case of *Spareham-Souter v Town and Country Development (Essex) Ltd 1976*. Instead they decided that the time started to run from when the damage occurred, whether it be discovered at that time or not. Applying this decision to the circumstances of the case, the damage had occurred in 1970 but the writ had not been issued until 1978. The claim therefore was statute barred as being made outside the six-year limit.

The series of cases considered with regard to negligence when local authorities, architects and builders were being sued for negligence many years after a building was constructed caused considerable alarm to these people and to their insurers. At the same time individual householders, whose biggest capital asset was their house, often found that there were serious defects in them as a result of negligence in their construction. This produced competing needs between householders, who sought protection against negligent construction, and architects and others, who wanted a known limit to their liability for negligence. Parliament tried to meet these competing needs by passing the Latent Damage Act 1986, which does not apply to claims for damages for personal injuries; it provided that new sections were to be incorporated into the Limitation Act 1980.

The original period of six years from the date of the cause of the action accruing is maintained. A further period of three years exists, which starts to run from the date on which the damage was discovered or ought to have been discovered: this date is the 'starting date'. Overlying the six-year and three-year periods is a fifteen-year 'longstop'. This bars any claim being made when fifteen years have expired from the date of the act of negligence which caused damage or even if no damage has yet been caused.

The provisions would apply in the following manner. Y built a house in April 1990 and in May 1992 X, the owner, discovers cracks in the walls which had occurred because of the defective foundations to the house. X has until May 1998 to bring an action. If the cracks did not occur until May 1997, more than six years after the foundations were constructed, which X discovered or ought to have discovered, then X has three years, May 2000, within which to bring an action. If, however, the cracks did not occur or were not discovered until April 2006 then no claim could be made as the fifteen-year longstop would bar any claim.

The benefit of these provisions for the owner of a building has been diminished by the House of Lords' decision in *Murphy v Brentwood District Council 1990*. Claims for economic loss with negligent building work can no longer be successful; the provisions in the Latent Damage Act 1986 which were introduced to deal with these problems are no longer applicable, as the event no longer gives rise to a cause of action.

7

Professional negligence

Circumstances in which a duty of care arises

The term 'professional negligence' is used in a wider sense than reference to the common law tort of negligence alone. It describes the liability of professional people in the circumstances where the law recognizes that they can be made to answer for the way in which they have performed their services as professional people.

The circumstances where professional people may be held liable for their services as members of their profession are by contract, the tort of negligence, and under the provisions in the Defective Premises Act 1972. It is possible for liability to arise on all these grounds; such liability could extend to different people. For example some failure to design a building properly, using reasonable skill and care, which led to a collapse would be a breach of contract, and negligence to those other than the client injured as a result of the collapse. If the building was a dwelling, there would be liability under the Defective Premises Act 1972.

Contract

The liability under a contract is restricted to the other party to the contract, from the doctrine of privity of contract (see p. 60). A person who is not a party to the contract cannot sue for breach of contract since English law does not, under the doctrine, recognize that that person has any rights or obligations under the contract. The obligation under the contract will depend on the express terms in the contract as to performance, failing which what is required from the professional person has to be implied. So if an engineer contracts to produce a design to meet a stated performance standard, that is what the engineer has undertaken to do; failure to produce that performance standard will be breach of contract. Where there is no stipulation as to stated performance the engineer is required to meet the standard implied by law, which is to use reasonable skill and care.

The engagement of a professional person is a matter of some importance and to leave the contract terms between the professional and the client to be those which are implied by law is not wholly satisfactory, particularly with larger works. Professional bodies therefore produce standard conditions of engagement which their members may use. The Association of Consulting Engineers has produced its own conditions of engagement, produced in different forms to meet various circumstances.

Tort

Liability under the tort of negligence is based on the decision in *Donoghue v Stevenson 1932*: there can be a duty owed to someone who is not a client of the engineer. In the case of *Bagot v Stevens Scanlon and Co 1964*, where the client sued architects he had engaged for failure to supervise the work properly, it was decided that there could not be liability in tort as well as that in the contract of engagement. The reason for seeking the right to sue for negligence was that the claim for breach of contract would be statute barred, being more than six years after the breach, under the Limitation Act 1939. A number of judges have questioned the correctness of that decision and in fact allowed claims for negligence. The present approach, however, as seen in the Court of Appeal decision in *Greater Nottingham Co-operative Society Ltd v Cementation Piling and Foundations Ltd and Others 1988* (see p. 180), is that if there is a contract, the claim may only be made under the contract.

The House of Lords' decision in *Murphy v Brentwood District Council 1990* (see p. 176) closed the flood of claims being made for economic loss on its own: the majority of cases decided on defective building work would not now be decided in the same way.

What that decision did not change was the principle in the House of Lords' decision in *Hedley Byrne and Co Ltd v Heller and Partners Ltd 1964* that there could be liability in negligence for a negligent misstatement. This principle has been used in a number of cases of professional negligence (see p. 226) and remains an important source of professional negligence both with regard to clients and others.

Defective Premises Act 1972

This Act has been little used since the development in the common law allowing a person to sue for negligence in building work gave a person stronger rights. The decision in *Murphy v Brentwood District Council 1990* (see p. 176) has reversed that development and the provisions in the Act are now likely to be used much more. The important provision regarding duty is to be found in Section 1:

(1) A person taking on work for or in connection with the provision of a dwelling (whether the dwelling is provided by the erection or by the conversion or enlargement of a building) owes a duty

(a) if the dwelling is provided to the order of any person, to that person; and

(b) without prejudice to paragraph (a) above, to every person who acquires an interest (whether legal or equitable) in the dwelling:

to see that the work which he takes on is done in a workmanlike manner or, as the case may be, professional manner, with proper materials and so that as regards the work the dwelling will be fit for habitation when completed.

First, this relates solely to dwellings; industrial and commercial buildings are not within the Act. The duty is owed not only to the person who placed the order but also to subsequent owners; it is not a duty based on contract. If an engineer was engaged to design the foundations of a dwelling by X, who then sold the dwelling to Y, who sold it to Z, the engineer is liable to Y or Z if during their periods of ownership a breach of the engineer's duty occurred.

Second, the duty is defined as having three points: workmanlike manner, proper materials, and that the dwelling will be fit for habitation when completed. There is specific mention of the duty extending to work being done in a professional manner: the duty does not therefore apply only to those concerned with the construction works. The engineer who reports on the ground conditions or designs the foundations or the roof structure owes the duty of care.

Sub-section 2 of Section 1 removes the duty of care where persons take on work on terms that they are to do the work to the instructions of another, subject to any duty to warn the other person of any defects in the instructions and there is a failure to discharge that duty. So a person who is asked to build a dwelling of unusual design or construction is under no duty other than to warn of any defect in the instructions.

Sub-section 5 of Section 1 states that the period of limitation for bringing an action is to be six years after the date when the dwelling was completed, subject to an extension if the person who has done the work does further work to rectify the work already done: then the six-year period runs from the date of the completion of the remedial works.

Standard of care

The standard of care required if a person is to satisfy the duty of care in negligence was defined in *Blyth v Birmingham Water Works Co 1856*:

Negligence is the omission to do something which a reasonable man, guided upon those considerations which ordinarily regulate the conduct of human affairs, would do, or doing something which a prudent and reasonable man would not do.

This is the test for ordinary individuals going about their everyday affairs – the reasonable person considered in the tort of negligence (see p. 175). With the professional person, this test is not wholly appropriate; instead the courts have applied the 'Bolam test', named after the decision in the High Court case of *Bolam v Friern Hospital Management Committee 1957*. Here a doctor administered electro-convulsive therapy treatment to Bolam without using relaxant drugs or any manual control and as a result Bolam broke his hip. He sued the Committee as employers of the doctor who had administered the treatment. In addressing the jury Mr Justice McNair said:

How do you test whether this act or failure is negligent? In an ordinary case it is generally said you judge it by the action of the man in the street. He is the ordinary man . . . . But where you get a situation which involves the use of some special skill or competence, then the test as to whether there has been negligence or not is not the test of the man on the top of a Clapham omnibus, because he has not got this special skill. The test is the standard of the ordinary skilled man exercising and professing to have that special skill. A man need not possess the highest expert skill; it is well established law that it is sufficient if he exercises the ordinary skill of an ordinary competent man exercising that particular art.

This test is used by the courts when deciding whether or not there has been professional negligence. It is applicable to all professions: there are no separate tests for different professions. Every member of a particular profession is required to meet, in any particular circumstances, the standard of the ordinary skilled member of that profession. If a professional person deals with a particular situation as an ordinary member of that profession would have, the person has fulfilled his or her duty of care and is not negligent. This is so even if someone should suffer some serious injury as a result of the professional person's actions. Although a leading member of a profession might not have acted in that way, it does not mean that the professional person whose actions are being called into question must be negligent.

When the jury applied the test to the claim of Bolam they decided that there had been no negligence: there were several acceptable methods of dealing with the patient using electro-convulsive therapy. The method the doctor used with Bolam was one of those accepted methods so there was no negligence by the doctor.

The defining of Bolam's test by the High Court was given approval by the House of Lords in the case of *Whitehouse v Jordan 1981*, which was a claim for medical negligence in childbirth. The doctor had followed normal medical practice in a case of difficult childbirth and his actions did not constitute negligence. During the Law Lords' consideration, comment was made on the attitude in the Court of Appeal, where the doctor's actions were described as errors of clinical judgement. The proper approach was by Bolam's test: did any error come within the due exercise of professional skill or not? Lord Edmund Davies said: 'If a surgeon fails to measure up to the standard in any respect (clinical judgement or otherwise), he has been negligent and should so be adjudged'.

A case of some interest to civil engineers, where the possibility of a higher standard of care being due from highly skilled and experienced engineers was considered, was *George Wimpey and Co Ltd v D V Poole and Others 1984*. The case was unusual since Wimpey went to court in order to prove that they had been negligent in some design work: Wimpey's insurance policy covered them when they were acting in different capacities. So one department of Wimpey's making use of the services of another department could sue that other department if their services had been performed negligently.

Wimpey were invited to tender for a design and construction contract (using the ICE Conditions of Contract) for the construction of a new quay. With the invitation was information about ground conditions. The design work was put into the hands of an experienced engineer who designed the quay wall. About ten years after the wall was constructed, cracking was noticed in the quay wall and remedial works had to be carried out. This movement was apparently caused by the long-term softening of clay, which had not been taken sufficiently into account in the design. Wimpey's construction department made a claim against Wimpey's design department on the ground of negligence. Wimpey's design department made a claim on the insurers, who were underwriters, on the basis that the department had been negligent and so were liable. The question was whether what the design department had done came within Bolam's test. If the design department had used reasonable care then there could be no liability, unless there had been some warranty given with regard to the design, and this had not been given. Wimpey sought to show that with a company of their size and high standing a more stringent and exacting standard was to be expected. If they were judged by this higher standard, they might be able to show that they had failed to reach it and so were liable. If, however, Bolam's test was the appropriate standard, what had been done with the design could come within the test as reasonable care.

The High Court judge refused to accept that there was any standard of care other than that laid down in Bolam's case. Wimpey's submission that a higher, more exacting standard ought to be applied to them was unsuccessful. Applying the reasonable care standard in Bolam's case, the judge decided that Wimpey's design department had not been negligent. The claim against that department by the construction department was not therefore one which the insurers had to meet.

The case of *Hedley Byrne and Co Ltd v Heller and Partners Ltd 1964* (see p. 177) plays such an important role in professional negligence, and is the principle on which recovery for economic loss on its own is allowed, that its application to the professional person requires consideration. The House of Lords' decision accepted that there could be liability for a negligent misstatement but in the particular circumstances the use of a disclaimer meant that Heller and Partners were not liable.

Lord Reid, the Senior Law Lord, considered the position of a person seeking information or advice from another:

> A reasonable man, knowing that he was being trusted or that his skill and judgement were being relied on would, I think, have three courses open to him. He could keep silent or decline to give the information or advice sought; or he could give an answer with a clear qualification that he accepted no responsibility for it or that it was given without that reflection or inquiry which a careful answer would require: or he could simply answer without any such qualification. If he chooses to adopt the last course he must, I think, be held to have accepted some responsibility for his answer being given carefully, or to have accepted a relationship with the inquirer which requires him to exercise such care as the circumstances require!

The other Law Lords were generally in agreement with this approach. Since this decision there has been an understanding that liability would not arise under the principle when a professional person was asked for advice in the form of a chance remark at, say, a social function. The courts have not allowed the principle to be used in every circumstance where a person suffers economic loss as a result of relying on some statement which events later show to have been negligent.

This reluctance is illustrated in the case of *Caparo Industries PLC v Dickman and Others 1990*, where Caparo bought shares in a company shortly after the company's audited accounts had been published. The accounts showed that the actual profits had fallen well short of those forecast, which caused the price of the shares to fall sharply. Caparo started buying shares and did so until they had taken over the company, when Caparo discovered that the accounts were inaccurate and misleading. Instead of a profit of £1.3 million there was a loss of £400 000. Caparo sued the firm of chartered accountants who had prepared the accounts.

In the High Court the judge decided that there was no liability since there was no duty of care owed. In the Court of Appeal, by a majority, it was decided that there was a duty of care owed to Caparo as shareholders but not as potential investors. The House of Lords decided that where a statement was put into general circulation, which might foreseeably be relied on by strangers for any one of a variety of purposes which the maker of the statement had no special reason to anticipate, there was no relationship of proximity between the maker of the statement and any person who relied on it. This is subject to the qualification that if the maker of the statement knew that the statement would be made known to others in connection with some transaction, and that person would rely on the statement, then there could be a relationship of proximity.

There was no duty of care owed by the auditors in auditing the accounts to any member of the public at large: there was no relationship of proximity. The duty of care was owed by the auditors, not to individual shareholders, but to the whole body of shareholders.

Breach of duty of care

Before considering the varying circumstances in which engineers may find themselves liable to a claim for professional negligence, and the decisions of the courts, we need to note that there are certain individuals who cannot be sued for professional negligence. The basis of this immunity is that of public policy: without this immunity individuals would be unwilling to accept certain duties, which would be contrary to the public interests.

So far as court proceedings are concerned, judges in the superior courts are immune; magistrates have a more limited immunity; witnesses are immune with regard to negligence claims in respect of their evidence; advocates are immune for negligence in the conduct of a case in court. The immunity of advocates was established by the House of Lords in *Rondel v Worsley 1967*. In the later case of *Saif Ali v Sydney Mitchell and Co 1978* the House of Lords limited this immunity so that a barrister is not immune when advising a potential litigant or in the preparation of the pleadings of a case.

The police have also been held to be immune in their investigations of crimes. The House of Lords' decision in *Hill v Chief Constable of West Yorkshire 1988* prevented the mother of a young woman who had been murdered by a multiple murderer suing the Chief Constable for negligence.

The immunity of most importance to the engineer is that of the arbitrator, which is based on the person acting in a capacity the law recognizes as being judicial: where professional people can show that they are acting in a judicial capacity, they will be immune.

The position of an architect when acting as a certifier was considered in *Sutcliffe v Thackrah 1974*. Before this case the belief was, based on an old Court of Appeal decision, that an architect was protected when acting as a certifier. Sutcliffe had engaged a firm of architects to design and supervise the construction of a house on land he owned. Payment was made to the builder by interim certificates, but the work was unsatisfactory: some interim certificates were issued which were not justified. The builder obtained payment on the certificates and then went bankrupt. Sutcliffe sued claiming negligence in the issue of the certificates. The defence that the architect was immune because of the function he was exercising, said to be semi-arbitral, was rejected. The House of Lords held that the architect was not immune. He owed a duty of care to his client with regards to the issue of the interim certificates. He had been negligent in that matter and so was liable.

State of the art

A court hearing will inevitably be heard some years after the event giving rise to a claim for professional negligence. The court has to avoid applying the state of knowledge current at the time of the hearing. The assessment by the court has to be made on the state of the art current at the time the event occurred: this is what the average member of a profession should have knowledge of at that time. Judicial comments have indicated that the average member of a profession should be aware of current developments, as reported in journals normally read by members of that profession. A professional person is not expected to be aware of developments described in another country's journals in foreign languages.

In the case of *Thompson and Others v Smith Shiprepairers (North Shields) Ltd 1984*, claims were made by employees of Smith Shiprepairers, who had lengthy service, for impairment of their hearing. They all worked where there was excessive noise but they were not provided with any form of protection until the early 1970s, by which time some had been exposed to the noise for thirty or more years. Harm caused by industrial noise was not the subject of any government information until 1963, when the Ministry of Labour issued a pamphlet; there was then a general awareness of the problem. Advice and means of protection were available.

Submissions were made to the court that industrial noise in a shipyard was excessive, well recognized and so required an employer to take action to protect employees from that risk. Failure to do so meant that the employer was negligent.

The High Court decided that employers were negligent when they failed to provide protection against industrial noise at a time when, in the same circumstances, a reasonable and prudent employer would have made such provision; regard being had to what they knew or ought to have known at that time. The employees were entitled to compensation for that degree of industrial deafness which arose after the date, 1963, when the employer became aware of the risk of industrial deafness.

The case of *Roe v Minister of Health 1954* dealt with a claim by a patient who became paralysed following a spinal injection. The anaesthetic injected was contained in a glass ampoule; the practice at that time was to store the ampoule in a bath of disinfectant. Before use the glass ampoule would be checked visually for cracks and if free of such cracks used. What was not known, but was revealed in the circumstances of the case, was that there could be fine cracks which were not detectable to visual examination.

The injection of the anaesthetic, which was contaminated with disinfectant, paralysed Roe from the waist down. It was claimed that there was negligence on the part of the hospital in failing to incorporate a colouring agent into the disinfectant so that any leakage through a crack not visible would be apparent.

In the Court of Appeal, Lord Denning, the Master of the Rolls, said that the doctor's failure to know that there could be undetectable cracks did not amount to negligence at that time. He said: 'We must not look at the 1947 accident with 1954 spectacles'. The decision was that there was no negligence on the part of the doctor, he had done what was common practice at that time. The claim of Roe was therefore dismissed.

Breach of liability to client

Liability to a client may arise either in contract or tort or both (see p. 211); liability may arise from a range of the functions of professional people to their clients. For the civil engineer, the two most important functions are those of design work and the supervision of works.

If a standard form of contract is used, such as the Association of Consulting Engineers' Conditions of Engagement, the terms are set out as to what services the professional person would provide for the client. If no standard form of contract is used, the implied term of reasonable skill and care applies in a range of matters, as may be seen from judicial decisions.

The case of *Sykes v Midland Bank Executor and Trustee Co Ltd 1971* dealt with a claim against a solicitor for professional negligence. The solicitor had been instructed by a firm of architects and surveyors to act for them in the acquisition of a lease to premises they wished to use in their practice. When the firm of architects and surveyors, after occupying the premises for some time, tried to transfer the lease they found that they could not do so. A clause in the lease restricted such transfer. The solicitor was held liable since he had failed to advise his client of the effect of such a clause. The Court of Appeal accepted that a solicitor would normally draw the client's attention to such a clause and give advice. The court rejected the submission that because the clients were architects and surveyors they did not need such advice. The fact that a client was an experienced business person did not remove the duty of the solicitor to warn of and advise on the clause.

The extent of the duty to advise a client properly is to be seen in the case of *Nye Saunders and Partners (A Firm) v Alan E Bristow 1987*. Mr Bristow wished to renovate a mansion that he owned and engaged Nye Saunders, a firm of architects, to obtain planning permission for the renovation. He told them that he could spend £250 000 on the renovation and asked for a written estimate of the likely cost for the works. The architects consulted a quantity surveyor and then submitted a schedule of costs totalling £238 000. The schedule did not contain any provision for inflation, which at that time was substantial, nor for any contingencies. It soon became apparent that the works would cost much more than the quoted sum: an updated figure of £440 000 was given to the client. For the first time this included a figure for inflated costs over the eighteen-month contract period. Mr Bristow immediately terminated the architects' engagement; the architects then sued for their fees.

The Court of Appeal decided that the architects were not entitled to their fees. There was a duty on them to warn Mr Bristow that the estimate they had given him did not take account of inflation. They were in breach of this duty. The fact that they had made use of the services of a quantity surveyor did not exonerate them: it was the architects' duty to warn the client that inflation had not been taken into account.

An unusual case where the High Court held an architect to be negligent for not appreciating a point of law was that of *B L Holdings Ltd v R T Wood and Partners 1978*. B L Holdings had a derelict site in Brighton which they intended to develop as an office. At that time an office development over 10 000 square feet could proceed only if in addition to planning permission an office development permit had been granted: this was to control office development on a national scale. Wood and Partners were appointed architects for the development. In their negotiations with the local planning authority they were told that the development would have to have car parking space but that this would not be included in the calculation to determine whether or not an office development permit was needed. The architects were surprised at this but did not inform the clients of their surprise at this decision. In a later discussion with the local planning authority it was agreed that an additional floor to provide residential accommodation for a caretaker would also not be included in the calculation. Eventually planning permission was granted for an office development which had a total area of 16 000 square feet, of which 10 000 square feet was office space. No office development permit was granted.

In 1972 the development was completed; a prospective tenant's solicitor queried the absence of an office development permit and the letting fell through. It was not until 1976, when the 10 000 square feet exemption was raised to 50 000 square feet, that the building was let. This resulted in a substantial loss to the clients, who sued the architects for breach of duty and negligence in failing to bring to their attention that an office development permit was needed.

In the High Court the judge held the architects to be liable: any competent architect would have been aware of this particular provision in planning law and that without an office development permit the planning application would be ineffective. At the very least the architects should have given warning and advice to the clients. The judge said 'it may be thought by some to be hard to require an architect that he know more law than the planning authority'.

The Court of Appeal held that the architects had not been negligent or in breach of their duty. The court disagreed with the judge's opinion as to what could reasonably be required of an architect in a difficult area of planning law. They did not disagree that the architects should have notified the clients of their surprise at the local planning authority's decision. Then the clients could have sought independent legal advice; the position could have been clarified with the local planning authority's legal staff or even by a court declaration.

The attitude of the High Court judge may seem strange: he said that the architects ought to have known that the local planning authority were acting incorrectly and that the planning permission was likely to be invalid. Whatever the planning law position, if the architects had communicated their fears to the clients they would have discharged their duty.

Another unusual case of liability to a client was *Cotton v Wallis 1955*. Wallis was an architect who was employed to supervise the building of a house and on completion to certify that the work had been done to his reasonable satisfaction. The specification required the contractor to use materials and workmanship to a stated high standard. The architect certified completion. The owner, however, was dissatisfied and claimed that the architect had acted negligently in certifying the work when, in the owner's opinion, it was of an inferior standard. The Court of Appeal refused by a majority to overrule the judge in the High Court who had decided that the architect was not negligent. The house was being 'built down to a price': this factor allowed the architect to accept work even though it was not of the highest standard.

Reliance on others

In the construction industry it is common practice to make use of various professional people's special skills and services for a particular development; sometimes these are obtained before any contract is let for the development. The person undertaking the production of all the information needed for tenders to be submitted may also call on the services of other professional people.

In the case of *Moresk (Cleaners) Ltd v Hicks 1966*, Moresk engaged an architect to design a building. The design supplied was of a reinforced concrete structure. The architect, who was not familiar with work of this kind, had sought the services of a structural engineer for the production of the structural design. The building was constructed in accordance with the architect's design. Within two years there were cracks in the structure and the roof purlins were sagging; these defects were due to faults in the design of the building. When Moresk sued, the architect pleaded that it was an implied term of his contract of engagement that he was entitled to delegate specified design tasks to qualified specialists.

The High Court rejected this defence: the architect had no power whatsoever to delegate his duty. He had no implied authority to use the services of any other person. The position would be different if the architect, or any other professional person, has express authority to use the services of other specialists.

The case of *Nye Saunders and Partners v Alan E Bristow 1987* (see p. 219) is relevant here: the architects' use of a quantity surveyor did not absolve them from the duty to advise the client that the schedule of costs prepared had not made any allowance for inflation. The duty to warn and advise on the likely effect of inflation was that of the architects.

Where a professional person has not made use of a specialist and possibly not made a charge for a service then, if the professional person is not undertaking any responsibility in that matter, there is a need to make this clear to the client. Otherwise it could be held that from the professional services normally expected from a professional person there was liability.

In the case of *Richard Roberts Holdings Ltd and Another v Douglas Smith Stimson Partnership and Others 1988*, Richard Roberts owned a dyeworks which they wished to extend. The Partnership were architects who had acted for them on a number of other projects, in addition to which a director was a friend of one of the partners. The new project included an effluent tank. On a previous project a consulting engineer with specialized knowledge of dyeing equipment had been used. No such appointment was made for this project but the architects could have available if they so wished technical advice from Holdings' senior staff. The architects designed an effluent tank which would cost some £35 000. Holdings told the architects to consider cheaper alternatives. While enquiries were being made, the main contractor proceeded with the work, including the construction of the effluent tank shell. It was not then possible, without demolition of the shell, to install a steel lining. The architects obtained an estimate of £15 000 for a tank lining of resin and glass fibre. Eventually an estimate from another contractor for £3240 for lining the tank with chopped strand matt and resin was accepted.

The architects asked the contractor to comment on the life expectancy of this form of lining but received no reply. Holdings accepted the estimate and made a contract direct with that contractor. The architects did not charge any fee with regard to the tank lining, which failed not long after installation. Holdings then sued, among others, the architects.

The High Court decided that the architects had been employed to design and to see to the alteration of the effluent tank. If they had wanted to limit their role in this work they should have done so expressly and in writing. They were not bystanders with regard to the choice of the lining to the tank. The architects had failed adequately to investigate the lining that was installed and to advise Holdings before the contract was made. The expertise of architects was to be able to collect information about materials of which they lacked knowledge and experience and to form a view on the topic. If they had felt unable to form a reliable judgement, they should have told Holdings this and advised them to seek advice elsewhere.

The fact that the architects did not charge a fee did not remove liability from them. They owed a duty of care and in the circumstances were in breach of that duty. Clearly to have told Holdings that they were not in a position to advise on the matter, or better still, to have in writing disclaimed any liability on the matter would have put Holdings on notice to take other steps in order to protect their interests.

Inexperience of the professional person

Inexperienced professional people, particularly younger members of a profession, may believe that because of their inexperience or youth, they ought to be judged differently. This is not the case: the judgement of any member of a profession is based on Bolam's test. It is not normally an accepted defence to claim that a person has limited experience. It might be different if a person giving advice or information made it clear that it was not a topic on which the person had knowledge and experience and it had to be accepted on that basis.

In the case of *Wilsher v Essex Area Health Authority 1988*, a baby who was born prematurely suffered, among other troubles, a deficiency of oxygen. The approved practice of administering oxygen was followed, but by mistake the junior doctor inserted a tube into a vein instead of an artery; this mistake was not detected by a senior doctor. The monitoring equipment failed to register the excess oxygen. The child's body had to cope with excess oxygen which it was claimed caused almost total blindness.

The Court of Appeal, dealing with the matter of liability, dismissed the concept of there being 'team negligence'. It was difficult to apply a uniform standard when the team would possibly contain a student nurse and an experienced consultant. By a majority the court decided that there could not be a different standard for a junior doctor; otherwise the right of a patient to complain of faulty treatment would depend on the doctor who dealt with the patient. One of the judges expressed the opinion that the law required trainees or learners to be judged by the same standard as their more experienced colleagues. Otherwise inexperience would be a frequent defence in a negligence action. If inexperienced doctors are called upon to exercise some specialist skill, then if they call for the advice and help of a superior it may well be that they are not negligent even if they had made a mistake. Another judge, while accepting that this was not the present legal position, thought that young inexperienced house doctors who are acquiring their initial medical experience ought to be judged by the standard of the position they held. He considered that, in all fairness, junior doctors could not be held to be at fault when they lack the skills they are seeking to obtain.

This case went on to the House of Lords, who ordered a retrial.

Skill of the client

A professional person whose services are given to a client who possesses some skill and experience in that subject may justifiably believe that if his or her service is accepted and later a fault is detected then the acceptance by the client is a relevant factor; what weight can be attached to this must depend on particular circumstances.

In the case of *Sykes v Midland Bank Executor and Trustee Co Ltd 1971* (see p. 218); professional people are under a duty to advise their clients on an unusual clause in a lease even when their clients are architects and surveyors who had both knowledge and experience of leasing premises.

An example of the experience of the client being accepted as a relevant factor is in *Worboys v Acme Investments Ltd 1969*. An architect had been engaged to provide a scheme by which as many houses as possible could be built on a site owned by the development company. An agreed fee of £2000 was to be paid in instalments. The first was paid immediately the scheme was accepted and the second instalment when 'half the buildings are built and finished'. Disagreement arose about the payment of the second instalment. Worboys sued for this payment. In their defence the developers alleged negligence against the architect. They claimed that the houses, which were to be sold as luxury houses at a then high price of £7500 had not sold because they had not been designed with a downstairs cloakroom, a feature that prospective purchasers would expect a house to have when sold at that price. This, the developers said, was negligence on Worboys part.

The Court of Appeal held the architect not to be negligent on this matter. One judge observed that the architect was dealing with a director of the developers who had twenty-five years' experience of development schemes and who of all people would know best whether houses of the type designed were saleable in the area without a downstairs cloakroom. He noted that the plans had been scrutinized on more than one occasion by the director, who knew what was wanted for that type of house. He clearly approved the plans and, in the judge's view, this broke the chain of causation of damage even if the architect was to blame. Another judge supported these views: it was unjust to blame the architect for a supposed inefficiency when the developers had accepted the plan and built the houses. The director could well appreciate that there was to be only one lavatory in the house. No objection was made to this.

The Court of Appeal also drew attention to the need, when a professional person is having to answer a charge of negligence, to have expert evidence put before the court so that a proper assessment may be made. Only in the obvious cases of omissions, such as the failure to provide a front door to premises, should the court deal with such a claim in the absence of expert evidence.

These two cases show that each set of circumstances will determine how much dependence can be put on the skill and experience of the client. For example, a structural engineer who was very experienced in a particular type of design, and who was engaged by another structural engineer to deal with that requirement in a project, could hardly avoid liability on the ground that he was dealing with another member of his profession.

Liability for design

What is possibly the greatest fear of any civil engineer is that he or she will produce a design which in some way is faulty with the result that a structure or a building collapses or has to be demolished because it is unsafe. This type of negligence occurs very infrequently but when it does it attracts a great deal of unfortunate publicity. Liability may arise under contract or in tort or both.

A leading case is *Greaves and Co (Contractors) Ltd v Baynham Meikle and Partners 1975*. Greaves were building contractors who undertook by means of a 'package deal' contract the construction of an oil storage warehouse complex, including a factory, warehouse and offices. The warehouse was to be used for the storage of barrels of oil, which would need to be moved safely from one point to another within the warehouse. The oil company made this purpose known to the building contractors, who therefore when they undertook to provide a building which would meet all the client's needs were agreeing to provide a building which would be fit for its known purpose. It was a contract which went beyond the obligation to use reasonable skill and care; it was a contract to provide a finished building fit for its known purpose.

Under the contract Greaves undertook to do everything which was necessary, so the client did not make use of the services of an architect, quantity surveyor, structural engineer or any other professional person. Because Greaves did not have a structural engineer on their staff they engaged Baynham Meikle to design the structure and in particular the first floor of the warehouse. The warehouse was to be a composite construction system in structural steel and concrete. The floor would be made of pre-cast concrete sections resting on the steel frame of the building with concrete then poured to bind the sections to form a solid floor. The form of construction was governed by the British Standard Code of Practice 1965, CP117.

When the structural engineers were appointed by Greaves there were discussions about the warehouse. It was made known to them that the first floor of the warehouse was to be used for the storage of filled oil drums and that fork-lift trucks were to be used to move these oil drums. The floor therefore had to be adequate to withstand the weight of the drums and the movement of the trucks. The designs were made and the warehouse built. A short while after it was put into use the floor cracked, which caused alarm to those employed there. The cracks seemed to be getting worse. Expert opinion was sought and attempts made to remedy the problem, without success. The building had a limited use because of this problem; the cost of remedial works was likely to be substantial.

The structural engineers believed that the cause of the cracking was the result of shrinkage of the concrete, a construction defect for which they were not responsible. The builders' view was that it was a design fault. In the High Court experts gave evidence for each party to support their beliefs. The judge decided that it was a design fault: the Council of British Standards Institution had issued a circular warning that CP117 required designers to satisfy themselves that there would be no undesirable vibrations caused by the imposed loading. Serious vibrations may result when dynamic forces are applied at a frequency near to one of the natural frequencies of the members. The judge decided that the structural engineer had not paid sufficient regard to this caution in using CP117 and had designed a floor which was not of sufficient strength to withstand the vibrations created by the use of the fork-lift trucks.

The Court of Appeal dismissed the resulting appeal. Using Bolam's test, the structural engineer had not used reasonable skill and care in the design and so was liable. There was also liability for breach of an implied term of the agreement that they would produce a design which was fit for its known purpose. They were fully aware of the purpose of use of the floor and they had warranted to produce a design fit for its intended purpose. The structural engineer was required to indemnify Greaves of the obligations they owed to the client.

The Court of Appeal took the opportunity, because of the High Court judge using certain words, to restate that there are not forms of negligence, such as 'gross' negligence. There is only one form of negligence and that is based on Bolam's test.

Another case involving design responsibility was that of *Independent Broadcasting Authority v EMI Electronics Ltd and BICC (Construction) Ltd 1980*. Independent Broadcasting Authority (IBA) wanted to have a television mast erected; EMI were main contractors and BICC were nominated sub-contractors for the design, supply and erection of the mast, which was to be 1250 feet high. The mast was to be of cylindrical construction, a form of construction not previously used. The mast was to have three lanes of stays. Because of the oscillations noted on another mast of IBA, BICC were asked to investigate this in order that the design data for the new mast could be confirmed. BICC confirmed that the structure would not oscillate dangerously; this assurance was given in a letter to IBA. The design work continued and when submitted carried a note that no allowance had been made for ice on the stays. The mast was constructed in accordance with the design.

In November 1966 IBA accepted the completed mast. In March 1969 the mast broke and collapsed. The weather was very cold: evidence showed that that type of weather was likely to occur every three or four years.

IBA sued both EMI and BICC for breach of contract and negligence. The High Court judge decided that the mast had broken because the design had failed to consider the effects on the mast of vortex shedding and asymmetric ice loading on the stays. The judgment was that this constituted negligence. An appeal was made to the House of Lords.

BICC were held liable for negligence in the design of the mast because they had failed to take account of the possibility of oscillations of the mast. The assurance given by them in the letter to IBA that they were well satisfied that the structure would not oscillate dangerously was a negligent misstatement under the principle in *Hedley Byrne and Co Ltd v Heller and Partners Ltd 1964* (see p. 177). It was an assurance given negligently, on which IBA had relied. EMI were also liable as they had contractually accepted responsibility for the design of the mast.

An engineer who undertakes a design responsibility is under a duty to use reasonable skill and care. This duty, however, is limited to producing a proper design unless the engineer has expressly undertaken some additional responsibility.

The case of *Holland Hannen and Cubitts (Northern) Ltd v Welsh Health Technical Services Organisation and Others 1985* came about because of a claim by Cubitts which was settled out of court. Part of that claim related to a bad floor design. A firm of consulting structural engineers had been retained to advise on the design and construction of the floors to a new hospital. In the High Court the structural engineers were held to be negligent.

The Court of Appeal decision, by a majority, was that the structural engineers had not been negligent. The issue of negligence was whether it was the duty of the structural engineers to foresee and warn their clients of the visual appearance that the floors might have when tiles were laid on them. The majority of the appeal judges were of the opinion that the visual appearance or aesthetic effect were things which came within the province of the architect and not the structural engineer. The duty of the structural engineer was to work out the deflections of the floor; the architect was then to work out whether a floor with those deflections would be visually attractive when the chosen floor finishes were used. No case of breach of contract or negligence had been made out against the structural engineer. The other judge differed from his colleagues: the structural engineer had an expertise to appreciate the likely profile of the floor when constructed to the design submitted and that it would be unacceptable to a reasonable building owner or the architect. He would have confirmed the High Court judge's opinion that the structural engineer had been negligent.

Negligent surveys

An important development in professional negligence concerns negligent surveys. After a number of conflicting decisions, the House of Lords gave an authoritive ruling in the case of *Smith v Bush 1989*. Mrs Smith, wishing to purchase a house with the assistance of a building society mortgage, paid to the society an inspection fee of £36.99. The application form to the society for the valuation survey carried a disclaimer of liability. The society instructed a firm of surveyors, Eric S Bush, to carry out a valuation survey, which put a valuation of £16 500 on the house. The surveyor in his report stated that no essential repairs were required: the survey was a visual inspection only and solely for valuation purposes. The survey report, a copy of which was given to Mrs Smith, carried a disclaimer of liability on the part of the surveyor. Mrs Smith relied on the valuation survey and did not have a structural survey carried out. She bought the house for £18 000 with the aid of a mortgage of £3500 from the society.

Mrs Smith was doing what many others do: relying on the survey being sufficient to justify the building society lending the money. This is a usual practice with modestly priced houses.

Eighteen months after Mrs Smith moved in, bricks from the chimneys fell through the bedroom ceilings causing considerable damage. This collapse had been caused by chimney breasts in the bedrooms being removed and the upper part of the chimneys left unsupported. The surveyor had noted the removals but had not checked in the roof space to see what had been done to support the chimneys.

The House of Lords had to decide whether the surveyor's omission was negligence; whether the disclaimer was a notice under the Unfair Contract Terms Act 1977; and whether if it was a notice it was fair and reasonably sufficient to disclaim liability. The survey was held to have been conducted negligently. The disclaimer in the surveyor's report was held to be a notice under the Unfair Contract Terms Act 1977 and therefore had to satisfy the test of reasonableness if it was to be effective. The Law Lords took the view that if the disclaimer was to be effective the whole pattern of house purchases had to be taken into account: it would not be fair and reasonable for building societies and surveyors to disclaim liability in such house purchases. The disclaimer was therefore not effective and Mrs Smith was awarded damages.

The House of Lords noted that the decision would be unlikely to apply in the case of valuation surveys of industrial property, large blocks of flats and expensive houses: here a structural survey would be necessary. In valuation surveys of such properties it would be reasonable for surveyors to limit their liability.

Construction operations

Professional negligence may arise with construction operations where the professional person fails to fulfil an obligation. For example engineers who negligently certified work as being satisfactorily completed when that was not the case would be liable to their clients.

The liability of an architect or engineer when an accident occurs in construction work depends on the circumstances. In the case of *Oldschool v Gleeson (Construction) Ltd and Others 1976* (see p. 103) a contractor's excavations undermined the foundations of a house causing the collapse of the party wall of a house. The design of the consulting engineer was held not to be unsound. The High Court also decided that it was not the responsibility of the consulting engineer to instruct the contractor as to the way in which the contract works were done. Even if a consulting engineer knew (or ought to have known) that a contractor was failing to take proper precautions so that there was a risk of damage to property, the duty that the engineer owed the contractor was limited to giving a warning to take the necessary precautions. In this case the engineer was held to have given a warning and so was not liable to the contractor.

This decision may be compared with that of *Clay v A J Crump and Sons Ltd and Others 1964* (see p. 103) where an architect agreed without making an inspection that it was safe to leave a wall of a building standing. This was a departure from the demolition proposals. The architect accepted the assurance of the demolition contractor; he visited the site but failed to inspect the wall. If he had he would have appreciated that it was unsafe to leave it standing. The architect's actions constituted negligence and he, together with the demolition contractor and main contractor, was required to pay damages to Clay who had been injured when the wall fell.

In the case of *Clayton v Woodman and Sons (Builders) Ltd and Others 1962* an architect was sued by a bricklayer when a wall collapsed. The accident occurred when the bricklayer was cutting a chase into a brick wall. When the architect visited the site to inspect the wall the bricklayer had suggested to him that a better way of dealing with the wall would be to demolish it and then rebuild it. The architect declined to order this change to the contract. The bricklayer continued cutting the chase and the wall fell, injuring him. It was a provision in the specification that the wall was to be supported while the chase was being cut, but this was not done.

The decision of the Court of Appeal was that the architect was not liable to the bricklayer for negligence. What the architect had done was simply to leave the contract to be performed in the required way. The fact that that was not done was not his responsibility. The architect owed no duty of care to the bricklayer.

The difference between this case and Clay's case is that with Clayton's case the architect did not change the contract or involve himself in the contract execution. In Clay's case the architect had varied the contract and involved himself in the contract works.

Liability to the contractor

When the House of Lords made their decision in the case of *Sutcliffe v Thackrah 1974* that an architect did not enjoy any immunity when acting as a certifier, and so could be sued by the client for negligence in wrongly certifying payment for work improperly done, there was a general understanding that the architect owed a duty to the contractor too, in effect holding a balance between the client and the contractor.

The case of *Pacific Associates Inc and Another v Baxter and Others 1989* arose from Pacific entering into a contract with the ruler of Dubai for dredging and reclamation work. The contractor was aware when he tendered for the work that there would be supervision by a consultant engineer acting for the client and that payment would be by certificates issued by the engineer. The contractors encountered a lot of hard material which made the work more difficult. They claimed that the tender information was inaccurate, which meant that the tender price was too low. A provision in the contract allowed for extra payment if the contractors encountered hard material during the dredging work which could not have been reasonably foreseen by an experienced contractor. The contractors made several claims under this provision, all of which were rejected by the engineer, who believed that the hard material was reasonably foreseeable. The contractors brought an action against the engineer claiming £45 million. It was alleged that the engineer was negligent or under a duty to act fairly and impartially in administering the contract and in breach of that duty by failing to issue certificates for payment to the contractors for the removal of the hard material.

The Court of Appeal rejected the claim. Where there was a contract between a client and an engineer there was a duty on the engineer to the client to use reasonable care and skill in overseeing the contractors' work, and there would be liability to the client, if the client was sued by the contractors, for economic loss suffered by the client because of the negligence of the engineer. In the case of the contractors, however, there was no such contractual relationship and in the absence of any assumption of liability in tort no claim could be made against the engineer. The court also observed that the contractors could under their contract with the employers claim for extra payment. There was an arbitration provision when, having followed the correct procedure, the contractors remained dissatisfied with the engineer's decision.

8

Land law

Freehold and leasehold land

The Law of Property Act 1925 altered substantially the law concerning land; its principal purpose was to simplify the law and so reduce the cost of conveyancing. This was achieved by reducing the number of legal estates in land to two, which are set out in Section 1 of the Act:

1 an estate in fee simple absolute in possession
2 an estate term of years absolute.

The estate in fee simple absolute in possession is that of freehold. The word 'fee' means that the estate is capable of inheritance. 'Simple' means that the estate is not restricted, such as being limited to male successors. 'Absolute' means that the estate is perpetual: it does not come to an end on the occurrence of some event. 'Possession' means not only physical possession but also the right to possession. It is usual to refer to the estate as fee simple. This estate for all practical purposes is absolute ownership.

The estate term of years absolute is usually referred to as leasehold; it arises when a person who holds an estate grants out of his or her estate a lease to another person. So a person who holds the freehold of land or a lease can grant a lease to another person.

Despite the description 'term of years', there can be a lease of less than a year, or for a year or from year to year. So there can be a lease for 999 years for building purposes, known as a ground lease, or a lease for, say, commercial premises for twenty-one years. Residential properties may have leases for a month or a week.

For a lease to exist there must be exclusive possession of the property and a stated beginning and end to the period of the lease. If there is not exclusive possession, the person using the property of another has a lesser right in law known as a licence.

The importance of leases and the need to maintain a fair balance between landlord and tenant has caused Parliament to make detailed provisions apply to their relationship. The Landlord and Tenant Act 1954 applies to leases of commercial and industrial properties, and the Rent Act 1977 to some residential properties.

Landlords of leased property, who have in effect 'lent' their land for a period of time, will protect their interest in the property by inserting provisions in the lease. These provisions, known as covenants, impose obligations on the tenant as to the way the property is to be used and the tenant's responsibilities with regard to maintenance of the property.

A breach of a provision in a lease allows a landlord to bring the lease to an end and require the tenant to leave the property. The Law of Property Act 1925 lays down a procedure which landlords must follow if they wish to exercise this right. This procedure gives the tenant a last chance to put right the breach of covenant.

Restrictions on the use and enjoyment of land

The well-known expression 'An Englishman's home is his castle' was true at one time; for a considerable number of years, however, this has not been the case. Landowners can now use their land subject to certain restrictions which have been imposed by common law and statute to the benefit of the public. Public interests override private interests.

Landowners must not cause nuisance to their neighbours by the activities they carry out on their land (see p. 153). If their activities do cause nuisance, the courts have powers to intervene and control the activities by way of injunctions and the award of damages. Under the rule in *Rylands v Fletcher 1868* landowners may be liable for harm caused by the escape of things brought on their land (see p. 166). Liability also arises when the owner of land next to a highway allows the property to create a danger to users of the highway, as we saw in the case of *Tarry v Ashton 1876* (p. 153). There may also be a duty of care owed under the common law tort of negligence.

Treasure trove

The finding of fossils, coins, articles of value and other specified things is regulated between the employer and the contractor (Clause 32 of the Institution of Civil Engineers' Conditions of Contract 6th edition: see p. 112). Between the employer and the contractor any such find is deemed to be the absolute property of the employer.

What this provision does not regulate is the find of treasure trove, which consists of a find of gold or silver (in manufactured form) which has been deliberately hidden and the owner of which is unknown. Treasure trove is restricted to gold or silver so other valuable metals or objects are excluded; the definition also excludes gold or silver in its state as an ore. If the gold or silver has been deliberately hidden by a person who intended to recover it later, and that can be substantiated, then the find is not treasure trove. The decision as to whether or not a find is treasure trove is made by a coroner's jury.

The importance of treasure trove is that any such find is claimed by the Crown. Clause 32 is inapplicable since there is no question of ownership by either the employer or the contractor. In practice the find goes to the British Museum which identifies and values the find. If the museum wishes to retain the find it does so, otherwise the find is returned to the finder. If the find is retained, its value is paid to the finder. This is not a legal requirement but a long-established practice so that finds of possible national interest are not concealed but are revealed promptly; they may then be evaluated and any necessary preservation works carried out. Where there is a failure to disclose the find or the full extent of it, the finder may not be rewarded, or be awarded only part of its value.

Statute

Landowners' rights to use their land have been reduced over time by provisions in Acts of Parliament. Public benefits have been considered to be of greater importance than the private interests of landowners. Parliament has passed legislation removing landowners' rights and controlling some of the ways in which they use their land.

Minerals

By ancient Acts of Parliament and also by common law gold and silver found in strata belong to the Crown. Oil in a natural strata is also claimed by the Crown: this was first provided by the Petroleum (Production) Act 1934 when exploration started in Britain. The Act has been subsequently amended. Coal was originally vested in the Coal Commission, in return for compensation, by the Coal Act 1938. Subsequently coal became vested in the National Coal Board, now British Coal, by later Acts of Parliament.

Water

Originally landowners had rights at common law to take water which flowed through defined channels in their land. The rights were not unlimited but allowed the landowner to take an unrestricted quantity for domestic use and to take water for non-domestic use provided that water was returned undiminished in quality and quantity. Now these rights are subject to the provisions in the Water Resources Act 1963, with later amendments. This restricts the abstraction of water, except by a licence granted by the controlling water body.

Other controls

The main form of statutory control is the Town and Country Planning Act 1990, as amended. Landowners are controlled with regard to the right to erect buildings and structures on their land, carry out certain activities on their land and the use to which they can put their land and buildings on their land. Buildings and structures which have been included in a list prepared by the Department of the Environment as being of architectural or historic interest are subject to special control: building work is subject to consent and requires the work and materials used to be consistent with the character of the building.

The Environmental Protection Act 1990 has updated the statutory law with regard to industrial activities carried out on land, which are now subject to authorization granted by the enforcing authority and subject to conditions.

Other statutes empower an authority to acquire land, compulsorily if necessary, for public purposes. Landowners are compensated for the value of the land taken; they are not allowed to resist the acquisition of their land for a public purpose authorized by an Act of Parliament. An example of this is the Highways Act 1980, under which a highways authority may acquire land, by negotiation or compulsorily, for the construction of a new highway or the improvement of an existing highway.

Licences in land

The Law of Property Act 1925 created two legal estates in land, the fee simple absolute in possession and the term of years absolute, more usually referred to as freehold and leasehold (see p. 230). The lesser legal right, a licence, is permission to go on land and to carry out some activities. Without this permission the person who goes on the land will be a trespasser. There are three main forms of licence: bare licence, contractual licence and licence coupled with an interest.

Bare licence

This simplest form of licence consists of permission given without any payment of money for a person to enter land. An example would be the owner of a field who allowed it to be used without charge for a charitable or public purpose. A bare licence allows the landowner to revoke the licence at any time, subject to the licensee having reasonable time to leave the land.

Contractual licence

This is also known as a licence for value. It is a contract; a simple example is a person who pays a fee or charge to watch a match or entertainment. As it is a contract the licensee has legal rights under the licence. Should the licensor seek to revoke the licence before it has fulfilled the purpose for which it was granted, the licensee may ask the court for an injunction to restrain the threatened revocation. If the revocation takes place, the licensee may sue for damages for the breach of contract. In some circumstances where a person has taken occupation of property without paying any charge or fee but performing services, the courts have held that this created a contractual licence, which entitled the licensee to obtain the assistance of the courts in remaining in possession.

Licence coupled with an interest

This is the highest form of licence. It is a two-stage licence: the first part is the right to enter the land and the second part the right to take some produce from the land or some other thing recognized by law. Examples include the right to enter land and take wood or dig peat or the right to re-enter land. In recent years the courts have shown a willingness to treat the expression 'interest in land' in a wider sense, which resulted in a person who could show some proprietary interest being held to have an interest in land. A licence coupled with an interest cannot be revoked; any attempt to do so may be restrained by a court injunction.

The matter of licences in land is important to civil engineering and building contractors. The contractors undertake to perform a contract on land owned by the employer. The contractors when taking possession of the site are not given a lease of the site, but have in law a licence to enter the land in order to perform their contractual obligations.

The leading case is that of *London Borough of Hounslow v Twickenham Garden Developments Ltd 1970*, which arose from a contract (JCT 1963 Edition) placed by the borough for the construction on their own land of a residential development of over 1000 dwellings. The date for completion of the contract was to be four years from the date of possession of the site being given to the contractors, which was 19 September 1966. In 1968 and 1969 there were prolonged labour troubles on the site, which was completely closed down by a strike that lasted several months. When the strike was resolved and the work resumed, the progress of the work did not satisfy the borough. The architect therefore in accordance with Clause 25 of the contract gave notice of his dissatisfaction as to the rate of progress and required within fourteen days the contractors to proceed regularly and diligently with the work. After this period had elapsed, the borough, as the party to the contract, gave notice to the contractors that as work was not proceeding regularly and diligently the borough were determining the employment of the contractors. The contractors, however, refused to accept this notice and challenged the borough on the ground that the architect had failed to issue a valid notice in accordance with the contract and so the contractors' determination of employment was invalid. The ground for this belief was that the architect had misjudged the progress of work and that in the circumstances he was expecting too much. The contractors took the view that the borough's action was a repudiation of the contract, which they refused to accept. The contractors therefore remained on the site and continued with the contract work. The borough started a legal action against the contractors, claiming that they were trespassing and requiring them to leave. An injunction was sought against the contractors to prevent them interfering with the borough's lawful possession of the site.

In the High Court, the judge in a lengthy judgment considered the legal position of a contractor taking possession of a construction site. He examined the previous judicial decisions and came to the conclusion that the contractors were occupying the site as contractual licensees as part of the contract to carry out the works for the borough. He was doubtful that the contractors' licence was a licence coupled with an interest in land. He was, however, firmly of the opinion that the contractors' licence could not be revoked since there was an implied obligation that the contract would not be revoked by the borough while the period of the contract was running. Unless the borough could establish that the architect's notice and the borough's notice were valid, the borough were not entitled to determine the employment of the contractors and require them to leave the site.

The judge decided that as the notices were based on disputed facts as to whether the contract works were being regularly and diligently proceeded with, then the injunctions sought by the borough could not be granted. He felt unable to accept that the borough would be successful in an action to determine the validity of the notices. With this doubt he was unwilling to grant injunctions, which are equitable remedies granted at the court's discretion.

This decision caused some surprise: some believed that any question as to the validity of notices should be decided by an arbitrator appointed under the arbitration clause in the contract. They also believed that the contractors could not ignore a notice to determine their employment and remain on the site. Such action prevents the employer putting another contractor on the site to complete the work.

Easements

English law recognizes that a landowner may have rights over the land of another: the most important is the right of easement, which is a right to use or restrict the use of another person's land. Easements exist in various forms and (unlike some parts of law) new forms may be recognized by the courts. As one judge said 'the class of easements is never closed'. The commonest forms of easements are rights of support, rights of way and rights of light.

Essentials of an easement

For an easement to exist there must be two plots of land. One plot, the servient tenement, is being used by the other plot, the dominant tenement. If one plot of land has a right of way over another, the plot with the right of way is the dominant tenement and the other is the servient tenement.

Other requirements are that the easement must accommodate the dominant tenement; that the two plots of land must not be both owned and occupied by the same person; and that the easement must be capable of forming the subject matter of a grant.

The range of rights recognized as being easements is extensive; some matters, however, have been refused recognition. For example there is no right to a view or to privacy. Although there is a right of support to a building, this does not extend to a right of weatherproofing.

In the case of *Phipps v Pears 1964*, a terrace house was demolished and a new house built. The new house was not built into the adjoining house but had a gable wall close to the wall of the next door house. The new gable wall was single brick only and had no external rendering or other form of protection. Subsequently the other house was demolished, which exposed the new gable wall to the weather. An action claiming that an easement of protection existed was dismissed. The Court of Appeal said that to allow such an easement to exist would prevent people demolishing their house if they so wished.

Also under this requirement the easement must be used without secrecy, without permission and without the use of force.

Creation of easements

There are a number of ways in which an easement may be created, some of more importance than others.

Statute

An easement may be created by an Act of Parliament, generally as one of a number of matters rather than a single matter.

Express grant or reservation

An easement may be created by the owners of the two plots of land executing a deed of grant. For example one owner may agree to allow a drain to be laid across her land which will serve another plot of land in different ownership.

An easement by reservation arises when land is disposed of and in the conveyance of sale the seller reserves for the benefit of other land he owns and occupies some right.

Implied grant and reservation

This depends on a court being satisfied that in the particular circumstances it is right to decide that it must have been intended that the easement should exist.

Implied grant arises when land was disposed of and it must have been the intention that some right would have been, but has not, granted. An example is the easement of necessity, where a person disposes of land without providing a right of way over land he retains.

Implied reservation follows the above but the person disposing of the land has failed to reserve for the benefit of land he or she has retained some right over the disposed. Again the easement of necessity may be the subject of the implied reservation.

Section 62 of the Law of Property Act 1925 provides that when land is conveyed then, unless a contrary intention is expressed, the conveyance is deemed to pass easements and privileges.

Presumed grant or prescription

A feature of English law is that, in certain circumstances, the use of something for a long period of time will be held to be a lawful use. At common law an easement may be established by a presumption that the use has existed from time immemorial and under the doctrine of lost modern grant. Time immemorial is fixed at 1189, the beginning of the reign of Richard I, and was fixed as the limit of legal memory by the Statute of Westminster 1, 1275. In order to succeed in a claim under time immemorial the court has to be satisfied that the right has existed since 1189. Few claims can satisfy this requirement.

The doctrine of lost modern grant is a legal fiction: a creation of law which is known not to be strictly true but is accepted as a means of resolving a difficulty. It was introduced to overcome the problem of proving a claim under time immemorial; it is based on a presumption that the right claimed had actually been granted but the deed of grant has since been lost and so could not be produced as evidence to the court. In practice a minimum of twenty years' use is required before the courts are prepared to apply the doctrine.

Most claims to an easement are established under the Prescription Act 1832, which specifies periods and conditions for an easement to exist. In the case of an easement, other than that of light, the use of twenty years as a right and without interruption means it cannot be defeated by showing that the use began after 1189. If the easement has been enjoyed for forty years as of right and without interruption the claim is absolute unless enjoyed by written consent. The twenty-year period does not establish a claim if its use started by oral or written permission.

In the case of an easement of light the requirement is that actual enjoyment suffices and there is only one period of time – twenty years. A claim for a right of light is defeated only if it is enjoyed by written consent or agreement.

Extinguishment of easements

Easements may be extinguished in a number of ways, such as an Act of Parliament or a deed of release executed by the owners of the two plots of land. It is also possible to extinguish an easement by implied release, where dominant owners by their actions indicate that they have released their right. Non-use of an easement does not in itself mean that an easement has been released.

If the two plots of land become owned and occupied by the same person, the easement ends: people cannot have an easement in their own land.

Right of support

A right of support is an easement. There is also another right of support which, unlike an easement, is not acquired but is a right of ownership of land: this is known as the natural right of support. It is of importance to civil engineers since the natural right of support needs to be taken into account when carrying out excavation work near to the boundary of adjoining land. Although not an easement, it is appropriate to consider it here.

Natural right of support

A natural right of support is a right of ownership of land; it is a right not to have the support provided by neighbouring land removed by the neighbour. If the support is removed by natural causes and not by the neighbour, no right of action arises. The natural right of support does not apply to buildings; it applies to land in its natural state. However, if the withdrawal of support would have caused damage even if a building had not stood on that land, then the action for withdrawal of support may include for the damage to that building.

In the case of *Redland Bricks Ltd v Morris 1969*, Morris owned eight acres of land where he carried on the business of growing strawberries; the value of this land was about £12 000. Adjoining it was land owned by Redland, where clay was extracted to a considerable depth and therefore the operation carried a risk of landslip. Redland were aware of this risk: their chief engineer and production director visited the site and gave instructions that when the quarry reached a certain distance from Morris's land extraction at that point should cease. This was done but the chief engineer's assessment was wrong: part of Morris's land slipped because of lack of support from Redland's land. The area of Morris's land affected was not great but there was a clear risk of further slips. Morris sued in the County Court claiming damages and an injunction to prevent further damage to his land. His claim was successful and he was awarded £325 and two injunctions. The first was to restrain Redland from withdrawing support and the second a mandatory injunction ordering Redland to take all necessary steps to restore the support to Morris's land within six months. Evidence suggested that the cost of this remedial work, which would consist of the construction of a retaining wall, would be in the region of £30 000.

Redland's appeal against the mandatory injunction, with its heavy expenditure, came before the House of Lords, who were agreed that a breach of the natural right of support had occurred for which Morris was entitled to damages and an injunction to restrain any further withdrawal of support. The mandatory injunction, however, was something they were unwilling to accept. They were critical of the injunction in two respects. The first was that the judge in the County Court had not been sufficiently specific in the injunction, in that Redland were not told in adequate detail just what was required of them by way of remedial works. The second criticism was that the judge had not taken into account the fact that the mandatory injunction would require the expenditure of some £30 000 to protect a property which had a value of only £12 000. This expenditure was unreasonable in the circumstances: a few thousand pounds would have been justified but not £30 000. The Law Lords therefore allowed Redland's appeal and discharged the mandatory injunction.

There have been further important cases on the natural right of support concerned with the abstraction of water percolating through the ground which resulted in a withdrawal of support to adjoining land. A leading case is *Langbrook Properties Ltd v Surrey County Council and Others 1969*, where Langbrook were developing a site of some three acres on which buildings had been erected. Surrey County Council were the highways authority for the area and acted as agents for the Ministry of Transport in the construction of a motorway, for which it was necessary to divert an aqueduct and reposition some water mains. These works required the digging of excavations that went below the water table level: pumping was necessary in order to keep them dry. Langbrook claimed that this extraction of water resulted in water being removed from beneath their land, which caused settlement resulting in cracking to their buildings. They claimed damages alleging negligence and nuisance. The High Court decided that neither Surrey County Council nor any of the contractors concerned in the works were liable. In the case of *Bradford Corporation v Pickles 1895* (see p. 155) the House of Lords had decided that it was not unlawful for a person to abstract water which flowed through his land, even if it was done with a malicious intent, provided the water was percolating through the ground and not flowing through channels. The High Court ruled that this decision bound it, in particular taking into account that in this case there was no malicious intent: what had been done was a normal constructional operation.

The correctness of the decision in Langbrook's case was confirmed in the case of *Stephens v Anglian Water Authority 1987*, where the water authority abstracted water percolating through their land which was near to that of Stephens. Stephens claimed that this caused damage to his property and he sued claiming damages for negligence. The Court of Appeal refused to allow the claim to proceed on the ground that the law was so clear on the matter as to preclude a claim being brought.

It may be thought that it is unfair that people whose property suffers damage as a result of their neighbour's action are denied a remedy at law. This view has some support by certain members of the judiciary, but as the authority of the House of Lords' decision in *Bradford Corporation v Pickles* has not been questioned since it was made, there is an obvious reluctance to overturn it.

The position is different if the abstraction is not only of water but also of part of the ground of the neighbour. An activity which results in the removal of part of the neighbour's land, with a consequent withdrawal of support, creates liability on the landowner on whose land that activity is being carried out: if pumping of an excavation leads to the removal of silt, running sand or other material, liability arises.

In the case of *Lotus Ltd v British Soda Co Ltd and Another 1971*, British Soda extracted salt on land which was near to that of Lotus, who had on their land a number of buildings including a factory where about 1300 workers were employed. British Soda's operation involved water being pumped down a borehole dissolving salt which lay in a strata; the brine was then pumped from another borehole. This process was continuous with some 250 000 gallons of brine being extracted each day. Severe damage was caused to buildings on Lotus's land and some had to be demolished. Lotus brought an action claiming damages and seeking an injunction to restrain the brine pumping operations.

The High Court accepted that the damage to the buildings was caused by the brine pumping. The court also considered previous relevant judicial decisions; it was accepted that if there could be liability for the removal of support by the extraction of wet sand, there could not be a significant difference in bringing about the liquefaction of a solid support and then removing the resulting liquid. There was therefore liability for the damage caused to the buildings. British Soda were required to pay damages and were made subject to an injunction restraining their brine extraction.

Acquired right of support

Unlike the natural right of support, an acquired right of support relates to buildings and must be created as an easement in one of the ways considered earlier. The simplest form of an acquired right of support exists with semi-detached houses: an easement will be implied from the fact that the houses were constructed in order to give support to each other. Neither owner may demolish his or her house without taking precautions to protect the right of support the adjoining house possesses. The fact that a right of support exists does not put the servient tenement under a duty to carry out works to maintain the support. Liability arises only if the servient tenement carries out work, such as demolition, which withdraws that support. The owner of the dominant tenement has the right to enter the servient tenement to carry out work necessary to maintain the support: this would be abating a nuisance.

In the case of *Bradburn v Lindsay 1983*, Bradburn purchased a semi-detached house. At this time the adjoining house (owned by Lindsay) was unoccupied and in a somewhat neglected state. The party wall between the two houses was (under the Law of Property Act 1925) divided with each owner of the houses having a right of support to the wall. The house remained unoccupied and its condition deteriorated: dry rot was to be seen. Bradburn therefore complained to Lindsay about the state of the house and the risk of the dry rot extending to his house. Lindsay, however, did nothing. Dry rot did penetrate to Bradburn's house and he had remedial works done to deal with the dry rot. Eventually the local council made a demolition order under the Housing Act 1957. The demolition of the house withdrew support to the party wall and exposed the roof space, part of which was now open to the elements. Bradburn sued claiming damages for negligence and nuisance.

The High Court decided that Lindsay owed a duty of care not to allow the house to deteriorate so as to permit the dry rot to penetrate to Bradburn's house. Damages were awarded to cover Bradburn's expenditure on this matter. The court was also satisfied that there had been a withdrawal of support to the party wall and that buttresses would have to be provided to provide support. The court ordered that this be done.

Right of light

A right of light can come into existence after actual enjoyment of a period of only twenty years (see p. 237); it relates solely to buildings. If a right of light does not exist, an adjoining landowner may erect a building on his or her land which obstructs the light of the neighbour's windows. No liability arises for such action. The fact that a building which had a right of light to its windows is demolished does not extinguish that right of light; a new building erected on the same site will have the same right.

An infringement of a right of light occurs when the obstruction is such that the amount of light left is insufficient to allow a room to be used for its ordinary purposes. This rule was laid down by the House of Lords in the case of *Colls v Home and Colonial Stores Ltd 1904*. It is still the test applied by the courts even though there have been developments which allow measurements of light to be made by instruments.

Restrictive covenants

Before we had any form of planning control some landowners would seek to exercise a degree of control over land they sold by imposing a restriction on the use of that land; this form of control applied to freehold land. If land was to be leased then whatever control the landlord wished to exercise could be done by inserting a provision to that effect in the lease.

Restrictive covenants are still used even though we now have a developed and comprehensive body of planning law. For example a residential developer may sell houses subject to a restrictive covenant that those houses may be used only for residential purposes. Any use of the houses for business purposes, even though no alterations are made to the houses, would be a breach of the restrictive covenant.

Restrictive covenants are private law matters concluded between private individuals: any breach of a restrictive covenant can be dealt with solely by a person who has the benefit of the restrictive covenant. A breach of planning law, however, is dealt with by the local planning authority using the powers given by the Town and Country Planning Act 1990.

A restrictive covenant is negotiated by agreement between two landowners, usually on the sale of land, and is set out in the conveyance of land or a deed. In a residential development the courts allow restrictive covenants to be created by means of a building scheme: this is based on the decision in *Elliston v Reacher 1908*. To come within the decision the restrictive covenant must apply to all the purchasers of the houses; all the houses must have been bought from the same seller; the intention must be that the benefit of the restrictive covenant must be applicable to all the houses; and there must be evidence to show that there was an intention to have a building scheme.

Restrictive covenants may lose their effectiveness; developments may mean that the covenants are an unreasonable restraint on the use of the land. There are therefore means available for the owner of land which is subject to a restrictive covenant to have it modified or discharged: the principal means is by application to the Lands Tribunal. Under Section 84 of the Law of Property Act 1925 the Lands Tribunal has power either to modify a restrictive covenant as it thinks fit, including the power to order compensation to be paid by the person seeking modification to the person having the benefit of the restrictive tribunal, or to discharge it.

To succeed before the Lands Tribunal the applicant must show that either the restrictive covenant has become obsolete, or that it would obstruct the development of land or that all those entitled to the benefit of the restrictive covenant have agreed to its discharge or modification, or that if it is discharged or modified it would not cause injury to those entitled to the benefit of the restrictive covenant. The Lands Tribunal must take account of development plans and any pattern of planning policy with regard to the granting or refusal of planning permission.

Land registers

Many rights can exist in land as well as the right of ownership: some system of recording these matters is essential. An efficient system allows those who are interested in purchasing land to search the registers and so discover what, if anything, is adverse to the purchase of that land. In this way people do not purchase land and then discover that it is subject to some restriction which prevents them using the land as they wish.

There are two systems of recording matters of importance affecting land: the Land Charges Act 1972 governs the national register and the Local Land Charges Act 1975 the local matters.

The Land Charges Act 1972 provides for registers to be kept in the name of the estate owner or other person whose estate or interest is intended to be affected: the search of the registers is against a named person. The Act prescribes certain matters which are required to be registered, including actions which are pending with regard to the land and petitions in bankruptcy, and land charges. The register of land charges includes a number of matters, such as second mortgages, a contract to buy the land and a restrictive covenant. Registration of that charge would have protected the person whose interest it was to have the charge registered and would have warned the prospective purchaser of its existence. The failure to make the necessary registration, in general, deprives the owner of that protection and allows the purchaser to buy free from that matter.

What has just been considered applies to land which is unregistered under the Land Registration Act 1925, as amended. The Act seeks to have a system of registration of all matters of importance affecting land and to record these matters on a certificate. The great benefit is that on a sale of the land the transfer of title is made by the name of the owner being struck off the certificate and the new owner's name inserted. It is therefore a less complicated and expensive way of transferring ownership of land than the traditional method with unregistered land.

The system operates by a register divided into three parts: the property register, which describes the land; the proprietorship register, which contains the name and address of the registered proprietor and the nature of his or her title; and the charges register, which contains details of matters such as mortgages, restrictive covenants and easements. If land is registered under the Land Registration Act 1925, registration under the Land Charges Act 1972 is not allowed. All the necessary information is on the register; failure to register means that a purchaser is not bound by that matter. A beneficial feature of the registration system is that there is a system of compensation if the Land Registry makes some mistake in the registration.

The Local Land Charges Act 1975 deals solely with matters that concern the land and public authorities. Registers are kept which record charges against named properties. If the district council, the authority responsible for keeping the registers, has done work to a property for which a charge has been made, that is entered in the register. Matters appertaining to planning, highway and sewerage are all contained in the register. If the district council issues a search certificate which contains an error, there is a system of compensation for purchasers.

Town and Country Planning Act 1990

The modern law of planning started with the Town and Country Planning Act 1947, the first comprehensive body of statutory law dealing with all aspects of planning. Before 1947 there were various Acts of Parliament that mostly dealt with new developments only and were often adoptive in that a local authority could decide whether or not to use the powers in their area.

Eventually all the law was consolidated into the Town and Country Planning Act 1971, which in turn has been amended. As planning law had become so voluminous Parliament has now passed the Planning (Listed Buildings and Conservation Areas) Act 1990, the Planning (Hazardous Substances) Act 1990, the Planning (Consequential Provisions) Act 1990 and the principal one, the Town and Country Planning Act 1990. All these Acts have been amended to varying degrees by the Planning and Compensation Act 1991.

The reasons for the frequent and often substantial amendments to planning law are that planning controls are used as a means of stimulating economic development, particularly in areas of deprivation, and from time to time events occur which indicate that existing laws are inadequate and require strengthening. Further changes to the law are inevitable: anyone working on something involving planning law needs to check that there has not been a recent relevant amendment.

Local planning authorities

Section 1 of the Town and Country Planning Act 1990 sets out the local planning authorities. In a non-metropolitan county the county council is the county planning authority and the district council the district planning authority. In a metropolitan county the district council is the local planning authority, because the Local Government Act 1985 abolished the metropolitan county councils created under the Local Government Act 1972. The 1985 Act also abolished the Greater London Council and so in London a borough council is the local planning authority.

Under Section 2 the Secretary of State for the Environment may make an order uniting districts for planning purposes; this power created the Lake District Special Planning Board and the Peak Park Joint Planning Board. Under Section 3 there is a joint planning committee for Greater London, which, however, is advisory only and has no administrative functions.

Sections 4 to 8 deal with special circumstances where some body other than the local authority has responsibility for planning. National parks are created under the National Parks and Access to the Countryside

Act 1949; if these areas are outside a metropolitan county, the county planning authority is to exercise all planning functions unless there is a joint planning board. The county planning authority is required to make an agency agreement for certain functions to be discharged by a National Park Committee. The Broads Authority is the district planning authority for the area which is its responsibility. In an enterprise zone, created under the Local Government, Planning and Land Act 1980, the enterprise zone authority is the local planning authority for the zone. In an urban development area, created under the Local Government, Planning and Land Act 1980, the urban development corporation is the local planning authority for such purposes as may be specified. Under the Housing Act 1988 a housing action trust is to be the local planning authority for the area which is its responsibility.

Where there are both county and district planning authorities, planning control generally is the responsibility of the district planning authority; a limited number of functions are the sole responsibility of the county planning authority. Both authorities share some functions.

Planning Officers are given delegated powers to make a decision on behalf of their authority: this decision binds the authority. All local authorities can use delegated power under Section 101 of the Local Government Act 1972; it is applicable to all local authority officers.

Development plans

The Town and Country Planning Act 1947 required each local planning authority to have development plans. A new concept of development plans was introduced by the 1968 Act, which was consolidated into the 1971 Act and is now contained in the 1990 Act. The abolition of metropolitan county councils and the Greater London Council meant that a development plan suited to the needs of the metropolitan district councils was needed: this has been done by the introduction of a unitary development plan.

Unitary plan

A unitary plan consists of a written statement indicating the authority's general policies for the development and use of land in their area or for any description of development or other use of land. The policies must have regard to the conservation of the natural beauty and amenity of the land improvement of the physical environment, the management of traffic, regional or strategic planning and current national policies. In preparing the unitary plan the authority are required to allow public participation. Before adopting it the authority are to make the plan available for public inspection and consider representations made to it. The Secretary of State for the Environment may make the plan subject to his or her approval. If objections are made, the authority must hold a local inquiry. The unitary plan may then be adopted either as originally prepared or having regard to the objections. The Secretary of State has extensive powers to intervene to ensure a proper plan is prepared.

Structure plan

The concept of a structure plan was introduced by the Town and Country Planning Act 1968. There was a slow introduction of this type of development plan but the whole of the county is now subject to structure plans. Structure plans, which apply only to non-metropolitan areas, are prepared by the country planning authorities. The plan is written statement formulating the authority's general policies in respect of the development and use of land in their area. It must include policies in respect of the conservation of the natural beauty and amenity of the land, the improvement of the physical environment, the management of traffic, regional or strategic planning, current national policies, the resources likely to be available, and any matter prescribed by the Secretary of State.

The plan contains diagrams, illustrations or other descriptive or explanatory matters. Certain matters are prescribed by the Secretary of State. The plan may be altered or replaced to take account of changes in the area.

The preparation of the structure plan is similar to that for the unitary plan: there must be public participation, consideration of representations and local inquiry to hear objections before the structure plan is adopted. The Secretary of State has extensive powers to secure that the structure plan is appropriate for the area.

Local plan

As with the structure plan, a local plan applies only in non-metropolitan areas and is prepared by the district planning authority. The local plan must be in general conformity with the structure plan; certain matters which are the responsibility of others have to be excluded. The local plan has to include policies similar to those in the structure plan; it is a written statement with a map illustrating each of the detailed policies and diagrams, illustrations or other descriptive or explanatory matter.

A local plan is in effect the detail of the strategic principles in the structure plan. The local plan has to conform to the structure plan: the county planning authority has to issue a certificate to this effect.

The preparation and adoption of a local plan has to comply with the usual provisions of public participation, representation, a right to object and the holding of a local public inquiry. The Secretary of State has extensive powers to ensure the production of a proper local plan.

'Development'

Anything which comes within the definition of 'development' under the Town and Country Planning Act 1990 generally requires planning permission. Undertaking something so defined without the necessary planning permission is a breach of planning law, which may be dealt with by enforcement action and prosecution in the criminal courts.

There are three main exceptions to the requirement that planning permission is needed for development. First, Crown land is not subject to planning permission, based on the principle that an Act of Parliament does not apply to the Crown unless it expressly does so or is a necessary implication of the Act. The 1990 Act does not so apply; there is, however, a system of consultation with local planning authorities.

Second, the Town and Country Planning (Use Classes) Order 1987 deems that a change of use of specified premises does not constitute development. This allows the change of use of a building from one industrial use to another, provided it comes within one of the prescribed classes, without planning permission.

Third, the Town and Country Planning General Development Order 1988 allows 'permitted development' subject to satisfying prescribed conditions. The most usual use of this exception is the extension of a dwelling house.

Section 55 of the 1990 Act defines 'development' as 'the carrying out of building, engineering, mining or other operations in, on and over or under land, or the making of any material change, in the use of any buildings or other land'. Added to this definition are certain matters which are to be considered as development and some others are specifically excluded. For example, works of maintenance, improvement or alteration of any building are excluded if they affect only the interior of a building or do not materially affect the exterior of the building.

The definition falls into two parts. The first is the carrying out of some activities which results in physical alteration to the land, which is of a permanent nature. The second part consists of activities which do not interfere with the physical characteristics of the land.

The words 'building', 'building operations' and 'engineering operations' are also defined in Section 336 of the 1990 Act. 'Building' includes any structure or erection, and any part of a building, as so defined, but does not include plant or machinery comprised in a building. 'Building operations' includes rebuilding operations, structural alterations of or additions to buildings, and other operations normally undertaken by a person carrying on business as a building. 'Engineering operations' includes the formation or laying out of means of access to highways.

The interpretation of 'development' has presented some difficulty to the courts: there is a body of case law which gives assistance in deciding whether a proposed development comes within 'development' and so requires planning permission. After some conflicting judicial decisions as to whether the demolition of a building came within the definition of 'development', Section 13 of the Planning and Compensation Act 1991 included demolition of a building in the definition of 'building operations'.

Any person who is unsure whether a proposal requires planning permission may, under Section 64 of the 1990 Act, apply for a determination by the local planning authority. Any such determination binds the local authority.

Application for planning permission

Provisions in the 1990 Act and orders made under it govern the making of an application, which has to be made in writing and provide specified information. The making of an application must sometimes be publicized. If the person making the application does not own the land concerned, the owner (if he or she can be found) must be notified.

An application may be made for either full or 'outline' planning permission. For full permission all necessary details must be submitted. The authority have the right to call for further information before making a decision. An application for 'outline' permission is a two-stage application. A plan indicating the affected land and requesting permission to build on it is submitted. If that is granted the permission is subject to a further application being made with regard to detailed matters, known as reserved matters. This saves the cost of preparing all the plans and information for a full application until it is known for certain that planning permission will be granted.

Fees have to be paid when an application is submitted: the amount of the fee depends on the type and the size of the proposed development.

A local planning authority has to notify in writing the applicant of their decision within eight weeks of the application being submitted; this period may be extended by the applicant agreeing in writing. Failure to give their decision in this time gives the applicant the right to appeal as if the application had been refused.

The Secretary of State for the Environment has the power to call in any application and determine the application, when an application concerns a matter of national importance or is a matter which causes strong local feeling.

Planning permission

Under Section 70 of the 1990 Act, a local planning authority when dealing with an application may grant planning permission unconditionally, grant it subject to conditions or refuse the application. The authority has to have regard to the provisions of the development plan, so far as material to the application, and to any other material consideration.

In considering their decision a local planning authority has to take into account any representations made by members of the public and the results of consultations with specified bodies. An application which comes within the terms of the development plan would normally be granted. Any refusal would be open to strong challenge.

If a local planning authority intends to grant an application which departs from the development plan, the authority's intention must first be advertised and any objections made considered. In some circumstances the Secretary of State must be notified and may call in the application and deal with it personally. The requirement to have regard to material considerations has been interpreted in a wide sense by the courts. Material considerations have been held to require consideration of private rights such as obstruction to a right of light. An application is assisted by a presumption the courts have indicated exists that permission should be granted rather than be refused.

The power to grant permission subject to conditions has been held by the courts to restrain the local planning authority to apply conditions which fulfil a planning purpose, fairly and reasonably relate to the permitted development, and must not be manifestly unreasonable. Conditions which do not satisfy these requirements may be declared to be invalid.

In the case of *R v Hillingdon London Borough Council ex parte Royco Homes Ltd 1974*, in granting planning permission to private developers to erect a block of flats on land they owned, the local planning authority imposed a condition that the flats were to be let at controlled rents, with security of tenure, to persons whose names were on the council's housing list. These conditions were held to be invalid: they exceeded the powers given to the council.

Section 90 of the 1990 Act provides that if an Act of Parliament requires that the authorization of a government department is required for a development to be carried out by a local authority or statutory undertaker, then that government department may direct that any necessary planning permission is deemed to be granted.

Section 91 requires a local planning authority to limit the duration of the planning permission: the development must be begun before five years have elapsed from the date of the permission being granted, or such longer or shorter period as they may direct. Under Section 92 where outline planning permission has been granted, the further application has to be made for reserved matters approval not later than three years from the date of the grant of outline permission. The development must be started not later than five years from the date of the outline permission or two years from the final approval of reserved matters, whichever comes later. Other periods may be substituted by the authority.

Appeals

When applications for planning permission are refused or granted subject to conditions to which the applicants object, they are likely to believe that the local planning authority have not considered their application properly or have dealt with it in some unsatisfactory way. The 1990 Act therefore allows two forms of appeal.

First, Section 78 allows the applicant to make an appeal to the Secretary of State for the Environment. The appeal must be made in the prescribed manner and within six months of being notified in writing by the authority of the decision. The Secretary of State has power to allow the appeal, dismiss it or allow it subject to conditions. The Secretary of State can deal with the application as if it had been made to him or her in the first instance and so may impose more severe conditions on the applicant than was originally the case.

The hearing of the appeal will depend on its importance. There may be a full public local inquiry, with the person appointed reporting to the Secretary of State, for who will make the decision. There may also be an inspector appointed from the Department of the Environment who makes the report after reading the written evidence and visiting the land. In the majority of appeals the decision is made by the inspector after conducting the appeal in the appropriate manner.

Under Section 288 an aggrieved person may challenge a decision of a local planning authority in the High Court. The action must start within six weeks of the decision. This form of appeal is used when the legality of the decision is open to question rather than where a decision is challenged because what was proposed was good planning practice.

Enforcement and stop notices

Breaches of planning control arise when a development is carried out without permission or the conditions or limitations in a permission are contravened. The local planning authority may then issue and serve an enforcement notice or a stop notice or both. Failure to comply with such notices constitutes a criminal offence.

In a breach of a condition in a granted planning permission, Section 187A of the 1990 Act (introduced by the Planning and Compensation Act 1991) allows the local planning authority to serve a 'breach of condition notice', which requires compliance with the conditions within a stated period of time of not less than twenty-eight days. If the notice is not complied with, a criminal offence occurs.

In a breach of planning control which consists of carrying out without planning permission building, engineering, mining or other operations in, on, over or under land, no action can be taken after four years from when the operation was substantially completed. This four-year rule also applies to a change of use of a building to use as a single dwelling. Subject to this, action cannot be taken for a change of use after the period of ten years has expired from the date of the breach.

Enforcement notices, which must be served on the owner and occupier of the land and any other person who appears to have an interest in the land, must specify the breach of planning control, the steps needed to remedy the breach and the period of time for compliance. An enforcement notice may be withdrawn or varied by the issuing authority. An appeal may be made to the Secretary of State against the service of the notice. Where a notice is not complied with the authority may take steps to enforce the notice.

As an enforcement notice does not become effective in less than twenty-eight days, the person who is in breach of planning control can continue that activity or that use for this minimum period without infringing the notice. In circumstances where this continuance would be extremely detrimental, the local planning authority may serve a stop notice, which is served after the enforcement notice and supplements that notice. A stop notice takes effect not earlier than three days after the date of service and not later than twenty-eight days from the date of service. When a stop notice is needed to come into effect earlier than three days, the local planning authority must serve with the notice a statement of the special reasons which led them to take that action.

The service of a stop notice can have a damaging effect on a development. A contractor may have to stop work and may then have a claim against the client for financial loss. The 1990 Act provides that compensation may be claimed by a person who occupies or has an interest in the land when either the stop notice or enforcement notice is withdrawn or the enforcement notice is quashed on certain grounds or the activity ceases to be a breach of planning control because the enforcement notice has been varied. Failure to comply with a stop notice is a criminal offence.

9

Highway law

Nature of a highway

At common law a highway is a way over which all members of the public have the right to pass and repass. This right has to be used by the public without licence or sufferance: there must not be a person who owns the highway and allows it to be used by his or her licence or suffers people to use it. Landowners may allow the public to use a way, which might be a properly constructed road, by their express permission or goodwill. The use by the public shows the difference between a highway and the easement of a right of way. An easement of a right of way is a right one plot of land exercises over another plot of land for the benefit of the owner of the dominant tenement (see p. 235). It is not a right available for the public to use.

Section 328 of the Highways Act 1980 defines 'highway'. Sub-section (1) states: 'In this Act, except where the context otherwise requires, "highway" means the whole or a part of a highway other than a ferry or waterway'. Unless the Act otherwide requires, a stretch of water is not a highway under the Act. At common law a highway includes those stretches of water over which the public have right of passage.

A highway, whether considered by application of the common law or statute, is a way where the public have right of passage. This right, however, may be limited in its use. A footpath is a highway but its use is restricted to a right of way on foot only. A bridleway is a highway where the use is restricted to a right of way on foot and a right of way on horseback or leading a horse, and with or without a right to drive animals of any description along the highway.

A highway may be created under the common law or by statute. Under the common law the creation is by dedication and acceptance. Dedication is where landowners dedicate for public use a passage over their land; this may be done by a formal deed of dedication, for example, making the deed in favour of the highway authority. Landowners may, however, dedicate by implication; they have not made a formal dedication but they are aware of the public's open use of their land as a passage of way and they do not take action to object to that use. At one time for the court to accept that there was implied dedication it was usual to produce as a witness the oldest inhabitant to give evidence as to the period of use. Under Section 31 of the Highways Act 1980, use without interruption for twenty years is now deemed to be dedication, unless there is evidence that there was no intention to so dedicate.

Dedication must be accompanied by use by the public at large without restriction, other than, for example, the use of a footpath by pedestrians only. If use is restricted to a particular group of the public, the way does not constitute a highway.

Landowners may be willing to allow the public to use a passage across their land but may be reluctant to thereby create a highway. The existence of a highway over the land would prevent proper development of the land unless the landowner can obtain an order for the highway to be extinguished or diverted, which may not be possible. Section 31 allows landowners to erect on their land a notice indicating that the way is not dedicated as a public right of way. That notice is evidence, in the absence of a contrary intention, that there is no dedication. Some landowners prevent a way becoming a highway by obstructing it once a year and then permitting its use only to those who acknowledge that it is not a highway.

Highways are more usually created by Acts of Parliament. The main one is the Highways Act 1980, which empowers a highway authority to create highways. The highway authority may acquire land, compulsorily or by negotiation, for the construction of a highway and provide associated matters such as street lighting.

Under the Highways Act 1980 the highway authority is responsible for the maintenance of most highways. There are, however, some highways where the responsibility is either that of the landowner over whose land the highway passes or that of landowners whose properties front on to the highway. In the event of the highway authority failing to maintain properly a highway, the maintenance of which is their responsibility, then they may be liable to any person who is injured as a result of that lack of maintenance.

Common law rights to use a highway

In our consideration of the law of torts we examined a number of cases which had dealt with the application of some torts to the use of highways. In the case of *Harper v G N Haden and Sons 1933* (see p. 151) the Court of Appeal ruled that an obstruction of a highway which is reasonable in both its extent and its duration will not be an unlawful interference. Where this is not the case, the interference will be unlawful and a public nuisance. The court also said that there had to be give and take with the use of highways. In the case of *Tarry v Ashton 1876* (see p. 153) occupiers of land which adjoins a highway are under a duty not to allow their land to become a danger to users of the highway. Negligence is a tort applicable to the right to use a highway, particularly with regard to construction operations.

Two cases need to be noted with regard to dangers caused to users of a highway by activities on adjoining land or the state of buildings on adjoining land. In the case of *Mint v Good 1951,* Good owned two houses which had a forecourt and a wall which separated the forecourt from the footpath of a highway. Mint, a ten-year-old boy, was walking on the footpath when the wall fell on him causing him serious injury. The Court of Appeal accepted that the wall had been in imminent danger of collapse: a reasonable inspection made by any competent person would have revealed this fact, therefore Good was liable. Lord Justice Denning stated the legal position of occupiers of premises which adjoin a highway:

> The law of England has always taken particular care to protect those who use a highway. It puts on the occupier of adjoining premises a special responsibility for the structures which he keeps beside the highway. So long as these structures are safe, all well and good; but if they fall into disrepair, so as to be a potential danger to passers-by then they are a nuisance, and, what is more, a public nuisance; and the occupier is liable to anyone using the highway who is injured by reason of that disrepair. It is no answer for him to say that he and his servants took reasonable care; for, even if he employed a competent independent contractor to repair the structure, and has every reason for supposing it to be safe, the occupier is still liable if the independent contractor did the work badly.

Thus occupiers are not to allow their structures which adjoin a highway to become dangerous to users of the highway. If that happens, the occupier is liable to anyone injured on that highway. The fact that the occupier used the services of an apparently competent independent contractor to execute repairs does not free the occupier of this liability; this is an exception to the general rule that a person is not liable for the torts of his or her independent contractor, which was the decision of the court in *Tarry v Ashton 1876* (see p. 153).

The second case is *Salsbury v Woodlands and Others 1969,* which is to be noted for the finding of liability for a hazardous operation on land which created a danger to users of a highway. Woodlands bought a house with an overgrown garden. Before moving in, he decided to have the garden attended to, including a 25 foot high tree felled. The tree was some 28 feet from a highway and near to some telephone wires. He engaged an apparently competent and experienced tree feller, Mr Coombe, to fell the tree. Coombe felled the tree in a manner which was held to be negligent. When the tree fell it brought down the telephone wires, which were thus suspended from a telephone pole on the opposite side of the road, and so formed a danger to users of the highway. A neighbour, Mr Salsbury, who had been watching the operation, realized the danger created by the loose wires stretched across the road and immediately started to coil them up. While he was doing this a car, which was being driven at a brisk pace, came up the road. Mr Salsbury, appreciating the danger to himself from the car catching the wires, threw himself to the ground, which caused injury to his back. He sued the car driver, Mr Woodlands and Mr Coombe.

The Court of Appeal decided that he succeeded against the car driver and Mr Coombe. The car driver was held either to have seen the loose wires or ought to have seen them and had failed to act in a prudent way. There was clear evidence that Mr Coombe had felled the tree in a negligent way and so he was liable. Mr Woodlands, however, was not negligent: he had appointed an apparently competent tree feller and was not liable for his negligent performance. No special liability arose with regard to the highway since if the felling of the tree had been done in a proper manner no danger to users of the highway could have arisen.

The special liability for dangers created on the highway does not change the principle and application of the tort of negligence. In the case of *Walsh v Holst and Co 1958,* Holst were building contractors carrying out work to premises occupied by an electricity board. Included in the work was the removal of bricks from a building which adjoined a highway. The contractors had erected a safety net to prevent anything falling from the work on to the highway. Walsh was walking on the highway when he was struck by a brick; the fall of the brick could not be accounted for. Walsh was unsuccessful in his claim against the contractors and the occupier. The Court of Appeal, by a majority, decided that since all reasonable precautions had been taken by the contractors Walsh's claim had to fail. This decision is in line with that of *Bolton v Stone 1951* (see p. 183), where Miss Stone was unable to recover damages for a serious head injury received when she stood on a highway and was struck by a cricket ball.

The carrying out of construction activities on a highway puts a duty on the contractor not to create a danger to users of the highway. This duty arises under the tort of negligence. Excavations are clearly a danger to highway users; the care required from a contractor will depend on the circumstances.

In the case of *Haley v London Electricity Board 1964,* the Board sent two employees to repair a cable in a pavement. They dug down to the cable; the intention was that the work would continue until the cable was repaired. The employees went off to have some tea and left the excavation open but guarded. The guard consisted of a wooden hammer placed so that the head was on the edge of the pavement and the handle rested on the railings. For a sighted person this was an adequate warning. Haley was a blind person walking on the pavement; when he came to the wooden hammer he failed to detect it with his white stick. He tripped over the handle, fell into the excavation and suffered serious head injuries which caused total deafness. The House of Lords refused to accept the Board's defence that no special duty was owed to blind persons unless the work was being done in the vicinity of a blind school or institution. The Board claimed that there was adequate warning to sighted persons and this was sufficient to discharge the Board's duty. The House of Lords said that the presence of blind people on the streets of London and other towns was not unusual and so those who created dangers on highways should provide adequate protection for them. The Board had failed to do this, they were in breach of their duty of care and so were liable to Haley. One of the Law Lords said that a contractor did not have to go to great expense to satisfy the duty of care: the use of folding wooden barriers as used by the telephone company would have been sufficient protection.

Haley's claim had been dismissed by the High Court and the Court of Appeal, who were both firmly of the opinion that the law was clear in that no special duty was owed to blind persons. The House of Lords, however, were unanimous that a special duty was owed to blind people.

Contractors need to take adequate precautions to guard their excavations in highways according to local circumstances. In the case of *Murray v Southwark London Borough Council 1966,* the council excavated in a road which was situated in an area where hooliganism was prevalent. The council had a night watchman for the work but he was also responsible for two other sites. One evening while the night watchman was at another site hooligans removed the warning lamps and the trestles he had placed over the excavation. The warning lamps had been interfered with on previous occasions. Murray was driving his car in a reasonable manner, that is at a reasonable speed and keeping a good look-out, when he drove into the excavation. Murray and his passengers were injured and sued the council for negligence. The decision was that the council were liable: they had failed to pay due regard to the previous acts of hooliganism in that area. Too much was required of the night watchman: a second ought to have been employed.

The second case, *Lilley v British Insulated Callenders Construction Co 1968,* shows that liability depends on the facts of the matter. British Insulated excavated in a main road situated in a quiet residential area which had not experienced any acts of hooliganism. Employees of British Insulated left the excavation at 8.30 pm with warning lamps and barriers properly positioned. At 10.30 pm Lilley drove into the excavation. Hooligans had removed the lamps and the barriers so that Lilley had no warning of the excavation. Lilley's claim for negligence failed. On the facts British Insulated were not negligent in not having a system of regular inspection during the night.

These two decisions show that the individual circumstances are most important. A failure to take appropriate steps in the circumstances will probably lead to liability for any accident. Construction work near to a school should be protected in a way sufficient to guard against inquisitive and mischievouse children. Failure to do so could well constitute negligence on the part of the contractor.

Method of working and system of warning

The carrying out of works on a highway inevitably creates some danger and difficulty to users of that highway. Contractors are expected to act in a reasonable way in order to minimize the difficulties and dangers their works will create. They are expected to use common sense and appropriate engineering skills. Failure to meet these requirements, which the law imputes, will make the contractor liable.

The case of *Parkinson v Yorkshire (West Riding) County Council 1922* is a good example of the requirement that work on a highway has to be done in a sensible engineering way. The council were resurfacing a road, one half of which, to a length of eight yards, had material spread on it; the other half was left as it was. At the end of the working day, the rolling in had not been completed: there was a large variation between the levels of the two halfs of the road. The newly laid material was disturbed by heavy traffic during the night. Parkinson lost control of his car because of the disturbed materials and overturned. His claim for negligence was successful.

The need to warn adequately of an obstruction in a road is to be seen in *Davies v Carmarthenshire County Council 1971*, where the council were widening a road. A lamp-post which had been by the side of the original road was not removed at first: it stood in the centre of the road being widened. A warning sign 'Road Works Ahead' was the only warning positioned to warn oncoming users of the road. Davies was driving her car along the road and, owing to the sun dazzling her, drove into the lamp-post. If the sun had not been shining, the lamp-post would have been visible at a distance of some 100 yards. The court held the council to be liable for negligence, but to 80 per cent only, Davies being contributorily negligent for the 20 per cent remainder. The council ought to have realized that leaving an obstruction in a busy road, with an inadequate warning, knowing that oncoming motorists would be driving against the setting sun would create a danger.

Highway authorities

The Highways Act 1980, as amended, defines highway authorities, which exercise various duties and powers with regard to the highways which are their responsibility.

Section 1 of the 1980 Act, as amended, makes the Minister of Transport the highway authority for trunk roads and other highways which are made the minister's responsibility. A road is designated as a trunk road not because of its size or manner of construction but because of its importance as part of the national road system.

In the Greater London area the borough councils are the highway authorities for all highways in their areas other than trunk roads, which are the responsibility of the Minister of Transport. Such highways were the responsibility of the Greater London Council until its abolition by the Local Government Act 1985, which also abolished the metropolitan county councils and made the metropolitan district councils the highway authorities for their areas.

Outside the metropolitan areas the county councils are the highway authorities for their areas, other than for those highways which are the responsibility of the Minister of Transport. The district council of these county council areas are not highway authorities in their own right.

In the case of toll roads constructed under the New Roads and Street Works Act 1991, the concession agreement between the highway authority and the concessionaire may authorize the concessionaire to exercise certain highway functions, specified in the agreement. Section 2 of the Act specifies certain functions that the concessionaire may not exercise. These are the power to make schemes or orders under the Highways Act 1980, the making of regulations or orders under the Road Traffic Regulation Act 1984, and other functions prescribed by the Secretary of State.

Various provisions in the Highways Act 1980 permit the delegation of functions to another highway authority. The Minister of Transport may delegate to another highway authority the functions with regard to trunk roads. Other highway authorities may make agreements between themselves as to different works to highways. The 1980 Act also contains provisions for the transfer of functions from the Minister of Transport to another highway authority when a trunk road ceases to be a trunk road.

Closure and obstruction of highways

Civil engineering works often require the closure of a highway, either permanently or temporarily, or that it be restricted. The means to achieve these requirements are found in the Highways Act 1980, the Town and Country Planning Act 1990 and the Road Traffic Regulation Act 1984, depending on the circumstances.

A legal principle which applies to highways is 'once a highway always a highway': it is not given to one section of the public to give away rights which another section of the public may wish to use, which means that non-use or little use will not extinguish the public right to a highway. Parliament has, however, given authorities and courts the power to extinguish the public right to use a highway, subject to certain restraints in order to protect the public's right to use the highway.

Highways Act 1980

Under Section 116 of the Highways Act 1980 a Magistrates Court may make an order that a highway, other than a trunk road or special road (more usually known as a motorway), which appears to them to be unnecessary or can be diverted so as to make it nearer or more commodious to the public, be stopped up or diverted. The application is made by the highway authority. Private individuals can, however, under Section 117, ask the highway authority to make an application on their behalf. If the highway authority agrees, that person has to pay the reasonable costs of the highway authority in making the application. Since the closure or diversion of a highway is a matter of importance and may substantially affect some members of the public, Section 12 requires the highway authority to give notice and inform the public of what is proposed. Before making an order diverting the highway the magistrates have to hear any person who would be aggrieved by the order; there must be written consent of the landowner over whose land the highway is to be diverted. The order is not to close a highway until the new highway has been completed, other than temporary closure.

An application may be made by the highway authority under Section 116 whether or not a development is proposed for the land over which the highway runs. In practice, most applications are made because of a possible development of the land and the presence of the highway would inhibit that development. Even without the possibility of a development Magistrates Courts can use their powers to accept that the highway is unnecessary or can be diverted so as to make it nearer or more commodious to the public.

Sections 118 and 119 of the 1980 Act contain separate provisions for the closure and diversion of footpaths and bridleways. The council may make an order stopping up a footpath or bridleway if they consider it is no longer needed for public use. The order, which is either submitted to and confirmed by the Secretary of State, or confirmed as an unopposed order, extinguishes the public right to use the path or way.

Section 118 deals with a council order according to whether it is opposed or not. If it is not opposed, the council has the power to confirm the order. If, however, there is opposition, the order must be submitted to the Secretary of State for confirmation. Neither the Secretary of State nor the council is to confirm an order unless satisfied that it is expedient to do so having regard to the public use of the path or way. There are certain provisions for the payment of compensation for the owners of land served by the path or way.

Section 119 gives a similar power to make an order for the diversion of a footpath or bridleway, when the interests of the owner of the land over which the path or way passes need to be considered. The diversion should be substantially as convenient to the public. An owner over whose land a path or way is to be extinguished may be called upon to defray or to make contribution to the expense involved in the diversion.

The making of an order under Sections 118 and 119 is subject to the procedure set out in Schedule 6 to the Act, which requires publication of the proposal to make an order, with opportunity to inspect documents relating to the proposal, and the holding of a public local inquiry if any objections have not been withdrawn.

Town and Country Planning Act 1990

A proposed development which has been given planning permission may not be able to proceed because of the existence of a highway; there are therefore means of stopping up or diverting the highway so as to permit the development to proceed, provided that is appropriate in the circumstances.

Section 247 of the 1990 Act empowers the Secretary of State to make an order authorizing the stopping up or diversion of any highway if it is necessary to do so in order to enable development to be carried out, which must be in accordance with planning permission granted under the Act or by a government department. The order may require the provision or improvement of any other highway; it may also direct that any highway provided or improvement made shall be a highway maintainable at public expense. As the order can be of substantial benefit to the developer and heavy expense may arise in the provision or improvement of a highway, the developer may be required to pay or make contributions in respect of the works provided by the order. The section may be used to authorize the stopping up or diversion of any highway which is temporarily stopped up or diverted under some other Act of Parliament.

This is an additional power to that considered with regard to the Highways Act 1980 (see p. 257). It is exercisable by the Secretary of State and not by a court, and only when a planning permission has been granted. A developer has therefore to make a request to the Secretary of State for an order to be made. The power may be used with regard to any highway. It may therefore be used for the stopping up or diversion of a footpath or of a highway used by vehicular traffic.

The stopping up or diversion of a highway is a statutory interference with a public right. In order to prevent unreasonable use of the power and to give those members of the public who will be affected an opportunity to make their views known, a prescribed procedure is set out in Section 252. Full details of the proposed order is to be published in at least one local newspaper and the *London Gazette*. A notice with these details is to be displayed in prominent positions at the ends of the highway which is to be stopped up or diverted. There has to be a period of twenty-eight days for objections to be made to the Secretary of State. If any objections are not withdrawn, the Secretary of State must cause a local inquiry to be held, consider the report of the person who conducts the inquiry and then may make the order with or without modification as he or she thinks fit.

Section 257 contains similar provisions to those in Section 247, but here the local planning authority has the power to make the order to stop up or divert. This power, however, is limited to footpaths or bridleways. Before exercising the power the local planning authority has to comply with the procedure set out in Schedule 14, which broadly follows the procedure just considered.

Road Traffic Regulation Act 1984

This Act has been amended by the Road Traffic (Temporary Restrictions) Act 1991; its provisions are widely used in order to allow civil engineering works to proceed. It is frequently necessary to close or restrict temporarily the use of a road so as to permit a building to be demolished, heavy equipment to be installed or connections to be made to services in the road. The laying of a sewer in a road would require some restriction of the use of the road, for the safety of both the public and those involved in the laying of the sewer.

Section 14 empowers a traffic authority by order temporarily to restrict or prohibit traffic on a road. The traffic authority must first be satisfied that the traffic on the road should be restricted or prohibited because works are to be executed on or near the road, or because of the likelihood of danger to the public, or of serious damage to the road which is not attributable to those works, or for enabling litter clearing and cleaning under the duty in Section 89 of the Environmental Protection Act 1990.

The traffic authority's power is not restricted to works being carried out on the road itself: they may be works near-by. Danger to the public is a sufficient reason for the traffic authority to exercise the power.

Section 14 allows the traffic authority to restrict or prohibit temporarily the use of a road, or any part of it, by vehicles, or vehicles of any class, or by pedestrians to such extent and subject to such conditions as they may consider necessary. So vehicles over a certain weight or size may be prohibited or there may be a total prohibition. Exceptions may allow certain vehicles, such as essential delivery vehicles, to use the road without being restricted or prohibited. The authority must have regard to the existence of alternative routes which may be used by traffic affected by the order.

Section 14 allows a traffic authority to use their power when there is a need to impose the restriction or prohibition without delay. This is done by the issue of a notice. Where a traffic authority either makes an order or issues a notice they may include provisions regulating traffic, including the suspension of parking provisions.

Section 15 specifies the duration of orders and notices: an order in respect of a footpath, bridleway, cycle track or byway open to all traffic for not more than six months; in any other case for not more than eighteen months. In the case of works on or near a road a longer period than eighteen months may be allowed if the traffic authority is satisfied it is needed; when the works are completed the order must be revoked. A traffic authority may renew an order; if there is insufficient time before eighteen months have expired for renewal to follow on immediately, the Secretary of State, at the request of the authority, may extend the original order for a period not exceeding six months. If the order was limited to six months, the Secretary of State may extend it, but if this is refused the traffic authority cannot make another order until a period of six months has elapsed from the ending of the original order.

The issue of a notice arises when there has been an emergency such as the collapse or the threatened collapse of a building or structure or the collapse of part of a road, which clearly requires prompt action: the traffic authority by the issue of a notice can achieve this. However, work which can be planned, and the likely period of restriction or prohibition known, is dealt with by making an order.

The duration of the notice depends on the reason for its need. If its issue is because of works being executed by the road or for litter clearing or cleaning, the period is not more than five days. If, however, the reason is danger to the public or serious damage to the road, the period is not more than twenty-one days.

The making of an order or the issue of a notice may have a serious effect on the users of the road. Section 16 of the Act allows the Secretary of State to make regulations regarding the procedure to be followed in the making of orders and notice; these include notification to the public.

Extraordinary traffic

Clause 30 of the Institution of Civil Engineers' Conditions of Contract 6th edition requires the contractor to use every reasonable means to prevent any of the routes to the site being subjected to extraordinary traffic (see p. 111). Extraordinary traffic is subject to Section 59 of the Highways Act 1980, whose provisions allow the recovery of expenses which are extraordinary having regard to the average expense of maintaining the highway. The proper officer of the highway authority submits a certificate that this expense has been or will be incurred in maintaining a highway which is maintainable at public expense. The extraordinary expense must have arisen because of damage caused by excessive weight or other extraordinary traffic on the highway; it is recovered from any person by or in consequence of whose order the traffic had been conducted.

For the excess expenses to be recoverable it is necessary for the court to be satisfied that the expenses have or will be incurred by the highway authority by reason of damage arising from the extraordinary traffic. Section 59 permits the person who is undertaking the works which will constitute extraordinary traffic to agree with the highway authority that damage is likely and to agree a sum to be paid for such liability. In the event of failure to agree the sum it may be determined by arbitration. When agreement has been made no proceedings may be brought to recover any other amount.

Proceedings to recover any sum of money, whether an amount agreed or not, have to be commenced within twelve months of the damage, or in the case of a building contract or work which extends over a long time not later than six months from the date of completion of the contract or work.

The provisions in Section 59, which existed in earlier Highways Acts, have often been examined by the courts; each case is dependent on its own particular facts. The certificate of the excess expense is not really open to challenge provided that the expense of repairing the road has been extraordinary compared with the average expense of maintaining a comparable highway in the neighbourhood.

The case of *Hill v Thomas 1893* explained the meaning of excessive weight and extraordinary traffic. Excessive weight can be simply the cargo carried by a single vehicle. Extraordinary traffic includes the continuous or repeated use of a road by vehicles belonging to the same owner, such that it is out of the common order of traffic which will cause damage to the road and increase the cost of maintenance of that stretch of road.

Thus a contractor who has heavy plant delivered to a site, and the weight of that item, plus the weight of the delivery vehicle, causes damage to a stretch of road, will incur liability under the provision dealing with excessive weight. If continuous use of the contractor's vehicles over a period of time results in damage to the road, which without that use would not have suffered damage, then liability arises for extraordinary traffic.

Section 60 deals with the situation where, because of works being carried out to services in a highway, it has been necessary to restrict or prohibit traffic and as a consequence traffic uses another highway of a lower classification. Those who are carrying out the works are to pay to the highway authority the cost of any strengthening works and making good of damage to that highway which thus occurred. Any dispute as to whether the cost was so incurred or was reasonable is determined by arbitration.

Improvement and building lines

When development of land adjoining a highway is being considered, the highway may be narrow and winding and insufficient for the traffic or it may have buildings on land adjoining it which by modern standards are too close to the highway. The Highways Act 1980 contains provisions which allow a highway authority to deal with these situations.

Section 73 allows a highway authority to prescribe an improvement line when they believe that a street, which is a highway maintainable at public expense, is narrow or inconvenient or without any sufficiently regular boundary line or it is necessary or desirable for the street to be widened. The making of an improvement line prevents any new building being erected or permanent excavation made nearer to the centre line of the street than is prescribed. This prohibition keeps land clear of buildings so that works of improvement may be carried out in the future and also avoids the payment of expensive compensation in the acquisition of land and buildings when the street is improved. Since the making of an improvement line may restrict landowners' use of their land there is a right of appeal to the Crown Court against the making of the improvement line or of conditions attached or of a refusal of consent to erect buildings within the prescribed area. A person whose property is injuriously affected by the making of an improvement line is entitled to compensation. An improvement line may be revoked by the highway authority. The making of an improvement line is subject to the provisions in Schedule 9, which require proper disclosure of the details of the improvement line to affected landowners.

Section 74 deals with building lines, which is a frontage line on one or both sides of a highway. The effect of the building line, which is prescribed by the highway authority, is to prevent the erection of any new building, other than a boundary wall or fence or permanent excavation below the level of the highway, nearer to the centre line of the highway than the building line. The highway authority may give their consent, subject to conditions or for a limited period, for the erection of a building beyond the building line. A building line has to be made in accordance with Schedule 9. A person whose property is injuriously affected by the making of a building line is entitled to compensation. If the highway authority believe that the building line is no longer necessary or desirable they may revoke it.

Highway authorities pay regard to a judicial decision when considering the making of improvement or building lines. It is in the case of *Westminster Bank v Beverley Borough Council 1971*, where the bank wished to develop land at the rear of their branch office in the centre of the ancient town of Beverley. The proposed development was to be an office extension; application for planning permission by the bank was refused on the ground that if the extension was built it would prevent the widening of the narrow busy road that the rear land adjoined. The highway authority had not, however, prescribed either an improvement or a building line for this land. The bank argued that if a highway authority wished to restrict development of land so as to be able to widen a highway sometime in the future, the authority should use their powers in the Highways Act. Parliament had made an Act which dealt with specific highway matters, and provided for compensation to be paid to any person whose property was injuriously affected by specified action, and so that Act should be used. It was not, the bank continued, open to the highway authority to use another Act of Parliament, the Town and Country Planning Act, which did not provide for compensation to be paid in order to achieve the same purpose.

The House of Lords decided that, contrary to the bank's submission, it was open to the highway authority to restrict the proposed development by the use of planning law even though the purpose was to achieve a highway improvement. Where two Acts of Parliament contained provisions which allowed the same purpose to be achieved, but only one Act required compensation to be paid, there was no duty to use that Act.

As a result of this decision the practice has developed of highway authorities refraining from making improvement and building lines. Instead they wait for an application to be submitted for planning permission and then require it to be amended in order to preserve land for highway improvement.

Operations on highways

The Highways Act 1980 contains many provisions which control construction operations on highways. Those that are of greater importance and more frequently encountered are the ones we shall consider. For knowledge of all of the provisions reference to the Act itself is necessary.

Builders' skips

Under Section 139 permission of the highway authority is required before any builders' skip can be deposited on a highway. The highway authority may grant the permission unconditionally or subject to conditions. The conditions may include the siting and size of the skip, its painted surface to make it visible to oncoming traffic, its lighting or guarding, the care and disposal of the contents and its removal at the end of the period of permission. Any person who deposits a builders' skip without this permission is guilty of an offence.

Section 139 requires the skip to be marked with the owner's name and address or telephone number, to be properly lighted and marked with reflective paint, and to be removed as soon as practicable after it has been filled. Failure to observe these requirements is an offence.

A person charged with an offence may plead that the offence was due to the act or default of another person. On a charge of failing to ensure that the skip was properly lighted during the hours of darkness it is a defence to prove that another person was responsible and that the owner took all reasonable precautions and exercised due diligence to avoid the offence. A further defence is to prove that all the conditions and requirements had been observed.

Nothing in Section 139 is to be taken as authorizing the creation of a nuisance or a danger to users of a highway or as imposing on a highway authority any liability for injury, damage or loss resulting from the presence of a skip on a highway.

Section 139 refers to the owner; it does not include a person who has hired a skip under a hiring agreement of less than a month.

In the case of *Lambeth London Borough Council v Saunders Transport 1974*, Saunders owned a builders' skip which they had hired to another person. A condition of the hire was that that person would be responsible for the proper lighting of the skip. When the skip was placed on the highway proper lighting was not provided. Saunders were charged with an offence. They pleaded that the offence was the act or default of another person and that they had taken all reasonable precautions and exercised due diligence. The court accepted this defence and Saunders were found not guilty.

In the case of *York District Council v Poller 1975*, the supervisor of the housing deparment of the council arranged for the hire of a builders' skip. A member of his staff told the owners of the skip that there was a 'blanket permit' in force authorizing the placing of the skip anywhere in the street where the skip was to be placed. The owners, understandably, accepted this assurance and deposited the skip in the street, but this information given to the owners was incorrect. The skip was therefore unlawfully placed in the street and the owners were prosecuted. The owners said that the council were the offenders since the owners had acted on the assurance of the council's officer that no permission was needed. The court agreed with this and the council were convicted for the offence.

Section 140 deals with the situation where a builders' skip has been properly positioned in accordance with the permission, and all the requirements and conditions observed, but the skip needs to be removed or repositioned. This could be because a traffic problem has arisen and the skip now forms an obstruction. The highway authority or a constable in uniform can require or cause the skip to be removed or repositioned. It is an offence not to comply with such a request. If either the highway authority or a constable in uniform cause the skip to be moved the owner is to be notified. The expense so incurred may be recovered from the owner.

Dangerous land adjoining a street

The carrying out of excavation work or the creation of a dangerous situation on land adjoining a street can make occupiers liable to anyone who comes on their land (see p. 189). Section 165 gives power to the local authority to deal with such a situation. This power is to prevent some injury being caused to a person rather than to secure compensation for an injured person. Section 165 allows the local authority to serve a notice on the owner or occupier of the land requiring the execution of works when the authority is satisfied that there is an unfenced or inadequately fenced danger on the land. If the person served with the notice fails to comply within the specified time, the authority may undertake the work and recover the expense involved. There is a right of appeal to a Magistrates Court against the notice.

Hoardings

It is standard practice for contractors to erect hoardings when undertaking works to buildings in a street, with the principal purpose of excluding unwanted visitors, probably with criminal intent. Local authorities, however, have to have regard to public safety. Sections 172 and 173 of the Act therefore require that a person proposing to erect or take down a building in a street must erect a close-boarded hoarding or fence to the satisfaction of the authority in order to separate the building from the street. The authority may, however, dispense with this requirement. There is also a right of appeal by a person aggrieved to the Magistrates Court.

Section 172 requires a covered platform for the hoarding, handrail, lighting and its maintenance in a good condition. A person who fails to observe these provisions is guilty of an offence.

Section 173 requires any person who uses a hoarding or similar structure in a street to see that it is securely fastened. Failure to fulfil this duty to the satisfaction of the authority is an offence.

Depositing building materials in streets

It is sometimes necessary when works are being carried out in a street to deposit building materials in that street, which could result in the contractor being held to be liable for public nuisance. The contractor would also be committing a criminal offence under the Highways Act 1980 in unlawfully causing an obstruction. Section 171 of the Highways Act 1980 allows this situation to be regulated so that if all the authority's requirements are observed, the contractor will probably not be liable in a civil action if someone collides with the deposited material.

Under Section 171 a person may, with the consent of the highway authority for a street, which is a highway maintainable at public expense, consent to a contractor temporarily depositing building materials, rubbish and other things in the street or making a temporary excavation, subject to conditions. There is a right of appeal to a Magistrates Court against a refusal of consent or the conditions in a consent. Section 171 requires the obstruction or excavation to be properly fenced and during the hours of darkness to be properly lighted and, if so required, to remove the obstruction and fill in the excavation. Traffic signals may have to be erected. Failure to comply with the provisions of the section is an offence.

Building operations affecting public safety

The carrying out of building operations in or near a street may put the public at risk. It is not unusual to see scaffolds being erected or dismantled in a street in a way which is quick and cost saving but not the safest of ways to undertake that task. There is therefore a need to control such activity.

Section 168 provides that if in the course of carrying out any building operation in or near a street there occurs an accident which gives rise to the risk of serious bodily injury to a person in the street, whether death or disablement to any person is caused or there would have been that risk but for the local authority or highway authority using the emergency powers in Section 78 of the Building Act 1984 to deal with a dangerous building or any other Act, then the owner of the land is guilty of an offence. If the offence arises because of the act or default of another person, then that person may be charged and convicted of the offence. There are defences available to a person charged with the offence, including that reasonable precautions were taken to secure that the building operation was carried out so as to avoid the danger; or that where the offence was due to the act or default of another person, that the person charged took all reasonable precautions and exercised due diligence to avoid the offence.

Section 168 does not replace any of the provisions in the Health and Safety at Work etc Act 1974 which might be relevant in such circumstances. For an offence to arise under Section 168 there must be a risk of serious bodily injury: an accident which does not give rise to this risk does not constitute an offence under Section 168.

Control of scaffolding on highways

The erection of a scaffold or other structure on a highway may well cause an obstruction to users of that highway, which might be unavoidable. It might, however, be avoidable or the extent of the obstruction be minimized if greater thought is given to the design of the scaffold. Section 119 requires that no person shall in respect of building works erect or retain on or over a highway any scaffolding or structure which obstructs the highway unless that person has a licence from the highway authority. The licence may be granted subject to terms.

A licence must be granted by the highway authority unless the structure would cause unreasonable obstruction or another structure erected in a different way would cause less obstruction. When an application is refused or granted subject to terms in which the applicant objects, an appeal may be made to a Magistrates Court.

A person granted a licence has to see that the structure is adequately lit at prescribed times, complies with directions as to the erection and maintenance of traffic signs, and other reasonable requirements. Failure to comply with the requirements of the licence is an offence.

The great benefit to the applicant for a licence is that provided the structure is in accordance with the licence, no criminal or civil proceedings lie with regard to any obstruction it may cause. Furthermore the highway authority are not liable. Section 119 does not deal with the safety of scaffolds or structures: it relates solely to the obstruction of a highway.

New Roads and Street Works Act 1991

This Act introduced the concept of toll roads and a system of control of street works. It repealed the Public Utilities Street Works Act 1950, which had governed street works.

As the provisions regarding street works for England and Wales occupy some sixty sections in the Act, with a number of supporting regulations, we shall consider only the main provisions to obtain a general understanding of the Act. The main aims of the Act are to control the breaking open of streets for installing or maintaining apparatus such as pipes and cables and for reinstating the street in a proper manner with a minimum of disturbance to road users.

Streets, street workers, street works licences and street works register

Sections 48 to 50 contain a number of definitions of terms which are used in the Act. A 'street' means the whole or any part of any highway, road, lane, footway, alley or passage; any square or court; and any land laid out as a way whether it is for the time being formed as a way or not. The meaning of a street under the Act is more extensive than is usually understood; it is not essential for a street to be a maintained highway for it to come within the scope of the Act.

'Street works' mean work, other than works for road purposes, executed in a street under a statutory right or a street works licence for placing apparatus, or inspecting, maintaining, adjusting, repairing, altering or renewing apparatus, changing the position of apparatus or removing it, or works incidental to such works. 'Undertaker' in relation to street works means the person by whom the relevant statutory right is exercisable or the licence under the relevant street works licence. This definition includes bodies such as British Gas who have statutory rights to place apparatus in land and others who are permitted to carry out street works by a street works licence.

'Street authority' means for a highway maintainable at public expense the highway authority, and for a highway not so maintained, the street managers. 'Street managers' means the authority, body or person liable to the public to maintain or repair the street, if there is more than the authority, body or person having the management or control of the street.

Under Section 50 the street authority may grant a 'street works licence' permitting a person to place or retain apparatus in a street and to carry out necessary works of repair and maintenance; it also permits the execution of any incidental works. The licence permits the licensee to execute works without obtaining the consent of any authority or person in their capacity of owner of apparatus affected by the works, which would otherwise be required. A person who executes street works which are not authorized by a street works licence or has a statutory right to execute such works is guilty of an offence. This provision does not apply to works for road purposes or to emergency works.

Section 52 deals with emergency works, which, on reasonable grounds, are necessary to execute because of likely danger to persons or property.

Section 53 requires a street works authority to keep a street works register, which is to show for each street information with regard to street works and other works which have been executed or are proposed to be executed. Other information may be prescribed for inclusion. The register is to be available for inspection at all reasonable hours free of charge.

Notices and co-ordination of works

If street works are to be carried out with minimum of disturbance to road users and for the street works authority to be aware of them, a system of notification is essential. Sections 54 to 60 set out these provisions.

When an undertaker proposes to execute street works, advanced notice must be given to the street works authority; the undertaker is to comply with their requirements regarding provision of information and other matters for the purpose of co-ordinating with any other proposed works. Failure to give notice is an offence.

When a street is to be broken up or any sewer, drain or tunnel beneath it broken into, not less than seven working days' notice must be given to the street authority. Failure to comply is an offence.

If the proposed street works are likely to cause serious disruption to traffic which could be avoided or reduced if the works were to be carried out only at certain hours, the authority may give directions regarding the times when the works may be done. Failure to obey these directions is an offence.

Where emergency works are needed, the undertaker does not need to give notice, unless the work involves breaking open a street for which seven days' notice would otherwise be required, then notice is to be given as soon as reasonably practicable and in any event within two hours. Failure to do so is an offence.

A matter of justifiable public criticism in the past has been that a road would have substantial road works carried out, then be reinstated, and shortly afterwards an undertaker would come along and tear up the road again. Section 58 aims to prevent that situation arising. The street authority may give notice that the execution of street works is to be restricted during the twelve months following the completion of any substantial road works. The notice has to be served on a number of specified authorities, stating the date, which is to be not less than three months, when the road works are to begin. The notice prohibits an undertaker breaking open the street except in limited circumstances. An undertaker who contravenes this provision is guilty of an offence and is liable to pay the reinstatement cost of the street authority.

Another justifiable public criticism has been that individual undertakers were concerned only with their own installations; one undertaker breaking open a street, installing apparatus and reinstating the road was followed a short while later by another undertaker who repeated the operation and the disturbance. The Act requires the street authority to use their best endeavours to co-ordinate the execution of works in the interests of safety, to minimize inconvenience to persons using the street, and to protect the structure of the street and the integrity of the apparatus in the street. A similar duty is placed on undertakers to co-operate with the street authority and other undertakers.

Streets subject to special controls

Special controls may sometimes be exercised. The street authority's consent (possibly including conditions) to some undertakers' works is necessary for a 'protected street', which is a special road or a street so designated by the street authority.

Streets with special engineering difficulties are also subject to special control: a plan and section of the proposed works must be agreed with the street authority. In the event of failure to agree the matter is settled by arbitration.

Streets designated as being 'traffic sensitive' are ones where the street authority may make special provision for street works. Where the street is traffic sensitive only for certain times or on certain days, limited designation may be made.

Execution of street works

When breaking open a street the undertaker has to ensure that the excavation, plant or materials used are adequately guarded and lighted; traffic signs reasonably required for the guidance of those using the street should be placed and maintained.

When an undertaker creates an obstruction which is greater in extent and for a longer period than is reasonably necessary, the street authority by notice may require reasonable steps to be taken to mitigate or discontinue the obstruction.

Section 67 requires that street works shall be under the supervision of a person having a prescribed qualification. Section 68 requires that undertakers shall afford the street authority all reasonable facilities for ascertaining that the undertakers are complying with all the duties imposed on them.

An undertaker is under a duty to reinstate the street as soon as reasonably practicable after the completion of any part of the street works. The undertaker is to notify the street authority before the end of the next working day following completion, stating if the reinstatement is interim or permanent. If the reinstatement is only interim, the permanent reinstatement must be made as soon as possible, not later than six months (or some other prescribed time) from the date of the interim reinstatement.

Some reinstatements have been of such a poor standard as to put road users in some danger. Cyclists and motor cyclists have been killed and seriously injured because of poor reinstatement works. The Act now contains measures which, if applied properly, ought to minimize such risks.

An undertaker must comply with specified materials, standards of workmanship and performance standards. The street authority may carry out investigatory works; this cost is borne by the undertaker if a failure is detected. The detection of a failure by the undertakers means that they have to bear the street authority's costs of a joint inspection to determine the nature of the failure and any necessary remedial works and of the authority's inspection of the remedial works. The authority may serve notice on the undertaker to carry out the remedial works within a period of not less than seven days, otherwise the street authority will carry out the work and recover their costs. Where the reinstatement is causing danger to road users the authority, without serving a notice, may carry out the necessary works and recover all their reasonable costs from the undertaker.

Charges, fees and contributions payable by the undertakers

The Act allows a street authority to be paid fees or recover costs incurred in connection with undertakers' works.

Under Section 74 an undertaker executing works in a maintainable highway may have to pay a charge to the highway authority where the works are not completed within a reasonable period, which is subject to the agreement of the undertaker and the authority. Failure to agree means that the matter has to be settled by arbitration. The period may be amended for events not reasonably foreseeable.

Under Section 75 an undertaker executing street works must pay to the street authority a fee for all or some inspections carried out by the authority.

The costs incurred by a traffic authority in making an order or issuing a notice under the Road Traffic Regulation Act 1984 (such as a notice in local newspapers and the provision of traffic signs) may be recovered from the undertaker whose works produced the need for this action.

Where street works have resulted in a highway being restricted or prohibited and the traffic diverted to an alternative route, the undertaker has to indemnify the highway authority of costs they have reasonably incurred in strengthening or making good damage to the highway.

Section 78 requires undertakers executing street works to make a contribution to the cost of making good long-term damage to a road.

Duties and liabilities of undertakers with respect to apparatus

The Act places obligations on undertakers to avoid unnecessary disruption to road use. Undertakers should keep an up-to-date record of apparatus in a street. Failure to do so is an offence.

An undertaker carrying out street works who finds apparatus belonging to another undertaker, which is either not marked or incorrectly marked on the records of that undertaker, is to inform that undertaker as soon as is reasonably practicable. If the undertaker who owns the discovered apparatus cannot be ascertained, the finder is to record the details and inform the street authority.

An undertaker who has apparatus in a street must maintain it with regard to the safety and convenience of persons using the street, the structure of the street and the integrity of apparatus of the authority in the street. The street authority and any other relevant authority are to be afforded reasonable facilities to see that this obligation is fulfilled.

Any undertaker whose execution of street works results in damage to other undertakers' apparatus or to a street shall compensate the other undertaker or the street authority. The obligation includes explosion, ignition or discharge from the undertaker's supply or service. It is not necessary to show that the undertaker had been negligent or that there had been a breach of statutory duty. This liability of an undertaker includes responsibility for employees, contractors and their employees. It does not, however, extend to a person whose own misconduct or negligence led to loss or damage to that person, or to a third party whose misconduct or negligence led to loss or damage. So there is no liability to a person who fails to make enquiries, or having made enquiries ignores the information given, and excavates where an undertaker's apparatus is and suffers loss or damage as a result of coming into contact with that apparatus.

10

Employment law

The contract of employment

A contract of employment (a contract of service) differs greatly from a contract of self-employment (a contract for services). The contract of employment gives the employer greater control over the work of the employee than is the case with a contract of self-employment (see p. 199).

An employee under a contract of employment enjoys certain legal rights and some assurance of continuity of employment. An employee normally has a right to holiday pay, sickness provision, membership of a pensions scheme, life assurance and, possibly, other benefits such as medical insurance. Self-employed people must make their own arrangements for these matters.

A self-employed person has, however, the benefit of paying income tax under Schedule D, at the end of the accounts year and not on a weekly or monthly basis under Schedule E. Claims for expenses are allowable under Schedule D which would not be under Schedule E.

Manual workers on a construction site are often working as self-employed; an increasing number of professional people also offer their services on this basis, which is attractive to employers when they have a limited need for extra assistance.

In the case of *Ferguson v John Dawson and Partners (Contractors) Ltd 1976* (see p. 201), although a self-employed contract had been made, the court decided that it was in fact a contract of employment. The courts reserve the right to look at the substance of the arrangement and not to be bound by its form or what the parties have agreed.

If, however, what the parties have agreed is genuine, the court will accept that a contract for services was made and proceed on that basis. In the case of *Massey v Crown Life Insurance Co 1978,* Massey worked from 1971 to 1973 under two contracts. Under one contract he was an employee; under the other he was a general agent and was not paid wages as an employee but received only commission and could also work as a freelance for other insurance brokers.

In 1973 Massey wished to become a self-employed person for taxation reasons; his employers, Crown Life, agreed to use these services. Massey made an agreement using the title 'John L Massey and Associates', which was registered under the Registration of Business Names Act 1916. Massey was repaid his contributions to the employers' pension fund and obtained the agreement of the Inland Revenue to treat him as self-employed. He therefore did not have deductions from his earnings from Crown Life for income tax or pension contributions.

In 1975 Massey was dismissed by Crown Life and given one month's notice. Massey made a complaint of unfair dismissal to an industrial tribunal, which first had to decide whether Massey was employed under a contract of employment and so entitled to have a complaint dealt with by an industrial tribunal. The decision was that Massey's work for Crown Life was not done under a contract of employment. Massey's appeal to the Employment Appeal Tribunal was also unsuccessful; he then made an appeal to the Court of Appeal.

The Court of Appeal agreed with both the industrial tribunal and the Employment Appeal Tribunal that Massey was not an employee. There was a written agreement, which the court accepted was genuine, under which Massey was to undertake the work he had done previously as an employee as a self-employed person. The agreement had changed Massey's status from employee to self-employed. He could not in order to claim the advantage of paying income tax under Schedule D say that he was not an employee and then when he was dismissed claim compensation for unfair dismissal.

One of the judges doubted that in the period 1971 to 1973 Massey had in fact been an employee: that arrangement, which allowed Massey to undertake work for others, could not have been a contract of service. The court also explained the distinction between this decision and that in Ferguson's case: in the latter the evidence regarding the contract was scanty. The contract was made by word of mouth only and so the court had to imply terms, which were consistent with it being a contract of employment only. In Massey's case, there was a written contract with explicit terms; furthermore the agreement had been made at Massey's request.

In the case of *Ready Mixed Concrete (South East) Ltd v Minister of Pensions and National Insurance 1968* (see p. 200), whether a contract of employment exists is determined by three conditions. These are that the person works for wages or other remuneration in return for his or her work and skill; the person agrees, expressly or impliedly, to be under the other person's control; and the other matters are consistent with the contract being a contract of employment. The judge also said that if there was doubt as to the rights and duties of the parties then a declaration of that kind would be helpful. In the Ready Mixed case the detailed agreement, together with the practicable arrangements, allowed the court to decide that the drivers were genuinely self-employed.

The courts have increasingly accepted that it is a common practice in the construction industry for workers to be self-employed. For manual workers the Inland Revenue 714 Certificate Scheme is strong evidence of this status. In the absence of a genuine written agreement, the status of the person has to be determined on the facts of the case. In Ferguson's case, Ferguson was a general labourer who was told it was a 'labour only' contract with no employment cards handed in. In Massey's case, Massey was an intelligent person holding a responsible commercial position who sought for his own benefit to change his status. The courts decided in one case there was a contract of employment and in the other a contract of self-employment.

Formation of a contract of employment

A contract of employment is formed in the same way as any other contract and is subject to the same rules of law (see p. 30). Manual employees may have their contracts made informally such as by word of mouth or letter. Other employees would have written contracts. Written contracts for the most senior employees may be negotiated individually with both parties' lawyers.

There is an increasing practice of using written contracts; they may contain terms intended to protect the employer's business interests and to establish the employee's rights.

Legality

Contracts of employment recognized by the courts must not be tainted with illegality, for example where the parties had deliberately set out to defraud the Inland Revenue. In *Ferguson v John Dawson and Partners (Contractors) Ltd 1976* (see p. 201), where Ferguson had been using a false name, one member of the Court of Appeal was of the opinion that this fact made the contract illegal. If he had persuaded the other judges, the court would have refused to have considered Ferguson's claim.

In order to protect an employee who has, knowingly or not, signed a written contract which seeks to deprive the employee of some statutory protection, Section 140 of the Employment Protection (Consolidation) Act 1978, for example, makes void in most circumstances any provision in a contract of employment or other agreement which seeks to exclude or limit the operation of any provision of the Act, or to preclude a person making a complaint to an industrial tribunal.

Offer and acceptance

Employers usually advertise and invite applications for a particular position, whose details are provided for applicant. After an interview the actual offer of employment is made, subject to conditions, such as satisfying a medical examination or the provision of suitable references. If any condition is not satisfied, the offer may be withdrawn, even if the person has actually started work.

The acceptance of terms of the offer has to be unqualified if a contract is to be created: clarity and precision are in the interests of both parties. If employees are required to work in other areas, the employer should state this in the contract.

In the case of *O'Brien and Others v Associated Fire Alarms Ltd 1969*, O'Brien and other workers were employed at the Liverpool branch office by Associated Fire Alarms, a national organization with branch offices throughout Britain. There was no express term in the contract of employment that O'Brien and the others would be required, if so called upon, to work at other branches.

O'Brien and the others had been based for several years at the Liverpool office, working throughout the Liverpool area but able to return to their homes each evening. When their work load diminished, they were asked to work in the Cumberland area, which would have meant that they would be able to return to home only at weekends. Their refusal to make the move led to their dismissal, which the employees claimed was because they were redundant. If correct this would mean that they were entitled to a redundancy payment. The employers disputed this claim: there was an implied term in the contract of employment that they would work in the Cumberland area, part of the region controlled from the Liverpool office.

The Court of Appeal refused to accept the employers' submission. There was no implied condition that the employees could be called upon to work in the Cumberland area. The only implied term was that they would work within daily travelling distance of their homes. As there was no work in the Liverpool area for the employees, they were redundant and entitled to redundancy payments.

The clearest way to avoid this difficulty would be by an express term in the contract requiring the employee to work when called upon throughout the country.

References

Although it is normal practice for a prospective employer to ask an intending employee to provide references on character and experience, there is no legal right for an employee to demand a reference. Some employers refuse to give references; others will do so only over the telephone. Where employers do give references they are under a duty to exercise care. Failure to exercise care can make the employer liable for damages to the employee.

In the case of *Lawton v BOC Transhield Ltd 1987*, Lawton had been employed by BOC for some ten years when he was made redundant. He obtained temporary work with another employer and the possibility of permanent employment subject to obtaining two character references. BOC provided an unfavourable reference and Lawton was dismissed by his new employer. He was out of work for two years and thus suffered a financial loss of some £7550. Lawton sued BOC, claiming that BOC had been negligent in providing an inaccurate and/or an unfair reference. BOC rejected this claim on the ground that they owed no duty of care to Lawton.

The High Court decided that the employers knew they were being asked to provide a character reference in connection with Lawton's future employment and that Lawton was relying on them to provide an accurate reference. There was a sufficient proximity between them for BOC to owe Lawton a duty of care to give opinions, based on accurate facts, which a reasonably prudent employer would have given. It was reasonably foreseeable that a failure to discharge this duty of care would lead to financial loss to Lawton. The High Court judge decided, however, that there had been justification for the opinions expressed and that the reference had been honest, accurate and not negligently prepared. Lawton lost his case.

There are two other cases of importance with regard to the matter of liability for the supply of a reference. In the first case, *Wishart v National Association of Citizens Advice Bureaux Ltd 1990,* Wishart was made an offer of employment 'subject to receipt of satisfactory written references'. One of the references led the Citizens Advice Bureaux to believe that Wishart had a poor record of attendance in his previous employment, apparently connected with ill health. After further enquiries and discussion within the Bureaux, the offer of employment was withdrawn. When Wishart sued the question was whether the standard for references was that of the reasonable employer or that of the particular employer. If any reasonable employer would have accepted that reference as satisfactory then, Wishart claimed, the Citizens Advice Bureaux should too. The Court of Appeal, however, decided that the test was whether the prospective employer decided that the reference was satisfactory. Mr Wishart's claim failed.

The second case, *Edwards and Others v Lee 1991,* dealt with the supply of a reference by a solicitor for one of his clients. Edwards made an arrangement with the client, Mr Hawkes, for Mr Hawkes to sell a car owned by Mr and Mrs Edwards and valued at £28 500. The car was handed over to Mr Hawkes. A short while later Mr Edwards was informed that the car was being offered for sale at £25 500. When questioned, Mr Hawkes was evasive and suggested that his solicitor, Mr Lee, be approached for a character reference. Mr Lee knew that Mr Hawkes was awaiting trial on a criminal charge of a similar nature to the matter causing concern to Mr Edwards. He could not, however, because of legal professional privilege reveal this fact. He provided a reference stating that he knew of no reason why Mr Edwards would not recover his money. Mr Edwards did lose his money and sued Mr Lee for this loss, claiming that the loss was a result of the false, misleading and negligent assurances given about Mr Hawkes's integrity.

The High Court decided that the solicitor should have asked his client if he could disclose his pending criminal trial, so removing the restraint of the legal professional privilege. If that had been refused, the solicitor ought to have considered whether he should give a reference. The court took account of the fact that when Mr Edwards asked for the reference he had not made it known to Mr Lee that he had doubts about Mr Hawkes's integrity and that he had considered cancelling the arrangement. The court held this failure to be contributory negligence, assessed at 50 per cent, and so awarded Mr Edwards £12 500 only as damages for the negligence of Mr Lee in giving the reference.

Incorporation of terms

When a contract does not set out in full all the terms, the practice is to incorporate the terms by reference in the contract to the document containing those terms, usually by referring in the letter of appointment that the contract is subject to the conditions of service set out in a national joint council agreement: this reference makes the document a contract document.

In the case of *Camden Exhibition and Display Ltd v Lynott and Another 1965*, Lynott and another employee of Camden Exhibition and Display were given a written statement under the Contracts of Employment Act 1963; it stated that the hours of work were to be in accordance with the working rules agreement of the national joint council. A rule in the agreement stipulated that overtime was to be that required for the due and proper performance of contracts and was not to be restricted but was to be by agreement between the employer and the workers concerned. This rule was important because Camden Exhibition and Display contracted to erect and dismantle displays to extremely tight contract times.

Lynott and his colleague were dissatisfied at a wage increase and in protest decided to stop working overtime. The legality of this action was then brought into question. The Court of Appeal stated that workers were expected to work their normal hours but were not required to work overtime. In this case the written statement had referred to the working rules agreement and therefore incorporated the rules into the contract of employment. In the circumstances Lynott and his colleague were found not to have been acting unlawfully. The main claim, which was dismissed, was that they had been inducing the other workers to break their contracts.

Express and implied terms

Under general contract law a contract might have terms agreed by the parties (express terms) or there may be terms implied by the courts. Contracts of employment may contain such terms. The rules considered earlier apply (see p. 54).

Express terms

A contract for a senior employee will contain express terms covering not only matters such as salary, hours of work and holidays but also the usual range of fringe benefits such as the provision of a car, life and medical insurance and expenses allowance.

An express term now often used is a restrictive covenant, excluding or limiting employees in working for a competitor or setting up in business similar to their employment for a period of time after leaving their employment. Originally such an express term was used only with employees engaged in research, or who had access to confidential information. Because of the easier access to confidential information to a wider range of employees, with the consequent risk of harm to the employer's business interests, greater use is made of restrictive covenants; a restraint of employment is permissible within limits.

In the case of *Nordenfelt v Maxim Nordenfelt Guns and Ammunition Co Ltd 1894*, Nordenfelt, a successful manufacturer of all kinds of armaments, sold his business for a large sum of money. He entered into a restrictive covenant that he would not for the next twenty-five years, directly or indirectly, engage in any similar business. Two years later, in disregard of his covenant, he set up in business manufacturing armaments in competition to the company, which therefore sought to restrain his breach of the restrictive covenant. The House of Lords decided that the main provisions of the restrictive covenant would be enforced. Some provisions were held to be too wide to be enforced.

The Law Lords stated that a restrictive covenant would be void unless it satisfies the test of reasonableness, which contains two rules:

1 That the restraint must be shown to be not unreasonable in the public interest.
2 That the restraint must be shown to be not unreasonable between the parties having regard to their interests.

The test of reasonableness has since been refined by the courts: the principle remains but, in general, a restraint of more than one year would be held to be unreasonable. What is reasonable restraint depends on the individual circumstances.

In the case of *Marley Tile Co Ltd v Johnson 1981,* a restrictive covenant sought to restrain an employee following termination of his employment working for a competitor over a wide area. In 1971 Mr Johnson joined Marley as a trainee; a restrictive covenant restrained him for the period of a year working in a similar capacity in named areas after his employment ended. Mr Johnson worked for Marley from 1975 to 1980 in Cornwall; in 1980 he went to Devon as manager, returning to Cornwall later that year. In March 1981 he gave notice and two months later started to work in Cornwall for a company which produced roof and flooring tiles. Marley sought to enforce the restrictive covenant.

The Court of Appeal accepted that the period of the restraint of one year was reasonable but that the area was too wide. Marley had over 2000 customers in Devon and Cornwall but the court decided that Mr Johnson could have known only a few of these. The restrictive covenant was unreasonable and could not be enforced by the courts.

In the case of *Anscombe and Ringland v Butchoff 1983,* a firm of estate agents in St Johns Wood, London, employed Butchoff. The restrictive covenant was that for a year after termination of his employment Butchoff would not undertake either alone or in partnership or as a member of a company not be interested directly or indirectly in the business of an auctioneer, valuer, surveyor or estate agent within a radius of one mile of Anscombe and Ringland's office. Butchoff left the firm's employment and shortly afterwards set up as an estate agent some 150 yards from the firm's office. Anscombe and Ringland sought to enforce the covenant against him.

The High Court decided that as Butchoff had never worked as a surveyor or valuer, that part of the restraint could not be justified. The part of the covenant which related to carrying on as an estate agent within one mile was, however, reasonable and so would be enforced.

In the case of *Court Homes Ltd v Wilkins 1983,* Wilkins was a building surveyor employed by Court Homes who were builders and developers.

Under his contract of employment, Wilkins could not set up in business, solely or jointly, directly or indirectly, within five miles of Court's registered office in Welwyn for a period of five years after leaving his employment. Wilkins left and set up a construction company with its registered office in Welwyn but its trading premises at Hatfield, more than seven miles from Court's offices.

The High Court refused to enforce the covenant. It was an unreasonable and unnecessary restraint on Wilkins, contrary to public policy and illegal as it sought only to stifle competition. Furthermore the restriction was invalid because the period of five years was too long.

From various judicial decisions, a restriction for a period of more than one year is likely to be held to be unreasonable. The area of restriction must depend on individual circumstances. In Anscombe and Ringland's case a restraint of more than one mile would very probably have been held to be unreasonable. The concentration of business in the London area would have meant that a restraint for, say, five miles would have been too restrictive.

Implied terms

In the absence of express terms in a contract of employment the courts will imply terms appropriate to the contractual relationship created, which puts both the employer and the employee under obligations to the other. These common law obligations seek to maintain the mutual trust and confidence essential to the contractual relationship: only when this state exists is the contract performing as it ought to be.

Employers' obligations

An important obligation for employers is to conduct themselves so as not to destroy or harm the relationship of confidence and trust between employers and their employees.

In the case of *Woods v W M Car Services (Peterborough) Ltd 1981,* Mrs Woods was the chief secretary and accounts clerk to the owner of a garage, which was taken over. The new employers took the view that she was overpaid. She was asked to accept a lower wage and to work longer hours; new conditions of employment were given to her and her title of 'chief' was removed from her job title. She refused to accept these changes and resigned. Mrs Woods then made a complaint of unfair dismissal on the ground that she had been constructively dismissed. Her claim was dismissed by the industrial tribunal.

The Employment Appeal Tribunal also dismissed her appeal against the industrial tribunal's finding, but observed that there existed an implied obligation that an employer should so conduct himself as not to destroy or seriously damage the relationship of confidence and trust between employer and employee. An employer who persistently attempted to vary an employee's conditions of service was acting in breach of the term so as to repudiate the contract of employment.

The Court of Appeal also dismissed Mrs Woods's appeal but did not challenge the observation of the Employment Appeal Tribunal. One of the judges did, however, say that an employer must not be put in a position, through the wrongful refusal of employees to accept change, so that the employer is prevented from introducing improved business methods in order to seek success in the enterprise.

The extent of the employer's duty to look to the employee's interests is illustrated in *Scally and Others v Southern Health and Social Services Board and Another 1991.* Dr Scally and other doctors were employed by the health board under contracts negotiated between the employers and a representative employees' body. The contract required the doctors to pay contributions to a superannuation scheme; to qualify for a full pension forty years' contributory service was necessary. Employees unable to contribute for forty years could pay additional contributions; this right, however, was subject to being taken up within twelve months of starting employment. Dr Scally and the other doctors were unaware of this right and so were not able to make the additional contributions. They claimed that the employers were in breach of contract in failing to notify them of the right.

The House of Lords decided that the employers were under an obligation to bring to the attention of the doctors the existence of this valuable right, which had been negotiated for the benefit of the doctors but was available only if the doctors took action to obtain the benefit, which they could not do unless the right was drawn to their attention. There had therefore been a breach of contract by the employers.

Employees' obligations

Obligations on the employee are to preserve the relationship of confidence and trust which the common law requires in a contract of employment. An important obligation is not harming the employer's business interests.

Not to cause harm to the employer's business interests

Employers are entitled to expect that their employees will not do anything that will harm the business. An employer whose business interests could be affected by an ex-employee would probably insert a restrictive covenant in the contract (see p. 277). The implied obligation includes not divulging trade secrets, working for a competitor or passing confidential information to competitors.

The case of *Hivac Ltd v Park Royal Scientific Instruments Ltd 1946* concerned a number of Hivac's employees who worked for Park Royal, a competitor, in their spare time. No evidence showed that the employees had actually passed on any trade secrets. The Court of Appeal was satisfied, however, that what was being done could be harmful to Hivac and granted Hivac an injunction restraining Park Royal from employing the workers in their spare time.

The matter of spare time working has been considered by the courts from time to time. There is a reluctance to prevent workers using their skill and ability to their own benefit in this way, but if it can be shown that spare time working would cause harm to an employer then that will be treated as a breach of an implied obligation of loyal service.

The use of confidential information after the employment has ended was considered in the case of *Faccenda Chicken Ltd v Fowler 1986*. Fowler, a sales manager, set up in business in competition with Faccenda; he knew their customers, the methods of delivery, pricing and quality of products. Faccenda claimed damages for breach of contract of employment in using Faccenda's sales information to the detriment or disadvantage of Faccenda and for abuse of confidential information.

The Court of Appeal dismissed Faccenda's claim and laid down guidelines. A distinction had to be made with regard to the use of confidential information during and after the period of employment. An employee using or disclosing confidential information would be in breach of an obligation to the employer. After the period of employment, the confidential information could be used unless it could be classed as a trade secret, which depended on the status of the employee: whether the employee was one of a restricted number who handled that information, or the employee regularly handled confidential information and recognized it as such. The nature of the information is relevant, as is the fact that the employer emphasized its confidential nature.

These are the guidelines the courts will use; the outcome of each case will depend greatly on the circumstances.

Obligation of fiduciary duty

An employee who is a director of a company is because of this position under a duty to protect the interests of the employer. In the case of *Cranleigh Precision Engineering Co Ltd v Bryant 1965,* Bryant was the managing director of a company. He acquired a patent which he used for his own purposes. The patent was of direct benefit to his employers, but he failed to disclose to his employers that he had the patent. The court decided that he was under an obligation to his employers to disclose its existence.

In the case of *Horcal Ltd v Gatland 1983,* Gatland was the managing director of Horcal Ltd, a company of building contractors. A customer asked Gatland to provide an estimate for work to be done to her home. This estimate, which was set on Horcal's headed notepaper, was accepted and the work done. Gatland kept for himself the payment for the work. Shortly afterwards Horcal made an agreement with Gatland for his employment to end. Included in the agreement was a payment of £5000 to Gatland for past service. When Horcal discovered what Gatland had done, they sued for the profit made by Gatland, some £2524, and for the return of the £5000. The profit was ordered to be returned but not the £5000. When the agreement was made Horcal were ignorant of what Gatland had done and Gatland might have decided to pay them the proceeds of the contract of work.

Employees' inventions

Employees engaged specifically for research work usually have an express term in their contracts of employment that any inventions discovered by them belong to the employers. There is, however, an implied term that if *any* employee makes a discovery, which could only have been made because of his or her employment, then that belongs to the employer.

The case of *British Syphon Co Ltd v Homewood 1956* dealt with this obligation. Homewood was in charge of his employer's design and development department but had no responsibilities with regard to research. He designed and developed a new form of soda syphon and patented it in his name. His employers brought an action claiming that the patent belonged to them. The court agreed that the discovery belonged to the employers as it came from Homewood's employment.

This decision does not mean that every invention by employees will belong to their employers. Where it can be shown that employees made the discovery in their own time, and it was not associated with their employment duties or the use of confidential information, then their employers have no claim on it.

Variation and discharge of the contract of employment

From time to time a contract of employment is varied, usually by the employer. An employer may be faced with economic difficulties which mean requiring employees to work longer hours or for less wages or both. Other variations may include requiring employees to work at a different place of work, to change their duties or their job title.

If the variation of a contract of employment has been agreed, that then constitutes the contract. If, however, there is no agreement but employees continue their employment the question arises as to whether acceptance is to be implied. Should an employee make no objection then, over a period of time, it could be held that there has been acceptance of the variation. Where there has been objection, the court will uphold the employee's contractual right.

The case of *Rigby v Ferodo Ltd 1987* examined the variation of a reduction of an employee's wages. Mr Rigby was a member of a union that in 1980 made an agreement with the employers as to methods and amounts of pay; this agreement became part of Mr Rigby's contract of employment. Because of severe financial problems the employers sought to make savings by the reduction of employees' wages. The union objected but were told that in the absence of agreement the wage cuts would be imposed. Mr Rigby was not dismissed and continued to work but was paid at the reduced wage rate. There was no indication that he accepted the variation to his contract.

The House of Lords decided that the employers had unilaterally imposed a wage cut, which constituted a repudiation of the contract. The repudiation had not been accepted by Mr Rigby and so the contract continued on its original terms. He was therefore entitled to claim the difference between the wages under this contract of employment and the wages actually paid to him. The Law Lords observed that the employers could have chosen to have terminated the employees' contracts and faced the consequences. Instead they employed the workers under contracts which entitled them to a certain level of wages but withheld from them a part of that entitlement.

This observation needs to be noted since an employer can give the agreed notice under the contract of employment and so end the contract. The dismissed employees may then be offered employment on varied terms. The employee has the choice of accepting or rejecting that offer. Whatever action the employee takes will clearly depend on the general economic situation.

The discharge of a contract of employment may be brought about by either the employer or employee giving the other the required period of notice. For professional people a period of notice is usually an express term of one month's notice in writing by either side. For more senior employees a longer period of notice may be specified. The loss of such an employee's services to an employer justifies a period of notice such as six or twelve months.

Where a contract of employment does not specify it, the period of notice is to be what is reasonable in the circumstances. In the case of *Hill v C A Parsons and Co Ltd 1972,* Hill was a senior engineer who had worked for his employers for thirty-five years; he was due to retire in two years. His employers wanted him to leave his trade union and join another, which he refused to do; he was dismissed and given one month's notice. Mr Hill brought an action claiming that he was entitled to more than one month's notice and sought an injunction restraining his employers from dismissing him. The Court of Appeal agreed that for a person of Mr Hill's status, age and length of service one month's notice was too short. Lord Denning, the Master of the Rolls, thought that for a professional man of his standing six months' notice was reasonable and, possibly, twelve months. The other judges agreed that in the circumstances six months' notice was reasonable. Mr Hill was granted the injunction he sought.

A contract of employment may be ended by frustration, which arises when an intervening event, which is the fault of neither party, makes the performance no longer possible (see p. 66). In the case of *Notcutt v Universal Equipment Co (London) Ltd 1986,* Mr Notcutt was almost 63 when in 1983 he suffered a coronary attack. In July 1984 his doctor wrote to the employers giving his opinion that he doubted that Mr Notcutt would work again. The employers then gave him notice to end his employment. Mr Notcutt claimed that this entitled him to sick pay for his twelve weeks of notice. The employers disputed this on the ground that his contract of employment had been frustrated by his illness before the notice to end the employment.

The Court of Appeal agreed that there had been frustration. Mr Notcutt's illness had totally incapacitated him from performing his contract. There was a change of such significance that if the contract were performed it would be a different thing from that contracted for.

Payment of wages

Before the Payment of Wages Act 1960, manual workers were to be paid in coin of the realm only; this was to prevent manual workers being paid in tokens or vouchers which could be spent only on the employer's premises. The 1960 Act, which allowed payment to be by coin of the realm, cheque or into the employee's bank account, was repealed by the Wages Act 1986, which allows the method of payment to be that agreed in the contract of employment. This Act also controls the way in which an employer may deduct from an employee's wages. 'Wages' is defined in the 1986 Act in a wide way and includes any fee, bonus, commission, holiday pay or other emolument.

Under Section 1 no deduction can be made unless it is required or authorized by a statutory provision or any relevant provision in the worker's contract or the worker has previously agreed to it in writing. These requirements do not prevent an employer making deductions in specified circumstances including an overpayment of wages or an overpayment of expenses. Employees who believe that an unauthorized deduction has been made from their wages may make a complaint to an industrial tribunal within three months of the deduction.

Section 8 of the Employment Protection (Consolidation) Act 1978 states that every employee is entitled to an itemized pay statement. Failure to provide such a statement empowers an employee to require a reference to an industrial tribunal.

Employment Protection (Consolidation) Act 1978

Most of what we have considered with regard to employment law has related to common law: what the parties have agreed in the contract of employment and the terms implied by the courts. In the early 1960s Parliament intervened in contracts of employment by requiring that certain duties were placed on employers and employees had certain rights. Further Acts of Parliament were consolidated into the 1978 Act, which has since been amended by several Employment Acts in the 1980s. Frequent parliamentary intervention in employment law appears to be inevitable, sometimes in order to comply with European Community directives.

Written statement of particulars of employment

The Contracts of Employment Act 1963 required that employees should be provided with a written statement setting out the terms and conditions of employment; this is confirmed in Section 1 of the Employment Protection (Consolidation) Act 1978, as amended.

The written statement has to be given to every employee, subject to limited exceptions, who works under a contract for not less than sixteen hours a week. For employees working between eight and sixteen hours a week, five years' service is necessary before they are entitled to a written statement. The statement has to be given not later than thirteen weeks after the employment started.

The statement must include the date when employment began and the date when the employee's continuous employment started; remuneration or method of calculating the remuneration; intervals at which payment is made; terms and conditions relating to hours of work, holidays and holiday pay, sickness and sick pay, pensions and pension schemes; period of notice the employee is entitled to receive and obliged to give to end the employment; and the title of the job the employee is employed to do.

The statement must inform the employee about the disciplinary rules of the employment, the person to whom an employee can appeal against any disciplinary decision and the redress available to an employee for any grievance during the employment.

Parliament wished to ensure that employees are given essential information regarding their employment. Certain rights, such as the right to a redundancy payment, depend on a period of qualifying weeks of employment; it is therefore essential to know when the employment started.

The Act allows an employer to refer in the employee's statement to another document, which must be readily accessible, which contains the required information. The Act requires that most amendments to the information must be notified within four weeks.

The written statement provides employees with prescribed information about their employment; it is sometimes referred to as a written contract. This is not correct unless some additional action has been taken to make it a written contract. In the case of *Gascol Conversions Ltd v J W Mercer 1974,* Mr Mercer was given the written statement as to his employment. He was asked to sign a receipt confirming delivery to him of the statement; this receipt stated that the statement formed the terms and conditions of employment. The Court of Appeal decided that this formed a written contract so that the terms and conditions were terms of the contract.

In the event of a failure by the employer to include the required particulars in the statement, an industrial tribunal may amend or substitute the particulars, which are then contained in the written statement.

Periods of notice to terminate employment

The common law position regarding the termination of employment, was considered to be uncertain and sometimes unreasonable (see p. 283). Employees who had worked loyally for their employers for many years could be dismissed on one week's notice or even less than one week. The Contracts of Employment Act 1963, and now the Employment Protection (Consolidation) Act 1978, stipulated minimum periods of notice. The employee's contract may provide for a longer period of notice.

When an employer dismisses an employee who has between one month and two years' continuous employment, the period of minimum notice is one week; where the period of continuous employment is more than two years, the minimum notice is one week for each year up to the maximum of twelve weeks. There is a minimum period of one week's notice when the employee terminates the contract, which applies whatever the length of employment, subject to any contract term requiring a longer period.

Employees may waive their right to the period of notice or they may accept payment in lieu of notice. It is accepted practice that when professional people are dismissed, they will be given payment in lieu of notice and so leave their employment immediately. Dismissed professional people might not give of their best when working out their notice and the employer's interests could suffer. Manual workers usually work out their notice: it is easier to check both their work and work output.

The statutory requirements of minimum notice periods do not affect the employer's right at common law to terminate the employment. If an employee's misconduct amounts to a fundamental breach of contract, the employer may dismiss the employee without notice.

Unfair dismissal

Unfair dismissal was introduced into employment law by the Industrial Relations Act 1971. When that Act was repealed, the unfair dismissal provisions were preserved in the Employment Protection (Consolidation) Act 1978, which excludes certain workers, including merchant seamen, fishermen, police officers, those who ordinarily work outside the United Kingdom and where the employer is a close relative of the employee. Subject to these exclusions Section 54 states that every employee has the right not to be dismissed unfairly by his (or her) employer.

Section 55 defines dismissal as first, the employee's contract is terminated by the employer by notice or without notice; second, where the employee's fixed term contract expires without being renewed under that contract; and third, where the employee terminates the contract, with or without notice, in circumstances such that the employee is entitled to terminate it without notice by reasons of the employer's conduct.

The first definition covers the normal procedure of dismissing employees by giving them the required period of notice or by dismissing them without notice because of a grave act of misconduct on their part. The second is where an employee under a fixed term of contract does not have that contract renewed. The third definition is usually referred to as 'constructive dismissal' and arises when the conduct of an employer is such that it is unreasonable to expect the employee to continue working for the employer. Parliament introduced this particular provision in order to prevent an employer making working conditions for employees so intolerable as to drive them out of their employment.

The leading case regarding constructive dismissal is *Western Excavating (EEC) Ltd v Sharp 1978*. Sharp took time off work, despite his employer's refusal to give him leave to be absent, in order to take part in a team contest. He was dismissed by the employers. His appeal under the employer's disciplinary procedure was allowed; the dismissal was withdrawn and a period of five days' suspension substituted. This loss of pay produced financial difficulties for Sharp and he asked for an advance on his accrued holiday pay. When this was refused he asked for a loan. This too was refused. He then gave notice to leave telling his employers that the circumstances forced him to resign. He was paid his holiday pay and left. He then made a complaint that he had been constructively dismissed. Both the industrial tribunal and the Employment Appeal Tribunal agreed that he had been constructively dismissed and awarded him compensation.

The Court of Appeal, however, said that both these tribunals had applied the wrong test. The test was whether the employer was guilty of conduct which went to the root of the contract or which shows that the employer no longer intends to be bound by one or more of the essential terms of the contract. If so, employees are entitled to treat themselves as discharged from any further performance of the contract, which means that the contract is terminated by the employer's conduct. The employees have been constructively dismissed. Employees must leave either with notice or without but they must decide soon after the employer's conduct, otherwise they have elected to confirm a contract.

A point of importance to civil engineers, who frequently work under fixed term contracts, is that under Section 142 unfair dismissal rights may be excluded, where the fixed term is for one year or more and the parties have agreed in writing that any right to claim unfair dismissal is excluded. A similar provision exists regarding the right to a redundancy payment but here the fixed term has to be two years or more. Employers use both provisions to preclude any claim for unfair dismissal or redundancy when the fixed term contract comes to an end.

What is unfair dismissal?

Section 57 of the Act defines the grounds on which a claim of unfair dismissal may be made. The employer is responsible for showing that the reason for dismissal was one of the specified reasons or was of some other substantial reason which justified the dismissal of an employee holding that position. The burden of proof in showing that the dismissal was fair rests on the employer: the employee does not have to prove that the dismissal was unfair.

The provision that the dismissal was of some substantial reason has been used by employers whose businesses were in financial difficulties. The dismissal of employees whose positions have been filled by others at lower salaries has been held to be fair in the employer's financial circumstances.

The specified reasons in Section 57 are

(a) related to the capability or qualifications of the employee for performing work of the kind he was employed by the employer to do, or
(b) related to the conduct of the employee, or
(c) was that the employee was redundant, or
(d) was that the employee could not continue to work in the position which he held without contravention (either on his part or on that of his employer) of a duty or restriction imposed by or under an enactment.

Section 57 states that where the employer has shown that the dismissal was for one of the stated reasons, the employer must satisfy the tribunal that in the circumstances it was reasonable to treat it as a sufficient reason for dismissing the employee. The equity of the matter and size and administrative resources of the employer must be considered.

The right of an employer to dismiss an employee for the reasons of capability or qualification would arise where an employee is incapable of performing satisfactorily the work he or she was employed to do, and where an employee is found not to have the particular qualification required for a job.

The conduct of the employee is probably the reason most often used to justify the dismissal. There is a system of warnings set out in the employer's disciplinary procedure, based on Code of Practice 1 Disciplinary practice and procedures in employment, produced by the Advisory Conciliation and Arbitration Service (ACAS). The Code suggests a system of four warnings: an informal oral warning, a formal oral warning, a written warning and a final written warning.

Redundancy is a reason which is used from time to time according to the financial position of the employer.

The final reason covers the situation where employees can no longer do the work they have been employed to do without breaking the law, for example, a lorry driver who has been disqualified from driving because of some traffic offence.

Section 58 makes the dismissal of employees unfair if the reason is because of their trade union activities.

Redundancy

The right of a dismissed employee to receive a redundancy payment was introduced by the Redundancy Payments Act 1965; previously the payment of any sum was at the employer's discretion. Dismissal for redundancy is now defined in Section 81 of the Employment Protection (Consolidation) Act 1978. Redundancy can be said to occur when an employer closes down or proposes to close down the whole or part of the business, or that the need for the employees to do their work no longer or will no longer exist.

Certain employees have no right to a redundancy payment even though redundancy is the reason for the dismissal. Included are employees who are over the state retirement age or have reached the normal retiring age for that employment; employees on a fixed term contract who have agreed in writing to give up the right to entitlement to a redundancy payment; a member of the employer's immediate family; civil servants; employees who have not worked for the employer for at least two years, since their eighteenth birthday, for sixteen hours a week or more or for at least five years for eight hours a week or more.

Parliament provided that where there are certain periods of short-time working or being laid off employees may claim that they are redundant; they are then entitled to a redundancy payment in the normal way.

The Act allows an employer to call for volunteers when redundancies are needed; they qualify for a redundancy payment. Employees working out their notice of redundancy may leave early, provided their employer agrees, and still be entitled to their redundancy payment. If the employer refuses to agree, employees may still leave without losing their redundancy payment provided that in the circumstances this was reasonable; the reasonableness of the employee's action may be determined by an industrial tribunal.

Employees given notice of redundancy may be made an offer by their employer to re-engage them under a new contract. Unreasonable refusal to accept the offer will disentitle the employee to the redundancy payment. Disputes are determined by an industrial tribunal.

The amount of redundancy payment depends on the employee's age, weekly pay and length of continuous service with the employer. The maximum number of years which may be claimed is twenty reckoned backwards from the employee's age. Each completed year of service of an employee aged between forty-one and sixty-five counts for one and a half weeks' pay; each year between twenty-two and forty counts for one week; between the ages of eighteen and twenty-one each year counts for half a week's pay.

An employee may therefore claim a maximum of thirty weeks: the maximum of twenty years at the one and a half weeks' rate. There is a reduction when employees are in their last year of employment before retirement.

The amount of weekly pay is what employees are entitled to under their contract. Where the wages vary because of piece-work or overtime, the amount is the average of the last twelve weeks' pay.

There is a maximum figure for a week's pay, which is usually adjusted annually. At present it is £198 per week, so the maximum payment is £5940. This payment is free of tax and does not affect the dismissed employee's right to unemployment benefit. Many employers make a larger payment than the statutory sum.

An employee does not usually need to apply for the payment. Where the employer does not make the payment, employees have the right to refer the matter to an industrial tribunal within six months of their dismissal. If the employer is insolvent, the employee will be paid by the Department of Employment.

Conciliation

Although Parliament has made provision for employers and employees to resolve disputes through industrial tribunals, it has sought to avoid and resolve disputes in employment matters by an independent body, the Advisory Conciliation and Arbitration Service (ACAS), which was set up by the Employment Protection Act 1975. ACAS has wide powers under the Act: it is to provide advice, on request or otherwise, without charge, to employers, employers' associations, workers and trade unions on industrial relations and employment matters as it thinks fit. ACAS is empowered to issue Codes of Practice for promoting the improvement of industrial relations. Several codes have been issued including one dealing with disciplinary procedures (see p. 288).

So far as unfair dismissal is concerned, the conciliation service of ACAS is confidential, impartial and without charge. The conciliation officer will act if both employer and employee request this service; even if no such request is made, the officer will act if there seems to be a reasonable prospect of success. An employee who has been dismissed but has not started the unfair dismissal complaint procedure may seek the conciliation officer's assistance.

The 1978 Act requires the conciliation officer to seek a settlement by obtaining reinstatement or re-engagement otherwise by way of compensation.

Industrial tribunals and their procedures

Industrial tribunals were created by the Industrial Training Act 1964; they have been given numerous responsibilities regarding employment matters. An industrial tribunal has a legally qualified chairman and two lay members selected for their knowledge of industrial relations, one from the employers' side of industry and the other from the trade union side.

Industrial tribunals result in a quicker, less expensive settlement of disputes and are conducted more informally than court proceedings. The knowledge and experience of industrial relations of the lay members is clearly helpful in the settlement of disputes. The tribunals are widely situated and conveniently accessible to complainants and witnesses; they usually sit in public.

Industrial tribunals are not outside the court system: either party may appeal to the Employment Appeal Tribunal, next to the Court of Appeal and then to the House of Lords. The Employment Appeal Tribunal has the standing of a division of the High Court: it comprises a High Court judge and two lay members with industrial relations experience.

Representation by a lawyer is not necessary in industrial tribunals. Complainants may represent themselves or be represented by another person, usually a trade union official. Allowances may be paid to complainants, their witnesses and to their representative, other than a paid representative. Costs are not normally awarded against a complainant, except where the complaint was unreasonable, frivolous or vexatious.

The procedure before an industrial tribunal, which is governed by the Industrial Tribunals (Rules of Procedure) Regulations 1985, starts with the dismissed employee, in the case of unfair dismissal, completing a form of complaint, which must be made within three months from the date of termination of employment. An industrial tribunal may, however, consider a complaint made outside the prescribed time if it was not practicable to do it in time.

In the case of *Dedman v British Building and Engineering Appliances Ltd 1974*, Dedman, without any previous warning, was told on 5 May 1972 that the activities of his department were being changed and consequently his employment was terminated immediately. He received a salary payment for the month of May and a further month's salary in lieu of notice. His National Insurance card was stamped up to 5 May. Dedman knew that he had some rights under the unfair dismissal provisions in the Industrial Relations Act 1971 but he was unaware that his complaint had to be made to an industrial tribunal within four weeks of his dismissal. He consulted a solicitor who failed to ensure that the complaint was made within the four-week period. The industrial tribunal, by a majority, decided to allow the complaint on the ground that it was not practicable for Dedman to make his complaint within the four-week period.

The Court of Appeal decided that the effective date of termination of the employment was 5 May, so the four-week period ran from that date. The court decided it was practicable for Dedman to have made the complaint within the four weeks, therefore his complaint of unfair dismissal could not be considered by the industrial tribunal.

The Master of the Rolls, Lord Denning, indicated that in deciding whether it had been practicable for the application to have been made within the prescribed time, the tribunal should inquire into the circumstances. If the man or his advisers were not at fault, so that there was just cause or excuse for not making the complaint, then it was not practicable for him to make his complaint within the prescribed time.

If dismissed employees are members of a trade union or they consult a lawyer then, if their claim is not made within the prescribed time, the tribunal will not accept a late complaint. If dismissed employees lose their right to have a complaint heard by an industrial tribunal, they may be able to sue their trade union or lawyer for the loss they have suffered.

Making the claim

The complaint of unfair dismissal is made by the dismissed employee submitting a form, obtained from Job Centres and unemployment offices, to the Central Office of the Industrial Tribunals. The Secretary of the Tribunals acknowledges receipt and sends a copy to the employer. The nature of the complaint has to be stated on the form, allowing the employer, within fourteen days, to indicate whether the employer intends to defend the claim and, if so, on what ground. The conciliation officer is also informed of the complaint so that assistance may be given if appropriate. The tribunal may order either of the parties to provide further and better particulars in order to clarify the matter.

The tribunal may hold a pre-hearing assessment, at the request of either party or because the tribunal believes it to be necessary. The tribunal may examine the documents and decide whether the complaint is likely to succeed. The complainant is told if it appears to be a weak case: if the complainant decides to continue and is subsequently unsuccessful, he or she may be ordered to pay the costs of the hearing.

Hearing

The procedure before a tribunal follows that of the courts but is much more flexible and informal. The employer's representative makes an opening statement setting out the facts of the case. The employer's witnesses may then give evidence, which may be subject to cross-examination, followed by re-examination.

The employee's representative then makes an opening statement and the witnesses give evidence. Both representatives sum up the case from their sides to the tribunal.

The tribunal makes its decision, which may be unanimous or by a majority. The decision has to be in writing and may be given at the end of the hearing by word of mouth. There is power given to the tribunal to review the decision.

Tribunal remedies
The remedies the tribunal may award are recommendations of reinstatement or re-engagement, or an order for compensation. With reinstatement or re-engagement, the employee has to agree and the practicality of the employer complying with such recommendation has to be taken into account. If employees contribute to their own dismissal, consideration must be given to whether it would be just to order reinstatement.

Employees who are reinstated must be treated as if they had not been dismissed. The tribunal's order has to specify the amount the employer has to pay for loss of earnings between dismissal and reinstatement, the rights and privileges which must be restored and the date of compliance with the order.

An order for re-engagement may be made when reinstatement has not been recommended; the employee must be re-engaged by the employer in comparable employment with similar requirements as for an order for reinstatement.

An order recommending either reinstatement or re-engagement which is not complied with entitles the tribunal to make an award of compensation, known as an additional award.

Where the tribunal does not make an order of recommendation, it must consider making an award of compensation, which is adjusted from time to time. The award is a basic award; a compensatory award may also be made if that is considered just and equitable.

The basic award is made to recognize the fact that the employee was dismissed unfairly. The amount of compensation is calculated on the same basis as redundancy, that is based on the employee's age, weekly pay, and length of service. At present the maximum basic award for unfair dismissal is £5940.

A compensatory award takes into account expenses reasonably incurred by the employee in consequence of the dismissal and the loss of benefits, such as pension rights. The maximum award is £10 000.

The maximum of the additional award, which arises only when an order of recommendation of reinstatement or re-engagement has not been complied with, is £5148.

In the case of the basic and compensatory awards the tribunal will reduce the amounts awarded if employees have contributed to their dismissal by their conduct or have failed to mitigate their loss arising from the dismissal.

The sums awarded are increased where the unfair dismissal was the result of trade union activities, sex discrimination or racial discrimination.

11

Industrial law

Trade unions

The legal position of trade unions has caused difficulties to both the courts and Parliament over the years. A trade union did not fit within the accepted definitions of companies, partnerships or individuals. There has also been the difficulty of distinguishing between a trade union and an employers' association. The main legislation is the Trade Union and Labour Relations Act 1974, which has been amended by a number of other Acts.

Section 28 of the Trade Union and Labour Relations Act 1974 contains a definition of a trade union. This is an organization, whether permanent or temporary, which

> consists wholly or mainly of workers of one or more descriptions and is an organization whose principal purposes include regulation of relations between workers of that description of those descriptions and employers or employers' associations.

Also included as trade unions are constituent or affiliated organizations or federations which meet the above requirements. Representatives of constituent or affiliated organizations are also to be treated as trade unions provided the organizations have a principal purpose which regulates relations between workers and employers or their organizations.

The organization need not be permanent although this is usually the case. The organization has to be mainly workers; its principal purposes must include regulation of relations between workers and employers or their organizations. So the setting up of a pressure group does not create a trade union. The requirement that the principal purposes must include the regulation of relations between workers and employers does not prevent a trade union having other purposes, for example providing financial benefits when a member dies or is without earnings because of sickness.

Independent trade unions

Under the Employment Protection Act 1975 in certain circumstances an employer is required to consult with a recognized trade union. A trade union cannot be recognized as such unless it is one which is an independent trade union. Under Section 30 of the 1974 Act an independent trade union is one which

(a) is not under the domination or control of an employer or a group of employers or of one or more employers' associations; and
(b) is not liable to interference by an employer or any such group or association (arising out of the provision of financial or material support or by any other means whatsoever) tending towards such control [and, 'in relation to a trade union', 'independence' and 'independent' shall be construed accordingly;]

The need for this definition arises from the formerly widespread practice of having a staff association which was dominated by the employer. The provision by an employer of accommodation, secretarial assistance, financial support or other support means that that organization is not an independent trade union.

Status of a trade union

A trade union is a collection of individuals but the courts have been unwilling to accept that this collection formed a company, with a separate legal entity, or a partnership. However, a trade union has certain legal rights and obligations.

Section 2 of the 1974 Act states that a trade union which is not a special register body cannot be a registered company under the Companies Act 1985. Any such registration is void: this prevents a trade union existing as a company. Section 2 also specifies the legal standing of a trade union: a trade union can make contracts, hold property, be sued and sue, have proceedings brought against it and have its property taken to meet court judgments, orders or awards. All these are considered to be necessary both for a trade union to function and for legal actions to be taken against it.

The union and its members

The relationship between a member and a trade union is that of a contract. The member by making an application to join agrees to accept the rules of the union which then form the terms of the contract. The courts over the years have sought to interpret the rules as being reasonable rules; those which were 'unreasonable' were to be struck down by the courts.

A form of control over a union which has been used has been the application of the *ultra vires* doctrine, that the union is acting or proposed to act in such a way as to be beyond its powers (see p. 44). In the case of *Goring v British Actors' Equity Association 1987*, the union conducted a referendum of its members following a proposal at Equity's annual general meeting that any member who worked in South Africa should be subject to expulsion. The objects of the union were that it was to be non-political and non-sectarian. The court decided that Mr Goring, a member of Equity who worked in South Africa, could not be expelled from the union. Although the referendum had resulted in the approval of the members it could not be acted on since it would be something beyond the union's power.

In the past a number of trade unions exercised strict control over the admission of individuals to union membership. When it was usual to have closed shops, this restriction meant that without membership of the appropriate union there was no chance of employment. The Employment Act 1980 therefore sought to limit the power of trade unions to admit or refuse admittance to applicants as the union wished.

Section 4 provides that every person who is, or is seeking to be, in employment by an employer, with respect to which it is the practice, in accordance with a union membership agreement, for the employee to belong to a specified trade union or one of a number of specified trade unions shall have the right (a) not to have an application for membership of a specified trade union unreasonably refused; (b) nor be unreasonably expelled from a specified trade union.

Refusal includes not only actual refusal but also implied refusal, which covers the situation where the application is not refused but is simply not processed. A member is unreasonably expelled if one of a number of reasons specified in Section 3 of the Employment Act 1988 applies. These include the failure of a member to take part in a strike or industrial action, whether called for by the union or not.

A member of a trade union who is refused admission or is expelled may, in addition to any right at common law, bring the matter before an industrial tribunal. The complaint must be made within six months. The tribunal, if satisfied that the complaint is well founded, may award compensation, limited to thirty weeks' pay. An industrial tribunal may deal with this type of complaint only if the member has been admitted or readmitted to membership when the tribunal comes to hear the complaint, otherwise the Employment Appeal Tribunal settles the compensation, which may then be fifty-two weeks' pay.

Collective agreements

A collective agreement is defined in Section 30 of the Trade Union and Labour Relations Act 1974:

> 'Collective agreement' means any agreement or arrangement made by or on behalf of one or more trade unions and one or more employers of employers' associations and relating to one or more of the matters mentioned in Section 29(1) above.

Section 29(1) details a number of matters including terms and conditions of employment; physical conditions of work; engagement, termination or suspension of employment; matters of discipline, membership or non-membership of a trade union of a worker and machinery for negotiation or consultation regarding the above.

The importance of a collective agreement is that it may form a legally enforceable agreement between the employer and employee, providing the terms of the contract between them, under Section 18 of the Trade Union and Labour Relations Act 1974.

A provision often found with collective agreements is that an employee shall not go on strike or take industrial action until some agreed procedure has been followed, which aims to avoid strikes called in the heat of the moment.

Strikes and other industrial action

A strike is a deliberate and total withdrawal of labour designed to bring pressure to bear on an employer. Other industrial action includes 'working to rule', when employees follow a specified procedure with such care that there is a reduction in output.

At common law a strike is a breach of contract: the implied obligation in the contract of employment is that an employee will be available for work. This is the case whether the employee gives notice or not of the intention to go on strike. Employees are not, of course, intending to end their employment but merely to suspend it; they hope that the strike or the threat of a strike will produce a settlement of a dispute and a resumption of normal employment.

Employers may, if they so choose, accept the withdrawal of labour as a breach of contract and inform the strikers that the contract of employment has been terminated by their action. Some employers serve notice requiring the strikers to return to normal working by a stated date otherwise their employment will be treated as ended: this is not strictly necessary if the employer decides to treat the withdrawal of labour as termination of the contract. However, service of a notice may result in a return to work, which might be the employer's aim.

Other industrial action may constitute breach of contract justifying dismissal depending on the circumstances. An employer may, when employees are failing to discharge their full duties, warn the employees that continuance of that conduct will be treated as breach of contract justifying dismissal. In the meantime the employer may make deduction for work not carried out. The exact rights of the parties in the case of industrial action depend on the circumstances, and in some circumstances the law is uncertain as to the rights of the employer.

In the case of *Miles v Wakefield Metropolitan District Council 1987*, Miles was a superintendent registrar of births, marriages and deaths in the council area. His duties required work for thirty-seven hours a week, including three hours on a Saturday morning. As part of industrial action for over a year he refused to work on Saturday mornings: this was in breach of his duties. He was told that if he failed to discharge his duties his salary would be reduced. He continued with his industrial action and his salary was reduced to take account of the failure to work the Saturday mornings. Miles brought an action claiming the salary withheld.

The House of Lords decided that Miles was not entitled to the full salary of his employment. The basis of the decision was that an employee was entitled to his remuneration under a contract of employment only if he was ready and willing to perform the duties required of him under his contract. Where he refused to perform the full duties of his contract then he was not ready and willing to perform his contract. Partial performance of the contract entitled the employer to refuse to pay the employee for work not done.

The Law Lords were not asked to decide what would be the position if employees worked to rule and the employer refused to pay employees for any of their work. They were, however, of the view that employees might be able to claim payment for the work they had actually done.

Ballots

The Trade Union Act 1984 required that before a trade union called a strike or other industrial action there had to be a ballot of its members. Failure to have a ballot means the trade union loses the legal immunity it has when calling a strike or other industrial action. Members of a union had sometimes been required to strike without being asked their views on that action, which caused them financial loss. Since 1984 Parliament has made a number of amendments to the matter of ballots.

Ballots must be conducted by means of written voting papers; completed by the people entitled to vote, comprising those who will be called upon to take part in the action. If a person who was not entitled to vote is later required to take part in the industrial action, the ballot will be invalidated.

The expense of the ballot may be recovered by the union from the government. The voting papers are to be provided to those entitled to vote at their place of work (or at a place more convenient to them) and immediately before, during or after their working hours. Postal votes are also available. The question on whether the person is prepared to take part in a strike or other industrial action must be answered by the word 'yes' or 'no'. Every ballot paper must carry the statement: 'If you take part in a strike or other industrial action, you may be in breach of your contract of employment'. The ballot should be conducted in secret.

A strike or other industrial action may be called on a national issue, when all the members are balloted. In a dispute at one place of work, only the members concerned take part. A ballot ceases to be effective four weeks after the date of the ballot. If, however, action is taken on the ballot and then suspended, its resumption does not require another ballot.

A member of a trade union may apply to the High Court claiming that a union has, without a ballot, authorized or endorsed any industrial action which has or will involve members of the union including that member. The High Court may then make an order restraining the union from inducing the members to take action.

Legal remedies for unlawful action

The right to bring an action against a trade union and claim damages for some harm caused by it dates back to the nineteenth century. An employer whose business interests had been harmed by a strike or other industrial action could sue the union responsible for the harm and recover damages. In the case of *Taff Vale Railway Company v Amalgamated Society of Railway Servants 1901,* a strike was called by the union which the company claimed caused them loss. The company was awarded £23 000 in damages. The House of Lords took the view that the union was not above the law.

As an award of that size, together with the risk of further actions, could destroy unions, Parliament passed the Trade Disputes Act 1906, which gave trade unions an immunity from similar legal actions. The present position of legal immunity is set out in the Trade Union and Labour Relations Act 1974, as amended, and the Employment Act 1982. For legal immunity to apply there must be a trade dispute on which the union has had a ballot before authorizing a strike or other industrial action. A trade dispute where unauthorized action by the union takes place deprives the union of the immunity, subject to a limit on the amount of the award which may be made.

A trade dispute is defined in Section 29 of the 1974 Act as a dispute between workers and their employer which relates wholly or mainly to one or more of the following:

(a) terms and conditions of employment, or the physical conditions in which any workers are required to work;
(b) engagement or non-engagement termination or, of suspension of employment or the duties of employment, of one or more workers;
(c) allocation of work or the duties of employment as between workers or groups of workers;
(d) matters of discipline;
(e) the membership or non-membership of a trade union on the part of a worker;
(f) facilities for officials of trade unions; and
(g) machinery for negotiation or consultation, and other procedures, relating to any of the foregoing matters, including the recognition by employers or employers' associations for the right of a trade union to represent workers in any such negotiation or consultation or in the carrying out of such procedures.

The importance of this classification is that when a trade dispute exists then a trade union may take action and, provided that action is authorized by a properly conducted ballot, the legal immunity applies.

Section 15 of the Employment Act 1982 provides that when proceedings in tort are brought against a trade union:

(a) that it induces another person to break a contract or interferes or induces any other person to interfere with its performance; or
(b) that it consists in his threatening that a contract (whether one of which he is a party or not) will be broken or its performance interfered with, or that he will induce another person to break a contract or to interfere with its performance; or
(c) in respect of an agreement or combination by two or more persons to do or to procure the doing of an act which, if it were done without any such agreement or combination, would be actionable in tort on such a ground;
then the trade union will be liable only if it was authorised or endorsed by a responsible official. The term responsible official is defined in some detail but it includes committees and union employed officials.

The provisions cover the breaking of a contract of employment by strikes or other industrial action, or threatening that such action will be taken, and action taken by two or more persons, which could constitute conspiracy, provided if one person only did the act there would be no right of action.

Trade unions do not have legal immunity in secondary action, inducement to use union only labour and action taken without the support of a ballot.

Secondary action is an inducement to breach or interfere with a contract of employment or a threat that a contract of employment will be broken where the employer under the contract is not a party to the trade dispute.

Inducement to use union only labour consists of measures taken to secure that a contract to supply goods or services is performed only by union labour. Any interference (or threats to interfere) with contracts of employment removes the legal immunity. An example would be where a trade union threatened to take action against a main contractor unless the main contractor made sub-contractors recognize or employ union labour.

Action not supported by a ballot consists of inducing a breach of contract or interfering with a contract or employment without a ballot being conducted.

In order not to destroy a trade union when action is taken against it where legal immunity does not exist the amount of damages which may be awarded is limited. Section 16 of the Employment Act 1982 sets these limits, which have upper figures of £10 000 to £250 000, according to the size of the union membership. These limits do not apply when the action brought against the trade union is for personal injury against any person for the torts of negligence, nuisance or breach of duty; or for breach of duty in connection with property.

Common law and industrial accidents

When an industrial accident occurs the injured worker, provided he or she is not wholly to blame for the accident, will seek an award of damages against the employer as the one primarily responsible, who will have the financial resources or insurance capable of meeting any award of the court.

It has now been established that employers owed a duty of care to their employees for injuries arising from their employment; this duty of care extends not only to employers personally but also to the acts of their employees.

The House of Lords in the case of *Wilsons and Clyde Coal Co v English 1938* defined the employer's duty of care as having three parts: the provision of a compentent staff; adequate materials; and a proper system and effective supervision. The Law Lords stated that the duty is not an absolute duty but is fulfilled by the exercise of due care and skill. It is a duty which is not fulfilled by entrusting its fulfilment to employees, even though selected with due care and skill.

The employer's duty of care does not need to guarantee that an employee will not be injured. The duty remains that of the employer even though the employer has selected with care and skill employees, such as foremen and supervisors, and instructed them to do what is necessary to discharge the duty. It is a personal or 'non-delegable' duty on the employer, even though employees work under the control of another person.

In the case of *McDermid v Nash Dredging and Reclamation Co Ltd 1987,* McDermid was a deckhand employed by Nash Dredging, a subsidiary company of a Dutch company, Stevin Baggeren BV. There were two captains, one British who was an employee of Nash Dredging, and the other a Dutchman who was an employee of Stevin, who operated a tugboat turn and turn about. McDermid was working on the tug, casting off the ropes which secured the tug to a dredger. The system was that he released the aft securing rope and then the forward rope. When he had done this he knocked twice on the wheelhouse and the tug-master would then move off. On this occasion he released the aft securing rope and went forward to release that rope. Before he could complete the task the Dutch tug-master put the boat in reverse. The rope snaked round his leg, took him into the water and caused such severe injury that his leg had to be amputated. He sued his employers.

Nash Dredging appealed to the House of Lords, claiming that the Dutch master was not an employee of Nash Dredging and so there was no liability for his failure. The Law Lords dismissed the appeal because employers owed their employees a duty to exercise reasonable care to ensure that the system of work provided was safe. This requirement meant that a safe system had to be devised and operated. This duty was one which was personal and non-delegable. It was no defence for employers to show that they had delegated the performance of this duty to a person, whether that person was an employee or not, even though the employer reasonably believed that that person was competent to perform it. Nash Dredging had delegated both the devising of a safe system of work and its operation to the Dutch tug-master. He had been negligent in failing to operate the system and this meant that Nash Dredging were liable to McDermid.

Provision of competent staff

Employers must take reasonable care in the provision of competent staff. If a contractor put an employee in charge of a crane and that employee's inexperience in its handling resulted in injury to another employee, the employer would be liable.

This duty may also extend to liability for the actions of an employee which results in injury to another employee. In the case of *Hudson v Ridge Manufacturing Co 1957* an employee was given to violent horseplay. Fellow employees complained to the foreman, who warned the employee to conduct himself properly. Despite this warning he still indulged in horseplay which injured Hudson, who sued the employers.

Hudson's claim was successful. The court held that the employers, through their foreman, had knowledge of the conduct of the employee. The foreman's warning had been inadequate which meant that the employers were liable.

In the similar case of *Coddington v International Harvester of Great Britain Ltd 1969,* however, Coddington was unsuccessful in his claim. The employee whose horseplay led to Coddington's injury had no past history of indulging in horseplay and so his employers had no knowledge of such conduct being likely to occur.

Adequate plant and equipment

Employers must take reasonable care not only to provide the necessary plant and equipment but also to maintain it: if some equipment which ought to have been provided has not been, and that absence has caused an accident, the employer is liable. What is required depends on the circumstances of each case.

In the case of *Paris v Stepney Borough Council 1951* (see p. 184), failure to provide protective goggles to an employee with good sight in only one eye made the employers liable.

In some circumstances the employee is expected to take reasonable measures after the equipment has been provided by the employer. In the case of *Smith v Scott Bowyers 1986,* Smith was an employee who was required to work in slippery conditions and was provided with a pair of wellingtons. From use the wellingtons lost their tread, but Smith did not apply to his employers for a replacement pair. During the course of his work he slipped and injured himself. He sued his employers claiming that they were liable as they had failed to provide him with protective clothing.

The court rejected his claim: the employers would be liable only if they had known (or ought to have known) that the employee was submitting himself to a risk of injury by failing to obtain new wellingtons. The failure to obtain a new pair was Smith's fault; this omission prevented him succeeding in his claim.

The duty on an employer to provide adequate plant and equipment is to exercise reasonable care; the employer is not required to guarantee the safety of plant or equipment. This was established in *Davie v New Merton Board Mills Ltd 1959,* where Davie in the course of his work needed to separate two pieces of a machine. For this purpose he selected a metal drift which appeared to be sound. When he struck the drift with a hammer a piece broke off and entered his eye. The drift had been given the wrong heat treatment in manufacture, so that it was too hard, but this fault was not detectable by any reasonable examination an employer could be expected to carry out. The employers had not bought the drift direct from the manufacturer but from a reputable supplier.

The House of Lords decided that Davie's claim failed. What was required of the employer was reasonable care only and that had been exercised by making the purchase from the reputable supplier.

This decision led to Parliament passing the Employer's Liability (Defective Equipment) Act 1969, which provides that if employees are injured in their employment by some defect in equipment provided by the employer and the defect was due to the fault of a third party, then the injury is attributable to the negligence of the employer. So if an employee is injured by the use of a tool with a manufacturing defect in it, the employee can sue both the employer and the manufacturer. If the manufacturer cannot be discovered, the claim is against the employer alone.

Safe place of work

Although it was not specified in the decision in *Wilsons and Clyde Coal Co v English 1938* (see p. 299), the employer's duty of care includes the provision of a safe place of work. Where work is being carried out on employers' premises, they have control over them and they have a clear duty of care.

Most contractors' work is carried out at premises which do not belong to them and are not therefore under their control, but they are still under a duty of care to their employees. The extent of this duty varies according to the nature of the premises at which the work is to be carried out. Lord Justice Pearce gave guidance on this point in the Court of Appeal decision in *Wilson v Tyneside Window Cleaning Co. 1958*:

> The master's own premises are under his control: if they are dangerously in need of repair he can and must rectify the fault at once if he is to escape the censure of negligence. But if a master sends his plumber to mend a leak in a private house, no one could hold him negligent for not visiting the house himself to see if the carpet in the hall creates a trap.

If contractors undertake work at industrial premises where, for all they know, there may be dangerous processes being carried out, failure to inspect the premises would constitute breach of duty of care. Contractors cannot simply instruct the workers sent there to look out for any dangers and to guard against them.

Safe system of working

It is not sufficient for an employer to provide a competent staff and proper premises and plant: the employer must organize a system which ensures that the staff and premises and plant work properly together. A system has to be appropriate to the work: if the circumstances change, the system has to be changed too.

A leading case is *General Cleaning Contractors Ltd v Christmas 1953*, where Christmas had been an employee of General Cleaning for some twenty years. He was cleaning windows at a commercial building. His method of working was to stand on the window sill which was six and a quarter inches wide and 27 foot above ground level. He held on to the sash of the window. The sash fell suddenly, causing him to lose his balance and fall to the ground. He sued his employers claiming damages for his injury. The House of Lords upheld his claim; they rejected the employers' claim that they were entitled to rely on the skill and experience of an employee such as Christmas.

In the course of the decision guidance was given as to what is an employer's duty as to a safe system of work. Lord Reid said:

Where the problem varies from job to job it may be reasonable to leave a great deal to the man in charge, but the danger in this case is one which is constantly found, and it calls for a system to meet it. Where a practice of ignoring an obvious danger has grown up I do not think that it is reasonable to expect an individual workman to take the initiative in devising and using precautions. It is the duty of the employer to consider the situation, to devise a suitable system, to instruct his men what they must do and to supply any implements that may be required such, as in this case, wedges or objects to be put on the window sill to prevent the window from closing. No doubt he cannot be certain that his men will do as they are told when they are working alone. But if he does all that is reasonable to ensure that his safety system is operated he will have done what he is bound to do.

This judgment makes clear that the responsibility for devising a safe system of work is that of the employer, who is not allowed to pass this responsibility on to employees. After a safe system has been devised the employer has to instruct the employees in its use. Any implements required in the system must be provided. If employees who have been properly instructed then fail to follow the system, that does not make the employer liable.

In the case of *Crouch v British Rail Engineering Ltd 1988*, Mr Crouch was a skilled mechanical fitter employed on general maintenance work, who could be required to work anywhere on the site. One day he was instructed to remove an extractor fan which was situated in premises five minutes' walk from his department. One of the securing nuts and bolts could not be removed with a spanner; he therefore used a hammer and chisel to separate this nut and bolt. A piece of metal flew off the chisel and entered his eye. He sued claiming that his employer had failed to provide him with protective goggles. The system operated was that goggles were available, if an employee thought that he needed them, from the employee's foreman and chargehand or from the stores.

The Court of Appeal decided that it was insufficient for an employer to provide a supply of goggles and then to leave it to employees to obtain them when their work put them at risk. Among various factors that should be taken into account were the frequency of use of goggles, the distance an individual worker might have to go to fetch the goggles and the experience and skill expected of employees. Because of the extensive area of work and the long walking distances involved, Mr Crouch should have had goggles in his kit. The damages awarded to Mr Crouch were, however, reduced by 50 per cent to take account of his contributory negligence. He knew that goggles were needed and were available; he could have collected them but he did not do so.

Breach of statutory duty

We have considered the common law duty of the employer to the employee. There is also the duty placed on an employer by statutory provision. From the point of view of an injured worker, to be able to sue for breach of statutory duty as well as for the common law duty is advantageous. The worker need only prove that a statutory provision applied in the circumstances and that provision was breached.

Reasonable care, as in the common law duty of care, does not enter into statutory duty.

The statutory provision must not only constitute a criminal offence but also give a right to sue for damages. Not every statute gives this right. Breaches of the Road Traffic Acts do not allow an injured individual to sue for breach of statutory duty, but only for negligence.

The construction industry is subject to a considerable number of statutory provisions. A few cases only therefore may be considered.

A case based on the Construction (Working Places) Regulations 1966 was *Smith v George Wimpey and Co Ltd and Another 1972,* where Wimpey were sub-contractors for the asphalting of a bridge being constructed as part of a motorway and John Laing and Son Ltd were main contractors. The bridge spanned a single line railway. Smith, an employee of Wimpey, was sent with a message to Laing's site office. This required him to cross the railway line using a well-trodden path down one side of the cutting, across the railway line and then up the other side of the cutting. Smith put his foot on a loose piece of rubble on the path, slipped and cut his hand badly on a piece of concrete.

Smith sued his employer and Laing. The action against Laing questioned the possible liability of the main contractors to those on the site who are not their employees under the provisions in the Construction (Working Places) Regulations 1966. These require sufficient safe access to every place at which any person at any time works, and that every contractor and employer of workers who are undertaking any operations or works to which the regulations apply to comply with the regulations.

The Court of Appeal decided that a main contractor is not under any duty in the regulations to sub-contractors' workers. The duty on main contractors is only to their employees. On the particular facts in the case Smith failed in his claim: Smith's accident was the type which occurred from time to time without negligence or breach of statutory duty.

Two cases dealing with accidents where safety belts had not been used by steel erectors are *Roberts v Dorman Long and Co Ltd 1953* and *McWilliams v Sir William Arrol and Co Ltd and Another 1962*. Both cases were brought by the men's widows.

Roberts was a charge-hand steel erector, engaged in the erection of a steel frame which was to be placed between two stanchions by the use of a crane. The frame did not fit properly and Roberts climbed to the top of the frame in order to assist in its placing. He sat on the frame 70 feet above the ground. He was not wearing a safety belt and the nearest available one was half a mile away. The crane moved the frame, Roberts lost his balance, fell to the ground and was killed.

Roberts' widow sued claiming that there had been a breach of statutory duty in the failure to provide Roberts with a safety belt. The Court of Appeal observed that as Roberts had not been provided with a safety belt he had no opportunity of making a choice as to whether to use one or not. This was a breach of a statutory duty and Mrs Roberts was successful in her claim.

McWilliams was working 70 feet above ground level fixing a staging. He was not using a safety belt. No safety belt was available for his use:

those that had been on the site had been removed to another site some days earlier. Evidence was given that McWilliams had used a safety belt only on rare occasions. As it was not his normal practice, there was a high degree on probability that he would not have worn a safety belt even if one had been available.

The House of Lords rejected Mrs McWilliams's claim: there had been a breach of statutory duty but this was not the cause of the damage suffered. Even if a safety belt had been provided McWilliams would not have worn it.

The obligation of employers to instruct their employees so that a breach of statutory duty is avoided is shown in the case of *Boyle v Kodak Ltd 1969*. Boyle was a skilled experienced painter, accustomed to working from ladders, who was sent to paint an oil storage tank. The Building (Safety, Health and Welfare) Regulations required both Boyle and his employers to ensure that any ladder used was to be secured at the top before use. On the side of the tank was an external metal staircase which gave access to the top of the ladder. Boyle did not make use of the staircase to secure the ladder, but went up the ladder which slipped and Boyle fell to the ground. Boyle sued his employers claiming, among other things, that there had been a breach of statutory duty. He was unsuccessful in both the High Court and the Court of Appeal. He then made an appeal to the House of Lords, who noted that Boyle had some knowledge of the regulations but that he had either not studied them or failed to understand their application in the circumstances in which he was working. His fault was merely that he had misapprehended his statutory duty. The employers had claimed that as Boyle was a skilled and experienced painter they were entitled to assume that he would comply with the regulations.

The Law Lords said that this was not enough. The employers ought to have realized that there was a substantial risk that a skilled worker might not be sufficiently familiar with the regulations to know what constituted a breach of them. There was a duty on the employers to instruct the employee what to do so as to avoid a breach of the regulations. Employers must know what was their duty under the regulations and take all reasonable steps to prevent their employees committing breaches. In these circumstances they could not claim that they had done all that could reasonably be expected of them. However, both Boyle and his employers were equally to blame, and Boyle's damages were reduced by 50 per cent for his contributory negligence.

Breaches of statutory duty can occur not only on construction sites but also in far less hazardous circumstances. Those who work in offices are protected by the Offices, Shops and Railways Premises Act 1963, which was the subject of *Wray v Greater London Council 1986*. Section 14 of the Act requires that a seat must be adequately and properly supported when in use. Wray, an employee of the Council, was sitting on a chair when a leg broke. Wray fell to the floor, suffering injuries for which he sued the Council.

The High Court rejected the Council's submission that no liability arose until they knew of the defect. Section 14 placed an absolute duty on employers; this duty had been breached and so Wray's claim was successful.

Health and Safety at Work etc Act 1974

The Robens Committee examined the effectiveness of the legislative controls for the protection of workers. Its report (published in 1972) was critical of the existing legislation, the way it was administered and the absence of a central body for carrying out research and for conducting investigations into serious accidents. Some of the report's recommendations were included in the Health and Safety at Work etc Act 1974, but Parliament realized that extensive changes in the vast body of health and safety law could not be made immediately. Changes are being made over a period of time and also take account of European Community Directives.

Administration

The Act required that there should be a Commission and an Executive. The Commission has a chairman and between six and nine other members, all appointed by the Secretary of State for Employment. Three ordinary members are appointed after consultation with organizations representing employers and three after consulting employees' organizations. For the other members local authority and professional bodies' organizations are consulted.

The Commission conducts or assists research, collects and distributes information, prepares reports as required by a Minister of the Crown and arranges for the approval of regulations. The Commission can direct that inquiries and investigations be carried out after accidents or similar occurrences.

The Executive is made up of three members, one of whom is the Director appointed by the Commission. The Executive administers the provisions of the Act and when required exercises any of the functions of the Commission.

Parliament took account of the need to have others than the Executive's inspectors involved in the enforcement of the provisions of the Act. Less hazardous premises are dealt with by local authority officers; this is an efficient system as these officers often visit such premises for the enforcement of other statutory provisions. The division of responsibilities between the Executive and local authorities is set out in the Health and Safety (Enforcing Authority) Regulations 1989. In general all premises where there are hazardous operations are under the control of the Executive; premises with few hazardous operations are under the control of local authorities. Thus a civil engineer's office is dealt with by the local authority; construction sites are dealt with by the Executive, usually by specially trained inspectors.

General duties

Section 2 of the Health and Safety at Work etc Act 1974 imposes on employers general duties with regard to the health, safety and welfare of their employees. This is based on broad principles which allow action to be taken without having to satisfy some precisely worded provision.

The general duties are set out in Section 2:

(1) It shall be the duty of every employer to ensure, so far as is reasonably practicable, the health, safety and welfare at work of all his employees.
(2) Without prejudice to the generality of an employer's duty under the proceeding subsection, the matters to which that duty extends include in particular –

(a) the provision and maintenance of plant and systems of work that are, so far as is reasonably practicable, safe and without risks to health;
(b) arrangements for ensuring, so far as is reasonably practicable, safety and absence of risks to health in connection with the use, handling, storage and transport of articles and substances;
(c) the provision of such information, instruction, training and supervision as is necessary to ensure, so far as is reasonably practicable, the health and safety at work of his employees;
(d) so far as is reasonably practicable, as regards any place of work under the employer's control, the maintenance of it in a condition that is safe and without risks to health and the provision and maintenance of means of access to and egress from it that are safe and without such risks;
(e) the provision and maintenance of a working environment for his employees that is, so far as is reasonably practicable, safe, without risks to health, and adequate as regards facilities and arrangements for their welfare at work.

The expression 'so far as is reasonably practicable' is used in each requirement; it is not defined in the Act but the test is not whether something can be done, that is either physically or financially, but how does the risk balance against the sacrifice involved. If an employer is required to take disproportionate measures to counter a risk, the requirement is not reasonably practicable. For instance, if there is a slight risk of injury to a worker in using a piece of equipment but the measure needed to guard against that risk would require heavy financial expenditure, that would not be reasonably practicable.

Sub-section 1 imposes a duty on an employer in the widest sense. A prosecution could be brought under this provision if other sub-sections did not apply.

Sub-section 2 sets out particular duties. With (a) a breach of the duty arises if maintenance is not carried out as the situation requires. This was used in the case of *Tesco Stores Ltd v Seabridge 1988,* where an employee of Tesco Stores suffered a severe burn to his hand from a control panel for a lift. The panel had four securing screws, three of which were missing. The employee's hand came into contact with live electric wires behind the panel. Evidence showed that the screws had been missing from the panel for a day or so, but employees had not reported this to the management. The system of checking the lifts had failed to find this defect. The court found Tesco to be in breach of the duty. The fact that the screws were missing from the panel was self-evident that the requirement had been breached.

General duties of employers and self-employed to persons other than their employees

Section 3 imposes duties on employers and self-employed to non-employees. The duties on self-employed are of particular importance to the construction industry. The duties are owed, among others, to members of the public. Contractors whose undertaking puts the public at risk are in breach of a duty under Section 3:

(1) It shall be the duty of every employer to conduct his undertaking in such a way as to ensure, so far as is reasonably practicable, that persons not in his employment who may be affected thereby are not thereby exposed to risks to their health or safety.
(2) It shall be the duty of every self-employed person to conduct his undertaking in such a way as to ensure, so far as is reasonably practicable, that he and other persons (not being his employees) who may be affected thereby are not thereby exposed to risks to their health or safety.
(3) In such cases as may be prescribed, it shall be the duty of every employer and every self-employed person, in the prescribed circumstances and in the prescribed manner, to give to persons (not being his employees) who may be affected by the way in which he conducts his undertaking the prescribed information about such aspects of the way in which he conducts his undertaking as might affect their health and safety.

In the case of *R v Swan Hunter Shipbuilders Ltd 1981*, the shipbuilders were constructing a warship, using about a thousand workers, many of whom were sub-contractors. The work required an extensive use of gases for welding: oxygen was taken from containers on the quay and distributed by pipes throughout the ship. Swan Hunter's safety officer was aware of the great fire risk if there was an escape of oxygen, particularly inside the warship because its numerous compartments were not well ventilated. The safety officer had produced a booklet warning of this danger and emphasizing the need to see that control valves were turned off when work was finished. This booklet was distributed to Swan Hunter's own employees but not to the sub-contract workers.

A control valve on an oxygen supply was not turned off when work finished at the end of a day. The next morning in the area where there had been this escape of oxygen some sub-contractors started to weld. A fierce fire broke out and several workers lost their lives. Swan Hunter were prosecuted under Section 3 and also under Section 2, for failure to conduct their undertaking as required by sub-section 1. The Court of Appeal upheld their conviction. There had been a failure to observe the duty since they had put the sub-contract workers at risk by failing to inform them of the risk of fire from the escape of oxygen.

In the case of *R v Mara 1987*, Mara and his wife were the sole directors of CMS Cleaning and Maintenance Ltd, which had made a contract for the cleaning of a retail foodstore. The work involved the use of electric cleaning machines including a polisher/scrubber. As the work was done early in the morning it interfered with delivery lorries using the loading bay. It was therefore agreed that the loading bay would be cleaned by an employee of the foodstore using CMS's polisher/scrubber. This employee was electrocuted. The fatality was caused by the defective condition of the cable, which had been damaged in several places and repaired by Mara with insulating tape. In this condition it was dangerous, particularly in wet conditions; the loading bay was usually wet when being cleaned. Mara was prosecuted under Sections 33 and 37 of the Act in that there had been a breach of duty under Sections 2 to 7, and that he had consented or connived to that breach. The breach of duty was a failure of his company to conduct its undertaking in such a way as to ensure that non-employees were not thereby exposed to risks to their health or safety. Mara was convicted in the Crown Court and appealed.

The Court of Appeal refused to accept the submission that Mara's company was not conducting an undertaking when their employees were not working at the foodstore. The fact that CMS left cleaning machines knowing that an employee of the foodstore would use the equipment constituted conducting an undertaking. That equipment included an unsafe electric cable, which constituted a risk to the foodstore's employees and was a breach of the duty under Section 3.

General duties of persons concerned with premises to persons other than their employees

Section 4 of the 1974 Act introduced an entirely new provision, which put duties on persons to those persons who are not their employees but use non-domestic premises as a place of work. Contractors' employees who go to work at premises not belonging to their employer may be covered by the provision in certain circumstances. A breach of this duty might therefore assist an injured worker in making a claim for damages.

The two most important sub-sections in Section 4 are set out below:

(1) This section has effect for imposing on persons duties in relation to those who –
- (a) are not their employees; but
- (b) use non-domestic premises made available to them as a place of work or as a place where they may use plant or substances provided for their use there,

and applies to premises so made available and other non-domestic premises used in connection with them.

(2) It shall be the duty of each person who has, to any extent, control of premises to which this section applies or of the means of access thereto or egress thereform or of any plant or substance in such premises to take such measures as it is reasonable for a person in his position to take to ensure, so far as is reasonably practicable, that the premises, all means of access thereto or egress therefrom available for use by persons using the premises, and any plant or substance in the premises or, as the case may be, provide for use there, is or are safe and without risks to health.

In the case of *Mailer v Austin Rover Group PLC 1989,* contractors were engaged by Austin Rover to carry out cleaning operations, including paint spray booths and the sumps underneath. Austin Rover gave the contractors instructions that paint thinners were not to be taken from a pipe in the booths, and entry was to be made to the sump with an approved safety lamp and only when no one was working above. Before the contractors' men started work Austin Rover closed the valve on the paint thinners' pipe but did not cap it. They also turned off the ventilation to the booths.

Despite the instructions, an employee of the contractors entered the sump while another employee was taking paint thinners from the pipe. The employee was not using an approved safety lamp. An explosion occurred and one of the contractors' employees was killed.

A prosecution by the factory inspector in the Magistrates Court against Austin Rover was successful: Austin Rover should have effectively isolated the pipe and had the ventilation turned on. Austin Rover's appeal against the conviction was made to a Divisional Court of the Queen's Bench Division of the High Court. This appeal was allowed; the factory inspector then appealed to the House of Lords.

The Law Lords indicated that whether premises are 'safe and without risks to health' depended on the purpose to which premises were being put. A building might be unsafe for normal use because of unstable walls. A building which was safe for normal use might become unsafe for overloading floors. What was required for an occupier of premises, in order to ensure that the premises were safe and without risks to health, was to see that the premises were reasonably safe. If the occupier had premises which were not a reasonably foreseeable cause of danger to any person acting in a reasonable way, it would not be reasonable to require the occupier to take any further measures against unknown and unexpected events.

In the particular circumstances Austin Rover could not reasonably have been expected to have taken measures to make their premises safe against unanticipated misuse. The appeal was therefore dismissed.

Although this case decided that contractors working at non-domestic premises cannot expect the occupier to take steps to guard against the contractors' unexpected activities, the position would be different if the contractors' activities were normal but the premises were unsafe and a risk to health.

General duties of employees at work

Sections 7, 8 and 9 contain provisions which place duties on employees. This is not found in previous legislation and indicates the intention of the 1974 Act to deal with workers' safety in the widest way. Over the years prosecutions have resulted from employees' carelessness, foolish conduct or simple stupidity. The fact that they can be prosecuted for breach of their duties still causes surprise to some employees.

Section 7 of the Act states:

It shall be the duty of every employee while at work –

(a) to take reasonable care for the health and safety of himself and of other persons who may be affected by his acts or omission at work; and

(b) as regards any duty or requirement imposed on his employer or any other person by or under any of the relevant statutory provisions, to co-operate with him so far as is necessary to enable that duty or requirement to be performed or complied with.

Employees must take reasonable care for the health and safety not only of themselves but also for other people. An employee who fails to use safety equipment and thereby puts himself at risk is in breach of the duty. The duty also extends to co-operation with the employer or others.

Section 8 imposes a duty on any person not to intentionally or recklessly interfere with or misuse anything provided for health, safety or welfare in accordance with the law.

Section 9 prohibits an employer from charging an employee for equipment or other thing provided in accordance with the law for the employee's health, safety or welfare.

Safety policies, committees and representatives

The Robens Committee Report asserted that the responsibility of safety at work should involve not only management but also workers: this is now done by safety committees and safety representatives.

Section 2 of the 1974 Act imposes a duty on nearly every employer to prepare and as often as is appropriate revise a written statement as to general policy with regard to health and safety at work of the employees. The organization and arrangement for that policy must be stated. The statement and any revision must be brought to the notice of the employees. The Employers' Health and Safety Policy Statements (Exceptions) Regulations 1975 excepts any employer who employs fewer than five employees.

Section 2 requires an employer, if so requested by the safety representatives, to establish a safety committee which is to keep under review the measures taken to ensure employees' health and safety at work. The Secretary of State may also prescribe other functions.

Section 2 provides for the appointment of safety representatives by recognized trade unions from among the employees. Safety representatives are to be consulted by the employer in making arrangements which will lead to the employer and the employee co-operating in promoting and developing measures to ensure employees' health and safety at work. The powers of safety representatives are set out in the comprehensive Safety Representative and Safety Committee Regulations 1977; these allow the safety representatives to investigate accidents, potential hazards and dangerous occurrences, to inspect the workplace at certain intervals and to investigate complaints. The safety representatives deal with the employer and are involved with inspectors of the Health and Safety Executive in all matters concerning the provisions of the Act.

Regulations

A number of matters concerning health and safety can be dealt with adequately only by making detailed regulations under Section 15 of the

Act. For example the Construction (Head Protection) Regulations 1989 specify what is an acceptable head protection, in which circumstances head protection is to be used, exempts a worker who is a Sikh and wears a turban while at work, requires all employers to provide suitable head protection for their employees, and head protection is to be readily available. Every employee and self-employed person is to wear suitable head protection.

Regulations may also be made for the purpose of laying down a procedure which is to be followed in order to satisfy a legal requirement. The Control of Substances Hazardous to Health Regulations 1988 are of general application and require that no work which is liable to expose anyone to substances hazardous to health shall be undertaken before an assessment has been made. This duty applies to both employers and self-employed people. The assessment has to evaluate the risk arising from the use of substances hazardous to health and then establish what must be done to meet the requirements. The assessment is to be reviewed if it is no longer valid or if there has been a substantial change in the work to which the assessment relates.

The regulations aim to prevent exposure of employees to substances hazardous to health; if that is not reasonably practicable, the exposure is to be adequately controlled. Finally, personal protective equipment is to be provided if other measures cannot prevent or adequately control exposure to these substances.

For certain substances specified limits must not to be exceeded. Where control measures are used these have to be properly maintained, tested at prescribed intervals and records kept. Where appropriate, there is to be health surveillance of employees at risk. Records relating to employees subject to health surveillance are to be kept for at least thirty years.

Regulation 12 is important: it requires an employer who undertakes work which exposes employees to substances hazardous to health to provide employees with suitable and sufficient information, instruction and training for the employees to know of the risks to health created by such exposure and the precautions to be taken. The employer is under the same duty to any other person who carries out any work in connection with the employer's duties under the regulations.

This last requirement covers, for example, contractors' workers who enter the employer's premises to carry out work such as installing monitoring equipment. They too are to be informed, instructed and trained as is appropriate.

Codes of practice

The Robens Committee recognized that it was desirable that accidents should be avoided where possible and that a good standard of safety practice would achieve this aim. Codes of practice are not legal requirements under the 1974 Act but are recommended good practice. Under Section 53 a code of practice includes a standard, a specification and any other documentary form of practical guidance.

Section 16 empowers the Health and Safety Commission to approve codes of practice prepared by the Commission or proposed by some other body. Approval by the Commission is subject to the consent of the Secretary of State. Codes may be revised or withdrawn.

The position of codes of practice in criminal proceedings is dealt with in Section 17. Failure to observe any provision in a code of practice does not in itself render a person liable to civil or criminal proceedings. Where, however, a person is charged with a breach of duty under Sections 2 to 7, any regulation or any existing statutory provisions then, if an approved code of practice applies to the particular provision, the code may be used in evidence. A failure to observe a provision in a code of practice may be accepted by the court as proof of a contravention of a statutory provision.

Prohibition and improvement notices

Before the 1974 Act the enforcing authority had little power to serve notices requiring the correction of a contravention of the relevant law. There was no power to serve a notice requiring that work be stopped when a danger existed which could result in death or serious injury to a worker. The 1974 Act dealt with these inadequacies by the introduction of prohibition and improvement notices.

Section 22 deals with prohibition notices; it applies to any activities which are about to be carried on by or under the control of any person, and to which the relevant safety laws apply. The inspector of the Health and Safety Executive or local authority may serve a prohibition notice when, in the opinion of the inspector, these activities carry risk of serious personal injury. The prohibition notice is served on the person having control of the activity. The notice must contain certain details so that the person served is fully aware of the grounds which have led the inspector to serve the notice. The activities must stop immediately, unless the contraventions have been remedied, if the inspector believes that the risk of serious personal injury is imminent. Otherwise the notice comes into effect at the end of a specified period. A prohibition notice may be withdrawn at any time and the period for compliance extended.

An improvement notice is less drastic in effect. Under Section 21 an improvement notice is served if an inspector believes that a person is contravening a relevant safety provision, or has contravened a provision in circumstances which make it likely that the contravention will be repeated. The notice must state the circumstances which led the inspector to that opinion, what constitutes the contravention and the period within which the matter is to be remedied, which must be not less that twenty-one days. An improvement notice may be withdrawn at any time and the period for compliance extended.

The service of either a prohibition or an improvement notice can have a most damaging effect on an employer: there is therefore a right of appeal against the service of either notice to an industrial tribunal (see p. 290). With an improvement notice the making of an appeal automatically suspends its operation until the appeal is determined or withdrawn. In the case of a prohibition notice the making of an appeal will suspend the notice only if the industrial tribunal so directs, and then only from the giving of that direction.

Enforcement

A breach of a provision in the 1974 Act allows the appropriate inspector to bring the offence before the criminal courts. The range of offences is set out in Section 33. The seriousness of the offence determines whether it will be dealt with summarily in the Magistrates Court or by way of indictment in the Crown Court. The powers of punishment are that on conviction in the Magistrates Court a fine not exceeding £2000 may be imposed; in the Crown Court the punishment may be an unlimited fine, or two years' imprisonment, or both, according to the offence. Crown Courts have imposed fines of many thousands of pounds.

Under Section 42 a court may deal with a convicted person by ordering, in addition to or instead of any other punishment, to take specified steps to remedy the matter within a fixed period which may be extended.

Offences are frequently committed by corporate bodies, such as registered companies, and they are prosecuted in the criminal courts. In order to permit individuals to be dealt with as being involved in the offence, Section 37 allows proceedings to be taken against any director, manager, secretary or similar people where that person had consented, connived or had by neglect committed the offence.

Factories Act 1961

Under Section 27 of the Factories Act 1961, certain provisions in the Act apply to building operations and works of engineering construction, which are defined in Section 176.

'building operation' means the construction, structural alteration, repair or maintenance of a building (including re-pointing, redecoration and external cleaning of the structure), the demolition of a building, and the preparation for, and laying the foundation of, an intended building, but does not include any operation which is a work of engineering construction within the meaning of this Act;

'work of engineering construction' means the construction of any railway line or siding otherwise than upon an existing railway, and the construction, structural alteration or repair (including re-pointing and re-painting) or the demolition of any dock, harbour, inland navigation, tunnel, bridge, viaduct, waterworks, reservoir, pipeline, aqueduct, sewage works, or gasholder, except where carried on upon a railway or tramway, and includes such other works as may be specified by regulations of the Minister.

Section 127 therefore applies to the usual circumstances found in building and civil engineering works.

Section 127 obliges any person who undertakes any building operations or works of engineering construction to notify (within seven days after beginning them) the district inspector of the nature of the operations or work, the name and address of the contractor and certain other matters.

This obligation applies only if the operations or works will take longer than six weeks.

Section 29 requires contractors, so far as is reasonably practicable, to provide and maintain safe means of access to every place at which any person has at any time to work, and every such place shall, so far as is reasonably practicable, be made and kept safe for any person working there.

Section 29 also requires that if people have to work where they are liable to fall more than two metres, then if secure hand-hold and secure foothold are not available, fencing or other safety measures must be provided.

In the case of *Dexter v Tenby Electrical Accessories Ltd 1991*, a contractor was engaged to install fresh air fans at the factory of Tenby Electrical. An apprentice electrician of the contractor went on the roof to complete the electric wiring, under the direct orders of his supervisor. He fell through the roof and suffered injury. The factory inspector brought a prosecution against Tenby Electrical in the Magistrates Court, which refused to convict Tenby Electrical. The magistrates believed that Tenby Electrical had not influenced the manner in which the contractor did the work. The factory inspector appealed to the High Court, which allowed the appeal and sent the case back to the Magistrates Court with a direction to convict Tenby Electrical. The High Court accepted that the duty under Section 29 was that of the occupier of the factory. This duty was not dependent on personal blame of the occupiers nor on their knowing of the circumstances in which the contravention had occurred.

Construction regulations

Under the Factories Act 1961, a number of regulations control a range of different activities associated with building operations and works of engineering construction. They apply to the circumstances covered by the definitions of building operations and works of engineering construction set out in Section 176 (see p. 314).

Regulations are enforced by prosecution in the criminal courts. The Health and Safety at Work etc Act 1974 enables improvement or prohibition notices to secure compliance with the regulations.

Each set of regulations comprises a comprehensive body of law dealing in detail with technical matters. There are many construction regulations: only four sets will be considered here.

The Construction (General Provisions) Regulations 1961

These regulations require that if more than twenty persons are employed, whether on the same site or not, an experienced and suitably qualified safety supervisor must be appointed. Safety supervisors need not be employees of the contractors; if they are, their employment duties must not prevent the efficient discharge of their safety responsibilities.

Excavations, shafts and tunnels receive special attention; an adequate supply of suitable timber must be available where a fall of earth, rock or other material could create danger. A competent person is to inspect at least once a day every excavation, shaft, earthwork or tunnel. Where the depth of the tunnel or trench is more than two metres deep an inspection is to be made at the commencement of every shift. A competent person must similarly inspect the execution of timbering work. Provision has to be made for escape from excavations, shafts or tunnels in case of flooding. Fencing too is required.

Transport on a site is dealt with in some detail, to ensure that the transport is safe to use. No one may ride on a vehicle in an insecure position.

Demolition is to be immediately supervised by a competent foreman, chargehand or employee experienced in that kind of work. Special mention is made of situations where the cutting of reinforced concrete, steelwork or ironwork is required.

The use of electricity or machinery is subject to precautions being taken to guard against various risks. Overhead electric cables, with their risk of contact with cranes, are to be protected by barriers or otherwise. Machinery has to be appropriately fenced.

The Construction (Lifting Operations) Regulations 1961

A number of regulations require that lifting appliances are to be properly constructed, properly maintained, adequately and securely supported and, so far as the construction allows, be inspected at least once a week by a competent person, who should make a report in the prescribed way.

No lifting appliance is to be operated except by a person trained and competent to operate that appliance, unless the operator is being trained under the supervision of a qualified person. Signalling must be done by a competent person; the signals given have to be distinctive in character so that the operator can see or hear easily.

Cranes and other lifting devices are to have safe working loads marked on them and must not be used if they are loaded beyond these. Specified cranes are to be provided with an approved type of automatic safe load indicator, which is to be properly maintained and tested by a competent person every time the crane is dismantled and erected.

Cranes and certain other lifting devices are not to be used unless they have been tested and thoroughly examined by a competent person within the previous four years. A report of the test and examination is to be prepared within twenty-eight days and sent to the district inspector of factories.

Chains, ropes and lifting gear must be of good construction, sound material, adequate strength, suitable quality and free from obvious defect. Their safe working load is to be marked on the article. Testing and examination is to be made by a competent person after any work has been done to the chain or other device.

Hoists are to be used for lifting persons only if they are provided with a cage. A hoist is to be protected by a substantial enclosure if there is a risk of any person being struck by a moving part. At any landing place gates are to be provided which shall be opened only for loading and unloading.

The safe working load is to be marked on the hoist. Hoists are to be tested and thoroughly examined by a competent person at least once a month and after they have been substantially altered or repaired. A report is to be prepared within twenty-eight days of the test and examination and a copy sent to the district inspector of factories.

The Construction (Working Places) Regulations 1966

These regulations deal with the construction and use of various scaffolds and the use of ladders. Regulation 6 is of considerable importance: so far as is reasonably practicable, there must be suitable and sufficient safe access to every place at which any person at any time works, which shall be properly maintained. This makes it an offence to permit a means of access to be used when it was foreseeable that certain weather conditions would make it slippery and dangerous. An offence also arises if the means of access was unduly littered with rubbish or equipment.

Scaffolds may not be erected, dismantled or substantially altered or added to except under the immediate supervision of a competent and experienced person. The construction of and material used in scaffolds is to be suitable for the purpose of use. Scaffolds are to be properly maintained and may not be used unless they comply with the regulations. Access to a scaffold which has been partly erected or dismantled is, if reasonably practicable, to be effectively blocked and a prominent warning notice indicating it is not to be used affixed near the point of approach.

No scaffold is to be used unless it has been inspected by a competent person within the immediately preceding seven days; it must also be inspected if weather conditions are likely to have affected its stability. A report is to be made by the person making the inspection.

As scaffolds are used for different purposes, there are suitable requirements as to the width and the provision of guard-rails and toe-boards. Scaffolds are not to be overloaded and should have the load evenly distributed.

Where it is not practicable to comply with the regulations and there is a risk of a person falling, safety nets or safety sheets should be provided unless employees are able to work using safety belts which are securely anchored.

The Construction (Health and Welfare) Regulations 1966

Where a contractor has more than five employees on a site, a sufficient number of suitable first-aid boxes are to be reasonably accessible at positions on the site where employees work. If there are more than fifty employees on site there shall be a person trained in first-aid treatment to a specified standard. The contents of first-aid boxes must conform to a specified list and standard.

A contractor who has more than twenty-five employees on a site has to notify in writing the local health authority, giving details of the works. A suitable stretcher or stretchers are to be provided and a responsible person appointed who is to be readily available during working hours whose duty shall be to summon an ambulance. On a site that lacks telephone or radio communication, a suitable vehicle capable of carrying a stretcher is to be available.

In the case of a site where more than 250 employees work, a contractor having more than 40 employees is to provide and maintain a first-aid room equipped to a specified standard.

Accommodation for workers to shelter in bad weather, for the storing of clothing, and facilities for heating water and taking meals are to be provided. Drinking water and washing facilities are to be provided. Sanitary facilities are to be provided to a scale appropriate to the number of employees on the site.

12

Insurance

Insurable interests

Insurance cover is a contract between someone who requires cover against a particular risk and the insurance company which provides that cover. It differs from other contracts in that people may not obtain insurance cover unless they can show that they have an insurable interest; this is an interest which is sufficient to be recognized by law and may exist with regard to an individual, a property or a legal liability. In the eighteenth century it was the practice to insure the lives of famous people; this was in effect a form of gambling and as such not a desirable practice. A statute was passed by Parliament requiring that there should be an insurable interest.

An insurable interest can exist without having to show ownership or some right to a thing. If individuals can show that they will suffer some damage, detriment or prejudice by the happening of an event that will be sufficient. The person may take out insurance against the risk and have the benefit of that insurance. The insurable interest must exist at the time the contract of insurance is made and also at the time the loss occurs.

In the case of a property which is let to a tenant and subject to a mortgage, the mortgagee, the landlord and the tenant all have insurable interests in the same property. Each will suffer in some way if the property is destroyed or damaged.

Another form of insurable interest is where an employer insures the lives of senior members of staff or insures against acts of dishonesty by employees who handle the employer's money.

For the civil engineer, insurance against professional negligence is a well recognized insurable interest. For the civil engineering contractor, the construction of some works, and all the associated risks, create insurable interests.

Insurance contracts and disclosure of material facts

A contract of insurance is a contract based on common law. There are also various statutes which apply to particular risks, such as motor insurance, and to insurance companies with regard to their financial stability.

The contract of insurance is made between a party seeking insurance cover, the insured, and a party providing that cover, the insurer. The consideration paid to the insurer for undertaking the risk is the premium. The benefit of the insurance contract for the insured is the payment of a sum of money or something of a similar nature on the happening of a specified event.

The usual form of insurance in the civil engineering industry is the indemnity, where the insurer undertakes to make good any financial loss which the insured has suffered, such as an award by a court of damages against a civil engineer for professional negligence. The purpose of indemnity insurance is to put the insured persons in the position they were in before the event which was the insured risk occurred. They are not permitted to make a profit from the insured event occurring: a person who has more than one insurance contract for the same risk cannot claim more than the true loss. The various insurers share the payment between them.

Form of contract

A contract of insurance is usually made on the insurer's standard form, but it can be made initially by word of mouth or by telephone. Generally the person seeking the insurance completes the proposal form provided by the insurer, who decides whether or not to accept the proposal or to accept it subject to conditions. It is the acceptance of the proposal by the insurer which makes the contract. The insured will then receive the policy, which contains all the details of the contract.

Uberrimae fidei

In completing the insurer's proposal form the insured person is required to answer a number of specific questions, usually including one which asks the proposer if there is anything else the insurers should be told. By these answers the insurer is able to judge the risk involved and whether to accept it subject to conditions.

Insurance contracts are *uberrimae fidei,* that is of the utmost good faith. There is an obligation to disclose all the information, known as material facts, which the insurer ought to have in order to make a proper assessment of the proposal and the risk involved. So a person seeking life assurance is under a duty to disclose on the proposal form all the material facts such as past medical history. A company seeking some form of business insurance is similarly under a duty to disclose all the material facts to the insurer.

Failure to provide all the material facts allows the insurer to avoid the contract. Once the material facts become known, which is usually when a claim is made under the policy, the insurer has the right to treat the contract as voidable. The contract is then null and void and no claim under the contract will be entertained.

The difficulty that has arisen in the past with regard to the disclosure of material facts has been that a person who answers all the questions on the proposal form has genuinely believed that no more was required; without in any way trying to conceal important facts the proposer has omitted to mention them. There is also the difficulty of deciding in particular circumstances just what constitute material facts.

As the failure to disclose the material facts allows the insurer to avoid the contract, which usually happens, people who innocently believed that some information was not relevant and so failed to mention it lose their right to claim, which gives the general impression that insurers are acting unfairly when they thus avoid liability. The question of what a proposer should treat as material facts is being examined by the Law Commission. Guidance may therefore be available in the future so that this difficulty can be avoided.

Examining some judicial decisions may help to show how *uberrimae fidei* is applied: each case depends on its own particular circumstances.

In the case of *Marene Knitting Mills Pty v Greater Pacific General Insurance 1976*, Marene took out insurance for their premises against loss by fire with Greater Pacific on 1 August 1973. The next day a fire occurred and Marene made a claim against the insurers. The insurers refused to meet the claim on the ground that there had been failure to disclose material facts, which were that Marene had suffered four previous fires of a serious nature. Clearly if Marene had disclosed the occurrence of these fires the insurers would have considered the matter of insurance cover in a different way. Marene claimed that the four previous fires had been suffered by a different business on different premises and the management had been changed, therefore they were not material facts.

The Judicial Committee of the Privy Council decided that, even allowing for the change of premises, Marene was carrying out the same business. Those four earlier fires were material facts which ought to have been disclosed. This meant that the insurers were entitled to act as they had done and avoid the contract.

In the case of *Woolcott v Sun Alliance and London Insurance Ltd 1978*, Woolcott bought a house in 1972 with the aid of a mortgage from a building society. A requirement of the mortgage was that the house would be insured through the building society, with the premiums being paid to the society. There was no separate proposal form for the insurance, which was part of the mortgage arrangement. The application form for the mortgage asked a question: 'Are there any other matters which you would wish to have taken into account?' Woolcott replied 'No'. Woolcott had a criminal record and for his last offence of robbery he had been sentenced to twelve years' imprisonment. A few months after obtaining the mortgage and the associated insurance the house was destroyed by fire. The insurers refused to pay the insurance cover on the ground that the failure to disclose the criminal record was a failure to disclose material facts. Woolcott sued.

The High Court accepted expert evidence from other insurers that they would have refused to issue a policy to a person with Woolcott's criminal record. This being so, the failure of Woolcott to disclose his criminal record, even though there was no specific question regarding moral character in the proposal form, was a failure to disclose material facts. His claim was therefore dismissed.

When obtaining insurance people frequently use the services of an insurance broker, who may fill in the proposal form for the client, with the client signing the form on completion. The question that arises here is who is responsible for a failure to disclose a material fact.

In the case of *McNealy v Pennine Insurance Co 1978,* McNealy, a part-time musician, wanted motor insurance. Part-time musician was one of the occupations which the insurers would not insure. The insurance brokers obtained insurance for McNealy without disclosing (or in fact knowing of) the part-time occupation. A claim was made against the insurers, who then discovered that McNealy had this part-time occupation and therefore avoided the policy on the ground of failure to disclose a material fact. The insurance brokers were then brought in on the ground that they owed a duty of care to McNealy.

The Court of Appeal decided that there had been negligence on the part of the brokers. They owed McNealy a duty of care to ensure that the proposal form was properly completed so that McNealy obtained the insurance cover needed. The breach of this duty of care made the brokers liable to McNealy.

A somewhat unusual case is *Horry v Tate and Lyle Refineries Ltd 1982.* Horry was an employee of Tate and Lyle when he was involved in an accident at work. He sued his employers, without being legally assisted or professionally advised or being helped by a union. Tate and Lyle's insurers followed the usual practice of making an offer to him in full settlement of his present and any future claim in connection with the accident. The insurers were aware that Horry was acting on his own, but they did not advise him that he should obtain independent advice as to whether the £1000 they had offered him was an adequate sum. They did not send him a copy of the medical report but simply read it to him over the telephone. Horry accepted the offer of £1000. Later he sought to withdraw from the settlement but the insurers declined to allow him to do so.

The High Court decided that the circumstances were such that the insurers were obliged to act so that Horry's interests were protected. The insurers had not acted in accordance with this duty and so Horry was entitled to have the settlement set aside.

Finally, *uberrimae fidei* is a continuing obligation: apart from any provision in the insurance contract, the insured when seeking renewal of the insurance is under a duty to inform the insurer of any change which might have occurred.

Other provisions

On many proposal forms is a provision that the proposer warrants the correctness of the statements made. If there is a breach of that warranty the insurer may use that as justification for avoiding the contract.

A further provision is known as an average clause, used in the insurance of property and contents. This situation comes about when an insurance contract is made to provide cover to, say, a building and the value of the building has increased. Failure to increase the insurance cover and pay the consequent increased premium allows the insurer to average the claim: the claim is reduced by the percentage that the building is under-insured.

The principle of subrogation applies to insurance contracts. This right, which exists at common law, allows the insurer to take the position of the insured and to have all the rights and remedies the insured had in the claim. At common law the right of subrogation arises after the insurer has paid the claim. It is usual, however, to have a term in the insurance contract allowing the insurer to exercise subrogation whether the claim has been paid or not.

In the case of *Lister v Romford Ice and Cold Storage Co Ltd 1957*, a father and son were employees of Romford Ice and Cold Storage. The son drove a lorry for the employers and his father was his mate. By negligent driving Lister junior knocked down and injured his father. Lister senior made a claim against his employers, which was paid by the employers' insurers, who then exercised the right of subrogation and in the employers' name sued Lister junior for breach of his implied obligation under his contract of employment that he would perform his duties in a proper manner. The insurers were successful in their claim and recovered the amount they had paid to his father.

This House of Lords decision alarmed trade unions: it had established a principle whereby employees could be sued for failure to perform their services properly. The insurers, however, took account of this concern and indicated that, except where there was fraud, similar actions would not be brought.

Insurances for civil engineers and civil engineering works

A civil engineer may seek insurance for both personal and professional reasons. An engineer in practice may think it desirable to have life assurance and permanent health insurance. While not required by law, insurance against professional negligence is generally considered essential: without this insurance cover the civil engineer is at risk of personal ruin.

Professional indemnity insurance

The public liability policy used with engineering works covers liability for the contractor in executing the contract works; it does not cover the engineer, who requires separate cover for professional competence. Professional people owe a duty of care under their contract to their client and to others under the tort of negligence (see p. 214).

The professional indemnity policy covers the legal liability of professional people for the negligent acts of themselves or their staff. Most insurances require cover of more than £1 million; it is usual to require the insured to carry an excess. The premium paid depends on the type of works undertaken, the experience of the engineer, the number of staff and the fee income.

Professional indemnity insurance has conditions similar to those found in other insurance contracts. Notification of an occurrence which might give rise to a claim must be made promptly. The importance of observing conditions in the policy is to be seen from the right of the insurer to avoid the contract for such failure.

The case of *Summers and Another v Congreve Horner and Co (Independent Insurance Co Ltd, Third Party) 1991* dealt with a failure to observe a condition in the professional indemnity insurance. Congreve Horner and Co, a firm of chartered surveyors, had a professional indemnity insurance which covered not only the partners but also the staff. The policy had a condition which required that liability would be excluded unless structural surveys were carried out by a member of staff who was a qualified member of one of a number of stated professional bodies, or was a person with not less than five years' experience of the work, or was a person nominated to carry out the work subject to supervision of that work by a person who was qualified under the policy.

Mr and Mrs Summers were interested in buying an expensive house and instructed Congreve Horner to make a structural survey of the property. The surveyors sent an assistant who was a graduate in surveying but had only three and a half years' experience and was not a qualified member of one of the stated professional bodies. The assistant was not under immediate supervision when making the survey. On the basis of the structural survey the Summers bought the house. Shortly afterwards they discovered defects which they believed should have been discovered by the survey. They sued for professional negligence.

The insurers disclaimed liability under the professional indemnity policy on the ground that the assistant did not come within any one of the three categories specified in the policy.

The High Court heard expert evidence regarding the way in which a structural survey was to be carried out and the interpretation of the exclusion clause in the insurance contract. The judge decided that for the assistant to come within the third category, since he failed to satisfy the requirements of the first two, he had to have at some time during the survey the attendance of a qualified person. This had not been done. The insurers were therefore entitled to avoid the contract for the failure to comply with the condition. The surveyors were left to meet the demand of £105 000 without the assistance of their insurers.

Civil engineering works

In Chapter 4 we saw that in the 6th edition of the Institution of Civil Engineers' Conditions of Contract, Clauses 21 and 23 require insurance cover.

Clause 21 requires the contractor to take out insurance for the works in the joint names of the contractor and the employer. The insurance is to cover the full value of the works and plant and equipment which is to be incorporated in the works; to this figure 10 per cent is added. The policy is to cover all loss or damage from whatever cause for which the contractor is responsible under the contract. The contractor is not liable for 'excepted risks' as set out in Clause 20. The period of the policy is to extend until a certificate of substantial completion has been issued. This type of policy is subject to a number of exceptions, the most important exception being that excluding loss from defective workmanship, materials or design. The matter of liability for design is one which comes within professional indemnity insurance.

Clause 23 deals with Third Party insurance. The policy is to be taken out by the contractor in the joint names of the contractor and the employer. The liabilities to be insured are death or injury to any person or loss or damage to any property. The policy does not include matters excluded in the clause: death or injury of any operative or employee of the contractors or any of their sub-contractors. These are covered by the Employers' Liability (Compulsory Insurance) Act 1969 or in some other way. Loss or damage to property does not apply to the works since these are the subject of insurance under Clause 21. A Third Party insurance policy must now include a cross-liability Clause 50 that the employer and contractor may be treated as separately insured. The amount of the insurance under the clause is to be at least the amount stated in the Appendix to the form of tender. The Third Party insurance is subject to a number of exceptions, the more important of which are set out in Clause 22.

Insurances required by statute law

There are a number of circumstances where Parliament has decided that there should be compulsory insurance. Failure to have such insurance is a criminal offence.

Employers' Liability (Compulsory Insurance) Act 1969

This Act makes it compulsory for employers, with a limited number of exceptions, to be insured against liability for personal injury or disease that any of their employees suffer in the course of their employment. Such insurance is to be with approved insurers; there must be a minimum of £2 million cover.

Without the protection of this insurance employees are at risk of not being able to receive from their employers the damages awarded to them by courts. It is therefore in their interests to know that the employer has obtained the insurance cover. There is a requirement that certificates confirming these insurance policies are to be displayed at each of the employers' premises.

In order to prevent an employee being deprived of the protection given by the insurance because of failure to satisfy some condition in the policy, as is possible in other insurance policies, policies under the Act prohibit certain conditions. So a condition which required the policy-holder to take reasonable care to protect employees against risks of bodily injury or disease in their employment is prohibited. Without such prohibition a breach of that condition would allow the insurer to avoid the policy.

Motor insurance

The Road Traffic Act 1972 requires that the driver of a motor vehicle on a road is to have insurance subject to a minimum requirement. Various insurances give the driver greater protection than that required by the Act.

The minimum requirement, usually referred to as 'Road Traffic Act only', provides cover for the use of a vehicle on a road and causing death or bodily injury to third parties. Better cover is provided by 'Third Party only', which gives the Road Traffic cover and adds to it damage to property with the cover applying wherever the vehicle is used within the limit of the policy. A 'Third Party, fire and theft' policy adds to these benefits by extending it to loss or damage to the vehicle caused by fire or theft.

The most extensive form of cover for the use of a motor vehicle is the comprehensive policy, which extends the cover so as to include accidental damage to the vehicle and financial payments for the death or injury to the insured. The loss of or damage to clothing or personal effects are also covered.

The premium paid for motor vehicle insurance is determined not only by the type of cover required but also by the record of the driver. A driver with a record of making several claims may be denied comprehensive insurance and made subject to a higher premium and be required to meet a substantial part of any claim.

A driver of a motor vehicle may not have insurance or a vehicle may not stop after an accident. In these circumstances a person injured by negligent driving either has no insurer against whom to make a claim or cannot trace the driver so as to bring an action. In order to meet the claims of people injured in these circumstances the Motor Insurers Bureau was established. The Bureau is financed by motor insurers. Where an injured person is successful in an action against an uninsured driver and is unable to recover any of the damages awarded, the Bureau pays the damages and costs. In the case of an untraced driver the Bureau will pay the injured person, provided the person would have been successful if a court action had been possible.

Glossary

Agent: A person who has authority to act for another known as the principal.
Arbitration: A means of resolving a dispute before an individual or tribunal, where the parties have agreed to such settlement.
Arbitrator: A person appointed by agreement of the parties to a dispute or by court order to settle a dispute.
Assignment: The transfer by agreement of some right or interest. The person making the transfer is the assignor and the recipient the assignee.
Attestation: The proper execution of a document by the signature of witnesses.
Award: A decision of an arbitrator which may be interim or final.

Bona fides: Good faith. Acting honestly, without fraud or wrongdoing.
Bill of quantities: A document setting out the works proposed to be executed and on which the contractor prepares his tender price.
Breach: A failure to fulfil an obligation, such as contractual.
Breach of warranty of authority: A person has held him/herself out as an agent for another when in fact the person had no authority to act.

Caveat emptor: Let the buyer beware. A rule that the buyer buys at his or her own risk.
Chattel: Property which does not form part of a freehold.
Claimant: The person who makes the claim to start an arbitration.
Condition: A term of importance in a contract.
Consideration: The thing given by a party to a contract.
Contra proferentum: A rule used by the courts when construing a document. The court is to construe the words in the document when some doubt arises with regard to the words.
Contributory negligence: The negligence of the person making a claim which contributed to the injury suffered by that person.
Counter-claim: An action brought by the person against whom an action has been started.

Damages: An award of money made in a civil action to compensate a person for the loss suffered by that person.
Deed: A written instrument stated to be a deed or executed as such and properly attested.
Defendant: A person sued in a civil action.
Discovery: Disclosure of the documents relevant to a civil action before the court trial.

Easement: A right to use or restrict the use of land which belongs to another person.
Estate: A term which is used to denote an area of land; a deceased person's property; and the extent of a person's interest in land.
Estoppel: A legal recognition that a person has by his conduct or some deed he has executed estopped or prevented himself from alleging certain facts.

Fee simple: One of the two legal estates in land. In practice equivalent to ownership of land.
Firm: A person or persons carrying on a business; a partnership.
Frustration: The ending of a contract by the occurrence of some intervening event.

General damages: Damages awarded by the judge which could not be previously ascertained.

Independent contractor: A person who has agreed to perform a given task; one who is not an employee.
Injunction: An order granted by a court ordering a person to do or not do something.

Lands Tribunal: A tribunal set up by statute to deal with certain matters concerning property.
Lease: A letting of land, and the instrument dealing with that letting.
Lessee: The person who accepts the grant of a lease.
Lessor: The person who grants a lease to another.
Licence: In the case of land, the authority to enter land without having the right to exclusive possession.
Lien: A right that a person possesses against the property of another to settle a debt owed to the person by the owner of that property.
Limitation: The periods laid down under the Limitation Act 1980 within which legal actions must be started.
Liquidated damages: An agreed amount to be paid when a breach of contract occurs, which is not a penalty.

Negligence: An action which fails to meet the duty of care owed to persons generally.
Novus actus interreniens: A new act intervening. Arises when a person has done an act which causes damage but a further act by another person has intervened. The effect may be that the first person will not be liable for the damage.
Nuisance: An unlawful interference with a person's use or enjoyment of that person's land; private nuisance. An unlawful interference within the rights of a section of Her Majesty's subjects; public nuisance.

Obiter dicta: Sayings by the way. Things said by a judge on a matter which the judge is not required to decide.

Official Referee: A judge who deals with cases of a technical nature, particularly construction disputes.

Penalty: A sum which is to be paid by provision in a contract for a breach of contract. It is not liquidated damages.

Plaintiff: The person who brings a civil action.

Pleadings: The documents which are exchanged in the preparation of a civil action.

Prescription: A claim to a right based on long use.

Privity of contract: The relationship between the parties to a contract which, in general, excludes those who are not parties to the contract from bringing an action based on that contract.

Quantum meruit: A claim for a reasonable sum to be paid for goods or service provided.

Queen's Counsel: A senior barrister who is appointed by the Lord Chancellor.

Quia timet: An injunction which may be granted by a court where a wrong has not yet occurred but the evidence suggests that unless the injunction is granted the wrong will occur. Used where construction works will cause a serious nuisance.

Ratification: Confirmation of a contract.

Ratio decidendi: The authoritative part of the judge's decision in a case.

Rectification: A court's correction of a document so that it expresses the parties' true intention.

Relator action: An action brought by the Attorney-General on behalf of a person or body claiming that a public right has been infringed. Used in actions for public nuisance.

Repudiation: The refusal of a party to a contract, either express or implied, to perform his or her obligation under the contract.

Res ipsa loquitur: The thing speaks for itself. The maxim applies where the circumstances were such that it was improbable that the accident would have happened without negligence by the defendant.

Rescission: An order of a court that a contract is to be cancelled and the parties to the contract be returned to their original positions. A remedy used where there has been innocent misrepresentation.

Simple contract: A contract which is not made as a deed. It may be made in writing, by word of mouth or conduct.

Special damages: Damages which are claimed in a civil action and which can be calculated.

Specific performance: An equitable remedy granted by a court ordering a person to perform his or her obligation under a contract.

Subpoena ad testificandum: An order requiring a person to appear in court and to give evidence.

Subpoena duces tecum: An order requiring a person to appear in court and to produce documents.

Subrogation: A right to bring and defend an action in the name of another person.

Third party: A person who is brought into a civil action by the defendant on the basis that the person has some liability. Third-party car motor insurance is the insurance cover a driver has for liablity to those who may be injured or harmed as a result of that person's driving.

Tort: A civil wrong which does not depend on a contractual relationship or trust.

Trespass: A tort, with regard to land, is where there is a direct interference with a person's right to exclusive possession.

Uberrimae fidei: Of the utmost good faith. An essential requirement in a contract of insurance.

Ultra vires: Beyond the powers. Arises when a corporate body enters into an agreement which it does not have the power to enter.

Variation order: An order issued by the engineer under a contract, which gives him the power to vary the contract in prescribed circumstances.

Vicarious liability: The liability of a person for the acts of another when acting within the person's authority.

Volenti non fit injuria: That to which a person consents cannot be considered an injury.

Warranty: A term in a contract which is of less importance than a condition and therefore a breach does not give the innocent party the right to withdraw from the contract.

Without prejudice: A form of words which in correspondence about a dispute is privileged and cannot be used as an admission of liability.

Index